This snapshot was taken of my father, Otto Emil Plath, as a young man. He has now been dead over six years. During his life he wrote many articles for scientific magazines, as well as a book titled, Bumblebees and their ways.

taken on our front porch in Jamaica Plain.

Aug. 23, 1934

As for me, I was born on October 27, 1932 in the Robinson Memorial hospital in Boston. I lived for a few years in Jamaica Plain, and then my family moved to Winthrop, a little fishing town on the edge of the great, salty ocean. I was brought upon the flat, sandy beaches and in the warm, fresh salty ocean air

Jan '1935

I was still in J. Plain in January, 1935, but left in the fall of the same year.

picture was in 1935 by Jamaica pond.

Around this time my little brother, Warren, was born on April 27, exactly 2½ years later than I was. We grew up happily together. When daddy died, Mother took a job teaching in high school, and Grammy rented her house and came to lift part of mummy's burden and take care of us while mummy taught. I came to know the Freeman's, David + Ruth, when mother took me to school for the first time. David was the oldest of us four children, then came me, Ruthie, and lastly, Warrie. We all ranged one yr. apart.

... child I had many gay experiences. My uncle Frank built a ...at and often took us riding on the wild blue waves. I ...developed a love for the stormy, turbulent ocean that few ...understand. I enjoyed lying for hours in the bright, white ...g at the sparkling blue-green waves bounding on the wet ...the silvery seagulls dipping for fish on the crest of a ...te-cap before it broke and washed among the pebbles. I ...much of the ocean, because it was an important part of ...ge and environment. And my love for it is hard to explain- ...seemed to be a spirit of a person to me, and nothing else in ...ascinated me as much as it, for nothing and noone has such ...ty as the rough, mysterious sea. ✝

Letters Home

Correspondence 1950–1963

Selected and Edited with Commentary

by Aurelia Schober Plath

Harper & Row, Publishers
New York, Evanston, San Francisco, London

Letters Home
by Sylvia Plath

811.5
P

Portions of this work originally appeared in *Mademoiselle*.
Some of the photographs originally appeared in *People*.

Photo reproductions by Jim Kalett

Grateful acknowledgment is made to Ted Hughes to reprint the following poems:

"Parallax" originally appeared in *Mademoiselle*, "Temper of Time" originally appeared in *The Nation*, "Winter Words" originally appeared in *Delta*, "Pursuit" originally appeared in *Atlantic*, "Metamorphosis" (later titled "Faun"), "Ode for Ted," "Song" and "Epitaph for Fire and Flower" originally appeared in *Poetry*, "The Lady and the Earthenware Head" originally appeared in *Pursuit* (Rainbow Press), "Battle Scene from the Comic Operatic Fantasy" originally appeared in *CSM*, "Departure of the Ghost" originally appeared in *Sewanee Review*.

"I Thought that I Could Not Be Hurt," "You ask me why I spend my life writing..." (fragment), "To Ariadne," "Gold leaves shiver..." (fragment), "Gold mouths cry..." (fragment), "Sonnet" (revised version), "Admonition," "Verbal Calisthenics," "Doom of Exiles," "Apparel for April," "Channel Crossing" Copyright © 1975 by Ted Hughes.

FIRST EDITION

Designed by Gloria Adelson

Library of Congress Cataloging in Publication Data

Plath, Sylvia.
   Letters home.

   Includes index.
   1. Plath, Sylvia—Correspondence. 2. Plath, Aurelia Schober. I. Plath, Aurelia Schober.
II. Title.
PS3566.L27Z53 1975   811'.5'4 [B]   74-1849
ISBN 0–06–013372–4

75 76 77 78 79 9 8 7 6 5 4 3 2 1

Contents

List of Illustrations

Acknowledgments

My first thanks go to my son Warren J. Plath, and his wife, Margaret, whose approval, moral support and assistance encouraged me to undertake this project and helped me throughout the two years it has been in process.

My friend, the author Mary Stetson Clarke, freely gave of her expertise; her faith in the purpose of the venture sustained me.

Deep gratitude is owed to each member of my understanding, loyal family, especially my niece, Nancy Benotti, who read all of the lengthy first version and whose youthful enthusiasm helped greatly.

Among the many supportive friends, these deserve special mention: Ilah Heath, Marion Freeman, and the poet-author Roberta Teale Swartz Chalmers.

I am deeply indebted to my editor at Harper & Row, Mrs. Frances McCullough, for her willingness and assistance far beyond the call of duty.

I am deeply grateful to Ted Hughes for generously giving me the copyright for this selection from Sylvia Plath's letters.

I gratefully acknowledge the generosity of the late Olive Higgins Prouty for the donation of her file containing her complete correspondence with my daughter.

This book is dedicated to my grandchildren: Frieda and Nicholas, Jennifer, and Susan.

Introduction

In answer to the avalanche of inquiries that has descended upon me ever since the publication of Sylvia's poems in *Ariel* and her novel, *The Bell Jar*, I am releasing a section of her intimate correspondence with her family from the time she entered Smith College.

It may seem extraordinary that someone who died when she was only thirty years old left behind 696 letters written to her family between the beginning of her college years in 1950 and her death early in February 1963. We could not afford long-distance telephoning, though, and Sylvia loved to write—so much so that she went through three typewriters in that same time.

Throughout these years I had the dream of one day handing Sylvia the huge packet of letters. I felt she could make use of them in stories, in a novel, and through them meet herself at the varied stages in her own development and taste again the moments of joy and triumph and more clearly evaluate those of sorrow and fear.

Along with the letters written to her brother, Warren, and to me, I have included correspondence with the late Olive Higgins Prouty (the novelist), for between Mrs. Prouty and Sylvia there existed a very special bond. Mrs. Prouty was not only the benefactress whose fund made Sylvia's education at Smith possible, she also was Sylvia's friend and came to her rescue when Sylvia suffered a breakdown in 1953. They found each other mutually fascinating as their relationship developed. After her marriage and the establishment of her writing career, Sylvia spoke of Mrs. Prouty as her "literary mother," in whom she could confide with complete trust and freedom.

Throughout her prose and poetry, Sylvia fused parts of my life with hers from time to time, and so I feel it is important to lead into an account of her early years by first describing the crucial decisions and ruling forces in my own life. As is often the case in a family having European roots (ours were Austrian), my father made the important decisions during my childhood and early girlhood. However, in the early 1920's, when financial catastrophe overtook our family as a result of unwise stock market investments, my father, broken in spirit and blaming himself most unjustly for his very human error, handed over the reins of management to my mother to the extent that my five-years-younger sister and my thirteen-years-younger brother grew up in a matriarchy. Nevertheless, ours was a peaceful, loving home, and I assumed that all marriages were like that of my parents.

Both my children were always asking me to "tell us about the olden days when you were a little girl," and I shared with them the unforgettable memory of my first day in school. Although my father spoke four languages and had lived in England two years before migrating to the United States, he and my mother spoke German at home. There were no children nearby to play with, so I too spoke only German. I told my children how isolated I felt at recess as I stood by myself in a corner of the schoolyard, listening intently to what the children were shouting to each other. The two words I heard most frequently were "Shut up!" so when I went home at the end of the school day and met my father, I answered his greeting proudly and loudly with "Shut up!" I still remember how his face reddened. He took me across his knee and spanked me. Weeping loudly over that injustice, I sobbed out, *"Aber was bedeutet das, Papa? Was bedeutet das?"* (What does that mean?) Then he realized I had not understood what the words meant; he was sorry, hugged me, and asked me to forgive him. It was my first and last spanking.

From that time on we always spoke English at home; my parents bought me all the books we used in school; father was our teacher, and mother and I studied together. By the end of the school term in June, I was given a "double promotion," moving from the first to the third grade—a great boon for me, for I left behind those who had made such sport of my early mispronunciations.

Perhaps I aroused Sylvia's interest in minority groups by my account of my early childhood in a primarily Italian-Irish neighborhood in Winthrop, Massachusetts, during World War I. Even though my father became an American citizen as soon as that privilege was possible, our name Schober, with its German sound, resulted in my being ostracized by the neighborhood "gang," called "spy-face," and at one time being pushed off the school bus steps and dumped on the ground, while the bus driver, keeping his eyes straight ahead, drove off.

I felt this prejudice was completely unjust for my parents' sake as well as my own, for they were ardent converts to American democracy. They believed every word their idol, Theodore Roosevelt, ever wrote or uttered and, because of him, voted the Republican ticket all their lives. Support at home compensated me for outside unpleasantness, as well as did success in the classroom; and family games, walks, visits on Sunday to the Museum of Fine Arts or to my paternal uncle's family in Jamaica Plain were the sweeteners of my childhood.

Then, too, I found my complete escape in the sugar-coated fiction of the day, wherein the poor and the virtuous always ultimately triumphed. I still possess one of Louisa May Alcott's own annotated copies of *Little Women* (given my father for me by a descendant of the Alcott family), worn to tatters, much of which I knew by heart. I read every one of Horatio Alger's stories, the novels of Harold Bell Wright, Gene Stratton Porter, and all the romantic historical novels I could find in the public library.

In my junior year in high school, I had the good fortune to have an inspirational English teacher who improved my taste. From then on Emily Dickinson's poetry became my new bible; the novels of Scott, Dickens, Thackeray, Eliot, the Brontës, Jane Austen, Thomas Hardy, Galsworthy, Cooper, Hawthorne, Melville, and Henry James—in fact, the world of American and English prose and poetry burst upon me, filling me with the urgency to read, read. I lived in a dream world, a book tucked under every mattress of the beds it was my chore to make up daily; a book in the bathroom hamper, and the family's stock answer to "What's RiRi [my nickname] doing?" was "Oh, she's reading *again*."

Fortunately, my mother was most sympathetic and when I was in college read my literature books too, saying cheerily, "More than one person can get a college education on one tuition." (I remembered that vividly when my daughter went to Smith and I, through her, broadened my horizons further in modern literature and art.) I completely identified with the characters in a poem or story, and my ever-growing wish became to open to other young people this wonder of multiple living through vicarious experience—to teach.

It never occurred to me to question my father's decision as to the type of education I should receive. I was to be a "business woman." Obediently, I signed up for a two-year course in the Boston University College of Practical Arts and Letters, doggedly applying myself to the vocational subjects, delighting in history, English composition and literature, as well as the courses in German language, literature and drama. I took on any part-time job I could get, for even the small tuition of that day was hard come by. I had worked in the public library since the age of fourteen and had my first full-time job the summer after high school in an insurance company, typing dull form letters eight hours a day five and a half days a week from wax dictation cylinders—a grim experience I vowed no child of mine would ever have to endure.

As soon as I had completed my two years of combined academic and vocational studies, I persuaded my father to allow me to sign up for two more years in order to prepare myself for teaching English and German, along with vocational subjects, on the high school level.

I now sought out more interesting summer positions, working at the close of my junior year (1927) for a professor at the Massachusetts Institute of Technology. He had a handwritten manuscript in German dealing with new principles of soil mechanics. As he had a publication deadline to meet, I usually worked into the early evening, so we often had dinner together before I left Boston for home. It was during these meals that I listened, fascinated, to his accounts of travel and colorful adventures, fully realizing that I was in the presence of a true genius in both the arts and sciences. I came away with my notebook filled with reading lists that led me to Greek drama, Russian literature, the works of Hermann Hesse, the poems of Rainer Maria Rilke, as well as the writings of great world philosophers. That experience was to affect me the rest of my life, for I realized how narrow my world had been and that self-education could be and should be an exciting lifelong adventure. It was the beginning of my dream for the ideal education of the children I hoped some day to have.

In 1929, after teaching English in Melrose (Massachusetts) High School for the year following my graduation from Boston University, I decided I would return to the university to earn a Master of Arts degree in English and German. In making out my graduate schedule, I learned that Dr. Otto Emil Plath taught the course in Middle High German that I wished to take. I had met Professor Plath briefly at one of the meetings of the German Club in the past and had learned that while his chief interest lay in biology and allied sciences, he was a gifted linguist and the only member of the faculty in the College of Liberal Arts to give this particular course. Dr. Plath greeted me cordially—a very fine-looking gentleman, I thought, with extraordinarily vivid blue eyes and a fair, ruddy complexion. When I brought up the subject of Middle High German, he said that he would enjoy conducting the class but would have to be assured that a minimum of ten students would sign up for it. I told him I would make it my responsibility to talk with all the students I knew who were interested in German, and by the beginning of the fall semester fifteen students had registered for the course.

I remember the last day of classes at the university very clearly, because when I went to say good-bye to my professors, Professor

An early photo of Otto Plath

Plath, who was alone in the German office at the time, played about with a pen on his desk for a bit, then, without looking at me, said that Professor Joseph Haskell and his wife, Josephine (both of whom had been my teachers in undergraduate courses) had invited him to spend the next weekend at their farm and had urged him to bring a friend along. Should I care to join him, he would appreciate it. It was a bolt out of the blue, but Mrs. Haskell was by that time a dear friend; I was ready for some fun and this promised to be interesting, at least.

I learned much about Otto Plath that weekend. He could be spontaneous, jolly, and certainly was confiding. He astounded me by telling me that he had married over fourteen years before. He and his wife had soon separated, and he had not seen her for thirteen years. Were he to form a serious relationship with a young woman now, of course he would obtain a divorce. He thought my A.M. thesis proved we had much in common and he said he would like to know me better. In response to this I told him that I had accepted a position as manager of the business office of twin camps for underprivileged children in Pine Bush, New York, for the summer, but added I would be happy to correspond with him and see him in the fall. In the voluminous correspondence that followed, he wrote me a brief story of his life, which I recall as follows:

Otto Plath grew up in the country town of Grabow, Germany (Polish Corridor territory), speaking German and Polish, and learning French in school. His citizenship papers indicate his nationality was uncertain. He told me his parents were German but that one grandmother was Polish.

His father was a skilled mechanic and worked at the trade of blacksmith. (I was told that when his father, years after his son's arrival here, came to the United States and took on a homestead grant in Oregon, he worked on some refinements of the McCormick reaper which were put to use.) As a young boy in Germany, Otto's "sweet tooth" and his inability to obtain money to purchase candy to satisfy it, led him to observe the nesting sites of bumblebees. These, he discovered, were usually built in the deserted nest of some rodent. At first, running the risk of being stung, he used to watch the bees emerge on a sunny morning from a particular spot in a field—easier to detect after hay had been cut in that area. Once they had left, he would insert a long, hollow straw into the nest below the ground surface and suck out the "wild" honey. Later, he dared to transfer such bumblebee colonies to cigar boxes and keep them in the family garden, thus having access to a constant supply of honey. His skill won him the name of *Bienenkönig* (bee king) from his contemporaries. Thus was born a lifelong interest in entomology.

Otto's grandparents, after emigrating to the United States, had settled on a small farm in Watertown, Wisconsin. Upon learning that this grandson was a top student in all his classes, they offered to send him to Northwestern College, Wisconsin, provided he would promise to prepare himself afterward for the Lutheran ministry. The opportunity appeared dazzling. Not only would he have the higher education which in Germany would be unobtainable for a boy in his circumstances, but he would escape military service, the thought of which he dreaded, for he was already a confirmed pacifist. At sixteen he arrived in New York, where an uncle owned and managed a combination food and liquor store. Otto lived with this family for a year, obtaining permission to audit classes in a grade school in order to learn to speak English in all subjects. He sat at the back of each classroom, making voluminous notes, talking with the children and the teachers after school. He promoted himself as soon as he felt he had mastered the vocabulary of that grade and within a year had progressed through all eight grades, all the while working for his uncle after school hours. The result was that he spoke English without a trace of foreign accent.

Because Otto refused to sell a certain kind of wine that cost more in one bottle of a particular shape than it did in a plainer bottle, his uncle wrote to the boy's grandparents, when his nephew was about to leave for Wisconsin, that "Otto is a good boy, but a poor businessman."

Otto's A-B record (majoring in classical languages) at Northwestern pleased his grandparents, but they did not realize what his extracurricular reading was doing to form his philosophy. Darwin had become his hero and when Otto entered the Lutheran seminary (Missouri Synod), he was shocked to find all Darwin's writings among the proscribed books. Worse still, this comparatively naïve newcomer to the land of the free discovered that most of the candidates for the ministry had never actually been verbally "called" or visibly given a "sign" from God that they had been "chosen" to preach His gospel. Instead, the students gathered in one of the dormitory rooms and discussed the varied and interesting ways each would announce he had been divinely informed. For six months, "miserable months of agonizing doubt and self-evaluation," he told me, Otto tried his best to conform, but succeeded only outwardly and that was not enough. He then decided that the ministry was not for him, but, with a flash of joy and hope that he could make it right with his grandparents, chose teaching for his profession. In this work he felt he could serve and hold to his integrity, be his own man.

However, another shock lay in store for him. His grandparents did not share his point of view; in their eyes he had broken his promise. If he adhered to this infamous decision, he would no longer be a part of the family; his name would be stricken from the family Bible. And so it was done. He was on his own for the rest of his life. When his parents and his three brothers and two sisters came to America, he visited with them only briefly, and by the time of our marriage, his parents were dead and all sibling connections severed. (His youngest sister, Frieda Heinrichs, however, for whom Sylvia's daughter is named, wrote me right after our marriage, and we two corresponded regularly until her death in 1966.)

From the fall of 1930 on, our friendship developed and deepened. Weekends found us hiking through the Blue Hills, the Arnold Arboretum, or the Fells Reservation. The worlds of ornithology and entomology were opening for me, and we dreamed of projects, jointly shared, involving nature study, travel, and writing. "The Evolution of Parental Care in the Animal Kingdom" was our most ambitious vision, planned to be embarked upon after we had achieved some lesser goals and had established our family of at least two children. I succeeded in interesting Otto at that time in the fine productions then given at the Boston Repertory Theatre—Ibsen, Shaw, and modern plays of that era—as well as sharing my enthusiasm for literature. I enjoyed teaching German and English in Brookline High School until January 1932, when Otto and I were married in Carson City, Nevada. Then I yielded to my husband's wish that I become a full-time homemaker.

Otto and I wanted to start our family as soon as possible, he hoping our first child would be a daughter. "Little girls are usually more affectionate," he said. As soon as I was certain I was pregnant, I began reading books related to the rearing of children. I was totally imbued with the desire to be a good wife and mother. At mealtimes we discussed the varying, and often conflicting, theories of child rearing. Had I been inclined to rigidity in the early training of my children, my husband, who believed in the natural unfolding of an infant's development, would have strongly opposed me. He constantly voiced his recollections of his mother's type of child care (he was the oldest of six children). I quietly followed the "demand feeding" accepted as modern today and labeled old-fashioned in the

Aurelia Plath, 1930, when she was teaching in Brookline, Mass.

1930's, though I would never confess to it in front of my contemporaries, who conscientiously followed the typed instructions of their children's pediatricians. Both my babies were rocked, cuddled, sung to, recited to, and picked up when they cried.

Sylvia was born October 27, 1932, a healthy eight-and-a-half-pound baby. At a luncheon that day, her father told his colleagues, "I hope for one more thing in life—a son, two and a half years from now." Warren was born April 27, 1935, only two hours off schedule, and Otto was greeted by his colleagues as "the man who gets what he wants when he wants it."

Otto thoroughly enjoyed observing the development of his daughter, both as a father and as a scientist. When he held her at the age of six months against a rope fastened verticially to a bamboo shade on the porch, he was delighted by the fact that her feet grasped the rope in the same manner as her hands—to him proof of man's evolutionary process as well as the gradual loss of flexibility when man started to wear shoes and used his feet only for walking.

The first year and a half of our marriage saw the expansion of my husband's doctoral thesis into book form. It was published in 1934 by the Macmillan Company, under the title *Bumblebees and Their Ways.* In 1933 Otto was invited to write a treatise on "Insect Societies," which appeared as Chapter IV in *A Handbook of Social Psychology.**
We worked together on this; my husband outlined the sections, listing authors and their texts to be used as reference (there were sixty-nine authors), and I did the reading and note-taking along the lines he indicated, writing the first draft. After that he took over, rewriting and adding his own notes. Then he handed the manuscript to me to put into final form for the printer. By this time I felt I had had an intensive and fascinating course in entomology.

Otto soon found the study he set up for himself in our apartment too gloomy as it faced north, so he moved all the materials he needed for the writing of "Insect Societies" into the dining room, where they remained for nearly a year. The seventy-plus reference books were arranged on top of the long sideboard; the dining table became his desk. No paper or book was to be moved! I drew a plan of the arrangement and managed to have friends in occasionally for dinner the one evening a week that my husband gave a course at Harvard night school, always replacing every item correctly before his return.

Social life was almost nil for us as a married couple. My dreams of

* Clark University Press, Worcester, Massachusetts, 1935.

"open house" for students and the frequent entertaining of good friends among the faculty were not realized. During the first year of our married life, all had to be given up for THE BOOK. After Sylvia was born, it was THE CHAPTER. Fortunately my family was welcome, and during the summer months preceding Sylvia's birth and the one following, they lived with us while renting their house in Winthrop.

Sylvia attached herself to "Grampy" at once and was his greatest delight. He wheeled her out into the Arnold Arboretum while Otto and I worked on "Insect Societies," and both Dad and Mother added their humor, love, and laughter to what would otherwise have been too academic an atmosphere. Sylvia was a healthy, merry child—the center of attention most of her waking time.

Otto insisted on handling all finances, even to the purchasing of meat, fish, and vegetables at the Faneuil Hall Market once a week, knowing that there he could get the best food at the lowest prices. Despite the fact that he was only sixteen when he arrived in the United States, the Germanic theory that the man should be *der Herr des Hauses* (head of the house) persisted, contrary to Otto's earlier claims that the then modern aim of "fifty-fifty" appealed to him. This attitude, no doubt, was inherent and reflected his own home life, where his mother, a rather melancholy person as he described her, was weighed down with the care of six children and an ulcer on her leg that never wholly healed (I did not understand the significance of that problem until the summer of 1940). His father, I was told, was energetic, jovial, inventive.

The age difference between us (twenty-one years), Otto's superior education, his long years of living in college dormitories or rooming by himself, our former teacher-student relationship, all made this sudden change to home and family difficult for him, and led to an attitude of "rightful" dominance on his part. He had never known the free flow of communication that characterized my relationship with my family, and talking things out and reasoning together just didn't operate. At the end of my first year of marriage, I realized that if I wanted a peaceful home—and I did—I would simply have to become more submissive, although it was not my nature to be so.

When I was pregnant in the winter of 1934–35, I told Sylvia that she was going to have a brother or sister (a Warren or an Evelyn) and that I wanted her to help me get ready for the baby. The project fascinated her, and once as she laid her ear against my side when the baby was moving, the thrust must have been audible to her, for her

Sylvia in Winthrop, Mass., 1936

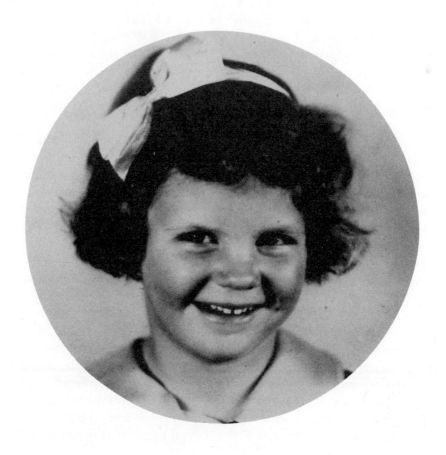

Sylvia, 1937

face lit up as she cried, "I can *hear* him! He is saying, 'Hó da! Hó da!' That means 'I *love* you; I *love* you!' "

I spent a week with Sylvia in my mother's home before the baby's birth in order to get Sylvia thoroughly established there with the grandparents she knew and loved so well. I left her on April 27, the day of Warren's birth. When told she had a brother, Sylvia pulled a wry face and pouted. "I wanted an Evelyn, *not* a Warren."

When we were reunited as a family, the one difficult period was when I nursed the baby; it was always then that Sylvia wanted to get into my lap. Fortunately, around this time she discovered the alphabet from the capital letters on packaged goods on the pantry shelves. With great rapidity she learned the names of the letters and I taught her the separate sounds of each. From then on, each time I nursed Warren, she would get a newspaper, sit on the floor in front of me and pick out all the capital letters to "read." In her baby book, I found the note that it was in July (at the age of two years and nine months), as we waited to cross the street to enter the Arboretum with Warren in the carriage, that Sylvia stared at the big STOP sign with fascination. "Look, Mummy," she cried, pointing to the sign, "Look! P-O-T-S. It says 'pots,' Mummy; it says 'pots!' "

Sylvia treasured a collection of small mosaic tile squares that had been given her and spent much time arranging them in designs. One Saturday, while I was baking in the kitchen, she was unusually quiet as she played with these in the living room. My husband went in there to see what she was up to, then called to me very excitedly. I stared in amazement for she had reproduced unmistakably the simplified outline of the Taj Mahal, the picture of which was woven into a mat in our bathroom. There were the four minarets terminating in domes like that of the center building—it was art without perspective, of course, but to us a definite sign of visual memory developing at an early age.

While Otto did not take an active part in tending to or playing with his children, he loved them dearly and took great pride in their attractiveness and progress. Once, as we looked in upon our sleeping two, he remarked softly, "All parents *think* their children are wonderful. We *know!*"

The year after Warren's birth, Otto began to draw more and more into himself and into his fears concerning his own health. There was ample reason. He was losing weight, had a chronic cough and sinusitis, was continually weary, and easily upset by trifles. He continued

Otto Plath, 1930

teaching—even in the summer—but the effort exhausted him, and he did his class preparation and correcting lying on the couch in his den. He steadily refused to consult a physician, pushing aside all such suggestions and pleas from me, my family, and his colleagues. He told me he had diagnosed his own case and that he would never submit to surgery. I understood the significance of what he said, for he had recently lost a friend who had succumbed after several operations to lung cancer.

I even telephoned my friendly family doctor in Winthrop, the town to which we moved in 1936, and asked him to drop in for a visit, but he said that in view of Otto's attitude it would be both unwise and unethical to do this. I sensed Otto's unspoken diagnosis: lung cancer.

Our move from Jamaica Plain in the fall of 1936 to Johnson Avenue, Winthrop Center, Massachusetts, had been a completely happy one for the children. They enjoyed living close to a beach and near their grandparents' home at Point Shirley, only a few miles away. The children enjoyed roaming over the "flats" at low tide, gathering shells or digging in the coarse sand. Warren was still a toddler and kept close to me, but Sylvia wandered off to explore shallow pools teeming with miniature sea life, and finding sizable rocks to climb.

From this time on, however, it was heartbreaking to watch a once-handsome, powerfully built man lose his vigor and deteriorate physically and emotionally. Appealing to him to get medical diagnosis and help only brought on explosive outbursts of anger. I kept an "upstairs-downstairs" household when both Otto and the children were indoors, partly so their noisy play and squabbling would not upset him, but mostly so that he would not frighten them, for he now occasionally suffered intense cramping spasms in his leg muscles, which would cause him to moan in pain. I had a local girl several mornings in the week take care of the ironing and general housework while I cooked, mended and did what work I had on hand for my husband—abstracting material to update his lectures, correcting German quizzes, and attending to his correspondence.

Otto was determined to keep on teaching and, apparently, kept himself functioning and controlled throughout these working sessions. However, his nerves paid the price when he came home, for on his return he often collapsed on the couch in his study, and many times I served him dinner there.

On the days Otto was home, he lived in this large study, and it was then I took the children to the beach so that they could run and shout and join their playmates, David and Ruth Freeman, whose mother, Marion, had become my closest and very understanding friend. Mr. and Mrs. Freeman, with their two children, David, six months Sylvia's senior, and Ruth, a year her junior, had moved into the neighborhood in the spring of 1937, and our two families became fast friends. The four children practically lived together in one home or the other—the relaxed, cheerful atmosphere of the Freeman home becoming a refuge in inclement weather when Otto was at home. Warren struggled hard to keep pace with the three older children, who were often impatient with him, but as time went on, the discrepancy diminished due to the youngest one's determination.

The largest bedroom upstairs in our home was made into a playroom. Here I invented the bedtime stories centered on Warren's favorite teddy bear, "The Adventures of Mixie Blackshort," which ran into nightly installments for several years. The children had their supper in this room, sitting at a little maple table by a large window, from where we once watched the thrilling progress of an eclipse of the moon. It was here that I read to them poems by Eugene Field, Robert Louis Stevenson, A. A. Milne, and over and over again from the children's favorite anthology, "Sung Under the Silver Umbrella." This reading progressed through Dr. Seuss's hilarious *Horton Hatches an Egg* to such books as Tolkien's *The Hobbit*. Both children made up their own rhymes and limericks, patterned on those I read to them.

After supper and their bath, they amused themselves in the playroom while their father and I had dinner. Then they would come down into the living room for about a half hour to be with us both before going to bed. This was the time Sylvia played piano for her father or improvised dances; both children would show him their drawings and recite the poems they remembered or the rhymes they had made up.

Sylvia's exuberant monopolizing of the luncheon conversation after each school session prompted Warren (then two and a half years old) to invent his "Other Side of the Moon" adventures (referred to years later in one of Sylvia's unpublished stories). The first tale beginning with "On the other side of the moon, where I was *nine* years old and lived before I met you, Mother," completely captured even Sylvia's attention.

At this time, Warren developed many allergies to foods, pollens, dust, etc. In the winter of 1938–39 he suffered two serious bouts with bronchial pneumonia and began having asthmatic attacks. Otto was

Sylvia and Warren Plath at the beach in Winthrop, Mass., 1940

Sylvia's latest ambition — Sept. '40

September, 1940: Sylvia dressed to help the nurse who was caring for her father, who died shortly after this picture was taken

steadily losing weight; his health continued to deteriorate, and between attending to him and Warren, I seldom knew an unbroken night's sleep. This was a period when my parents took care of Sylvia whenever Warren was ill. Her attachment to Grampy deepened, for he not only played games with her but took her swimming with him, an event she later described as a memorable experience with "daddy." It was the beginning of her fusion of characters that occurred periodically in her writing. The first example of this takes place in an unpublished story, "Among the Bumblebees," where the fusion of father and grandfather occurs several times, the story ending with her recollection of her father in his final illness. The swimming episodes with her grandfather are here attributed to her father:

First father would go for a swim himself, leaving her on the shore. . . .
After a while she would call to him, and he would turn and begin swimming shoreward, carving a line of foam . . . cleaving the water ahead with the powerful propellers of his arms. He would come to her and lift her onto his back, where she clung, her arms locked about his neck, and go swimming out again. In an ecstasy of terror, she would hold to him, her soft cheek prickling where she laid her face against the back of his neck, her legs and slender body trailing out behind her, moving effortlessly along in her father's energetic wake.

One morning in mid-August 1940, while preparing to leave home for summer school teaching, Otto stubbed his little toe against the base of his bureau. When he returned home, limping, that afternoon, I asked to see his foot. To our dismay, the toes were black and red streaks ran up his ankle. There was no protest this time as I rushed to telephone my doctor, who came to the house within an hour. He was very grave about the situation, ordered my husband to keep his foot elevated and not to leave his bed for any reason. The doctor took blood and urine samples back to his laboratory, calling me later to report a far-advanced state of diabetes mellitus. The announcement burst upon me like a clap of thunder—so this was his illness—not cancer at all, but an illness which, treated in time with insulin and diet, could be lived with and controlled. I began to hope wildly—the only question was did we have *time?*

From that day on life was an alternation of hope and fear; crises were interspersed with amazing recoveries only to give way to crises again. Otto developed pneumonia, was rushed to the Winthrop hospital, returned home after two weeks with a practical nurse. I sent Warren to his grandparents' home, where his young Uncle Frank took him sailing and fishing. Sylvia wanted to remain with us, so the friendly nurse cut down an old uniform for her and called Sylvia her "assistant," who could bring Daddy fruit or cool drinks now and then, along with the drawings she made for him, which gave him some cheer.

On the nurse's first day off, Otto suggested that I get out into the sun with Sylvia for an hour; he had all his needs supplied on the table next to his bed. She and I ran along the beach together for only about a half hour, because I felt uneasy about having left my husband. I then took Sylvia over to the Freemans' house, where she was invited to remain for supper. On my return home I found Otto collapsed on the staircase. He had left his bed to go downstairs into the garden to look at his flowers. Somehow I half dragged, half carried him to his bed. It was a Wednesday and the doctor could not be reached. I gave Otto his insulin injection; he was so exhausted he could eat very little supper. In the middle of the night he called me and I found him feverish, shaking from head to foot with chills, his bed clothes soaked with perspiration. All the rest of that night I kept changing sheets, sponging his face, and holding his trembling hands. At one point he caught my hands, and holding on, said hoarsely, "God knows, why have I been so cussed!" As tears streamed down my face, I could only think, "All this needn't have happened; it needn't have happened."

The next day the doctor came with the renowned diabetic surgeon, Dr. Harvey Loder, from the New England Deaconess Hospital. Dr. Loder listened carefully to my account of the past years of deteriorating health and the events of the day before. He made a careful examination and as he came out of the room, he told me that amputation from the thigh of the gangrened foot and leg would be necessary to save Otto's life.

As I handed Dr. Loder his hat, he murmured, "How could such a brilliant man be so stupid."

On October 12 the amputation was performed in the New England Deaconess Hospital. I had arranged for a private room and nurse. The report was very favorable, and I attended some lectures to learn about the care of diabetics. We began making plans for the future which would have to be prefaced by Otto's getting adjusted to a prosthesis and learning how to walk with it. Dr. Daniel Marsh, then president of Boston University, wrote my husband, "We'd rather have you back at your desk with one leg than any other man with two." Students volunteered in great numbers to donate blood; everyone was encouraging and helpful. The late Dr. Irving Johnson, and Otto's former graduate student and friend Carl Ludwig, carried on my husband's teaching assignments, refusing to accept any remuneration.

The children were going to school regularly, and my mother or Marion Freeman cared for them during the hours I spent with Otto in the hospital. Marion advised me to explain the operation to Sylvia and Warren, for she had heard children in the neighborhood talking about the amputation; therefore, it seemed best for me to prepare them. I emphasized the fact that we hoped that after this Daddy would be well. Warren accepted the news very quietly, perhaps not sensing the reality of it; Sylvia, wide-eyed, asked, "When he buys shoes, will he have to buy a *pair*, Mummy?"

I had talked with the doctors concerning the type of help a wife must give to restore confidence to a husband who has been mutilated by surgery and I understood the compelling necessity to make him feel a "whole man" and completely acceptable to me. As the days went by, however, Otto avoided any discussion about coming home or trying the prosthesis. The reality of his operation depressed him, and I realized the road ahead would be long and would require much patience.

On November 5, when I left Otto after finding him much weakened, I was told that his condition was serious. My telephone was ringing when I returned home; it was Dr. Loder, who informed me that an embolus had struck in a lung and caused my husband's death as he slept.

I waited until the next morning to tell the children. It was a school day, and I went into Warren's room first. As I looked at the sleeping little boy, only five and a half years old, I thought of both children now having to live the rest of their lives with but one parent. I knew that I would have to earn a living, and my mind leapt to the offer my generous parents had made me. "Should Otto not recover," they had said, "we will come to live with you so that you can return to teaching and the children will be cared for when you are away." My parents were very young to be grandparents; my mother only eighteen years my senior. They were healthy, optimistic, strong in their faith, and loved the children dearly. My young brother, only thirteen years Sylvia's senior, and my sister would be close to us—the children would have a sense of family and be surrounded with care and love. This much I could be sure of. All this passed through my mind before Warren, of his own accord, awoke. I told him as quietly as I could that Daddy's sufferings had ended, that he had died in his sleep and was at rest. Warren sat up, hugged me tightly, crying out, "Oh, Mummy, I'm so glad *you* are young and healthy!"

Then I faced the more difficult task, telling Sylvia, who was already reading in her bed. She looked at me sternly for a moment, then said woodenly, "I'll never speak to God again!" I told her that she did not need to attend school that day if she'd rather stay at home. From under the blanket which she had pulled over her head came her muffled voice, "I *want* to go to school."

After school, she came to me, red-eyed, and handed me a piece of paper, which told me there had been troubling comments from her classmates regarding the possibility of a stepfather. On the paper, in shaky printing, stood these words: I PROMISE NEVER TO MARRY AGAIN. Signed:_____. I signed at once, hugged her and gave her a glass of milk with some cookies. She pushed a kitchen chair against the one I was sitting on, sighed as if relieved and, leaning against my arm, ate and drank with relish. That done, she rose briskly, saying matter-of-factly, "I'm going to find David and Ruth."

I looked at the rumpled "document" I had just signed, which Sylvia had left on the kitchen table, apparently without further thought or doubt, and knew that I never should marry again unless, in years to come, I would have the opportunity to marry a man I respected, loved, and trusted to be a good father to my children and *whom the children wanted to have for their father.* This was the explanation I gave Sylvia when, as a college student, she had come to know a classmate whose once-widowed mother had remarried very happily for herself and her children. "That document never *kept* you from marrying again, did it?" she queried anxiously. I assured her that it had not.

At the request of Dr. Loder, I permitted an autopsy to be performed when he assured me that Otto could still be given the "normal" funeral that he had once stated was his wish. When I viewed Otto at the funeral parlor, he bore no resemblance to the husband I knew, but looked like a fashionable store manikin. The children would never recognize their father, I felt, so I did not take them to the funeral, but placed them in the kind, understanding care of Marion Freeman for that afternoon. What I intended as an exercise in courage for the sake of my children was interpreted years later by my daughter as indifference. "My mother never had time to mourn my father's death." I had vividly remembered a time when I was a little child, seeing my mother weep in my presence and feeling that my whole personal world was collapsing. *Mother*, the tower of strength,

This picture was taken by mother in our back yard. It is in about July, (Aug 1940) and the flowers are beginning to appear in their full glory. They are the ones that daddy planted, and many artists come to paint them. My hair has turned brown, and I wear it in long braids. I am dressed in the uniform that daddy's nurse gave me after he died. Just as I began the sixth grade in Winthrop, mother took a better job-training medical secretarys in Boston University (P.A.L.) And we sold our house and moved to a cosy white house in Wellesley. We felt mingled regrets and anticipation as we bade good-bye to the Freeman's,

August, 1946

we are now happily settled in our little white house on elmwood Road in wellesley. I have made many new friends and also a place for myself. this picture was taken in our living room by Betsy Powley, one of my closest friends. This was taken just before beginning the 9th grade. I have cut my hair much shorter, now. For the past three years I have been going to scout camp. The first two summers to Weetamoe, N.H. And this summer Betsy and I both went to camp storrow on cape cod (near the ocean) and had a perfectly super two weeks there.

this is a picture of me sitting on our front-door step in wellesley, holding my favorite "whisky jug." I have taken piano lessons for five years, but have dropped them in order to practice viola so I can be in the school orchestra. I also have acquired an

1946 extraordinary cat that came disguised as a common Tiger alley cat! I call him Mowgl

Excerpts from a scrapbook autobiography Sylvia made in high school

And so there comes a time in your
senior year at high school when, because
you like the ocean and the wind and
sand, someone grins and drives you
down to the sea; and because you
like poetry, someone gives you a poetry
anthology for graduation; and because
that someone is collegiate and
quite lovely, you invite him to
your senior prom and write to
him every day for a whole summer
long fat letters
with little colored
pictures in the
margins. And
no matter how
you change or grow
up, there was a time
when someone was
terribly important.

my one refuge, *crying!* It was this recollection that compelled me to withhold my tears until I was alone in bed at night.

The week after Otto's death both children came down with measles, Warren having the added complication of pneumonia and Sylvia developing sinusitis. My father, who had been cost accountant for the Dorothy Muriel Company, lost that position at this time, along with all its other employees, when the company changed ownership. He was beginning to have serious difficulty with his eyesight, and the ophthalmologist informed me that progressive macular degeneration was the cause—a grim prognosis lay in the near future for him.

The whole family, including my brother and sister, were together for Christmas, making that event a joyous one for the children.

In January, through the kind efforts of a former classmate, I obtained a $25-a-week substitute teaching position in Braintree High School, teaching three classes of German and two of Spanish daily. I left home at five thirty each morning, commuted to Jamaica Plain to my friend's house, then she drove me to Braintree High School, where she held a full-time teaching post. Three times a week I took private lessons in Spanish from a young teacher in Emmanuel College in Boston. Few teaching positions were available and by the end of the spring term I was very grateful to accept an opening in the Junior High School in Winthrop for the coming September.

The following school year I began having difficulty with a duodenal ulcer I had developed during the last two years of my husband's illness. At the Winthrop Junior High School, in addition to a full teaching program, I was put in charge of all the monies in the entire school: the weekly banking by the pupils (in the second term this was expanded to the purchase of war stamps and bonds by the pupils and teachers), the class and athletic dues. The responsibility of handling and accounting for other people's money weighed heavily upon me. Along with the air raid drills that occurred frequently after December 7, 1941, and our entry into World War II, this was a tense time.

In the summer of 1942, I was invited by the dean of the Boston University College of Practical Arts and Letters to develop a course in Medical Secretarial Procedures. I looked upon the appointment as providential, for it would enable us to leave Winthrop and move as far west of Boston as was possible for a person who had to commute to the city daily. Warren's frequent bouts with bronchitis and Sylvia's sinusitis, we thought, might have been aggravated by their proximity to the sea.

It was a serious step to take, for I was leaving the security of a good state pension and starting at the small salary of $1,800 a year (which was not increased for three years) and carried no benefits at this time, but I felt that the children's health was more important than my financial future. I vowed that I would make the course interesting, yes, fascinating, by presenting the stenographic skills as only the first step up a ladder. I wrote to my sister-in-law's husband, Walter Heinrichs, M.D., who outlined for me a basic course upon which I was to build: nomenclature of disease, basic anatomy and physiology, record keeping and account keeping in a medical office, applied psychology, pertinent problem solving. I added a brief history of the evolution of medicine itself as it emerged from witchcraft, superstition, and religious practices (my A.M. thesis gave me some insight into this as I had written about the personality and work of Paracelsus from sources in English and German literature). I took a course at Harvard Evening School in biology, as well as a general course given for medical secretaries, borrowed medical journals, extracted case histories from these and made up a collection of medical correspondence and records.

By October 26, 1942 (the day before Sylvia's tenth birthday), I had sold the Winthrop house and purchased a small, six-room, white frame house in Wellesley. There were many reasons why I selected Wellesley. Our new home was in a modest section of the town; then the real-estate evaluation and taxes were low. The school system had a fine rating, and Wellesley College, which admitted outstanding students on a town scholarship, might in the future hold opportunity for Sylvia. As my husband had no pension and his $5,000 life insurance had to be used to pay his medical and funeral expenses and for part of the down payment of our new home—the Winthrop house having been sold at a loss—we were operating on a tight margin and had to plan very carefully.

Our proximity to my sister's home in Weston delighted us all, and my father, who was by now employed in the Brookline Country Club as maître d'hôtel—a position he could manage even with his restricted vision—was able to join us on weekends. As a car was essential in this suburb, we were grateful that Grammy possessed a secondhand one and, when necessary, was a willing chauffeur.

In Winthrop Sylvia had been promoted to the sixth grade, but when I discovered that all the children in that grade in Wellesley were nearly two years older than she, I asked the principal to place Sylvia in the fifth grade. She was very understanding and agreed with my multiple reasons for the request, adding, "It is the first time in my

Sylvia wearing a Girl Scout uniform in her Wellesley home, 1946

teaching experience that a mother has requested an all-A pupil be put *back* a grade." However, it worked out well, for the texts and methods differed completely from those in Winthrop. Sylvia made forty book reports that year for her own enjoyment; became an enthusiastic Girl Scout along with the others in that grade, and continued to take piano lessons, which she had begun at the age of seven.

Sylvia's 1944 and 1945 diaries—I always slipped a diary into her Christmas stocking—are full of accounts of school events, shared activities with her friends, especially with Betsy Powley, whose family always had the latchstring out for Sylvia. There were weekend visits in Winthrop with the Freemans and in the summer, camping, swimming, and sailing. Sylvia was writing rhymes constantly and making sketches to accompany them, which she hid under my napkin to surprise me when I came home from teaching. At this time she thought of possibly becoming an illustrator, a dress designer, a writer. Her original illustrated cards with her own verses for occasions of family celebration were a delight for the recipient and have been carefully preserved, as have the original paper dolls for which she made exquisite costumes.

Grampy was so proud of the special-occasion cards she made for him and the poems she had published in the school paper that he carried them in his billfold until they wore out, proudly showing them to his friend, the author William Dana Orcutt, who was interested in Sylvia's progress.

The junior high school years (1944–47) were the "awkward years" for Sylvia, physically. At fifteen years of age, she attained her full height of five feet nine inches, but it was not until her sixteenth year that she began adding curves to her tall frame. Years later, she said she was glad she had not been "pretty" at this time, or rushed to go steady, for it was in junior high that she developed work habits and skill in her favorite fields of endeavor, art and writing, winning prizes from the "scholastic awards" competitions each year.

My pack-rat tendencies led to recovery of an old theater program, the first play I took the children to. Sylvia was twelve, Warren, nine and a half. The play was Margaret Webster's production of *The Tempest*. I told the children I would buy good tickets for us all, including Grammy, of course, if they read the play and could tell me the story of it. I gave Sylvia my copy of Shakespeare's complete works and handed Warren Charles and Mary Lamb's version, feeling he was a bit young for Shakespeare. He was indignant and read the play in the original.

The diary for 1945—the end of the war—was the last *dated* diary. Sylvia now asked me to give her each Christmas an undated journal, because, "When the big moments come, one page is not enough."

These were the days when we still were together enough to enjoy long talks about books, music, paintings—how they made us feel. We were critical of our verbal and written expression, for we shared a love of words and considered them as a tool used to achieve precise expression, a necessity for accuracy in describing our emotions, as well as for mutual understanding.

As soon as my children were old enough to comprehend it, I shared with them the belief my husband and I had held concerning the importance of aiming and directing one's life toward an idealistic goal in order to build a strong inner life.

I explained to them that their father, who felt regret when he accidentally stepped on an ant, had told me he could never bear arms. He would do any type of menial work to fulfill compelled military service, but he could never take another's life.

Back in our Winthrop days I had read Matthew Arnold's "The

Forsaken Merman," to the children, which Sylvia recalled in a published reminiscence years later, noting the impact of the lines as she wrote:

A spark flew off Arnold and shook me, like a chill. I wanted to cry; I felt very odd. I had fallen into a new way of being happy.

Together she and I read Edna St. Vincent Millay's "Renascence," and Sylvia was particularly moved by the lines

> A man was starving in Capri;
> He moved his eyes and looked at me;
> I felt his gaze, I heard his moan,
> And knew his hunger as my own.

Between Sylvia and me there existed—as between my own mother and me—a sort of psychic osmosis which, at times, was very wonderful and comforting; at other times an unwelcome invasion of privacy. Understanding this, I learned, as she grew older, not to refer to previous voluntary confidences on her part.

Both Sylvia and I were more at ease in *writing* words of appreciation, admiration, and love than in expressing these emotions verbally and, thank goodness, write them to each other we did! (I held off because as she entered her late teens, her response to my spoken praise would be, "Oh, *you* think I'm wonderful [or look lovely] because you're my *mother!*")

Sylvia read almost all the books I collected while I was in college, used them as her own, underlining passages that held particular significance for her. In *A Short History of Women* by Langdon-Davies, among the several sections underscored by her are these two: the first from the section of Contents;* the second from the Epilogue, "The Future."†

Life began without sex; animals simply divided in two and went their way. What advantage did the life-force gain by the evolution of sex? . . .

Sex is the result of specialism in performing the labour of living. . . .

Thus the possession of two sexes gives an animal or a plant a start in the race for evolution. Thus sex is seen to be three things, rejuvenation, division of labour, *increased ability for variation.*

. . . for once both sexes use their reason equally, and have no unequal penalty awaiting the exercise of their emotions, then women cannot fail to dominate. Theirs is the stronger sex once nature and art cease their cruel combination against them, because it possesses a greater singleness of pur-

* John Langdon-Davies, *A Short History of Women* (New York: Viking Press, 1927), p. ix.
† *Ibid.*, pp. 381–382.

pose and a greater fund of imagination, for those are the two properties which all men must forfeit under the institutions and necessities of our industrial civilizations. . . .

. . . perhaps the world will be happier in the new régime. But all this is of only partial value as speculation on the future; for men and women are purely relative terms, and long before the tendencies of our times work to their logical conclusions, men and women, as we know them, will have ceased to exist; and human nature will have forgotten the "he and she." According to our own personal feelings we may regret that we shall not live to see that time, or congratulate ourselves on living at a time which antedates it.

I was very grateful for the flow of communication that existed between Sylvia and me, especially during the years of her adolescence; yet I fully expected this to change as she grew more mature and felt that her intimate confidences would then be shared with selected members from among her peers.

The following poem, written at the age of fourteen, was inspired by the accidental blurring of a pastel still-life Sylvia had just completed and stood up on the porch table to show us. As Warren, Grammy, and I were admiring it, the doorbell rang. Grammy took off her apron, tossed it on the table, and went to answer the call, her apron brushing against the pastel, blurring part of it. Grammy was grieved. Sylvia, however, said lightly, "Don't worry; I can patch it up." That night she wrote her first poem containing tragic undertones.

I THOUGHT THAT I COULD NOT BE HURT

I thought that I could not be hurt;
I thought that I must surely be
impervious to suffering—
immune to mental pain
or agony.

My world was warm with April sun
my thoughts were spangled green and gold;
my soul filled up with joy, yet felt
the sharp, sweet pain that only joy
can hold.

My spirit soared above the gulls
that, swooping breathlessly so high
o'erhead, now seem to brush their whir-
ring wings against the blue roof of
the sky.

(How frail the human heart must be—
a throbbing pulse, a trembling thing—
a fragile, shining instrument
of crystal, which can either weep,
or sing.)

Then, suddenly my world turned gray,
and darkness wiped aside my joy.
A dull and aching void was left
where careless hands had reached out to
destroy

my silver web of happiness.
The hands then stopped in wonderment,
for, loving me, they wept to see
the tattered ruins of my firma-
ment.

(How frail the human heart must be—
a mirrored pool of thought. So deep
and tremulous an instrument
of glass that it can either sing,
or weep.)

Her English teacher, Mr. Crockett, showed this to a colleague, who said, "Incredible that one so young could have experienced anything so devastating." When I repeated Mr. Crockett's account of this conversation to me, Sylvia smiled impishly, saying, "Once a poem is made available to the public, the right of interpretation belongs to the reader."

In her diary, however, she wrote:

Today I brought a group of original poems to Mr. Crockett. . . . In class he read aloud four of them, commenting mainly favorably. He liked "I Thought That I Could Not Be Hurt" above the rest and encouraged me greatly by remarking that I had a lyric gift beyond the ordinary.

I was overjoyed, and although I am doubtful about poetry's effect on the little strategy of "popularity" that I have been slowly building up, I am confident of admiration from Mr. C!

In the poems written between the ages of fifteen and seventeen, there is a long one that explains her somewhat, ending,

You ask me why I spend my life writing?
Do I find entertainment?
Is it worthwhile?
Above all, does it pay?
If not, then, is there a reason? . . .

> I write only because
> There is a voice within me
> That will not be still.
> (1948)

Sylvia had begun writing for the "It's All Yours" section in the magazine *Seventeen*. Margot Macdonald, then editor of this section, wrote personal notes on several of the forty-five rejection slips Sylvia received. The editor made the comment that although Sylvia's writing held promise and present merit, she still had to learn to "slant" her subject matter and treatment toward the requirements of the particular publication from which she hoped acceptance. She advised Sylvia to go to the library and read every *Seventeen* issue she could find and discover the "trend." This Sylvia did, and in August 1950 she had her first story published, "And Summer Will Not Come Again," for which she was paid $15. In November of the same year, *Seventeen* published her poem, "Ode on a Bitten Plum."

As she critically surveyed her long list of rejections and the short, but growing, one of acceptances, Sylvia discovered that her exuberant, joyous outbursts in both poetry and prose brought rejection slips, while the story or poem with pathetic twist was found more acceptable. More people would identify with the plain heroine beset

Sylvia, summer 1949

with doubts and difficulties. The old adage to "get your hero up a tree, throw stones at him, then let him extricate himself" still held true at this time. Advice and experience in regard to writing led her now into an examination and analysis of the darker recesses of self.

The beginning of the appeal of the tragic muse is heard in a poem written in the spring of 1949:

TO ARIADNE
(deserted by Theseus)

Oh, fury, equalled only by the shrieking wind—
The lashing of the waves against the shore,
You rage in vain, waist deep into the sea,
Betrayed, deceived, forsaken ever more.

Your cries are lost, your curses are unheard by him
That treads his winged way above the cloud.
The honeyed words upon your lips are brine;
The bitter salt wind sings off-key and loud.

Oh, scream in vain for vengeance now, and beat your hands
In vain against the dull impassive stone.
The cold waves break and shatter at your feet;
The sky is mean—and you bereft, alone.

The white-hot rage abates, and then—futility.
You lean exhausted on the rock. The sea
Begins to calm, and the retreating storm
But grumbles faintly, while the black clouds flee.

And now the small waves break like green glass, frilled with foam;
The fickle sun sends darts of light to land.
Why do you stand and listen only to
The sobbing of the wind along the sand?

Similarly, Sylvia discovered that the "problem" story sold well. In "The Perfect Setup" (*Seventeen*, October 1952), she handled the problem of religious discrimination (WASP withdrawal from a Jewish neighbor). Her heroine, a baby-sitter, Lisa, reluctantly obeys the WASP mother's orders to keep her children away from those cared for by Lisa's newly made Jewish friend, working for a Jewish family. Lisa goes through the difficult task of explaining the WASP mother's attitude to her friend and ends with a feeling of self-loathing for having allowed herself to become allied with this narrow, hypocritical attitude:

You know how sometimes you could slap yourself for a stupid remark you made or a big chance you missed to do the best you could? Well, right then

I wanted to worm my way down into that sand until I was covered all over and couldn't see the lines of foam Ruth was making out there in the water. I just sat there with the whole summer turning sour in my mouth.

As Sylvia herself explained in the personal note at the close of her prize story in *Mademoiselle* (August 1952), her summer jobs provided her with an amazing variety of characters "who manage to turn up dismembered, or otherwise, in stories." This is a keynote to be remembered in connection with much of her writing.

While I considered my children *good* children, I accepted sibling teasing and rivalry as natural processes in development. There was the usual loyalty to each other against outsiders, but there were many times when each made the other miserable; and Sylvia, as the older, was the more dominant and the more culpable. In my notes about my children, there is this statement made by Warren at the early age of four, "saying scathingly to his sister, 'You're the *most* person who doesn't know any better!' " Sylvia's diary entry at fourteen, contains this observation: "It's so nice to know long words! I'm trying to make them a part of my vocabulary—they're so-o-o handy. *Exemplī gratia:* This morning I told Warren that he was 'ostentatiously, obnoxiously superfluous,' and he hadn't the slightest idea of what I meant."

Throughout her high school years, Sylvia was very uncritical of me. The remark I treasured most and wrote in my journal was made by Sylvia when she was fifteen. "When I am a mother I want to bring up my children just as you have us." (This charitable attitude, however, was not to last, and I was vividly reminded of my own hypercritical judgment of my parents throughout *my* undergraduate years at college!)

Between Sylvia and Warren there were often arguments just for the sake of discussion. While she was still an incorrigible tease, they nevertheless experienced periods of very close sharing, too. In her diary, 1947, Sylvia wrote: "Warren and I spent a pleasant evening— he writing poems for his 'Spring Booklet,' and I drawing pictures for each page while we both listened to 'The Fat Man,' 'The Thin Man,' and 'People Are Funny' [radio programs]."

When in 1949 Warren went to Phillips Exeter Academy in New Hampshire on a four-year scholarship, the children's relationship changed completely. In that year Warren grew six inches, generously topping Sylvia's height, to her great delight. As he won distinction in subjects she herself did not study, she now came to respect and admire him. His appreciation of all her writing and art work, as well as his growing understanding of her as a person, resulted in an ever-deepening concern for each other's welfare and a friendship that endured.

Sylvia was naturally drawn to people who were interested in literature and in creative writing. Time after time, however, such relationships became strained when Sylvia won a prize or had something published. To outsiders it seemed as though she won so easily; they did not know what constant practice and effort it took. (I remember mailing for her three different "volumes" of poetry and dozens of stories that were all rejected.) We came to realize that it is the rare friend who genuinely rejoices in another's success.

She was soon to become wary of dating boys who "wanted to write." Invariably, no matter how able they were in other areas, her appearance in print would inject a sour note in the relationship. Sylvia was conscious of the prejudice boys built up among themselves about "brainy" girls. By the time she was a senior in high school, she had learned to hide behind a façade of light-hearted wit when in a mixed group and, after a triple date, was exultant as she reported to me, "Rod asked me what grades I got. I said airily, 'All A's, of course.' 'Yeah,' he replied, grinning, as he led me out to the dance floor, 'You *look* like a greasy grind!' Oh, Mummy, they didn't believe me; they didn't believe me!"

The high school years were such fun. The sharing meant so much, for Warren had gone to Exeter and I missed him terribly. When Sylvia would come home from a dance, I could tell by the way she ascended the stairs how the evening had gone. If she came up slowly and started to get ready for bed, the event had not been "special," but if her step was a running one and she'd hurry into my bedroom, whispering excitedly, "Mummy, are you awake?" ah, then she'd picture the evening for me, and I'd taste her enjoyment as if it had been my own.

In Sylvia's scrapbook-journal, the entries illustrated with snapshots, clippings, and various memorabilia, there is her account of the summer of 1950, when she and her brother took a farm job together.

And so there are summers every year, but the one which brought my first job is unique. Warren and I went up to Lookout Farm [in Dover, Mass.] right after I graduated. . . . Every day we biked up together early in the morning, left our bikes at Wellesley College usually and hitched a ride with one of the other hands. I can never go back to those days spent in the fields, in sun and rain, talking with the negroes and the hired hands. I can only remember how it was and go on living where I am.

But the companionship with my favorite brother is something that was worth more than all the previous summers put together . . . this Farm Summer will always be The First Job and the sweetest.

This summer of farm work was the beginning of her interest in botany and it was then she found deep satisfaction in working with growing plants and the sweet-smelling earth. In one of her unpublished manuscripts she referred to this summer's experience:

I am now firmly convinced that farm work is one of the best jobs for getting to know people as they really are. As you work side by side in the rows, your hands move automatically among the leaves and your thoughts are free to wander at will. What, then, is more natural than to drift into conversation with your neighbor? It is really amazing what a receptive ear can do by way of encouraging confidences. . . .

The farm episode produced a poem, "Bitter Strawberries," and an article, "The Rewards of a New England Summer," both published in *The Christian Science Monitor.*

In the poem, a discussion between the strawberry pickers dealt with the impending threat of war, the act of human destruction figuratively suggested in the last lines:

> We reached among the leaves
> With quick, practiced hands,
> Cupping the berry protectively before
> Snapping off the stem
> Between thumb and forefinger.

It was rewarding, at last, to receive not only notice of the acceptance of her poem and article, but the added comment from Herbert E. Thorson, Editor, Family Features Page: "We hope that you will try us again soon with articles and essays for these columns."

Her article closed with these words:

When you see me pause and stare a bit wistfully at nothing in particular, you'll know that I am deep at the roots of memory, back on the Farm, hearing once more the languid, sleepy drone of bees in the orange squash blossoms, feeling the hot, golden fingers of sun on my skin, and smelling the unforgettable spicy tang of apples which is, to me, forever New England.

A few closely written, stapled sheets, entitled "Diary Supplement" could have been titled "Reflections of a Seventeen-Year-Old," and are dated November 13, 1949.

As of today I have decided to keep a diary again—just a place where I can write my thoughts and opinions when I have a moment. Somehow I have to keep and hold the rapture of being seventeen. Every day is so precious I feel infinitely sad at the thought of all this time melting farther and farther away from me as I grow older. *Now, now* is the perfect time of my life.

In reflecting back upon these last sixteen years, I can see tragedies and happiness, all relative—all unimportant now—fit only to smile upon a bit mistily.

I still do not know myself. Perhaps I never will. But I feel free—unbound by responsibility, I still can come up to my own private room, with my drawings hanging on the walls . . . and pictures pinned up over my bureau. It is a room suited to me—tailored, uncluttered and peaceful. . . . I love the quiet lines of the furniture, the two bookcases filled with poetry books and fairy tales saved from childhood.

At the present moment I am very happy, sitting at my desk, looking out at the bare trees around the house across the street. . . . Always I want to be an observer. I want to be affected by life deeply, but never so blinded that I cannot see my share of existence in a wry, humorous light and mock myself as I mock others.

I am afraid of getting older. I am afraid of getting married. Spare me from cooking three meals a day—spare me from the relentless cage of routine and rote. I want to be free—free to know people and their backgrounds—free to move to different parts of the world so I may learn that there are other morals and standards besides my own. I want, I think, to be omniscient . . . I think I would like to call myself "The girl who wanted to be God." Yet if I were not in this body, where *would* I be—perhaps I am *destined* to be classified and qualified. But, oh, I cry out against it. I am I—I am powerful —but to what extent? I am I.

Sometimes I try to put myself in another's place, and I am frightened when I find I am almost succeeding. How awful to be anyone but I. I have a terrible egotism. I love my flesh, my face, my limbs with overwhelming devotion. I know that I am "too tall" and have a fat nose, and yet I pose and prink before the mirror, seeing more and more how lovely I am . . . I have erected in my mind an image of myself—idealistic and beautiful. Is not that image, free from blemish, the true self—the true perfection? Am I wrong when this image insinuates itself between me and the merciless mirror? (Oh, even now I glance back on what I have just written—how foolish it sounds, how overdramatic.)

Never, never, never will I reach the perfection I long for with all my soul— my paintings, my poems, my stories—all poor, poor reflections . . . for I have been too thoroughly conditioned to the conventional surroundings of this community . . . my vanity desires luxuries which I can never have. . . .

I am continually more aware of the power which chance plays in my life. . . . There will come a time when I must face myself at last. Even now I dread the big choices which loom up in my life—what college? What career? I am afraid. I feel uncertain. What is best for me? What do I want? I do not know. I love freedom. I deplore constrictions and limitations. . . . I am not as wise as I have thought. I can now see, as from a valley, the roads lying open for me, but I cannot see the end—the consequences. . . .

Oh, I love *now*, with all my fears and forebodings, for *now* I still am not completely molded. My life is still just beginning. I am strong. I long for a cause to devote my energies to. . . .

Just now I don't care where I end up at college. I have a new formal, a row of dates with a fine, sensitive boy, an eye for color and form in the springtime, and two nicely-shaped legs to pedal my bike to school. Art & writing are always with me. I love people. And a few of them love me back. I am the one who creates part of my fate, and I'll fight destiny all the way. So!

A fragment from Sylvia's high school diary

PART ONE

September 27, 1950–June 1953

Sylvia's letters from Smith show the effort of a conscientious student striving for high grades, partly to satisfy herself and build up her own image and partly to prove herself worthy of the generous financial aid she was receiving from various sources: the Olive Higgins Prouty Fund, the Nielson scholarship, and the Smith Club in Wellesley. Added to this effort was her need to project the image of the "all-around" person; i.e., the student who not only did well scholastically but was socially acceptable by both sexes, and the service-oriented person who made a contribution to her peer group and the community. To all this, Sylvia added her own burning desire: to develop creatively in her chosen field—writing—and to win recognition there. The pressure that developed from her involvement in all these areas was periodically overwhelming, both physically and psychically.

⤙*First letter written from Smith*⤚

SMITH COLLEGE
NORTHAMPTON, MASS.
SEPTEMBER 27, 1950

Dearest Mummy,

Well, only five minutes till midnight, so I thought I'd spend them writing my first letter to my favorite person. If my printing's crooked, it's only because I drank too much apple cider tonight.

Even though I don't have much finery adorning my room yet, it seems that it's pretty much home. Tangible things can be awfully friendly at times. Even though I've only been here since three, an awful lot seems to have happened. I kind of like getting a quiet first acquaintance with my room and the girls.

I feel that I've wandered into a New York apartment by mistake . . . the maple on my desk feels like velvet. I love my room and am going to have a terrific time decorating it.

I lay down for half an hour and listened to the clock. I think I'm going to like it—the ticking is so rhythmic and self-assured that it's like the beat of someone's heart—so-o-o it stays on the bureau.

. . . After our little get-together, at which a delightful extrovert freshman from Kansas kept us in hysterics, we three freshmen sat and talked. After which I left them in their room on the first floor, drifted into conversation with Ann [*Davidow*] on the second, and finally arrived here at 11:30. Girls are a new world for me. I should have some fascinating times learning about the creatures. Gosh, to live in a house with 48 kids my own age—what a life! There are (don't faint) *600* in my class. Mrs. Shakespeare [*the house mother*] is very sweet. In fact, I like everything. . . .

Love, Sivvy*

SEPTEMBER 28, 1950

Dear Mummy,

. . . so far, I've gotten along with everyone in the house. It's good to see more faces familiar to me. I love my room, my location, and am firmly convinced that the whole episode here is up to me. I have no excuse for not getting along in all respects. Just to find a balance is the first problem.

We had our college assembly this morning. I never came so close to crying since I've been here when I saw the professors, resplendent with colors, medals, and emblems, march across the stage and heard adorable Mr. Wright's stimulating address. I still can't believe I'm a SMITH GIRL! . . .

The whole house is just the friendliest conglomeration of people imaginable. Gerry—one gorgeous creature—just got a picture and writeup in *Flair* as representative of Eastern Women's Colleges. People are always talking about Europe and New York. Lisa told me about how good it is not to work *too* hard, but to allot time for "playing with the kids in the house." Seems she's done a neat job of adjusting. I hope I can really get to *know* her sometime. She has quite a friendly attitude, and I could talk to her about almost anything.

Love, ME

SEPTEMBER 29, 1950

Dear Mummy,

The most utterly divine thing has happened to me. I was standing innocently in the parlor, having coffee after supper, when a senior said, sotto voce, in my ear, "I have a man all picked out for you." I just stood there with that "Who, me?" expression, and she proceeded

* [*"Sivvy" was Sylvia's family nickname.*]

Sylvia's high school graduation photo, 1950

to explain. Seems she met this young guy who lives in Mass. but went to Culver Military Academy. He is a freshman at Amherst this year, tall, cute and—get *this*—HE WRITES POETRY. I just sat there burbling inarticulately into my coffee. She said he should be around in a few weeks. God, am I thrilled. The hope, even, of getting to know a sensitive guy who isn't a roughneck makes the whole world swim in pink mist.

The food here is fabulous. I've had two helpings of everything since I got here and should gain a lot. I love everybody. If only I can unobtrusively do well in all my courses and get enough sleep, I should be tops. I'm *so* happy. And this anticipation makes everything super. I keep muttering, "I'M A SMITH GIRL NOW."

ME

SEPTEMBER 30, 1950
(MIDNIGHT)

Dear Mummy,

. . . my physical exam . . . consisted in getting swathed in a sheet and passing from one room to another in nudity. I'm so used to hearing, "Drop your sheet," that I have to watch myself now lest I forget to dress! My height is an even 5'9"; my weight 137; my posture, good; although when my posture picture was taken, I took such pains to get my ears and heels in a straight line that I forgot to tilt up straight. The result was the comment, "You have good alignment, but you are in constant danger of falling on your face."

. . . Then quickly back to the house to pick up the much-awaited mail. There was that lovely letter from you and *two* from Eddie* [*Cohen*]! . . . I'm so pleased with your news; it's all so happy—especially about Exeter. [*Grammy and I had visited her brother, Warren, there.*]

. . . After supper, we gathered around the piano and sang for a good hour. Never have I felt so happy, standing with a group of girls—with piano, Lisa's accordion, and two ukuleles—singing my favorite popular songs. It was such a wonderful feeling. No home life could make up for the camaraderie of living with a group of girls. I like them all.

After singing, two girls from our Annex house came up to my room for the purpose of studying. However we got in the process of learn-

* Eddie Cohen, a Chicago boy who wrote Sylvia a fan letter when her first story, "And Summer Shall Not Come Again," was published in *Seventeen*.

ing the Charleston . . . Ann Davidow stayed to do her Religion homework. We drifted into discussion, and she is the closest girl yet that I've wanted for a friend. She is a free thinker. We discussed God and religion and men. Her parents are Jewish. I find her very attractive—almost as tall as I, freckle-faced, short brown hair and twinkling blue eyes.

. . . The sensitive guy I told you about in the card has not yet materialized. I'll give him a month. I've fallen for him already merely because of the poetry angle.

Love, Sivvy

OCTOBER 1, 1950

Dear Mother,

. . . Ann Davidow, the lovely Jewish girl I told you about, got me a date from Amherst. . . . It was a triple date, and when the boys came, I was relieved to see that mine was 6 feet tall, slender, and cleancut. . . . I don't know just what chance of fate threw us together, but my first "blind date" sure was lucky. . . . Bill and I separated from the crowd and went down the hall to his room. It was lovely—a fireplace, records, big leather chairs. And somehow we got to talking very frankly. He surprised me by hitting rather well on a few points of my personality which I usually keep hidden. But there was a sensitivity about him which appealed to me in comparison with the hearty, roughneck, drinking crowd, so I talked quite openly. His manner is somewhat reminiscent of Warren. . . . He didn't even approach me, which is another thing in his favor. After we discussed several important things which I don't exactly recall—something about ego and religious belief—he got up abruptly, and we went to another house to dance. After a few dances, he led me, equally abruptly, out of the house, and, by mutual consent, we walked around the campus. Nothing is as beautiful as a campus at night. Music drifted out from the houses; fog blurred the lights, and from the hill, it looked as if we could step over the edge into nothingness . . .

Never, since I have come here, have I been in such an island of inner calm. I like people, but to learn about *one individual* always appeals to me more than anything. We sat and talked out in the cool dark of the steps, and I told him how I felt about being at ease. Seems he felt the same way. So we went home at 12:30 with the others, and

I felt very happy. To think that I didn't have to torture myself by sitting in a smoke-filled room with a painted party smile, watching my date get drunk! This guy was gentle and sweet. He goes out for crew, so I told him all about Warren. . . .

. . . Back at Haven [*House*], we stood for a while outside; the other couples were all coming up the walk, kissing each other regardless of onlookers. So he just smiled and looked at me, saying, "Some people just don't have any inhibitions," and kissed the tip of my nose briefly.

So that was that . . . said he was glad to know I lived at Haven so he wouldn't have to go scouting the campus for me.

Among his various observations: I live "hard," am dramatic in my manner, talk sometimes like a school girl reporting a theme, and have a Southern accent!

Don't mind my rambling. The first college date is a big thing and I really feel a part of life now.

Love, Sivvy

OCTOBER 3, 1950

Dear Mother,

Just got your Sunday letter this morning, so I thought I'd drop you a line. Your letters are utterly fascinating and they mean so much since I don't get much mail or have too much time to write coherently . . .

I wish I really did have only 18 hours of classes. With 24, I find myself hard pressed. I am enclosing a copy of my schedule, which may enlighten you somewhat. You see, I have six hours in both Art and Botany, which fills it in rather heavily . . .

. . . I am nowhere as physically exhausted as I was at first. In fact, I see a little order in the chaos already. Wait for a few weeks till I build up study habits and sleep habits . . . Just now I can't look ahead more than a few hours at a time. But that, I tell myself, is as it should be. Rome was not built in a day, and if I accept confusion as a normal consequence of being uprooted from home environment, I should be able to cope with my problems better.

Today should have been Mountain Day [*a random, beautiful day in October when classes are suspended so that students can go mountain climbing*]. The tree outside my window is pure shining gold. Oh, what joy to have no studies and to bike to the mountains!

Love, Sivvy

{Postcard}

Dear Mother,
    . . . If *only* I don't appear as stupid to my profs as I do to myself!
                                                        Love, Sivvy

{Postcard}

OCTOBER 5, 1950

Dear Mum,
    Don't worry that I'm sacrificing valuable time writing to you.
These cards take only a sec. Just before I hop to bed, thought I'd send
you a snatch of verse.

>Gold leaves shiver
>In this crack of time;
>Yellow flickers
>In the shrill clear sun;
>Light skips and dances,
>Pirouettes;
>While blue above
>Leaps the sheer sky.
>
>Gold leaves dangle
>In the wind.
>Gold threads snap.
>
>In giddy whirls
>And sweeps of fancy
>Sunlit leaves plane down.
>
>Lisping along the street
>In dry and deathless dance,
>The leaves on slipshod feet
>Advance and swirl
>   frisk
>   dip
>   spiral,
>   circle
>   twirl.
>
>Brief gold glitters
>In the gutters;
>Flares and flashes

Husky rushes;
Brisk wind hushes
    hushes
      hushes.

And in that moment, silent, cold
Across the lawn—dull pools of gold.

. . . As nasty as it is to have a sinus cold at the present moment, I have become philosophical and decided that it is a challenge.

. . . It is an Indian summer day—blue-skied, leaves golden, falling. Some girls are studying—some few. So I sit here, sheltered, the sun warming me inside. And life is good. Out of misery comes joy, clear and sweet. I feel that I am learning . . . I almost welcome this quiet solitude, since I feel still too shaky for much energetic work.

. . . I've dropped Warren a letter, but haven't heard from him yet. How I love that boy! Your cards are so sweet and sunny. . . .

This Austin [*the poet?*] was a sweet boy, but evidently likes short blondes, so I fear I must either cut myself in two or be sweet to Bill Gallup, who evidently has taken quite a fancy to me. He was talking to some girls over at Amherst about me this Sat. and one of them said later, "My *deah*, you made a great impression on him." Naturally, I blushed modestly.

God, today is lovely! My cold is still runny, but with plenty of sleep and nosedrops I should be well rid of it soon. By the way, do you suck those buffered penicillins or swallow with water? . . . I don't want to kill myself by taking them the wrong way!

Cheerio! Sivvy

. . . This weekend I went out Saturday with Bill. We doubled with Ann Davidow—that nice girl I told you about. We went over to Amherst as usual. Honestly, I have never seen anything so futile as their system of dating. The boys take their dates up to their rooms, usually to drink. After the first hour, the groups break up, and couples wander from fraternity to fraternity in search of a crowd into which they can merge or a "party" which they can join. It is like wandering from one plush room to another and finding the remains of an evening scattered here and there. I cannot say I give a damn about it. Bill, at least, is very sweet and thoughtful—nowhere as superficial as most of the boys I've run into over there. We were both quite tired and not in the mood for any party glitter, so we went to the suite, and I curled up on the red leather couch and dozed while he stretched out in a chair. He had built a fire and put on some good records, so for about two hours I rested, my eyes closed. We didn't even talk. At least both of us were tired at the same time. I almost have to laugh when I think back on it now. What would my house-mates say if they knew what an entertaining evening I spent? I don't suppose they would realize that I had a better time under the circum-stances than I could have had by straining to achieve a bright, empty smile in a crowd all night.

Sunday night I did the rather unwise thing of accepting a blind date to Alpha Delta (God, these Greek names are foolish!).

. . . My date had pictures and scrapbooks of his girl—a Smith girl spending her junior year abroad—around the room. So I was more or less just a date. It's funny, but the whole system of weekends seems more intent on saying: "I went to Yale" or "Dartmouth." That's enough—you've gone somewhere. Why add, "I had a hell of a time. I hated my date." You see, I don't think people with ideals like our mutual friends, the Nortons, frequent the bars where I have hitherto made my appearance (drinking Cokes). As for what I wore—my aqua dress Sat., and my red skirt and black jersey last night. This next weekend I have vowed to stay home and sleep and study. I wonder if I will ever meet a congenial boy. Oh, well—

OCTOBER 19, 1950

Dear Mum,

Another mild, orange-gold October day. Just to think I'm almost 18! I get a little frightened when I think of life slipping through my fingers like water—so fast that I have little time to stop running. I have to keep on like the White Queen to stay in the same place.

Today I have experienced the pin-point arranging of time. I painted my first art assignment . . . I did it hurriedly—a splashed color impression of Chapel Meeting, but I got a thrill out of thinking how much I may improve.

. . . That rest care at the infirmary was a lifesaver. Life looks so bright when you're rested and well.

Sylvia, Warren, and Aurelia in the backyard, before Sylvia left for Smith, 1950

Sylvia going off to Smith, September 5, 1950

OCTOBER 27, 1950
18TH BIRTHDAY

Dear Mum,

I couldn't wait another minute before writing you how touched I was to get my birthday package, which just came. I walked into the house after my last class, and there it was, so I ran upstairs to open it.

The Viyella maroon blouse is a dream (no wonder you are bankrupt) and the socks are warm and fit just right. I think I'll share the cake with the freshmen in the house tomorrow . . . the bureau scarf just *makes* the room. This is my first birthday away from home, so I was rather overwhelmed by the packages. This morning I got three cards . . . and my favorite gift of the day—a letter from and a picture of my brother! His snapshot now occupies a prominent place on my bulletin board. He is the handsomest, most wonderful boy in the world. I'm so proud of him . . .

Love, Sivvy

OCTOBER 31, 1950

Dear Mother,

Well, I have just come from a half hour session with Miss Mensel [*Mary Elizabeth Mensel, director of scholarships and student aid*]. I was really foolish to ask you what I should say to her. It all poured out during the course of the conversation. Really, she is the dearest person—not beautiful—freckled and gray-haired, rather—but with a keen, vital twinkle in her blue eyes. She wants to meet all the scholarship girls in the freshman class and get to know them so she can describe them and their needs to the Board. In other words, she is the personal medium through which the Board gets to know who we are and what we deserve. So I found myself telling her how stimulating my courses are—how the French relates with History and Art with Botany. How I want to take creative writing and art courses. I even said how I love my house and the girls in it—the older ones, too, who could give us a sort of perspective on college life. And about how nice it was to get dressed up and go out on weekends or just go bike riding through the countryside. I had to keep myself from getting tears in my eyes as I told her how happy I was. I only hope I can live up to my courses and get good grades . . . I was afraid I would be stiff and nervous at first, but my enthusiasm washed all that away, and I just flooded over and told her how stimulating it was here. She agrees that I am in a superlative house [*Haven House: the house mother,*

Mrs. Shakespeare, created a warm, relaxed, gracious atmosphere; this was a home for the students, rather than a dormitory] and also stressed the point about getting out on weekends so as not to go stale.

Now I come to the most thrilling part—about whose scholarship I have. The thing is Miss Mensel likes the girls to establish contact with their benefactors so the people who give out the money are rewarded by a flesh-and-blood case. And whom should my $850 come from but *Olive Higgins Prouty!!!* Miss Mensel said it was very seldom given to freshmen, but with my enjoyment of writing and my prize from the *Atlantic Monthly* (I'm afraid my *Atlantic Monthly* Honorable Mention has increased its prestige too much), Olive Higgins Prouty would be very pleased to hear from me and learn about my achievements and future plans and also about the impact Smith has had on me. Now I will plunge into those darn critical English themes with renewed vigor and go through my art exercises with that "means-to-an-end" gleam in my eye. If only I can meet all the opportunities! Just now I feel rather overwhelmed at the things Smith offers. Olive Higgins Prouty. Isn't she the one who dramatizes *Stella Dallas*? The fascinating thing is that she lives in Brookline, Mass.

I just can't stand the idea of being mediocre . . . I'll be studying and sleeping all Thanksgiving, I fear. About the going out angle—I'll plan on going out Saturday night and staying home the others. After all, I can go out all the time here, but my family isn't seen so often. . . .

As for Bob [*a high school boyfriend*] . . . frankly I hardly have time to give him a second thought . . . I am so busy finding out about Smith that I have no time to be either homesick or lovesick. Boys are strictly secondary in my present life. . . . I find myself numb as far as feeling goes. All I'm trying to do is keep my head above water, and emotions are more or less absent or dormant for the while. It's a good thing to have one less distraction.

If only I'm good enough to deserve all this!

Love, Sivvy

NOVEMBER 8, 1950

Dear Mother,

. . . I was rather embarrassed in English today when my teacher said to let the rest of the class work at a story analysis once in a while—that I was explaining too much. It's so annoying to sit back and watch people fumble over a point you see clearly. English is not too challenging, I fear.

Love, Sivvy

Dear Mother,

I was up in my room talking with a lovely girl . . . (she's one of the people I really can tell things to) . . . expounding on the misery and inferior feeling of being dateless this weekend. Bill *had* asked me out, but I had refused—he just isn't my sort—no spark . . . when the phone rang. It was Louise—three boys had just dropped over and would I go out tonight. So I threw on my clothes, all the time ranting . . . on how *never* to commit suicide, because something unexpected always happens. Turned out that my date was a doll . . . I now feel terrific—what a man can do. Oh, well, I'll do my homework before class tomorrow.

Love, Sivvy

Dear Mother,

There are times when schoolwork definitely should be put aside, regardless. And tonight was one of them. I have been working pretty steadily, so I decided I owed it to myself to hear Dr. Peter Bertocci of B.U. speak on "Sex Before Marriage." Naturally, the title of the lecture drew hordes, and the browsing room was packed to the gills. I have to hand it to the man: he knows what a college crowd needs—none of this dodging the issue, either. I quickly lost my consciousness of the fact that he has an unpleasantly raspy voice and became lost in the sound maze of his contentions. . . .

As for the substance of his talk, it was not to dictate, but to set up a pattern of inquiry in our own minds. His lecture was phrased so that you could apply your own history and ideals with the case histories and questions which he brought out.

Naturally my mind was receptive to clear, cold logic—no "Emile" around to make my emotions fight reason. [*The French version of her father's middle name, Emil, was the name she gave to a boyfriend who inspired her first prize-winning story, "Den of Lions."*] In fact, since I haven't really enjoyed myself with a boy since "Emile," my emotional problems are vague and dormant. Maybe it's a good thing. I have thrown all my energy, physical and mental, into Smith. Perhaps that would be a temporary sort of sublimation. The part that is hardest is this interregnum between boys. I need rather desperately to feel physically desirable at all times and mentally desirable in cases where I admire a boy for his ideas, too; but just now I am lacking any object of affection—no one to pour myself into except a close girl friend. . . . And I talk with her only too rarely.

In other words, this is a period of sterility emotionally. Mentally, it is a fertilization of the soil in my mind . . . who knows what may bloom in the fruitful season later on? Enough symbolism. I am happy, which is strange, as I realize myself socially and emotionally unfulfilled. But with my old resilient optimism, I know deep down inside that when I find a *real* companion in a boy, I will be only too glad I had this period of static waiting to increase my sense of pleasure.

As to my subjects—I'm beginning to see light. I love them all. I'm being stretched, pulled to heights and depths of thought I never dreamed possible—and what is most wonderful—this is only a beginning. The future holds infinite hope and challenge. I somehow can't keep from singing to myself, no matter how weary I am. Sunshine which I had when I was little seems to have been restored by Smith, and I know that, in the cycle of joy and sorrow, there will always be an outlet for me. I can never lose everything—all at once. Once I get my scholarship firmly established, I may have time to turn my attention more thoroughly to art and creative writing. Even now I am greatly encouraged to find that the black, immovable wall of competition is not so formidable when broken down into small human units. I am finding myself still in upper brackets as far as marks go. Sure, I work hard, and so do hundreds of others. But my sane weekend life has kept me healthy and able to cope with most daily work. I'm getting study habits, keeping up. When I get that down to a science, I can weekend with relative impunity.

Above all, I'm happy—knowing that from pain comes understanding, I rejoice in whatever happens. Strangely enough, I am rather well-adjusted, I think, and enjoying life more fully than I ever have.

If only I can weld the *now*—where I'm living so hard I have no energy to produce—into art and writing later on! It's like animals storing up fat and then, in hibernation or relaxation, using it up. I have a feeling that my love of learning, of people, of wanting to perfect techniques of expression may help me to reach the goals I choose to set. Can you make any sense out of this? Maybe you can analyze the ramblings of your child better than she can herself.

Love, Sivvy

NOVEMBER 27, 1950

Dear Mum,

Well, I didn't know just when the wave of homesickness would hit [*on return to Smith after Thanksgiving holidays*], but I guess it was when I walked into my room—empty and bare. Only three or four girls were in the house . . . Gosh, I felt lonely! I had so much work I should have done, and my schedule for the week looked so bleak and unsurmountable; but I have now snapped out of my great depression—the first real sad mood I've had since I've been here. I am now writing this in the cosy living room with a girl beside me and music coming out of the radio. What one human presence can mean!

I realize that for all my brave, bold talk of being self-sufficient, I realize now how much you mean to me—you and Warren and my dear Grampy and Grammy! . . . I am glad the rain is coming down hard. It's the way I feel inside. I love you *so*.

Sivvy

NOVEMBER 30, 1950

Dear Mum,

By the way, I'm almost famous! There is a bulletin board in College Hall (where the President and all the deans work), which has weekly clippings of Smith girls "in the news." Yup, some news hound dug up my poem ["*Ode to a Bitten Plum*," Seventeen, *November 1950*] and it and my face shine out.

I had a strange experience in history today. As I always sit in the middle seat in the front row, it seems as if Mrs. Kafka is talking directly to me. I felt the oddest thrill. History is becoming rather vital and fascinating . . .

DECEMBER 1, 1950

. . . Wrote a long letter to Mrs. Prouty last night which took up a few hours of thought and time, but, good heavens, *she* is responsible for all this!

{Excerpts from the letter to Olive Higgins Prouty were published in the Smith Alumnae Quarterly, *February 1951, reprinted below.}*

At first I didn't want to let myself hope for Smith, because a disappointment would have been hard. But more and more I became aware of how much fuller my life would be if I were able to live away from home. There would be a beginning of independence, and then the stimulation of living with a group of girls my own age. After weeks of waiting and indecision, I heard from Smith that I was being awarded a scholarship . . . so I went about the house for days in a sort of trance and not quite believing myself when I heard my voice saying: "Yes, I'm going to Smith."

And here I am! There are times when I find myself just letting the sights and impressions pour into me until the joy is so sharp that it almost hurts. I think it will always be this way. There is so much here, and it is up to me to find myself and make the person I will be. I still remember the first evening when we had our freshman meeting. I was separated from the girls I knew in my house, and as I stood bewildered on the steps of Scott Gym, watching 600 strange faces surge at me and pass by like a flood, I felt that I was drowning in a sea of personalities, each one as eager to be a whole individual as I was. I wondered then if I could ever get behind the faces and know what they were thinking, dreaming, and planning deep inside. I wondered if I would ever feel that I was more than a name typewritten on a card.

But even now I smile at myself. For with the studying and with the ability to isolate and differentiate one person from another, and with the increasing sense of belonging, I find myself at the beginning of the most challenging experience I've ever had.

As for my courses, I have never felt such a sharp sense of stimulation and competition. I am especially fortunate in my instructors—all of whom are vital and alive with enthusiasm for their particular subjects. In art we sketch the same trees that we analyze in botany. In French we follow the ideas of men who were influenced by the events and times we read about in history. And in English—which has always been my favorite subject—we read and do critical essays. . . . As you can see, my courses fit together like a picture puzzle, and life has suddenly taken on deeper perspective and meaning.

I don't just see trees when I bike across the campus. I see shape and color outwardly, and then the cells and the microscopic mechanisms always working inside. No doubt all this sounds a bit incoherent, but it's just that excitement which comes when you are increasingly aware of the infinite suggestions and possibilities of the world you live in.

The people here are also another source of amazement and new discovery. I don't think I've ever been so conscious of the dignity and capacity of women. Why, even in my house there is a startling collection of intelligent, perceptive girls—each one fascinating in her own way. I enjoy knowing people well and learning about their thoughts and backgrounds. Although I have never been able to travel outside the New England states, I feel that the nation—and a good part of the world—is at my fingertips. My acquaintances come from all sorts of homes, all sorts of localities, and as I get to know them better, I learn about all varieties of past personal history. . . .

I wonder . . . if I have revealed even a small part of my love for Smith. There are so many little details that are so wonderful—the lights of the houses against the night sky, the chapel bells on Sunday afternoon, the glimpse of Paradise from my window. All this and so much more. . . . I just want you to understand that you are responsible, in a sense, for the formation of an individual, and I am fortunate enough to be that person.

DECEMBER 4, 1950

. . . I am learning a lot. There is the sort of person who has problems and never tells them to anyone and thus no one ever knows them; there is the sort of person who has problems and tells them to one understanding person, and there is the sort of person who fools everyone, even herself, into thinking there are no problems except those shallow material ones which can be overcome.

All this, as you may have gathered, leads up to my date last night. As I said, I doubled with Patsy. It was ordinary enough, driving over with the couples—my date looked rather old (in fact, his hair was somewhat reminiscent of Mr. Crockett's) and he had a rather good-looking face. It developed that he and I like English and that he was majoring in Political Science. So as we all sat around the fire, I decided to stab in the dark and see if I could get to know him better. I told him how I like to write and draw and know people more than just on the surface, and I said I'd like him to tell me all about the things that ever had hurt or bothered him so I'd be able to understand him better. Well, it was just a try, but evidently he was rather overwhelmed by the fact that I could be so intelligent and yet not be ugly or something, and as we danced after cooking our supper over the fireplace in their room at the Fraternity House, he told me that he was twenty-five, disabled in the last war. Naturally that bowled me over, so I asked if he could tell me at all about it.

Pat had said that his roommates don't *really* know him because he keeps everything to himself, so I was rather amazed that he would confide in me.

At his suggestion, we went for a walk so we could talk better, and he told me a little about fighting in the Marianas and about what it is like to have to kill someone or be killed. Then he asked when my father died, and when I told him, he said his died two weeks ago and that he had been with him for the last days. It seems his father was the best patent attorney in Missouri—clients from England even, and this guy adored him . . . So he told me how he felt about him and said that the other girls he'd been out with since didn't give a damn, etc.

Naturally nothing like that had ever happened to me before, and I guess he was so overwhelmed with the idea that at last someone was interested in him as a person, not just as a date, that he seemed to think we should have intercourse. Of course, I was in rather a bad position, having gaily gone on a walk, but I told him quite forcibly that I wouldn't oblige—all of which made a scene, and I asked him how many other girls he had known, and he said he would tell me the truth, that the Marine Corps wasn't the place to be a gentleman and that ideals didn't quite matter when you slept and lived in the mud. So I learned about the girl in Hawaii and about the English nurse when he was in the hospital for two years.

. . . I came home in rather a fog. I don't know just how things will work out or whether I should see him again. I am just beginning to realize that you can't ostracize a person for having relations with a lot of others. That doesn't automatically cancel out their worth as human beings. . . . I would like your opinion on the matter, as I don't quite know what to make of it, never having run into anyone quite so determined before.

It's sickening to see all the uniforms on campus and hear that Amherst won't even be here next year. I am *so* tired, and I'm looking so forward to being with the family this Christmas.

Keep smiling. (*Why* do I always inspire males to pour out their life story on my shoulder? I guess I just ask for it.)

DECEMBER 7, 1950

Dear Mum,

Your letter and one from Olive Higgins Prouty came in the same mail . . . I was thrilled to see Mrs. Prouty's scratchy, almost illegible hand. Her letter is one I will always keep. She thinks I have "a gift for creative writing" and wants me to send her some of my poems and drop in to have a cup of tea when I come home on vacation. [*Their meeting inspired an (unpublished) manuscript written for—and rejected by—Reader's Digest, "Tea with Olive Higgins Prouty."*] She even said she's having my letter typed up with carbons to send to some of her alumnae friends. It makes me feel so wonderful that I could even partly express to her how I felt about Smith, and as Miss Mensel said, it's nice to have a scholarship mean more than a grant of money.

Love, Sivvy

Dear Mother,

. . . I have been rather worried about a friend of mine. . . . Her usual gaiety has been getting brighter and more artificial as the days go by. So yesterday, after lunch, I made her come up to my room. At first she was very light and evasive, but at last her face gave way and melted. It seems that since Thanksgiving she hasn't been able to do her work, and now, having let it slide, she can only reiterate, "I can never do it, never." She hasn't been getting enough sleep, but has been waking up early in the morning, obsessed by the feeling she has to do her work, even if she is in such a state that she can only go through the motions. . . . She finally told me that she had realized she was not intelligent enough for Smith—that if she could do the work, nothing would matter, but her parents were either deceiving her into thinking she was creative or really didn't know how incapable she was. The girl was in such a state of numbness that she didn't feel any emotion, I guess, except this panic. I got scared when she told me how she had been saving sleeping pills and razor blades and could think of nothing better than to commit suicide.* Oh, mother, you don't know how inadequate I felt. I talked to her all afternoon . . . If only I could make her sleep and personally supervise her for a few days! I can't say anything to Mrs. Shakespeare or anyone here, because [she] would only put up a mental barrier, thinking they wouldn't understand. But I have been thinking of writing a note to her parents (she admitted that it would be more convenient if she took the car and killed herself at home . . .) telling them a bit of how tired she is and how she needs rest before she can do her work. For her mother kept telling her she was foolish and could do it all. But her mother couldn't really see how incapable the poor girl is of thinking in this state.

Oh, well, maybe it's none of my business, but I love the girl and feel very inadequate and responsible. If you were her mother, she would be all right.

Love, Sivvy

* Actually, the girl in question was not suicidal; perhaps Sylvia's earlier Thanksgiving depression was influencing her words here. Yet when Sylvia found herself in a similar state two years later, razor blades and sleeping pills were her first thoughts.

Dear Mother,

. . . You no doubt wondered what that Special Delivery letter from our favorite magazine was about. I can picture you feeling how thick it was and holding it up to the light. Well don't get *too* excited, 'cause it's only a third prize, but it does mean $100 (one hundred) in cold, cold cash. Seriously, I'm kind of dazed. I did love "Den of Lions" and Emile's name sure worked as a lucky piece. It seems my love affairs always get into print, only I doubt if anyone will recognize this one. *This* time I've *got* to get a good photograph—or snapshot. I'll bring home the documents to be signed when I come home in a week and a half. Could you have that old roll of film developed? It would save expense if I had a good snapshot of myself on it.

Honestly, Mother, can't you see it now? An illustration for it and everything? I'll show you the letter from the editor (very conventional and *Seventeenish* and "hope you have a long, successful career," etc.) when I see you. I'm dying to see what got 1st and 2nd prize. Oh, well, you can't always hit the top! But Clem's mother better watch out. I'll be Sarah-Elizabeth-Rodgering her out of business in no time. [*Sarah-Elizabeth Rodger: the novelist and highly successful writer of magazine fiction. Her son, Clement, was a classmate of Warren's at Exeter and Harvard.*]

FEBRUARY 21, 1951

Although you brushed with almost hysterical gaiety over your ulcer—I am only too aware that Fran's [*my doctor's*] "demotion" was caused by trouble. I don't want you to worry about things, Mummy. Is it money? or Warren? As for money, I have good news. Marcia [*Brown*] and I got a double-decker on the second floor, and that will be $50 less for the year. (I slept in one when I visited her, and managed quite well.)

[Undated; written early February 1951]

Dear Mother,

. . . As for my weekend, I thought I'd wait to tell you after it happened . . . I left Saturday morning to go to Yale with Dick Norton [*a family friend and Yale student who became an important boyfriend*], who wrote and asked me to drop down for a day or two, for God knows what reason. I think he thought it would be a nice thing to do—show little "cousin" round the campus. But I did have a good time and learned a great deal.

It rained all day Saturday, so we sat and talked in his room. He knows everything. I am so firmly convinced that knowledge comes through science that I would like to get some elementary books of physics or chemistry or math and study them this spring vacation and this summer. Perhaps Warren could help me. For I am the strange sort of person who believes in the impersonal laws of science as a God of sorts and yet does not know what any of those laws are . . . All that I write or paint is, to me, valueless if not evolved from a concrete basis of reasoning, however uncomplex it must be . . . Poetry and art may be the manifestations I'm best suited for, but there's no reason why I can't learn a few physical laws to hold me down to something nearer truth.

I came away last night feeling desperately eager to learn more and more. It's so easy to be satisfied with yourself if you aren't exposed to people farther advanced . . . I kept asking Dick to tell me about his interview results in sociology, and about what he met up with at the mental institution and all. It was a process of assimilation and taking on *my* part and, of necessity, nothing reciprocal. But he has an amazing mind and a remarkable group of highly developed skills— dancing, skating, swimming and so on. So I felt a bit guilty to take up two days. You'll have to admit it was a rather unselfish gesture on his part . . .

Love, Sivvy

-{Postcard}-

FEBRUARY 25, 1951

Just thought I'd tell you something that surprised me a bit. A senior said to me at lunch, "Congrats for being up on the College Hall Bulletin Board again." (Smith girls in the news, you know!) So, full of curiosity, I hurried over. You should have seen it. I stood for a full five minutes laughing. It was one of those cartoon and personality write-ups titled "Teen Triumphs." There was a sketch of a girl s'posed to be me—writing, also a cow. It said, and I quote: "BORN TO WRITE! Sylvia Plath, 17, really works at writing. To get atmosphere for a story about a farm she took a job as a farmhand. Now she's working on a sea story." Then there's another sketch of me saying, "and I'll get a job on a boat." Not only that. "A national magazine has published two of her brain children, the real test of being a writer. The little Wellesley, Mass. blonde has won a full scholarship* to Smith College." All this effusive stuff appeared in the Peoria, Illinois, *Star* on January 23. Beats me where they got the sea stuff. I just laughed and laughed.

<{Postcard}>

Dear Mother,

I think I shall start a new scrapbook about myself, what with all my little attempts at writing being blown up rather out of proportion. Imagine, one awestruck girl greeted me yesterday with, "I hear you're writing a *novel*. I think that's just wonderful!" Whereupon I felt like telling her I was my twin sister and never wrote a damn thing in my life. I've got to get to work if I'm to live up to my "reputation." At least Olive Higgins Prouty can feel I really *do* write. Seems that scholarship was rather well chosen. Hope the dear is content.

Love, Sivvy

April 18, 1951

Dear Mother,

When I consider that there are but 45 days left to my freshman year in college, I feel frightened. At the same time that I wish the tension and exams were over, so do I realize that I am thus wishing my life away. And as I look ahead I see only an accelerated work-pattern until the day I drop into the grave. One encouraging thing— we had a talk on taking honors this morning in chapel, and the twelve hour week appeals to me no end. I will *definitely* honor! This twenty-four hour schedule runs *me,* and I am sick of having to do work in isolated pieces with no time to follow thru various absorbing facets of it.

I am extremely lost as to which courses to take next year. I *must* take a practical art and a creative writing course, but I am still unde-

* While Sylvia's scholarships to Smith were generous, she was never granted a *full* scholarship.

cided as to my major. I should also take both an English lit and a history of art course in case I choose one or the other. Also I should take science and govt or sociology, which leaves me in conflict. Sometimes I wonder whether or not I should go into social work. If I did that, I could earn my own living—or if you could get me started secretarially next summer, I might lay in summer experience for that "U.N. job." The question is—shall I plan for a career? (ugh—I hate the word) or should I major in English and art and have a free lance career? If I ever catch a man who can put up with the idea of having a wife who likes to be alone and working artistically now and then. I would like to start thinking about where I'll put the emphasis for the rest of my brief life.

If I get battered and discouraged in my creative course next year, I don't care. Olive Higgins Prouty said I "had something." Mr. Manzi, my art teacher, spent an hour telling me how he liked what I was turning out in art (before supper, too, and he's a gourmet, at that).

As for jobs . . . Marcia and I are seeing about one for two friends, baby sitting in Swampscott. Wish us luck!

Love, Sivvy

MAY 6, 1951

Dear Mum,

. . . I was quite amused to receive your comments on the story along with Eddie's [Cohen] and Dick's [Norton]. Dick, I think, was perhaps a bit impressed and actually said he liked it. He is such a dear. I got a charming long letter from him all about it, saying how he showed the thing to various and sundry of his friends.

Eddie was also surprisingly sweet and laudatory, and his criticisms were all extremely valid. It's funny, but he said some things that I had never thought of—about how he thought it should have gotten 1st, but 17 probably put it on a lower level because of the fuzzy characterization of Emile and the not-strong-enough explanation of Marcia's decision. He also thought the metaphors were "lovely writing" but too overdone—inhibiting straight action and dialogue. I can't say it as well as he did, but I can see his points completely.

As for me, I think practice will help me grasp even larger situations. This new experience with children [summer baby-sitting job] might prove writable, too.

Love, Sivvy

Dear Mother,

Sometimes I think the gods have it in for me. Things have been much too smooth and placid so far. Anyhow, I'm over my cold, pretty well caught up in everything except Art, when—bang!

I got my program pretty well settled for next year with my advisor (who is also my Botany teacher), when, as I was striding cheerfully and skippingly out of his office, I slipped on the smooth stone floor and fell on my ankle, which gave a nasty and protesting crunch. The train of events involved my throwing my arms about dear Mr. Wright's neck and getting him to half-carry me downstairs to his car. The doctor taped it, and I had it x-rayed this morning for a possible break.

Needless to say, what with a huge English paper due tomorrow and this divine weekend tottering in the balance, I feel all too close to tears. But self-pity isn't appreciated by people who have the use of their two feet, so I swallow my salty sobs and grin bravely.

If it's a break, I'll have to have a cast. That would definitely finish the idea of my going anywhere. If it's only a bad sprain, I'll call Dick and ask him if I can limp down. If he doesn't want me down, I'll ask him up, and if he doesn't want me either way, he's a bad doctor and a poor sport.

Seriously, I will ask for Mondays off [*from summer baby-sitting job*]—because there is nothing I'd rather do than see Dick. I really do think he's the most stimulating boy I've ever known, and I don't care much about anybody else anyway. I suppose I might be conservative and say that I adore him and worship his intellect and keen perceptions in almost every field. But I still think that if he ever saw me with noseguards on, flailing impotently in the water, or with skates on, standing on my ankles, that his enthusiasm in my direction might cool rapidly. . . .

However, I have a rather odd feeling that the more I see Dick the more I like him and the more I like him the more I want to show him things and get his reactions on things. Of course, I could always play safe and withdraw myself into a protective little shell so I won't feel too sad when he wearies of my company and browses in greener fields. Ah, me!

. . . Pray it's not a break, dear Mummy! [*It wasn't.*] And if so, I *will* keep my chin up. If you ever want to call me, try between six and seven, as I am usually here for supper. Love you very much.

Sivvy

Dear Mother,

. . . If only you could be here today! I never have seen such lovely weather in my life! . . . As I write at my desk in front of the open window I can hear the subdued murmur of twilight birds, see leady silhouettes of treetops, and one evening star . . .

As you probably know, I'm going to the Yale Commencement and Dick will probably drive me home on the second of June after my last French exam . . . By the way, Dick has the queer idea that daughters grow to be like their mothers. You better not be so capable and wonderful, because the poor boy doesn't know that I'm rather an awkward hybrid. I pointed out the discrepancy in our noses as an indication that like does not *always* breed like. He also thinks I have negroid features . . . say, we get compliments we ain't even used yet.

I am *definitely* majoring in English. My schedule, tentative as it is, looks pretty good so far.

SWAMPSCOTT, MASS.
JUNE 20, 1951

C'est la vie!

Dear Mother,

Say, but I feel that I'm cut off from all humankind. I don't even know how I can last one week. I feel like putting my head on your shoulder and weeping from sheer homesickness. They say not to let children be tyrants over you. Fine, but I'd like to know just how you get a thing done on your own if you are continually to "keep an eye" on them while they play when they want you to put them up on swings or play ball, or if I should maybe run after them all the time just so they'll think I'm on the job.

Last night I couldn't sleep and couldn't sleep just because I wanted so badly to spill over to someone. My day begins at 6 or 6:30 with the first cry or bright face bursting in the door. Mr. and Mrs. M. sleep downstairs with the baby who is just a toddler and who "loves to get into everything." The 4-year-old girl is a "me-do," always doing death-defying leaps after big brother on the trapeze. After I get the two older ones washed and dressed, I go down and help with breakfast, after which I do dishes, make beds, pick up and mop the kids' rooms, do laundry in the Bendix and hang it out, watch the children. There is no cook here, so a woman comes three days a week. I just hope she makes lunch for the kids and me on those days. She is very capable and I don't know just whether I'll be in her way or not when I clumsily monkey about in the kitchen. But I'd love it if you could tell me how to cook some meats and vegetables . . . 'cause I cook our lunches when Helen (the lady) isn't here. (Hah!) After lunch the two youngest are supposed to have naps, while the boy plays around by himself. I *hope* to be able to rest in my room for an hour then, although I will do the ironing whenever there's time—just for the kids who change clothes every day so every day there's wash and ironing to do. I get the supper for myself and the children and hope I feel more like eating as the days go by. After supper, I wash the baby and put her to bed. The two oldest play out till after seven, whereupon I call them in, bathe them and put them to bed. If I have my way, they'll all be out of the way by eight, by which time I shall probably be so dead that I can no more look at a book than anything . . .

Do I ignore their fights? Do I try to break them up? How do you inspire kids with awe and respect? By being decisive? By being ominously quiet?

Outside it is lovely. From my window I can see the beach. So I sit here exhausted, seeing no way out, seeing only slavery from six in the morning till eight at night . . .

One sure thing, I don't feel like traveling to Brewster [*Cape Cod, to see Dick*]. My face is a mess, all broken out; my tan is faded, my eyes are sunken. If I could be pretty, I wouldn't mind so much. But I shall do my best and try to keep the letters heading that way cheerful . . .

Do write me now and then, but don't expect to hear from me too often . . .

Your bewildered . . . Sivvy

JULY 7, 1951

Dear Mummy,

. . . I feel very sorry I don't write more often, Mumsy, because your letters are great sustenance to me. I miss you and home and Warren, and wouldn't mind so much if I felt I was *learning* anything, or writing or drawing something worthwhile . . . When there is no one around to make you feel wanted and appreciated, it's sort of easy to talk yourself into feeling worthless. I haven't really *thought* about anything since I've been here. My reactions have been primarily blind and emotional—fear, insecurity, uncertainty, and anger at *myself* for making myself so stupid and miserable.

. . . *Seventeen* sent two brief mimeographed copies of eulogistic letters about my story. I laugh a bit sadistically and take them out to read whenever I think I'm a worthless, ungifted lummox—some gal by the name of Sylvia Plath sure has something—but who is she anyhow?

> "My head is bloody, but unbowed,"
> May children's bones bedeck my shroud.

x x Sivvy

P.S. I *will* grow up in jerks, it seems, so don't feel my growing pains too vicariously, dear. Love you all heaps.

AUGUST 4, 1951

In spite of getting in at 2 o'clock this morning, I arose before eight and whipped up breakfast per usual . . . The occasion last night was a double date for a "beach party" with Marcia. . . . I ended up with a Junior at Dartmouth, who is a life guard for the Corinthian Yacht Club. We all went down to the beach where many other couples had congregated, and it turned out that my date had a guitar and could strum out songs like nothing at all. I actually drank some cold beer, which tasted pretty good . . .

My boy liked skiing better than anything else in the world, but he was so gifted in all physical attributes—such as swimming, football, Charlestoning, singing, pool playing, and so on, that I guess I bored him, perhaps. But I realized how much of the active life I've missed. Ski jumping must be a great religion. . . . I suddenly envied him very much for the life he leads. Boys live so much harder than girls, and they know so much more about life. Learning the limitations of a woman's sphere is no fun at all.

Love, Sivvy

AUGUST 11, 1951

Dear Mummy,

I can't tell you how much our stay at 26 Elmwood [*home*] meant to me this last Tuesday. You did a faultless job at having the house clean-swept and uncluttered. I love every corner of that dear place with all my heart. I was wondering if my stay in this mansion would sour or embitter me in regard to my relatively small lodgings. On the contrary—I associate home with all the self-possession and love which is an intrinsic part of my nature and find a great overwhelming pleasure in coming back from my travels in the realm of adult independence to lay my head in blissful peace and security under my own hospitable roof. You and Grammy and Grampy and Warren are so lovely to be around after long months away from all companions, save Marcia. Thanks again for being such a dear and understanding mummy. Marcia loves you, too . . .

AUGUST 17, 1951

[*Cooking automatic now; children amenable.*]

. . . I really am enjoying myself, especially since I got those wonderful pastels. Already, I've done a big, full-sized self-portrait which came out sort of yellowish and sulky, but the face isn't bad at all. Quite traditional. Thought that when I get home, I could cut it down. I love the hard pastels—much more precise than the soft and cleaner cut. Only thing I've got to get over is the "rubbing" habit. I liken it to putting too much pedal on a sloppily played piano piece—it only serves to blur mistakes. Next subject: Freddie. He's the only one around here who can sit still. [*Pen-and-ink drawings of all three children accompanied "As a Baby-Sitter Sees It" in the* Christian Science Monitor.]

AUGUST 22, 1951

Dear Mum,

Dick has come and gone again, and this time our encounter was sane and rained upon.

As soon as Dick came, before noon, a clap of thunder . . . and it began to pour. We ended up by cooking and eating at Lane's house. The afternoon was spent in biking to Castle Rock and Marblehead, getting soaked by another shower and finishing our food by a roadside in the car. Not quite what I had planned. However . . .

Dick left at seven, and I felt the sudden need for some vicious activity, no doubt to get rid of a few months of physically barren living. Even a regular cadence of weekend dating provides enough male friction or magnetism, taken in small doses, at a distance. And that system can cope with this emotional business. . . .

. . . I wondered what on earth I could do, standing in my room alone. Finally I had it! I looked at the angry gray ocean, darkening in late twilight. So I put on my bathing suit and ran barefoot down to the beach. It is a queer sensation to swim at night, but it was very warm after the rain, so I splashed and kicked and the foam was strangely white in the dark. After I staggered out, I put on my sweatshirt and alternately ran and walked the length of the beach and back.

As I walked into the house, my purpose accomplished, I said goodnight to the M.'s who gasped, "You went swimming *alone?*"

They must think I'm crazy, what with never having a date, reading every spare minute and going to bed early. But what the heck do I care. They leave on the cruise in three days, and I'll be on my own for the rest of my time here.

So-o-o, only about twelve more days . . . There is so much I want to do and so little time to do it in!

x x Sivvy

AUGUST 24, 1951

. . . I finally know definitely that I will be home on Monday, the third of September . . . I feel I owe myself a brief respite of leisure and no rushing around. Heaven knows I have enough to do with the Cape job-hunting prospect, the driving appointment, the 10-minute speech [*to give before the Wellesley Smith Club*] and the few stories that I *must* write.

What do you think of the following merely descriptive lines:

> The acid gossip of the caustic wind,
> The wry pucker of the lemon-colored moon,
> And the sour blinking of the jaundiced stars . . .

Or have I degenerated horribly in my verbal expression?

x x x Sivvy

{Note on back of envelope}

Caution: To be read at leisure, sitting down—in a good light—slowly—[*All the girls at Haven House were invited to Maureen Buckley's coming-out party.*]

Dear Mother,

How can I ever, ever tell you what a unique, dreamlike and astounding weekend I had! Never in my life, and perhaps never again, will I live through such a fantastic twenty-four hours. Like years, it seems—so much of my life was involved.

As it is, I'll start out with an attempt at time sequence. Saturday afternoon, at 2 p.m., about 15 girls from Smith started out for Sharon [Connecticut]. Marcia and I drew a cream-colored convertible (with three other girls and a Dartmouth boy). Picture me then in my navy-blue bolero suit and versatile brown coat, snuggled in the back seat of an open car, whizzing for two sun-colored hours through the hilly Connecticut valley! The foliage was out in full tilt, and the hills of crimson sumac, yellow maples and scarlet oak that revolved past— the late afternoon sun on them—were almost more than I could bear.

At about 5 p.m. we rolled up the long drive to "The Elms." God! . . . Great lawns and huge trees on a hill, with a view of the valley, distant green cow pastures, orange and yellow leaves receding far into blue-purple distance.

A caterer's truck was unloading champagne at the back. We walked through the hall, greeted by a thousand living rooms, period pieces, rare objects of art everywhere. On the third floor (every room was on a different level) most of the girls slept. Marcia and I and Joan Strong (a lovely girl, daughter of a former headmaster of Pomfret) had the best deal. We lived across the way at "Stone House," a similar mansion. Marcia and I had a big double bed and bath to ourselves in a room reminiscent of a period novel, with balconies, gold drapes, and another astounding view. We lay down under a big quilt for an hour in the gray-purple twilight, conjecturing about the exciting, unknown evening fast coming.

Joan, Marcia, and I were driven in a great black Cadillac by one of the Buckley chauffeurs to the Sharon Inn where a lovely buffet supper was prepared for the 20–30 girls. After supper, Marcia, Joan, and I skipped and ran along the lovely dark moonlit road to our mansion. Another hour of lying down (reminding me of Scarlett O'Hara before the ball) and then the dressing. I struck up a delightful conversation (while ironing my black formal) with the Filipino houseboy.

Again the chauffeur. Up the stone steps, under the white colonial columns of the Buckley home. Girls in beautiful gowns clustered by the stair. Everywhere there were swishes of taffeta, satin, silk. I looked at Marcia, lovely in a lilac moiré, and we winked at each other, walking out in the patio. Being early, we had a chance to look around. The patio was in the center of the house, two stories high, with the elm treetops visible through the glassed-in roof. Remember Mrs. Jack's patio? [*Isabella Stuart Gardner Museum, Boston, Mass.*] The same: vines trailing from a balcony, fountains playing, blue glazed tiles set in mosaic on the floor, pink walls, and plants growing everywhere. French doors led through a tented marquee built out on the lawn. . . . Two bars and the omnipresent waiters were serving champagne. Balloons, Japanese lanterns, tables covered with white linen—leaves covered ceiling and walls. A band platform was built up for dancing. I stood open-mouthed, giddy, bubbling, wanting so much to show you. I am sure you would have been supremely happy if you had seen me. I know I looked beautiful. Even daughters of millionaires complimented my dress.

About 9:30 we were "announced" and received. There was a suspenseful time of standing in fluttering feminine groups, waiting for the dancing to begin, drinking the lilting, bubbling, effervescent champagne. I began to wish I had brought a date, envying the initial security of the girls that had, wondering if I could compete with all the tall, lovely girls there.

Let me tell you, by the end of the evening, I was *so* glad I hadn't hampered my style by a date and been obligated like the girls who did.

I found myself standing next to a bespectacled Yale Senior. (The *whole* Senior class at Yale was there—it was just about All-Yale to All-Smith!)

Maureen's brother is a senior. (*Ten* children in the Catholic family, all brilliant, many writers!)

I decided I might as well dance instead of waiting for a handsome man to come along. The boy was . . . a scholarship Philosophy major, admitting a great inferiority complex. We got talking over champagne, and I had just about convinced him that he should be a teacher when we went back to dance. "Darn," I thought, "I can see me bolstering inferiority complexes all night."

At that point a lovely tall hook-nosed freshman named Eric cut in. We cooled off on a terrace, sitting on a couch, staring up into leaves dramatically lighted. Turned out we both love English. Great deal in common.

Back to floor with Carl [*the philosophy major*], who asked me to Cornell weekend. I refused: nicely. Eric cut in.

Next I had a brief trot with the Editor of the *Yale News*. No possibilities there. About then the Yale Whiffenpoofs sang, among whom was one of Dick's old roommates, who grinned and chatted with me later.

Now, suddenly, a lovely grinning dark-haired boy cut in. "Name?" I asked. The result was a sort of foreign gibberish. Upon a challenge, he produced a card bearing the engraved "Constantine Sidamon-Eristoff" [*later a member of the Lindsay administration in New York*] . . .

He was a wonderful dancer and twirled so all I could see was a great cartwheel of colored lights, the one constant being his handsome face. Turned out his father was a general of the Georgian forces in the Russian Caucasus Mountains. He's a senior at Princeton.

I was interrupted in a wild Charleston (champagne does wonders for my dancing prowess. I danced steps I never dreamed of and my feet just flew with no propulsion of mine) by a tall . . . boy, who claimed his name was Plato. By that time, I was convinced that everyone was conspiring against me as far as names were concerned. Turned out he really *was*—Plato Skouras whose father is a Greek—head of 20th Century Fox productions. Plato did the sweetest thing anyone has ever done. In the midst of dancing on the built-up platform amid much gay music, he said, "I have a picture I want to show you." So we crossed through the cool, leaf-covered patio, the sound of the fountain dripping, and entered one of the many drawing rooms. Over the fireplace was a Botticelli Madonna.

"You remind me of her," he said.

I was really touched. . . . I learned later that he has traveled all over the world. Speaks several languages, including Greek . . . A devout Catholic, I learned that he believes in the Divine Revelation of the Bible and in Judgment Day, etc. You can imagine how much I would like to have really gotten into an intense discussion with him. As it was, I had a lovely dialogue. Imagine meeting such fascinating, intelligent, versatile people! At a party, too.

From there followed a few more incidental people, and, saving best to last, my Constantine. Again he cut in, and we danced and danced. Finally we were so hot and breathless that we walked out on the lawn. The night was lovely, stars out, trees big and dark, so guess what we did—Strauss waltzes! You should have seen us swooping and whirling over the grass, with the music from inside faint and distant.

Constantine and I really talked. I found that I could say what I meant, use big words, say intelligent things to him.

Imagine, on a night like that, to have a handsome, perceptive male kiss your hand and tell you how beautiful you were and how lovely the skin was on your shoulders!

I would have taken it all with several grains of salt had we not gone farther. I came out with my old theory that all girls have lovely hair, nice eyes, attractive features and that if beauty is the only criterion, I'd just as soon tell him to go and pick someone else and let me out.

He said he'd take me home, and so we drove and drove along in the beautiful night. I learned a great deal about him, and he said the most brilliant things. I learned about Jason and the Golden Fleece—the legend having been written about the Georgian people—who were a civilized culture, like China, while the Russians were "still monkeys." I learned about his ideas of love, childbirth, atomic energy . . . and so much more.

I asked him what happened when a woman got old and her physical beauty waned, and he said in his lovely liquid voice, "Why she will always be beautiful to the man she married, we hope."

. . . when I asked him what I should call him, he told me three names.

"I like Constantine best," I said. "I like to say it, because of its good sound."

"I have a dear Grandmother who is 92 years old," he said, "and she always calls me Constantine. I do believe it's because she likes the feeling of the name rolling from her tongue."

He sang for a while, and then the bells struck four o'clock in a church tower. So I asked if I could tell him my favorite poem. I did, and he loved it.

Oh, if you could have heard the wonderful way he talked about life and the world! That is what made me really enjoy the dear remarks he made about me.

Imagine! I told him teasingly not to suffocate in my long hair and he said, "What a divine way to die!" Probably all this sounds absurd and very silly. But I never expressed myself so clearly and lucidly, never felt such warm, sympathetic response. There is a sudden glorying in womanhood when someone kisses your shoulder and says, "You are charming, beautiful, and, what is most important, intelligent."

When we drove into the drive at last, he made me wait until he opened the door on my side of the car and helped me alight with a ceremonial "Milady . . ."

"Milord," I replied, fancying myself a woman from a period novel, entering my castle.

It was striking five when I fell into bed beside Marcia, already asleep. I dreamed exquisite dreams all night, waking now and then to hear the wind wuthering outside the stone walls, and the rain splashing and dripping on the ivy-covered eaves.

Brunch at Buckleys' at 1 p.m. on a gray, rainy day: About 30–40 of the girls and a few men had the most amazing repast brought in by colored waiters in great copper tureens: scrambled eggs, bacon, sausages, rolls, preserves, a sort of white farina, coffee, orange juice. Lord, what luxury! Marcia and I left, went back to our mansion and lay snuggled side by side in the great double bed under a warm quilt in the gray afternoon, talking and comparing experiences, glowing with happiness and love for each other and the world!

At 3 p.m. the chauffeur picked us up. Five girls drove back in the big Cadillac. I sat up front beside the driver and wrapped myself in silence for two hours of driving through rain and yellow leaves.

Back here. I can't face the dead reality. I still lilt and twirl with Eric, Plato, and my wholly lovely Constantine under Japanese lanterns and a hundred moons twining in dark leaves, music spilling out and echoing yet inside my head.

To have had you there in spirit! To have had you see me! I am sure you would have cried for joy. That is why I am spilling out at such a rate—to try to share as much as I can with you.

I wonder if I shall ever hear from Constantine again. I am almost afraid he was a dream, conjured up in a moment of wishful thinking. I really loved him that evening, for his sharing of part of his keen mind and delightful family, and for listening to me say poetry and for singing—

Ah, youth! Here is a fragmentary bit of free verse. What think you?

> gold mouths cry with the green young
> certainty of the bronze boy
> remembering a thousand autumns
> and how a hundred thousand leaves
> came sliding down his shoulderblades
> persuaded by his bronze heroic reason.
> we ignore the coming doom of gold
> and we are glad in this bright metal season.
> even the dead laugh among the goldenrod.

The bronze boy stands kneedeep in centuries,
and never grieves,
remembering a thousand autumns,
with sunlight of a thousand years upon his lips
and his eyes gone blind with leaves.

Very rough. But I've got an evolving idea. Constantine is my bronze boy, although I didn't know him when I wrote it.

I've got to work and work! My courses are frightening. I can't keep up with them. See you the 19th.

Love,
love,
love,
Sivvy

SMITH COLLEGE
NORTHAMPTON, MASS.
OCTOBER 15, 1951

I finished *one* story ["*The Perfect Set-Up*"] for *Seventeen,* at least, for my first English paper. The due date is again Dec. 15. I'll bring it home to be typed and notarized on Thanksgiving. I want to wait until she criticizes it, so I can rework it. It's the one about the two baby-sitters . . .

OCTOBER 20, 1951

Dear Mum,

. . . The two letters you forwarded were, as you no doubt guessed, from dear old Eddie [*Cohen*] and a rather unceremonious return of poems from the *Saturday Review of Literature.* I guess I don't quite measure up to Edith yet, dear me! The blow was mitigated by the coincident arrival of the most beautiful two-page letter I've ever been written. Yes, Constantine did not vanish like a leprechaun with the bubbles in the champagne! I gave him "two weeks." I found myself writing schoolgirlishly in my notebook: "Dear Constantine: Ever since I danced with you on the lawn under the stars and elm leaves, and talked so intensely about the Georgian tribes, the purpose of life, and the possibility of the world's end, I have hoped to see you again to renew the enchanting four hour acquaintance we had." I laughed at myself for such foolishness, and felt that I would never hear from him, that all the delightful perceptive lyrical things we said were a dream, an ephemeral passing of two jaunty sloops in the night.

I'll bring his letter home when I come. The substance is that he has invited me to come to Princeton on November 3rd. After a first reaction of a loud scream and a sitting suddenly on the floor, I gathered myself together and thought of pros and cons.

Difficulties:

(1) I'll be going away two weekends in a row. Bad policy for work. (Redeeming factor: This coming weekend at home will be partial rest and work. I am working every minute this weekend. If I *do* go, I won't go away again till after Thanksgiving.)

(2) The trip is arduous and expensive. I would leave about 7 Sat. a.m., takes 5 hours or more. (Rationalization: I have spent no money on social life. A prospect like Constantine is a potential. A trip like that is an experience, an emancipation, a new world.)

Now, I am asking you, would you mind my going? I plan to build up into the lovely creature I really am during the next two weeks. It would be my one fling this semester as far as train fare is concerned. Constantine is the *one boy* I have met . . . (after Dick) that I could really become greatly interested in. As far as my future life is concerned, doesn't it bear a whirl?

I run the risk of disillusionment, as does Constantine, of a "beer taste" after a "champagne ambrosia." Daylight and football games will be a test of sorts to see if the exciting rapprochement of Japanese lanterns and church bells through trees at five in the morning will hold water.

Do write quickly and tell me if you are in favor or not. Wait till you read his letter!! I hope you really like it.

OCTOBER 21, 1951

If maturity consists partly in making judicious and important decisions, then I am more mature than Methuselah. After all the excited business I wrote you about Constantine, I have decided not to go. The factor of decision was that the English written was postponed until Tuesday, November 6. I already had a government written on that Wednesday (7th) which I had thought I could study for Monday and Tuesday. I am really glad that the written was postponed, because it makes my tripping off to Princeton an academic impossibility. Everybody has read Constantine's letter and is urging me to go. Maybe I'll marry into Russian society, etc. But wisdom has won the day. I am going to write him a diplomatic letter, suggesting that we arrange to meet soon again. If I do get a chance to see him again, I shall be very happy. If not, I will curse the fate that held so tantalizing a prospect before my eyes and then made me say, "no." At this stage, it's hard to decide which is more important—possibilities of future life, or present tasks. A balance is sometimes hard to achieve. There are so many fascinating, intelligent men in the world. I do want to see Eric and Constantine again. I'm so lucky I went to Maureen's party. Her brother, by the way, just published a book, *God and Man at Yale*— Will [*Bill*] Buckley. Her whole family is amazing, terribly versatile and intellectual.

I'm giving up the idea of *Mademoiselle* this year. Next year I'll be clever and write it *before* school begins. As it is, I'm on a treadmill of back work. Feeling really great, though. Mucus only in morning. I love you and Constantine and Smith, and am ricocheting between supreme despair at the one short life I've been dealt (and the endless permutations possible. Which to choose?) and dizzy joy at feeling well and making the wise, if unromantic, decision about Princeton.

One thing about sinus—if you feel like a depressive maniac while you have it, there is a renaissance of life when you can breathe again.

Can't *wait* to see you Friday.

Love,
Your incorrigible Sivvy

NOVEMBER 3, 1951

Dear Mother,

. . . I'm enclosing a sonnet composed when I should have been reading the Mass. It's supposed to be likening the mind to a collection of minute mechanisms, trivial and smooth-functioning when in operation, but absurd and disjointed when taken apart. In other words, the mind as a wastebasket of fragmentary knowledge, things to do, dates to remember, details, and trifling thoughts. The "idiot bird" is to further the analogy of clockwork, being the cuckoo in said mechanism. See what you can derive from this chaos . . .

Love, Sivvy

SONNET

All right, let's say you could take a skull and break it
The way you'd crack a clock; you'd crush the bone
Between steel palms of inclination, take it,
Observing the wreck of metal and rare stone.

This was a woman: her loves and stratagems
Betrayed in mute geometry of broken
Cogs and disks, inane mechanic whims
And idle coils of jargon yet unspoken.

Not man nor demigod could put together
The scraps of rusted reverie, the wheels
Of notched tin platitudes concerning weather,
Perfume, politics, and fixed ideals.

The idiot bird leaps up and drunken leans
To chirp the hour in lunatic thirteens.

⟨Postcard⟩

As you may imagine, I felt pretty low today when I got my [*rejection*] letter from *Seventeen*. I hadn't realized the subconscious support I was getting from thinking of what I would do with my $500. I guess I'll really have to hit those True Stories. By the way, I suddenly got an inspiration for the "Civic Activities" section of my application blank. I am starting next Monday to teach art to a class of kids at the People's Institute, volunteer work (make it sound impressive). Next year I hope for either mental or veterans hospital. . . . I feel suddenly very untalented as I look at my slump of work in art and writing. Am I destined to deteriorate for the rest of my life? . . . *Do* write for Dr. Christian. [*The radio show had a writing contest.*] Every year you will, until you win. You have the background and technical terms. Go to it!

FEBRUARY 28, 1952

I have found a vocational interest. Today our creative writing class heard the president of the Hampshire bookshop speak on the publishing house business. It sounds like just what I want. You teach me shorthand and typing, and I work up in all sorts of jobs (variety of angles—publicity, secretarial, editorial, reading manuscripts, juvenile departments, etc.). I was overwhelmed with enthusiasm; still want to work in veterans hospital, though. But English majoring and Press Board *can* lead to a practical end. See if you can get any contacts!

MARCH 7, 1952

Maybe your daughter is slightly crazy, maybe she just takes after her illustrious mother, but in spite of the fact she has three wicked

writtens next week, she is just now feeling . . . very virtuous because she refused three weekends this weekend—Frosh Prom at Yale,
Junior Prom at Princeton, and a blind date from MIT . . .

Just finished delivering my best baby yet—a story (only 7 pp.)
about a vet with one leg missing and a girl meeting on a train.
Dialogue discipline, you know . . .

I am very excited at being one of the three soph finalists for secretary of Honor Board, one of the big all-campus organizations up here,
specially fascinating because it deals with psychological breaking of
Honor System. . . .

MARCH 17, 1952

Dearest-Mother-whom-I-love-better-than-anybody,

I have so much to tell you I hardly know where to start . . . I was
one of the 16 girls in the college up for the college elections . . . Unfortunately my good friend and I who were both up for Sec. of Honor
Board lost to the third girl . . .

Friday morning I shot out of here like a bat out of Hades, got off
right at the Medical School and ran to Dick. First thing I did was to
call you, but you had gone . . . Dick and I sat and talked and talked
and read Hemingway aloud for *seven solid hours* without even
eating. . . .

◄{Postcard}►

APRIL 10, 1952

Got straight A on that old English exam I took way back when,
with a "This is an excellent paper" from the august Elizabeth Drew
herself! So happy I didn't go to Princeton. Last night I sat up to type
the 16-page story "Sunday at the Mintons' " that I'm sending to *Mlle*
just for fun. You would be interested to see the changes. I made it a
psychological type thing, wish-fulfillment, etc. so it wouldn't be at all
far-fetched. Tonight I hear Robert Frost, tomorrow, Senator Mc-
Carthy. Also wrote two poems this weekend which I'll send eventually: "Go Get the Goodly Squab in Goldlobed Corn" . . . Life is
terribly rushed what with Press Board, work, and all these lectures—
but fun.

⊰Sylvia and I were reading Auden, Yeats, and Spender together at this time.⊱

APRIL 30, 1952

You are listening to the most busy and happy girl in the world. Today is one of those when every little line falls in pleasant places.

. . . I have just been elected to Alpha Phi Kappa Psi, which is the Phi Beta Kappa of the Arts. So I am one of the two sophs chosen for creative writing ability! We all got single roses and marched out in chapel today. Also, I think I will get at least one sonnet published in the erudite *Smith Review* this next fall!

. . . at the first Alpha meeting after lunch today two girls came running up to me and said how would I like to be on the Editorial Board of the *Smith Review* next year, and my, how they just loved my sonnet: Eva. (What a life!)

. . . None other than W. H. Auden, the famous modern poet, is to come to Smith next year (along with Vera Michelis Dean) and may teach English, or possibly creative writing! So I hope to petition to get into one of his classes. (Imagine saying, "Oh, yes, I studied writing under Auden!")

. . . Honestly, Mum, I could just cry with happiness. I love this place so, and there is so much to do creatively, without having to be a "club woman." Fie upon offices! The world is splitting open at my feet like a ripe, juicy watermelon. If only I can work, work, work to justify all my opportunities.

Your happy girl,
Sivvy

MAY 12, 1952

Today I got a letter from The Belmont [*Summer hotel at Cape Cod*] confirming my job. So all is set. Dick is much pleased, too. I really hope I earn a lot of money.

An English major here got a Fulbright this year to study in England after she graduates! Also, the Rotary scholarships are good. Find out anything you can. We will be applying for those in a year or so.

If only I can get all my work done before these exams! I must get good marks in them, plus writing up forty senior personals to all the papers for graduation, and doing each day's press board, plus keeping up Honor Board work, plus going to showers, dinners, etc. Really, though, I am leading a gloriously country-clubby life in spite of my work. I have at last gotten thinner, and you should see my tan!

Love, Sivvy

The Belmont Hotel, Cape Cod
June 11, 1952

Your amazing telegram [*telegram announcing $500 Mademoiselle prize for "Sunday at the Mintons'," which I forwarded*] came just as I was scrubbing tables in the shady interior of The Belmont dining room. I was so excited that I screamed and actually threw my arms around the head waitress who no doubt thinks I am rather insane! Anyhow, psychologically, the moment couldn't have been better. I felt tired—first night's sleep in new places never *are* peaceful—and I didn't get much! To top it off, I was the only girl waitress here, and had been scrubbing furniture, washing dishes and silver, lifting tables, etc. since 8 a.m. Also, I just learned since I am completely inexperienced, I am not going to be working in the main dining room, but in the "side hall" where the managers and top hotel brass eat. So, tips will no doubt net much less during the summer and the company be less interesting. So I was beginning to worry about money when your telegram came. God! To think "Sunday at the Mintons' " is *one* of *two* prize stories to be put in a big national slick!!! Frankly, I can't believe it!

The first thing I thought of was: Mother can keep her intersession money and buy some pretty clothes and a special trip or something! At least I get a winter coat and extra special suit out of the Mintons. I *think* the prize is $500!!!!!!!!!

ME! Of all people! . . .

So it's really looking up around here, now that I don't have to be scared stiff about money . . . Oh, I say, even if my feet kill me after this first week, and I drop 20 trays, I will have the beach, boys to bring me beer, sun, and young gay companions. What a life.

Love, your crazy old daughter. (Or as Eddie said: "One hell of a sexy dame"!)

x x x Sivvy

June 12, 1952

No doubt after I catch up on sleep, and learn to balance trays high on my left hand, I'll feel much happier. As it is now, I feel stuck in the midst of a lot of loud, brassy Irish Catholics, and the only way I can jolly myself is to say, "Oh, well, it's only for a summer, and I can maybe write about them all." At least I've got a new name for my next protagonist—Marley, a gabby girl who knows her way around but good. The ratio of boys to girls has gotten less and less, so I'll be lucky if I get tagged by the youngest kid here. Lots of the girls are really wise, drinking flirts. As for me, being the conservative, quiet, gracious type, I don't stand much chance of dating some of the cutest ones . . . If I can only get "in" as a pal with these girls, and never for a minute let them know I'm the gentle intellectual type, it'll be O.K.

As for the *Mlle* news, I don't think it's really sunk in yet. I felt sure they made a mistake, or that you'd made it up to cheer me. The big advantage will be that I won't have to worry about earning barely $300 this summer. I would really have been sick otherwise. I can't wait till August when I can go casually down to the drug store and pick up a slick copy of *Mlle*, flip to the index, and see ME, one of two college girls in the U.S.!

Really, when I think of how I started it over spring vacation, polished it at school, and sat up till midnight in the Haven House kitchen typing it amidst noise and chatter, I can't get over how the story soared to where it did. One thing about *Mlle* college fiction— although that great one last year by the Radcliffe girl was tremendous and realistic—I remembered the first issue I read where there were two queer part-fantasies, one about the hotel the woman kept for queer people, and the other about an elderly married couple. So I guess the swing of the pendulum dictated something like good old Henry and Elizabeth Minton. Elizabeth has been floating around in my head in her lavender dress, giggling very happily about her burst into the world of print. She always wanted to show Henry she could be famous if she ever worked at it!

One thing I am partly scared and partly curious about is Dick's reaction when he reads the story in print. I'm glad Dick hasn't read it yet, but Henry started out by being him and Elizabeth me (and they grew old and related in the process). But nevertheless I wonder if Dick will recognize his dismembered self! It's funny how one always, somewhere, has the germ of reality in a story, no matter how fantastic . . .

I get great pleasure out of sharing it [*her feeling about the story*] with *you*, who really understand how terribly much it means as a tangible testimony that I *have* got a germ of writing ability even if

Seventeen has forgotten about it. The only thing, I probably won't have a chance to win *Mlle* again, so I'll try for a guest editorship maybe next year or my senior year, and set my sights for the *Atlantic*. God, I'm glad I can talk about it with you—probably you're the only outlet that I'll have that won't get tired of my talking about writing . . .

Speaking again of Henry and Liz, it was a step for me to a story where the protagonist isn't always ME, and proved that I am beginning to use imagination to transform the actual incident. I was scared that would never happen, but I think it's an indication that my perspective is broadening.

Sometimes I think—heck, I don't know why I didn't stay home all summer, writing, doing physical science, and having a small part-time job. I could "afford" to now, but it doesn't do much good to yearn about that, I guess. Although it would have been nice. Oh well, I'll cheer up. I love you.

Your own Sivvy

June 15, 1952

Dear Mother,

. . . Do write me letters, Mommy, because I am in a very dangerous state of feeling sorry for myself . . . Just at present, life is awful. *Mademoiselle* seems quite unreal, and I am exhausted, scared, incompetent, unenergetic and generally low in spirits . . . Working in side hall puts me apart, and I feel completely uprooted and clumsy. The more I see the main hall girls expertly getting special dishes, fixing shaved ice and fruit, etc., the more I get an inferiority complex and feel that each day in side hall leaves me further behind . . . But as tempted as I am to be a coward and escape by crawling back home, I have resolved to give it a good month's trial—till July 10 . . . Don't worry about me, but do send me little pellets of advice now and then.

June 17, 1952

Dear Mum,

. . . It's my week's anniversary here, and I am celebrating the beautiful blue day by spending my morning hour . . . down on the beach. Needless to say, I am in a little more optimistic mood than when I last wrote you . . . The characters around here are unbelievable, and I already have ideas churning around in my head. One learns so much by keeping quiet and listening. I hope I'll be able to really get a lot of story material out of this. At least I'll be able to spout authentic dining hall lingo and thereby give a semblance of reality and background. Chin up and take it easy.

June 21, 1952

. . . I've got an idea for a third story for *Seventeen* called, of all appropriate things, "Side Hall Girl." I even have a heroine named Marley who is, of course, me. The ending would be very positive and constructive. I hope I can get time and energy to write it. If I mull it over in my head for a week or so, trying to organize the chaotic incidents which pile on me every day, I should be able to sit down and type it up on some girl's typewriter in a few days and send it to you to type and get notarized. Ambitious? You bet. . . .

Would I like to win a summer at Breadloaf! But that is really a dream, because *boys* usually win those things, and my style needs to mature a lot yet. I'm glad to have catapulted out of the *Seventeen* arena, though.

June 21, 1952

. . . As for side hall, they've done the best they can for me as far as station is concerned, and I figure I deserve a "bad break" what with all my good fortune winning prizes and going to Smith. My different hours give me an excuse for not hanging around with some of the more snobby cliques, and well, I just don't care what people think about me as long as I'm always open, nice, and friendly.

Love to you all,
Sivvy, your Side Hall philosopher

June 24, 1952

. . . Last night I went on a "gang" birthday party at the "Sand Bar" where we sang and talked for a few hours. There were about forty of us kids from the hotel. I managed by some magic to get myself seated next to a fellow in his first year at Harvard Law—and he was just a dear . . . The best part was when we came back. It was a beautiful clear starry night, and Clark went in to get me two of his sweaters to wear because it was cold, and brought out a book of T. S. Eliot's poems. So we sat on a bench where I could just barely read the print, and he put his head in my lap and I read aloud to him for a while. Most nice. The only thing is I am so inclined to get fond of someone who will do things with me like that—always inclined to be too metaphysical and serious conversationally—that's my main trouble . . . So glad to hear the check from *Mlle* is real. I hardly could believe it. Just now I am mentally so disorganized that I can't retain knowledge or think at all. The work is still new enough to be tiring, what with three changes a day into uniforms, and I am so preoccupied by mechanics of living and people that I can't yet organize and assimilate all the chaos of experience pouring in on me. In spite of everything, I still have my good old sense of humor and manage to laugh a good deal of the time . . . I'll make the best of whatever comes my way.

JUNE 25, 1952

Just a note to let you know I'm still alive, although in a state of suspended animation. Never, it seems to me, has work worn me out so much. . . . I can't *think*, I can just perform mechanical acts. So no more going out for me. I won't be asked, anyway, because I'm just not the beer-brawl type, even if I do have fun now and then at those aimless soirees. I am still captain of my soul, will send you money orders of my "great intake" in cash every week or two to be safe. We slave so for every dollar that I figure I can't take any risks.

I have definitely decided to come home August 10. It is the only reasonable way out I can see. I will have stayed two months, slaved for $200 (−$10) and will need a good month to recuperate physically and mentally. With all my important and demanding school offices, I can't afford to crack up. . . . I figure if I leave then I can get my science done at home in 30 days at the rate of 25 pages a day (in the morning) and really get continuity. Now I'm always so tired that I just can't *retain* anything except what kind of eggs people like for breakfast . . . Well, tell me what you think of my schemes.

Your maturing Sivvy

[*Sylvia suffered another deep-seated sinus infection at The Belmont; therefore she returned home in mid-July. After recovering, she read an intriguing ad in the* Christian Science Monitor, *advertising for a mother's helper and companion for a teen-age daughter. Sylvia tele-*

phoned and talked with a Mrs. Michael Cantor. Each liked the other's voice, and July 21 found Sylvia in the Cantors' large, lovely home in Chatham. While she worked busily every morning doing housework and helping with the meals, she soon became a "part of the family." It was a thoroughly happy experience, lasting six weeks.]

. . . I can hardly believe it's August already, and that my magazine is reposing in my closet, well read. . . . On Wednesday, my day off, Grammy and Grampy called for me, proudly bearing the First Copy I had seen [Mademoiselle *story, "Sunday at the Mintons' "*]. I drove them to Brewster where Dick met us at the cabin . . . spent a half hour talking before he left for work . . . I left Grammy and Grampy at the cabin because they were comfortable reading and had had enough of the beach, and took the car alone for a blissful two hours at the Brewster beach with a bag of cherries and peaches and the Magazine. I felt the happiest I ever have in my life. I read both stories and already feel that I have outgrown mine, as I saw a great many errors, artistically, and am already beginning to think out about the tremendous job I'll do on the next one. I read it . . . chortled happily to myself, ran out on to the sand flats and dog-trotted for a mile far out alone in the sun through the warm tidal water, with the foam trickling pale brown in fingers along the wet sand ridges where the tide was coming in, talking to myself about how wonderful it was to be alive and brown and full of vitality and potentialities, and knowing all sorts of wonderful people. I never have felt so utterly blissful and free.

Yesterday . . . I stopped at the Bookmobile that stops once a week in Chatham to sell books. I got talking to the most fascinating little, sallow, cynical, brilliant woman who runs it. When she asked where I went to college, she said, "Oh, Smith. That's a great handle. Snob appeal. You'll be using it all your life. It does things for you." . . . I was at her feet with questions pouring out. She has written Western pulps, Western love stories, and will have a "dowager story" in the *Ladies' Home Journal* this fall. She also writes juveniles and had a blurb up on the wall advertising her latest for 12–14-year-old boys. Her name is Val(erie) Gendron, and she lives in a little ramshackle house in South Dennis. I plan to haunt her every Friday if I get a minute. Boy, would I like to bike over to her house on some day off and talk with her for hours. She really has been through the mill, I guess.

Love, Sivvy

Dear Mummy,

. . . After supper Mrs. Cantor kindly drove me over to South Dennis for my evening with Val Gendron. I don't know when I've had such a wonderful time in all my life. It was like a dream of an artist's Bohemia.

Val lives in a rickety old "half house" (one door, two windows), painted barn red with a white trim . . . and has carved a flower garden and vegetable garden out of the pine woods around her . . . When I arrived, she came to greet me, slouching slender and fragile in the doorway in her old plaid lumber shirt and paint-stained dungarees.

. . . Val ground some savory-smelling coffee and made a pot, got out a mound of grapes and a . . . cake, put the whole feast on a tray and led the way up a steep narrow flight of stairs to her "workshop."

. . . I just stood on the threshold and gurgled in fatuous delight. She had erected the walls, made the door and bookshelves, painted and done everything herself.

. . . Well, we got talking . . . Val telling me about her job in New York, regaling me with anecdote after anecdote of her skyrocketing position in a bank and why she quit—all hilarious.

. . . She got out her outline of her latest Western novel, not yet accepted, and let me read a short story and lots of her correspondence with her two agents—both her letters to them and theirs to her—all neatly dated and filed. And she told me so much in the course of the evening, we didn't stop talking till midnight . . . She drove me back in her old jalopy—us yelling to each other all the way, over the noise of the engine.

She knows lots of people: Rachel Carson and she are friends as of this summer, and she went to school with Hemingway's sister—all sorts of tales. I learned so much, so very much from her, and I agree with all she says about writing. [*Val inspired Sylvia's self-imposed "discipline," 1,500 words every day—"like doing scales and exercises."*] I must tell you in detail when I see you.

I left her at 12:30 after five of the most wonderful hours I have ever spent—completely fond of the dear, skinny, dark-haired woman.

She had been so tremendous to me—"criticized" my story and all, and been so generous with herself and her work.

x x x Sivvy

Turning down invitations to stay with the Norton group in the Brewster cabin or with grandparents in Falmouth, Sylvia returned home, hoping to plunge into the study of a required physical science course, to prepare herself for an examination in it in order to be freer in the fall semester to elect courses in English and art that appealed to her more. She discovered she had set herself too difficult a task in the short time remaining and decided to give up the attempt, which meant taking the course in the fall term. The prospect worried her a great deal.

Sylvia returned to Smith, but not to Haven House, where she had been so happy for two years. She went to a co-op, Lawrence House, to room with Mary, a studious and brilliant girl. No very close relationship developed between them. Sylvia waited on table at lunchtime and had one hour of "watch" a week, plus occasional weekend duties.

SMITH COLLEGE
NORTHAMPTON, MASS.
SEPTEMBER 25, 1952

Physical Science shouldn't be too bad—Mr. Sherk gave me a friendly grin when he saw me, so the initial sheepishness has worn off me. Mr. Davis, my creative writing teacher, I adore. He is the sort that can make you feel the urge to think and work and *create* until it kills you. I want to do so much for him. And Mr. Patch, my Medieval Lit Unit prof., is the most imposing literary lion I have ever seen—a great 6'5" gray-haired man, who seems to live in the ruddy vitality of the Middle Ages. He is terrifying and magnificent. The ten of us taking the unit meet in his library and sit around on chairs, comfortably. . . . I feel at once pitifully stupid, inadequate and scared—and *determined* to succeed in the enormous intellectual honesty, ambition and discipline that honoring requires.

⊰{Postcard}⊱

SEPTEMBER 29, 1952

It is amazing what a difference a good night's sleep can make in my psychological outlook on life. From the lonely, scared, bewildered creature I was for the first few days, I am now sure that everything will work out for the best. I have decided to drop Art II as much as I hate to, because I want to do as well as possible at my work, while getting to know the girls in the house, and concentrating on Press Board and *Smith Review*. My creative writing and Patch unit promise to be wonderful and demanding.

OCTOBER 6, 1952

Dear Mummy,

Wow! Speak of appropriate psychological moments for getting unexpected good news, this was one. I wandered lazily downstairs just before lunch today and glanced casually in my mailbox. Two letters from you. I opened the little one first, looked at it, puzzled for a few minutes before it suddenly dawned on me what the contents were. I never even cherished the smallest hope of getting one of the third prizes [*from* Seventeen *for "Initiation"*] this year—as you know, I figured out the relative deadline for their decision by my other story and had long since given up thinking about it.

This news makes me feel that I am maybe not destined to deteriorate, after all.

I have been too busy getting used to the routine of the house and doing the pile of beginning work on Press Board to really plunge into my studies, and, as a result, I have been feeling very far behind and scared about my courses. Sort of a beginning paralysis. . . . I never realized how important doing well in studies was to me until I got behind this last busy week. . . .

Your last big morale-building letter was most appreciated. You are the most wonderful mummy that a girl ever had, and I only hope I can continue to lay more laurels at your feet. Warren and I both love you and admire you more than anybody in the world for all you have done for us all our lives. For it is you who has given us the heredity and the incentive to be mentally ambitious. Thank you a million times!

Your very own Sivvy

[*Written on back of envelope of letter of October 6*]: So your old favorite idea "Heather-birds' Eyebrows" worked out after all! I am amazed, but strange are the ways of the world, especially publishing.

["Heather-birds' Eyebrows": Sylvia, carrying out orders during high school sorority hazing, asked people on the bus what they ate for breakfast. When she told me of the delightfully imaginative reply given by an elderly gentleman, I exclaimed, "There! You have a story!" And from this incident developed the plot for "Initiation," which won second prize ($200) in Seventeen's short-story contest and was published in the January 1953 issue.]

OCTOBER 11, 1952

Dear Mother,
. . . I have written a thank-you and sent a snapshot to *Seventeen*. That magazine has really been awfully good to me, and I am really aghast at this last fling of mine. I still can't believe it is true, and I have completely forgotten the plot and detail of my story. I was most interested to hear your quotes. It was as if someone else had written it.
. . . The house is really lovely—very attractively decorated downstairs and closer to everything. The girls are all wonderful—they work, get good marks in general, and hold extracurricular offices. There is a delightful atmosphere of economy, and everyone understands the words, "I can't; I'm broke."

NOVEMBER 5, 1952

. . . I hope, by the way, that you are feeling better, able to sleep, and aren't letting finances or Grampy's retiring bother you. I really wish you would give up teaching Sunday School [*brief, simplified course in comparative religion*]. You work like a fiend all week teaching, and Sunday should be a day of rest. You should pamper yourself, have a long late breakfast, read, listen to music, lounge a little. I also hope you are wise about the extent and lateness of your baby-sitting. Do feel free to tell me any problems that are bothering you. It takes my mind off myself to think of other people.

NOVEMBER 6, 1952

Dear Warren,
. . . My [*Princeton*] date was the perfect example of the absolute sheep, and I thought I could have fun with him, and it was all right

until he started talking. He was by all means the most pathetic speci-
men of manhood I have ever met. . . . As much as I tried to conceal
my brilliance, he guessed I was not as neutral as I seemed. His confession of his own inadequacies, in an attempt to be serious, was not
only pitiably revealing of his lack of thinking and values, but was
evidently quite a strain on his mental powers, and I use the word
loosely. . . .

No doubt, some of the boys at Princeton are intelligent and nice, but
all the ones I saw are spoiled, sheepish socialites, who get drunk all the
time and don't have an original or creative impulse—they are all
bloodless like mushrooms inside, I am sure . . .

I am terribly disappointed that Stevenson lost the election. I don't
remember knowing who you were for, except for Pogo or Krajewski.
But poor mother was for Eisenhower.

. . . My work is overwhelming. Don't know how I have the time
to goof off writing letters, but I have two papers due every week from
now till Thanksgiving. I'll have to work most of the vacation on my
back work, too. Ah me, life is grim. If I live till Xmas, it will be a
miracle . . .

Love you dearly,
Your galley slave sister, Sivvy

NOVEMBER 6, 1952

I have written to Bread Loaf [sic] to see if they have any tuition
scholarships, but I doubt it . . . I would love to go to Summer
School . . . to Harvard, too, perhaps. I would also like only a part-
time job or one that would only last a short part of the summer, so I
could read and write and work on research for my thesis. I think that
it is important that I have such a chance to think and work. I plan to
write my application for *Mademoiselle* as soon as I get home on
Thanksgiving, because I won't have a minute till then.

All for now. Keep your lovely letters coming—do so appreciate
them.

x x x Sivvy

[*Shortly before this letter was written, there was an account published in the papers of the suicide of one of Warren's classmates at
Exeter. Sylvia, shocked, telephoned me about it. Here in this letter is
the first sign of her magnifying a situation all out of proportion.*]

96

Brace yourself and take a deep breath—not too nice:

NOVEMBER 19, 1952

. . . God, will I be glad to get home for a few days of rest. I am
sorry to have to admit it, but I am in a rather tense emotional and
mental state, and have been tense and felt literally sick for about a
week now . . . a physical manifestation of a very frustrated mental
state. The crux of the matter is my attitude toward life—hinging on
my science course. I have practically considered committing suicide to
get out of it, it's like having my nose rubbed in my own slime. It just
seems that I am running on a purposeless treadmill, behind and
paralyzed in science, dreading every day of the horrible year ahead
when I should be revelling in my major. I have become really frantic:
small choices and events seem insurmountable obstacles, the core of
life has fallen apart. I am obsessed by wanting to escape from that
course. I curse myself for not having done it this summer. I try to
learn the barren dry formulas. Sick, I wonder why? why? why? I feel
actually *ill* when I open the book, and figure I am *wasting* ten hours a
week for the rest of the year. It affects all the rest of my life; I am
behind in my Chaucer unit, feeling sterile in creative writing. My
whole life is mastered by a horrible fear of this course, of the dry
absurdities, the artificial formulas and combinations. I ask myself
why didn't I take Geology, anything *tangible* would have been a
blessing. Everyone else is abroad, or falling in love with their courses.
I feel I have got to escape this, or go mad. How can I explain the
irrevocable futility I feel! I don't even *want* to understand it, which is
the worst yet. It seems to have no relation to anything in my life. It is
a year course. I have wondered, desperately, if I should go to the
college psychiatrist and try to tell her how I feel about it, how it is
obsessing all my life, paralyzing my action in every other field. Life
seems a mockery. I have the idea that if I could get out of this course,
even for second semester, I would be able to see light ahead. But I
can't go on like this. I have a paper and two exams after Thanksgiving, too. And I will have to study and rest all the time I am home.
Luckily I haven't gotten sinus yet; that would be another form of
escapism. When one feels like leaving college and killing oneself over
one course which actually nauseates me, it is a rather serious thing.
Every day more and more piles up. I hate formulas, I don't give a
damn about valences, artificial atoms and molecules. It is pseudo-
science—all theory; nothing to grasp. I am letting it ruin my whole

life. I am really afraid to talk it over with a psychiatrist (symbol of a parent, or priest confessor) because they might make me drop my activities (Press Board in particular) and spend half my time pounding formulas and petty mathematical relationships (which I have long since forgotten) into my head, when I basically *don't want* to learn them. To be *wasting* all this year of my life, obsessed by this course, paralyzed by it, seems unbearable. I feel that absolved of it—with some sign of light ahead—I could again begin to love.

Oh, Mother, I hate to bother you with this, but I could cry. Life is so black, anyway, with my two best friends, Dick and Marcia, so far removed I hardly see them. And this course: I actually am worried over my mental state! What earthly *good* is this going to do me in my future life? I hate it, find it hideous, loathsome. I have built it up to a devouring, malicious monster. Anything but formulas, anything but. And it is only a grade I course. God, what a mess my life is. And I know I am driving myself to distraction. Everything is empty, meaningless. This is not education. It is hell; and how could I ever persuade the college authorities to let me drop a year course at the half year? How could I convince the psychiatrist I would go *mad* if I didn't escape from these horrible formulas and, for me, dry, useless chunks of memory? My reason is leaving me, and I want to get out of this. Everybody is happy, but this has obsessed me from the day I got here.

I really am in a state of complete and horrible panic. I feel on the one hand that I *must* get out of this course: I can't reconcile the memory and rote with my philosophy of a creative education, and I am in a very embarrassing position as far as the authorities of the college are concerned: I have managed to make a pretty good impression so far, but to have me go insane over what I thought was a horrible, wasteful course would only make them expel me or something. Every week I dread opening my science book; it is the *subject* of the course that annihilates my will and love of life. Not the fact that if I studied more I could take it calmly. Of course I am behind a few chapters (I skipped them to keep abreast of the present work) but I feel that if I *only* could drop it second semester (how I would fill the science requirement I don't know!) I could at least see the light of life again. Even now I have a unit paper due—a new week's work of science to vomit over. I am childish? Maybe, but the series of hideous adjustments thrown in my lap this year doesn't help. Science is, to me, useless drudgery for *no purpose*. A vague, superficial understanding of molecules and atoms isn't going to advance my understanding of life. I can't deny that to myself.

Oh! Every fibre of me rebels against the unnecessary torture I am going through. If only I *wanted* to understand it, but I *don't*. I am revolted by it, obsessed. How can I ever explain this to anyone plausibly, even the psychiatrist? I am driven inward, feeling hollow. No rest cure in the infirmary will cure the sickness in me.

I will wait till Thanksgiving before getting actively desperate. But oh! how very desolate and futile and trapped I feel!

Love,
Your hollow girl, Sivvy

[*During the Thanksgiving recess, Sylvia caught up with her work and seemed to regain confidence and buoyancy.*]

[UNDATED; WRITTEN ABOUT DECEMBER 1, 1952]

Dear Warren,

So glad I have a few minutes to write my favorite man. There is so much to tell you. Life is certainly looking up for your old sister, even if she is practically in danger of flunking an amateur science course because she can't seem to understand beautiful euphonic words like erg, joules, valences, watts, coulombs and amperes. . . .

Dick is coming home [*from the sanatorium*] for a few days for Christmas, at the time of the Cotillion, darn it, so I will have to give up the idea of going and stay home, the way he did for me last year when I was sick. But really, dances aren't as important as people, and I'll be glad to see him. I am leaving with him by train or plane for the sanatorium right after Christmas for a few days. I will be living with the family of a doctor who writes novels and short stories in his spare time and meeting all sorts of tubercular New York truck drivers, so it should be lots of fun. . . . Wot a giddy life!!

The best thing happened the day after you left Thanksgiving. Did mother tell you? I went to Perry's [*Dick Norton's brother*] for supper and he had two roommates home from Yale. One is engaged to be married this Christmas, and Perry said over the phone that the other one, Myron Lotz, was first in his class at Yale (Perry is second). I envisioned a short, dark little boy with glasses. What was my amazed surprise when I walked into the Nortons' living room and saw a tall, handsome guy get up and grin. Honestly, I don't think I've ever been so immediately attracted to anyone. He looks anything but the brilliant scholar. Guess what he does in the summer! He pitches for the Detroit Tigers, and last summer he earned $10,000! Isn't that amazing? Not only that, he comes from Austro-Hungarian immigrant parents who work in the steel mines and can hardly speak English. And he is going through Yale in three years, starting Yale Med School next fall. Did you ever hear of such a phenomenal character? Best of all, he is coming up to our Lawrence House Dance with me the weekend of December 13, so we'll really have a chance to get to know each other. Keep your fingers crossed that my beautiful intellectual charm will captivate the brilliant lug. Maybe you could help me with information about the Detroit Tigers. I don't even know what league they're in! Ah, me . . .

Well, I must needs go to bed now. Remember that I love you, baby, as Mickey Spillane would say. And I do hope you let me know what you are doing and thinking about. After all, there is no one in the world but us who has shared our particular common past and childhood—everything from the feast and the beast and the jelly bean to skalshalala meat, remember? And it is not every sister who has such a tall, handsome, brilliant brother to be proud of. Wonder what you'd think of Myron. Of course he has had women going gaga over him at baseball games and talking about their hopechests, but I don't have to worry about scaring him away, because I'm the last one to get matrimonial avarice in my eye. Poof, for a few years yet, anyway. There is so much to do in life anyway. Anyway.

Write if you get work.

Lots of x x x x x x
Sivvy

DECEMBER 15, 1952

Dear Mother,

. . . We [*Sylvia and Myron Lotz*] changed then, for the cocktail party, and walked over to the professor's house. On the way we decided to keep on walking for a while longer, and so walked up to the mental hospital [*Northampton*], among the buildings, listening to the people screaming. It was a most terrifying, holy experience, with the sun setting red and cold over the black hills, and the inhuman, echoing howls coming from the barred windows. (I want so badly to *learn* about *why* and *how* people cross the borderline between sanity and insanity!)

. . . Sunday . . . as we went walking out in the fields, we saw some airplanes landing close by, and so hiked over to watch them landing like toy gliders at a small airport. As we approached the field, a tall, lean, blue-eyed man with a moustache came toward us . . . We chatted for a while and he showed us his private plane . . . and [we] listened to the pilot describe his experiences. He looked at us: "I'm going up this afternoon, want to come?" I stared at Myron, who gave me an understanding, benevolent grin: "She'd sure like to, sir," he told the pilot. So we went back, and they strapped me into the two-seater little plane . . . We taxied across the field, bumping along, and it felt like being in a car. I didn't believe we would go up, but then, suddenly, the ground dropped away, and the trees and hills fell away, and I was in a small glass-windowed box with a handsome, mysterious pilot, winging over Northampton, Holyoke, Amherst, watching the small, square, rectangular colored fields, the toy houses, and the great winding, gleaming length of the Connecticut River. "I am going to do a wing-over," he said, and suddenly the river was over my head, and the mountains went reeling up into the sky, and the clouds floated below. We tilted rightside up again. Never have I felt such ecstasy! I yelled above the roar of the motor that it was better than God, religion, than anything, and he laughed and said he knew. "You fly it," he told me, and I took the stick and made the craft climb and tilt. For half an hour we were up . . .

Today I am probably going to the infirmary because of my insomnia, so don't worry if you get a notice. I have an appointment with the psychiatrist this afternoon about my science, and will ask her if I can go up there for a few days to rest and get rid of a slight sore throat. Also, Mary Ellen Chase called me this morning and I hope to see her sometime this week, too. [*In her little book, "Recipe for a Magic Childhood," which she gave Sylvia on December 18, 1952, Mary Ellen Chase wrote: "For Sylvia Plath with admiration and confidence." She recommended Sylvia for a Fulbright grant in 1955 and in 1957 for an instructorship in English at Smith College.*]

x x x Sivvy

-{*Telegram*}-

JANUARY 5 [?], 1953

BREAK BREAK BREAK ON THE COLD WHITE SLOPES OH KNEE ARRIVING FRAMINGHAM TUESDAY NIGHT 7:41. BRINGING FABULOUS FRACTURED FIBULA NO PAIN JUST TRICKY TO MANIPULATE WHILE CHARLESTONING. ANYTHING TO PROLONG VACATION. NOR-

TONS WERE PLANNING TO MEET ME SO WHY NOT CALL TO CHECK. MUCH LOVE. YOUR FRACTIOUS FUGACIOUS FRANGIBLE SIVVY.

[*After the Christmas holidays, Sylvia and Dick had gone to Ray Brook, New York, where Dick was being treated for tuberculosis. Sylvia borrowed skis and without any previous professional instruction skied on the advanced slope. Result: a collision and a broken fibula. Her grandmother was the first to read the telegram and looked at me, puzzled. "What does she mean?" she asked. "She's broken her leg!" I exclaimed. "Oh, no! Where does she say that?" Grammy queried.*]

JANUARY 9, 1953

. . . All in all, my leg has made me realize what a fool I was to think I had insurmountable troubles. It is a sort of concrete symbol of limitations that are primarily mental, or were. And now that I see how foolish I was in succumbing to what I thought were mental obstacles, I am determined to be as cheerful and constructive about my mental difficulties as I am going to be about this physical one. Naturally I will be a bit depressed and blue at times, and tired and uncomfortable, but there is that human principle which always finds that no matter how much is taken away, something is left to build again with.

JANUARY 19, 1953

Dear Mother,

Well, the world has a miraculous and wonderful way of working. You plunge to the bottom, the way I did this fall, and you think that every straw must be the last . . . Then you break your leg, decide to be gay and merry, and the world falls like a delicious apple in your lap . . .

First of all, my petition for auditing science without credit went through . . . As you may imagine, during my agonies of this fall, I felt that I could see no light ahead for the rest of the year. Now I will be taking a course in Milton instead of the hated science, and concentrating heart and soul on modern poetry and creative writing. Isn't it wonderful?

This is my three weeks' anniversary, and I have proved that a broken leg need not handicap a resourceful woman. Thanks so much for your encouraging letter. It was just what I needed. Oh, mummy, I am so happy. If a hideous snowy winter, with midyears and a broken leg is heaven, what will the green young spring be like? How can I bear the joy of it all!

Much overflowing love,
Your own Sivvy

FEBRUARY 21, 1953

Dear Mother,

Well, this will go down in history as Plath's Black Month. Myron called last night, car hasn't been delivered yet, so no weekend date . . . The cast came off Thursday night, and I felt as if the doctor were lifting a coffin lid when I saw the hairy yellow withered corpse of my leg lying there. The emotional shock of admitting it was my leg was the hardest (ugh). He took an x-ray and said the leg wasn't completely mended (which was also a nice shock). . . .

Thursday night I felt like hell; took a razor and sheared off the worst of the black stubble and the skin of course is all coming off and raw, my ankle is swollen and blackish green, and my muscles have shriveled away to nothing. Needless to say I am never going skiing again. I am going to live in a southern climate the rest of my life and play tennis (a nice safe sport), bicycle, swim, and eat mangoes . . . From the way things look now I'll be lucky to go to junior prom in my long black dress with a taped ankle . . . To make myself feel better I wrote two villanelles today and yesterday: a rigid French verse form I've never tried before, where the first and third line have to be repeated as refrains. They took my mind off my helpless misery and made me feel a good deal better. I think they are the best I've written yet, and of course sent them off blindly, one to *The Atlantic* and one to *The New Yorker*. Oh hell. Life is so difficult and tedious I could cry. But I won't; I'll just keep writing villanelles.

Love, Sivvy

FEBRUARY 23, 1953

Manuscript came yesterday, and I can't thank you enough. When I am rich and famous I will hire you for my private secretary and baby-tender, and pay you scandalously high wages and take you on monthly jaunts in my own shocking pink yacht. Needless to say, I love you very dearly.

x x x Sivvy

Dear Mother,

. . . Had a sad, longing . . . letter from Dick. He told me last fall that he wanted me to tell him all about my dates so he wouldn't imagine things. I did so as painlessly as possible, yet I should have realized that in his heart he wouldn't want to hear about them . . . I never went steady with him or committed myself in any way other than that I liked being with him more than any other person, but I always went out with the other persons. Also, I went out all last summer . . . and he wasn't bothered. Now, at the sanatorium, I have taken on an unusual importance as I am the only girl he knows, and he is inhibited from making new contacts. If he were in the real world he wouldn't feel so sorry for himself. I really Don't Want to go up there spring vacation at all, but if they will go for only a day and two nights, I might be persuaded . . . The thing I am afraid of is that he will try to extort a promise to him to try again when he comes out . . . I know as well as I've known for a long time now, deep down, that I could never be happily married to him: physically I want a colossus . . . mentally, I want a man who isn't jealous of my creativity in other fields than children. . . . I have always been very rational and practical about the prospect of marriage; . . . I'm not leaping rapidly into anything for some time yet . . . Graduate school and travel abroad are not going to be stymied by any squalling, breastfed brats. I've controlled my sex judiciously and you don't have to worry about me at all. The consequences of love affairs would stop me from my independent freedom of creative activity, and I don't intend to be stopped.

Love, Sivvy

Your lovely long letter came today, and I am once again forcibly made aware of what a superlative mother you have been to me. In the great whirlpools of responsibility you have had these last ten years and more of "bringing me up right," you deserve the most verdant laurels. Honestly, I appreciate your rational understanding of me so much. In return I have always felt I can be completely honest with you, and want more than anything to make you proud of me so that some day I can begin to repay you for all the treats you've given me in my two decades of life . . .

Last night and yesterday I finished this month's *Mlle* assignment: a story I just wrote about a Big Weekend: I took a dance at Harvard

Med School to get the bizarre touch they like so well, and tried to make it quick-moving and sophisticatedly glittery, somewhat like "Den of Lions," only much smoother, dramatic and better. I feel I've come such a long way since then. Mailed that with my "Ideal Summer" this morning; thanks again for saving me by typing it . . .

. . . I was sitting in [the] bone clinic last Monday and started talking to a freshman from Newton. She exclaimed, "Oh, you write for *Seventeen* and *Mademoiselle*, don't you? I have read all your things, and felt so proud you were going to Smith, too!" . . . As I left I heard her telling the nurse: "Oh, she's a wonderful writer, does stories for all sorts of magazines." Really, does one's heart good. Sometimes I feel so stupid and dull and uncreative that I am amazed when people tell me differently.

Glad you like the villanelles . . . felt that I am getting more proficient with the singing, uncrowded lyric line, instead of the static adjectival smothered thought I am usually guilty of.

{Plans for a weekend at Yale with Myron Lotz}

MARCH 3, 1953

Dearest one,

. . . *The* dress is hanging up in my window in all its silvern glory, and there is a definite rosy cast to the skirt (no, it's *not* just my attitude!). Today I had my too-long hair trimmed just right for a smooth pageboy, and I got, for $12.95, the most classic pair of silver closed pumps . . . With my rhinestone earrings and necklace, I should look like a silver princess—or feel like one, anyway. I just hope I get to be a Junior Phi Bete this year so I can use it for my Phi Bete dress, too. (Do you realize that I got the ONLY A in the unit from Mr. Patch!)

. . . God, how I wish I could win the *Mlle* contest. This year would be so ideal while I'm still in touch with college. . . . Bye for a while,

Your busy loving, silvershod Sivvy

MARCH 6, 1953

Dear Mother,

As far as I'm concerned, things look very promising for a rich companionship between Mike [*Myron Lotz*] and me with the understanding that there are no strings attached and there is complete freedom for both of us . . . Mike and I don't feel ready to make final choices for a few years yet . . . This is very nice, because I get a chance to see how Mike works out in Med. School and what he wants to do with the rest of his life. He is still very young at heart and changing into being a man and needs encouragement and affection, which I certainly am glad to give. . . . For me and for him, love is difficult to define, but it is a very slow, growing, rational thing. I have to know a great deal about anybody and be able to predict reasonably the future life I'd have before I could ever commit the next fifty years of my life.

MARCH 9, 1953

The most tantalizingly sad thing happened this afternoon. I really can't help but sit down and immediately spill it over to you. I got my two villanelles back from *The New Yorker* today with a rejection that wasn't even mimeographed, but that was written in pencil and initialed by one of the editors. It said, and I quote: "Although we were impressed by many things in 'Doomsday,' I'm sorry to say the final vote went against it, as well as the other poem. We were somewhat bothered by the two rhymes that break the scheme—especially 'up,' which is not even an assonant rhyme here. Do try us again and thanks for letting us see these."

Honestly, I've never come so blasted close, and it's almost worse than missing out altogether. "Final vote"! Those heartless men! Ah, well, to keep my courage up, I immediately sent them the third villanelle. The worst they can do is reject that, too.

MARCH 17, 1953

Dearest Progenitor,

Even though I am very weary and very longing for sleep and very behind in papers, I felt such a sudden burst of love and happiness and joy in love seething all day in me that I could not help but want to share some of it with you. There is so much to flow over merrily with, and I feel violets sprouting between my fingers and forsythia twining in my hair and violins and bells sounding wherever I walk.

Why should I be so elated even if tired? Because I have two good strong legs, the doctor and x-ray said so yesterday; because I revised my villanelles the way *The New Yorker* man suggested, and it is true they are much better and I am going to send them back and see what he says; because I will probably get the coveted position of *Hampshire Gazette* Correspondent for next year in the News Office, which will mean earning about $150 or $200—the most lucrative job in the office; because I have many good, warm friends—Marcia, Enid, and talented others; because one Myron Michael Lotz thinks I am brilliant-creative-and-beautiful-all-at-once; because one promising Raymond Wunderlich [*of Columbia Medical School*] has just written and asked me to come to New York sometime this spring for ballet and other cultural delights; because I just got a check from the *Springfield Daily News* and bought three coveted books and six modern art postcards at the Hampshire Bookshop: the huge black-and-white modern art–covered *New Directions* (14), James Joyce's *Dubliners* [*she planned to write her senior thesis on Joyce*], and *The Basic Writings of Freud*; because life in general is rich and heterogeneous and promising if I work hard.

MARCH 14, 1953

Got back the *Mlle* manuscript today. This is a bad time for me as rejections go. Also, I don't see how I have any sort of a chance to be an editor this June. Twenty top girls from Smith are trying out . . .

My personal rejection from *The New Yorker* has made me realize how hard I want to work at writing this summer. I'll never get anywhere if I just write one or two stories and never revise them or *streamline them for a particular market*. I want to hit *The New Yorker* in poetry and the *Ladies' Home Journal* in stories, and so I must study the magazines the way I did *Seventeen*. Speaking of *Seventeen*, I wrote them as you suggested . . . asking if I could submit stories and poems on a professional basis. It would be a great triumph for me to get a story in there on a regular basis. If I can consciously gear things to them the way I did that "Initiation" story, I don't see why I couldn't produce prolifically . . .

Your rejected daughter, Sivvy

UNDATED; POSTMARKED MARCH 21, 1953

Dear Warren,

. . . The great W. H. Auden spoke in chapel this week, and I saw him for the first time. He is my conception of the perfect poet: tall, with a big leonine head and a sandy mane of hair, and a lyrically gigantic stride. Needless to say he has a wonderfully textured British accent, and I adore him with a big Hero Worship. I would someday like to touch the Hem of his Garment and say in a very small adoring voice: Mr. Auden, I haveapomeforyou: "I found my God in Auden."

> He is Wonderful and
> Very Brilliant, and
> Very Lyric and Most
> Extremely Witty.

. . . There are a million things I want to talk to you about, since I haven't written you for a long time. Looks like you and I will both be home this summer, so I hope we can help mother with the cooking and work since grammy is evidently pretty out of the running now, and I look so forward to being with you all the summer: I hardly ever see you during the year, and you are still my Very Favorite Person! We will have a fun summer together. It will help the fact that my social life will obviously be Nil. At least now and then we can Do Boston together, alleys and all, because you are a Big Man and can protect me. . . .

Much love,
Sivvy

{From a Smith College theme, "The Ideal Summer," spring 1953:}

. . . I have run through my roster of friends, relatives, and favorite professors, and my choice for a fellow wanderer is, strange as it may seem, my 18-year-old brother, Warren. . . .

. . . Warren and I have a rather wonderful friendship and enjoy each other as if we were chosen comrades, not merely related. Furthermore, Warren starts Harvard on scholarship next fall, and, as a culturally and intellectually stimulating companion, he is also ideal.

APRIL 11, 1953

Dearest Mother,

I am at present beginning a long, funny poem which the first stanza of I here reproduce. I am trying to get a rollicking rhythm. Sometimes, I fear, it is not only rollicking, but also supremely irresponsible:

Dialogue en Route

"If only something exciting would happen!"
Said Eve the elevator-girl ace
To Adam the arrogant matador
As they shot past the forty-ninth floor
In a rocketing vertical clockcase
Fast as a fallible falcon.

⊰{Telegram}⊱

APRIL 24, 1953

BIRTHDAY GREETINGS. MY PRESENT IS FOLLOWING NEWS. HARPERS MAGAZINE
JUST GRACIOUSLY ACCEPTED THREE POEMS FOR 100 DOLLARS IN ALL. MADE-
MOISELLE SENT TEN DOLLARS FOR RUNNER-UP IN THIRD ASSIGNMENT. BEST
LOVE TO YOU. SIVVY

APRIL 25, 1953

Dearest Mum,

Well, tomorrow is your birthday, and *Harper's* conveniently came
across just in time for me to tell you the news I wanted to: that I got
my first real professional acceptance! Even now I still can't believe it!
Although the lovely check for $100 came today. The poems they
accepted are two of the villanelles, "Doomsday" and the one you like
so much, "To Eva Descending the Stair." The third was one I wrote
last spring, called "Go Get the Goodly Squab." I was most surprised
about that one because the *Atlantic* had already rejected it, and the
Smith College Jury for the annual poetry contest overlooked it completely last year . . . It is one of my favorite exercises in sound, so
I'll be most pleased to see it in print in the future. . . .

. . . Now I can really plan to live in Cambridge [*for the summer*], I
think. In the same mail I got a $10 check for being one of the ten
runners-up in *Mlle*'s last assignment, so all my extra work and your
kind typing really paid off.

. . . Mentally, I dedicate this *Harper's* triumph to you, my favorite
person in the world.

. . . The *Atlantic* and *The New Yorker* remain my unclimbed
Annapurnas. Of course, in *Harper's* I shall be in excellent literary
company. Really, I just couldn't sleep all last night, I was so excited.
Can't you just hear the critics saying, "Oh, yes, she's been published

in *Harper's.*" (Don't worry, I'm not getting smug. I'm just happy that my hard work has gotten such a plum of a reward.)

x x x to my birthday mummy—Sivvy

. . . Yesterday I was elected Editor of the *Smith Review* for next year—the one job on campus that I really coveted with all my heart. So now, with my prize financial job on the *Gazette*, I'm carrying my full number of points and have the two activities I . . . wanted above all.

Last night I will never forget. W. H. Auden came to our unit of Modern Poetry and for two hours sat and read and analyzed one of his longest poems . . . to hear the brilliant play of minds, epigrams, wit, intelligence and boundless knowledge was the privilege of my lifetime. Miss Drew's living room took on the proportions of a book-lined sanctuary, and I never felt such exaltation in my life. The English Department in this place is unsurpassed anywhere, and this year, with the symposium and W. H. Auden, was a plumcake of letters and arts genii. . . .

. . . Tell me what you think about the poems . . . any resemblance to Emily Dickinson is purely intentional.

ADMONITION

If you dissect a bird
    To diagram the tongue
You'll cut the chord
    Articulating song.

If you flay a beast
    To marvel at the mane
You'll wreck the rest
    From which the fur began.

If you pluck out the heart
    To find what makes it move,
You'll halt the clock
    That syncopates our love.

PARALLAX

Major faults in granite
    Mark a mortal lack;
Yet individual planet
    Directs all zodiac.

Tempo of strict ocean
    Metronomes the blood.
Yet ordered lunar motion
    Proceeds from private flood.

Diagram of mountains
    Graphs a fever chart;
Yet astronomic fountains
    Exit from the heart.

Drama of each season
    Plots doom from above;
Yet all angelic reason
    Moves to our minor love.

VERBAL CALISTHENICS

My love for you is more
    Athletic than a verb,
Agile as a star
    The tents of sun absorb.

Treading circus tightropes
    Of each syllable,
The brazen jackanapes
    Would fracture if he fell.

Acrobat of space
    The daring adjective
Plunges for a phrase
    Describing arcs of love.

Nimble as a noun,
    He catapults in air;
A planetary swoon
    Could climax his career.

But adroit conjunction
    Eloquently shall
Link to his lyric action
    A periodic goal.

Dearest Harvard Man,

"Oh, I on-ly date a man if his shoes are white"—I am so proud of you that I can hardly keep from leaping up and down and shouting liddle 'ip-'oorays all over the Smith campus. So Harvard came across with a National! And best of all, they won't Let You Work during the year. That is what I call princely. . . .

Tell me, now, how much is left for you to cover? Will mother have to pay anything? I hope not, because she is really down to rock bottom, and I gather from her letters that she is having ulcer trouble, although she is very brave and gay about eating baby foods again. I hope that I too can pay for everything next year, in spite of summer school (I just wish Harvard would come across for me too on June 1!) and New York.

Now, I think you and I should have a plan to make mother rested and happy this summer, in spite of the fact that she is teaching. As you know, the house is being decorated (for which I'm infinitely glad, as now I can bring boys home without keeping the lights down very dim and hoping they won't see the spots and tears in the wallpaper, and you can feel proud to bring girls home during college). And, obviously, this is a big financial chunk out of mother's almost non-existent bank account. So if we can continue to completely support ourselves these next years (if ONLY my *True Story* [*she wrote several for* True Story] would pay, I'd keep our pot of caviar boiling by writing more such sordid money makers). Ironically enough, all my attempts to earn money by prostituting my talent, e.g., by writing hundreds of Lucky Strike jingles, have been silent, while Big Money has come from all my attempts at artistic satisfaction without care for remuneration, e.g., *Mlle* and *Harper's.*

One thing I hope is that you will make your own breakfasts in the a.m. so mother won't have to lift a finger. That is the main thing that seems to bother her. You know, as I do, and it is a frightening thing, that mother would actually Kill herself for us if we calmly accepted all she wanted to do for us. She is an abnormally altruistic person, and I have realized lately that we have to fight against her selflessness as we would fight against a deadly disease. My ambition is to earn enough so that she won't have to work summers in the future and can rest, vacation, sun, relax, and be all prepared to go back to school in the fall. Hitherto, she's always been rushed and tired, and her frailty worries me . . .

After extracting her life blood and care for 20 years, we should start bringing in big dividends of joy for her, and I hope that together we can maybe plan to take a week down the Cape at the end of this summer. What do you think about that?

If we could go after I get out of summer school at the last week in August, or right after Labor Day when expenses are down, we could read, relax, and just be together. I don't know where the car will be, or what you think about it, but we could both chip in and treat her to a week in a cabin, maybe around Brewster, or Falmouth, or somewhere. Let me know what you think about this little light bulb of a plan. . . .

. . . Really, you and I have it good. Food, clothes, best schools in the country—our first choices, and all sorts of prizes, etc. Seems we lead a charmed plathian existence. Just hope the world doesn't blow up and queer it all before we've had our good hard lives lived down to the nub.

So much remains to talk about: philosophies of life, aims, attitudes. At least we can be best companions, all honesty and help each other. I am so proud of you and want the very best for you in the world. Hope that you can profit by all my mistakes, and a few of my lucks and successes!

Be good, and keep a cool and level head (soaking it in beer often helps).

One thing, when you get all success like us, you have to be damn careful because many people secretly would like to see you fall off your proud stallion into the mud, because, no matter how good friends they are, they can't help but be a bit jealous. I find it expedient to keep quiet about the majority of my publications, for instance, because friends can rejoice with you for just so long without wishing they were in your place, and envying you in spite of themselves. It's sad, but that's the way it goes. . . .

Much much love and more felicitations,

Your very proud

Sivvy

{Telegram to Sylvia from Mademoiselle*}*

[NO DATE]

HAPPY TO ANNOUNCE YOU HAVE WON A MADEMOISELLE 1953 GUEST EDITORSHIP. YOU MUST BE AVAILABLE FROM JUNE 1 THROUGH JUNE 26. PLEASE WIRE COLLECT

IMMEDIATELY WHETHER OR NOT YOU ACCEPT AND IF YOU WANT HOTEL RESERVA-
TION. GIVE MEANS AND COST OF TRANSPORTATION HERE AND HOME IN SEPARATE
WIRE IF NECESSARY. LETTER FOLLOWS ON YOUR ACCEPTANCE WIRE. MARYBETH
LITTLE, COLLEGE BOARD EDITOR

MAY 13, 1953

Dearest Progenitor,

. . . The month sounds strenuous but challenging and lots of fun.
I've already sent in the names of four writers, one of whom I will meet,
interview and be photographed with. My tentative choices are: J. D.
Salinger (*Catcher in the Rye* and tremendous stories); Shirley "The
Lottery" Jackson; E. B. White of *New Yorker* fame; and Irwin Shaw.
Hope one of those luminaries consents to be seen with me. . . .

MAY 15, 1953

I hope maybe you can write a bit this summer . . . articles about
your teaching job . . . for one of the women's magazines. I'd love to
edit for you . . . Of course, sharpening up writing again, once it's
rusty, is very painful and almost prohibitive, as the "Oh, why should
I waste my time doing something that will never be published" attitude is easy to have.

But you deserve to pamper yourself increasingly now that the
hardest 20 years of your life are over, and you deserve all the returns
you can get from your wonderful selfless work and help to Warren
and me, who love and admire you more than anyone else . . . You
have managed to create a warm, loving, intelligent family unit, where
pride and love in mutual achievement make us all very close. I never
know anyone for long before I start holding forth with pride about
Grammy and Grampy and you and Warren. Smith and all the opportunities now opening only make me want to affirm my rich heritage
all the more!

Love, Sivvy

[*The two days at home between her last examination at Smith and
her departure for New York were crammed with frantic activity, including the completion of an assignment for* Mademoiselle.]

NEW YORK, N.Y.
JUNE 4, 1953

Dear Mother,

So incredibly much has happened so quick and so fast these last three days.

. . . From my window I look down into gardens, alleys, to the rumbling Third Avenue El, down to the UN, with a snatch of the East River in between buildings. At work at night at my desk, I look down into a network of lights and the sound of car horns wafts up to me like the sweetest music. I love it.

. . . Whooshed up to the sixth floor of 575 Madison; spent morning with other Eds filling out endless forms and job data in mirrored dark-green and pink conference room, which is our headquarters . . . I talked with Rita Smith, Fiction Editor (also sister of Carson McCullers!), Polly Weaver, Jobs and Futures Editor (who had my job on Press Board when *she* was at Smith), and Betsy Talbot Blackwell, fabulous Editor-in-Chief.

. . . Afternoon—rewrote poetry squibs again [*Article: "Poets on Campus," thumbnail accounts of interviews with Alastair Reid, Anthony Hecht, Richard Wilbur, George Steiner, and William Burford*].

. . . Assignments announced. One of my best friends from Washington State is Editor-in-Chief. I'm Managing Ed and moved my typewriter into Cyrilly Abels' office today. At first I was disappointed at not being Fiction Ed, but now that I see how all-inclusive my work is, I love it.

I work in her office, listen surreptitiously to all her conversations on telephone and in person, read all copy and do a lot of "managing"—deadlines, dirty work, etc., but it is fun. Her secretary is a girl I knew at Smith last year, so all is relatively un-tense now, almost homey, in fact.

I have to write comments on all the stuff I read. Just got through criticizing Elizabeth Bowen's speech she gave the very day I talked to her—intellectually stimulating. Also will have a chance to criticize poetry, etc., so my fiction interests are included here, too.

. . . affairs scheduled include fashion tours (e.g. John Frederics hats), UN and *Herald Trib* tours, movie preview, City Center ballet . . . TV show, dance at St. Regis Roof and dinner—sounds exotic, what? . . . Love,

Your managing ed, Syrilly

. . . Work is continuous. I'm reading manuscripts all day in Miss Abels' office, learning countless lots by hearing her phone conversations, etc. Reading manuscripts by Elizabeth Bowen, Rumer Godden, Noel Coward, Dylan Thomas, et al. Commenting on all. Getting tremendous education. Also writing and typing rejections, signed with my own name! Sent one to a man on the *New Yorker* staff today with a perverse sense of poetic justice.

. . . Have a horrible feeling I probably won't get into O'Connor's course [*Frank O'Connor's prestigious course in creative writing at Harvard summer school*]. Send "Mintons" . . . AND the first section from one of my creative writing assignments this year called "The Birthday." . . . Erase comments if possible, or better still, retype, and send . . . I'm dubious about getting in as all people in U.S. will no doubt try to.

. . . Life happens so hard and fast I sometimes wonder who is me . . . Love hearing from you. Letters mean much. So much to do, and a month is such an infinitesimal amount of time.

August issue will be full of us all—several pictures, also *last word*—introduction to whole issue which I just got finished writing in my capacity as managing editor. Poet feature all done. Looks great.

Wearily, still amazedly that there are so many people and animals in the big huge world.

Your citystruck Sivvy

Love specially to Warren, whom Mrs. Prouty also thinks is wonderful and would like to meet. How is he? I miss him more than anybody and am learning a lot about the world that I will tell him.

Saw a yak at the zoo and a soft-nosed infinitely patient eland . . . Will go again when more kinds and different names are awake . . . it was twilight when I went. But I heard a heffalump snore. I know I did.

Love and more love,

s.

Dear Mother,

. . . My job in the office is, I am sure, the most valuable I could ever have. Met Santha Rama Rau yesterday (she's a very good friend of Miss Abels), went to lunch with Miss Abels and Vance Bourjailly (he's the co-editor of a new and wonderful literary periodical, *Discovery*) and had a lovely talk. . . . Paul Engle, poet-teacher of a new program at Iowa State, where you can get your MA in creative writing, dropped in, talked, read some of my poems . . . and said he'd send us booklets describing the Iowa graduate program. He's co-editor of the O'Henry collection this year.

Lots of the other girls just have "busy work" to do, but I am constantly reading fascinating manuscripts and making little memo comments on them and getting an idea of what *Mlle* publishes and why. I am awfully fond of Miss Abels and think she is the most brilliant, clever woman I have ever known. . . . Thoughts are with you and Warren at [*Exeter*] graduation this weekend [*June 13–14*]. . . . Really, I couldn't have come with the cost of it. Money goes like water here, and I rebel against ever taking taxis, but walk everywhere. . . .

Your rested daughter,
Sivvy

UNDATED—LATE JUNE, 1953

Dear Warren,

 . . . I have learned an amazing lot here: the world has split open before my gaping eyes and spilt out its guts like a cracked watermelon. I think it will not be until I have meditated in peace upon the multitude of things I have learned and seen that I will begin to comprehend what has happened to me this last month. I am worn out now with the strenuous days at the office and the heat and the evenings out. I want to come home and sleep and sleep and play tennis and get tan again (I am an unhealthy shade of yellow now) and learn what I have been doing this last year.

I don't know about you, but I've realized that the last weeks of school were one hectic running for busses and trains and exams and appointments, and the shift to NYC has been so rapid that I can't think logically about who I am or where I am going. I have been very ecstatic, horribly depressed, shocked, elated, enlightened, and enervated—all of which goes to make up living very hard and newly. I want to come home and vegetate in peace this coming weekend, with the people I love around me for a change.

Somehow I can't talk about all that has happened this week at length, I am too weary, too dazed. I have, in the space of six days, toured the second largest ad agency in the world and seen television,

Sylvia interviewing Marianne Moore for **Mademoiselle,** *1953*

Sylvia talking with Elizabeth Bowen on a Mademoiselle *assignment, summer 1953*

kitchens, heard speeches there, gotten ptomaine poisoning from crab-
meat the agency served us in their "own special test kitchen" and
wanted to die very badly for a day, in the midst of faintings and
hypodermics and miserable agony. Spent an evening in Greenwich
Village with the most brilliant, wonderful man in the world, the
simultaneous interpreter, Gary Karmirloff, who is tragically a couple
of inches shorter than I, but who is the most magnificent lovable
person I have ever met in my life. I think I will be looking for his alter
ego all over the world for the rest of my life. Spent an evening
listening to an 18-year-old friend of Bob Cochran's read his poetry to
me after a steak dinner, also at the Village. Spent an evening fighting
with a wealthy, unscrupulous Peruvian delegate to the UN at a Forest
Hills tennis club dance—and spent Saturday in the Yankee Stadium
with all the stinking people in the world watching the Yankees
trounce the Tigers, having our pictures taken with commentator Mel
Allen; getting lost in the subway and seeing deformed men with short
arms that curled like pink, boneless snakes around a begging cup
stagger through the car, thinking to myself all the time that Central
Park Zoo was only different in that there were bars on the windows—
oh, God, it is unbelievable to think of all this at once—my mind will
split open.

. . . do you suppose you could meet your soot-stained, grubby,
weary, wise, ex-managing editor at the station to carry her home with
her bags? I love you a million times more than any of these slick ad-
men, these hucksters, these wealthy beasts who get dronk in foreign
accents all the time. I will let you know what train my coffin will come
in on.

Seriously, I am more than overjoyed to have been here a month; it
is just that I realize how young and inexperienced I am in the ways of
the world. Smith seems like a simple, enchanting, bucolic existence
compared to the dry, humid, breathless wasteland of the cliffdwellers,
where the people are, as D. H. Lawrence wrote of his society, "dead
brilliant galls on the tree of life." By contrast, the good few friends I
have seem like clear icewater after a very strong, scalding martini.

. . . Best love to you all—you wonderful textured honest real
unpainted people.

Your exhausted, ecstatic, elegiac New Yorker,

Sivvy

Sylvia, Spring 1954

PART TWO

Summer 1953–August 12, 1955

My mother and I met a tired, unsmiling Sylvia on her return from her month as guest editor for Mademoiselle in New York City. I dreaded telling Sylvia the news that had come that morning—that she had not been accepted as a student in Frank O'Connor's short-story writing class.

I knew Sylvia would see it as a rejection of her as a competent or even promising writer, despite all the writing honors and previous publications she had to her credit. At this point, success in short-story writing was her ultimate goal, and Sylvia was too demanding of herself.

As we left the station I said as casually as possible, "By the way, Frank O'Connor's class is filled; you'll have to wait for next summer before you register for it again." I could see Sylvia's face in the rear-view mirror; it went white when I told her, and the look of shock and utter despair that passed over it alarmed me.

From that point on, I was aware of a great change in her; all her usual joie de vivre was absent. My mother tried to reassure me that this was no doubt temporary, a natural reaction to the strains of the last year. There had been no respite at all, so we encouraged her to "just let go and relax." We packed picnics and drove to beaches in New Hampshire and Massachusetts. At home, she would sunbathe, always with a book in hand, but never reading it. After days of this, she finally began to talk to me, pouring out an endless stream of self-deprecation, self-accusation. She had no goal, she said. As she couldn't read with comprehension anymore, much less write creatively, what was she going to do with her life? She had injured her friends, "let down" her sponsors—she went on and on.

Sylvia's self-recrimination even extended to reproaching herself for having published "Sunday at the Mintons'," one of the two prize-winning stories in the August 1952 edition of Mademoiselle. She felt it had been unkind to the young friend who supplied the germ of the characterization of Henry, one of the two characters in the story. This reaction might be considered a foreshadowing of her emotional recoil from The Bell Jar when that autobiographical novel appeared in London in 1963, shortly before her death.

In an effort to pull herself together, Sylvia, who had by this time decided not to attempt any courses in Harvard Summer School, felt that some form of scheduled activity would keep her from feeling that the whole summer was being wasted. Her plan was that I should teach her shorthand for an hour each morning so that she could "get a job to support my writing—if I can ever write again." For four lessons we worked together. But her disjointed style of handwriting did not lend itself well to the connected strokes of the Gregg system, and I was relieved when she agreed with me that this was a skill she could manage to live without. Later, I regretted that we even attempted it, for the abortive experience just added to her increasing feeling of failure and inferiority.

One unforgettable morning, I noticed some partially healed gashes on her legs. Upon my horrified questioning, she replied, "I just wanted to see if I had the guts!" Then she grasped my hand—hers was burning hot to the touch—and cried passionately, "Oh, Mother, the world is so rotten! I want to die! Let's die together!"

I took her in my arms, telling her that she was ill, exhausted, that she had everything to live for and that I would see to it that she wanted to. We saw our own doctor within an hour; she recommended psychiatric counseling, and the long summer of seeking help began.

The first psychiatrist unfortunately reminded Sylvia of a handsome but opinionated date she felt she had "outgrown," and did not inspire her with confidence. He insisted that a series of shock treatments would be beneficial. I felt so inadequate, so alone. A kind neighbor took Sylvia and me to the hospital for the treatments; it was she who sat with me, holding my hand as we waited for Sylvia to reappear, for though I had pleaded to accompany her, I was not allowed to do so.

The consultations with the referred psychiatrist, an older man, gentle and fatherly, gave me a ray of hope. He prescribed sleeping tablets, which he told me to administer each night, and which I kept locked in a metal safety case. Sylvia still talked to me constantly in the same self-deprecating vein, becoming very agitated at times as she noted the approaching date of the fall term at college.

On August 24, a blisteringly hot day, a friend invited us to a film showing of the coronation of Queen Elizabeth II. Sylvia said she wanted to stay home with her grandparents, who had recently returned from the Cape, but urged me to go. She looked particularly well this day; her eyes sparkled, her cheeks were flushed. Nevertheless, I left her with a sense of uneasiness, feeling that her buoyancy was contrived.

I found it difficult to concentrate on the slow-moving, archaic ceremony on the screen, and in the middle of it I all at once found myself filled with terror such as I had never experienced in my life. Cold perspiration poured down me; my heart pounded. I wanted to get out of my seat and rush from the theater. I forced myself to remain quiet until the close, then begged my friend to drive me home at once. Propped against a bowl of flowers on the dining-room table was a note in Sylvia's handwriting: "Have gone for a long walk. Will be home tomorrow."

Grammy came from her room, distraught, saying, "We had no idea she was so ill, she should not have been left alone." Grampy was crying. The nightmare of nightmares had begun.

The report of Sylvia's disappearance, which I phoned to the police, was issued over the radio. Then I discovered that the lock to my steel case had been broken open and the bottle of sleeping pills was missing.

At noon on the third day, while we were eating lunch, Warren was the first to discern a moan coming from the region of our basement. He dashed from the table before any of the rest of us could move, and then we heard his shout, "Call the ambulance!" He had found his sister, returning to consciousness in the crawl space beneath the downstairs bedroom, the entrance to which had always been blocked by a pile of firewood. A partially empty bottle of sleeping pills was by her side.

In minutes she was carried into the ambulance, and we followed to the Newton-Wellesley hospital. When I was allowed to see her, there was an angry-looking abrasion under her right eye and considerable swelling. Her first words were a moaned "Oh, no!" When I took her hand and told her how we rejoiced she was alive and how we loved her, she said weakly, "It was **my** last act of love." While her voice was weak, her speech was completely coherent and rational. I told her that she was now to think only of complete rest and that with medical care, recovery would follow. She replied, "Oh, if I only could be a freshman again. I so wanted to be a Smith woman."

The next weeks were anxious ones; her desire to live had not reasserted itself. She was transferred to the psychiatric wing of the Massachusetts General Hospital, where association with other patients much more severely disturbed than she caused her to regress.

As soon as the news of our finding Sylvia was made public, I received a sympathetic telegram from Mrs. Prouty, who was vacationing in Maine. One of Sylvia's deep concerns throughout her illness had been that she had not proven herself worthy of the scholarship help given her. Now Mrs. Prouty again held out hope for us all, for her telegram read: HAVE JUST LEARNED SYLVIA HAS BEEN FOUND AND IS RECOVERING AT HOSPITAL. I WANT TO HELP. AM WRITING. OLIVE H. PROUTY

Several letters and visits followed; Mrs. Prouty had herself suffered a breakdown, and during this period she and Sylvia became especially close.

SEPTEMBER 2, 1953

My dear Mrs. Plath:

. . . It is good news to know that your general practitioner finds no trace of psychoses, though I know well that a neurosis can be long drawn-out and requires even more wise handling because recovery is just around the corner and the wrong kind of treatment may delay it.

I think your idea of Sylvia's going to Provincetown with your friend, who is a trained nurse, is excellent—at least as a first step. Of course Sylvia doesn't want to see anyone now. It will take some time, you say, for her face injury to heal. (Poor child! I am so sorry!) Certainly you do not want to send your sensitive child to a place of closed doors and restraint. I heartily agree! But when she is physically stronger, should she not have the constructive help and advice of some wise doctor who has had experience with a nervous breakdown such as hers? I value my nervous breakdown (of some twenty-five years ago) because of what I learned about living from Dr. Austen Riggs (a very great philosopher as well as doctor) of Stockbridge,

Olive Higgins Prouty at home, August 1969

Mass., where I went to get away from home and too much solicitation and care from those dearest to me. Like Sylvia I felt I had become a burden and wanted to get away to relieve them. So I went to Stockbridge and in time recovered completely. I am better equipped to meet life because of my nervous illness. I wish Sylvia might benefit by a recovery similar to mine . . .

You have been through a terrific ordeal and I know well you are still terribly anxious and beset by all the decisions to be made and also by Sylvia's suffering. I wish I could help relieve your anxiety about Sylvia's future, but I am very hopeful there will be no disfiguring scars left on either her body or soul.

Sincerely
Olive H. Prouty

{*Sylvia was now at McLean Hospital, Belmont, Massachusetts*}

OCTOBER 22, 1953

Dear Mrs. Plath,

I went to see Sylvia yesterday, and we went out to lunch together. She met me with a smile, looking very pretty in her blue suit and her hair lovely. After lunch at the Hartwell Farms, we stopped at various fruit stands on our way back to the hospital where I had an appointment with Dr. B. Dr. B. said that Sylvia's weaving was the best in the shop, though Sylvia had told me it was "awful." Later, she showed it to me and it is really exquisitely done. She gave me the typing I had asked her to do and that, like the weaving, was flawless. Dr. B. suggested that she is a perfectionist, which accounts for her self-depreciation if she falls short of perfection in anything she does. I didn't leave her until darkness began to fall. She asked me to send her more manuscript to copy—also said she would like a beginner's book in Culbertson contract [*in the game of bridge*]. Isn't that encouraging? I shall mail her one today . . .

Sincerely,
Olive H. Prouty

{*The following letter is from Mrs. Prouty to Dr. William H. Terhune*}

WALNUT ST.
BROOKLINE, MASS.
NOVEMBER 2, 1953

Dear Will,

. . . Dr. H. says Sylvia will recover completely in time. There are no schizophrenia symptoms, no psychosis of any kind, and no fear the present neurosis will develop into a more serious mental condition . . .

I would like Sylvia to go to you finally, but one of the doctors at McLean said to me, "If she is improving *here*, why change her?" Because the treatment at McLean seems to me so unconstructive (though I didn't tell him this). None of the patients are given a schedule. No occupational therapy or outdoor exercise is required. No stimulating mental effort is provided (like the little green books at Silver Hill). No philosophy of living is offered and no instruction as to how to live wisely when one is well again . . .

Sylvia received insulin therapy and after several weeks showed definite signs of improvement. She submitted to a series of shock treatments toward the end of her stay at McLean, but her understanding psychiatrist promised to be with her throughout the treatment, and Sylvia's faith in her doctor was without reservation.
By the fifth of December she seemed to be her normal self. To see her eyes light up again and a genuine smile accompany her first

embrace of me was cause for deep thanksgiving! She told me that she was determined to return to Smith for the second semester: "I know I can do it, Mother! I know I can do it!"

Sylvia handed me this following letter in the spring of 1954, saying, "I never sent this. However, I kept it as a record of how I felt about things at the time, looking back at last summer."

BELKNAP HOUSE,
McLEAN HOSPITAL,
BELMONT, MASS.
DECEMBER 28, 1953

Dear E.

The rather enormous lapse in time between the date of this letter and the date of your brief-but-eloquent plan for me to write needs an explanation. I don't know just how widely the news of my little scandal this summer traveled in the newspapers, but I received letters from all over the United States from friends, relations, perfect strangers and religious crackpots; and I'm not aware of whether you read about my escapade, or whether you are aware of my present situation. At any rate, I'm prepared to give you a brief résumé of details. . . .

I worked all during the hectic month of June in the plushy air-conditioned offices of *Mlle* magazine, helping set up the August issue. I came home exhausted, fully prepared to begin my two courses at Harvard Summer School, for which I'd been offered a partial scholarship. Then things started to happen. I'd gradually come to realize that I'd completely wasted my Junior year at Smith by taking a minimum of courses (and the wrong courses at that), by bluffing my way glibly through infrequent papers, skipping by with only three or four exams during the year, reading nothing more meaty than the jokes at the bottom of the columns in *The New Yorker* and writing nothing but glib jingles in an attempt to commune with W. H. Auden. I had gaily asserted that I was going to write a thesis on James Joyce (when I hadn't even read *Ulysses* through thoroughly once) and take comprehensives in my senior year (when I wasn't even familiar with the most common works of Shakespeare, for God's sake!). Anyhow, there I was, faced with the impossible necessity of becoming familiar with the English language, which looked as coherent as Yiddish to me, in the short sweet space of one summer. When I had come to think psychology, sociology, philosophy . . . were infinitely more worthwhile, valuable, and unattainable.

To top it off, all my friends were either writing novels in Europe, planning to get married next June, or going to med. school . . . The one or two males I knew were either proving themselves genii in the midst of adversity . . . or were not in the market for the legal kind of love for a good ten years yet and were going to see the world and all the femmes fatales in it before becoming victims of wedded bliss.

Anyhow, to sum up my reactions to the immediate problem at hand, I decided at the beginning of July to save a few hundred $$$, stay home, write, learn shorthand, and finesse the summer school deal. You know, sort of live cheap and be creative. Truth was, I'd counted on getting into Frank O'Connor's writing course at Harvard, but it seemed that several thousand other rather brilliant writers did, too, and so I didn't; so I was miffed and figured if I couldn't write on my own, I wasn't any good anyhow. It turned out that not only was I totally unable to learn one squiggle of shorthand, but I also had not a damn thing to say in the literary world; because I was sterile, empty, unlived, unwise, and UNREAD. And the more I tried to remedy the situation, the more I became unable to comprehend ONE WORD of our fair old language.

I began to frequent the offices and couches of the local psychiatrists, who were all running back and forth on summer vacations. I became unable to sleep; I became immune to increased doses of sleeping pills. I underwent a rather brief and traumatic experience of badly given shock treatments on an outpatient basis.

Pretty soon, the only doubt in my mind was the precise time and method of committing suicide. The only alternative I could see was an eternity of hell for the rest of my life in a mental hospital, and I was going to make use of my last ounce of free choice and choose a quick clean ending. I figured that in the long run it would be more merciful and inexpensive to my family; instead of an indefinite and expensive incarceration of a favorite daughter in the cell of a State San, instead of the misery and disillusion of sixty odd years of mental vacuum, of physical squalor, I would spare them all by ending everything at the height of my so-called career while there were still illusions left among my profs, still poems to be published in *Harper's*, still a memory at least that would be worthwhile.

Well, I tried drowning, but that didn't work; somehow the urge to life, mere physical life, is damn strong, and I felt that I could swim forever straight out into the sea and sun and never be able to swallow more than a gulp or two of water and swim on. The body is amazingly stubborn when it comes to sacrificing itself to the annihilating directions of the mind.

So I hit upon what I figured would be the easiest way out; I waited until my mother had gone to town, my brother was at work, and my grandparents were out in the back yard. Then I broke the lock of my mother's safe, took out the bottle of 50 sleeping pills, and descended to the dark sheltered ledge in our basement, after having left a note to mother that I had gone on a long walk and would not be back for a day or so. I swallowed quantities and blissfully succumbed to the whirling blackness that I honestly believed was eternal oblivion. My mother believed my note, sent out searching parties, notified the police, and, finally, on the second day or so, began to give up hope when she found that the pills were missing. In the meantime, I had stupidly taken too many pills, vomited them, and came to consciousness in a dark hell, banging my head repeatedly on the ragged rocks of the cellar in futile attempts to sit up and, instinctively, call for help.

My brother finally heard my weak yells, called the ambulance, and the next days were a nightmare of flashing lights, strange voices, large needles, an overpowering conviction that I was blind in one eye, and a hatred toward the people who would not let me die, but insisted rather in dragging me back into the hell of sordid and meaningless existence.

I won't go into the details that involved two sweltering weeks in the Newton-Wellesley hospital, exposed to the curious eyes of all the student nurses, attendants, and passers-by—or the two weeks in the psychiatric ward of the Mass. General, where the enormous open sore on my cheek gradually healed, leaving a miraculously intact eye, plus a large, ugly brown scar under it.

Suffice it to say that by fairy-godmother-type maneuverings, my scholarship benefactress at Smith got me into the best mental hospital in the U.S., where I had my own attractive private room and my own attractive private psychiatrist. I didn't think improvement was possible. It seems that it is.

I have emerged from insulin shock and electric (ugh) shock therapy with the discovery, among other things, that I can laugh, if the occasion moves me (and, surprisingly enough, it sometimes does), and get pleasure from sunsets, walks over the golf course, drives through the country. I still miss the old love and ability to enjoy solitude and reading. I need more than anything right now what is, of course, most impossible, someone to love me, to be with me at night when I wake up in shuddering horror and fear of the cement tunnels leading down to the shock room, to comfort me with an assurance that no psychiatrist can quite manage to convey.

The worst, I hope, is over . . . Somehow, all this reminds me of the deep impression the movie "Snake Pit" made upon me about six years ago. I only hope I don't have any serious relapses and get out of here in a month or two.

. . . I can now have visitors, go for drives, supervised walks, and hope to have "ground privileges" by the end of this week, which means freedom to walk about the grounds alone, to frequent the Coffee Shop, and the library, as well as the Occupational Therapy rooms.

. . . I long to be out in the wide open spaces of the very messy, dangerous, real world which I still love in spite of everything . . .

As ever,

syl

The following was written more than three years after her own breakdown when Sylvia, married to Ted Hughes, was studying on a Fulbright grant in Cambridge, England. S. was the son of a dear friend. His mother had written me about his being deeply depressed and asked my advice about urging him to get psychiatric counseling.

NOVEMBER 29, 1956

Dearest Mother,

I was most moved by your account of S. . . . I suddenly "felt myself into" his state where he must feel, as I felt, only a little over three years ago, that there is no way out for him scholastically. I wish you could somehow concentrate on him—have him over alone for a weekend, get him to talk, break down whatever sick reserve and terror he has and even get him to let go and cry.

If you think you can, use me as an example. I'm sure he thinks that even though I went to a mental hospital, I never had any trouble about *marks*. Well, tell him I went through six months where I literally couldn't read, felt I couldn't take courses at Smith, even the regular program . . . Tell him I went back without a scholarship for my half year. I know only too well how it is to have nothing anybody says help. I would have felt almost better if people had not tried to be optimistic when I honestly believed there was no hope of studying and thinking. I am sure he is not that badly off.

Find out what his marks *are*. Is he in danger of failing? If not, tell him that (even in our competitive American society) while marks may get scholarships, people are judged by very different standards in life. If he tries to *enjoy* his studies (I assume he is now taking some courses he likes), he will be enriched throughout life. Try to give him a life-perspective . . . walk out in nature maybe and show him the trees are the same through all the sorrowful people who have passed under them, that the stars remain, and that, as you once wrote me, he must not let fear of marks blind him to the one real requirement of life: an openness to what is lovely among all the rest that isn't. Get him to go easy on himself; show him that people will love and respect him without ever asking what *marks* he has gotten.

I remember I was terrified that if I wasn't successful writing, no one would find me interesting or valuable.

Get him to see that he must like his work for itself first . . . tell him to force himself every time he does a paper or exam to think, "Whatever mark I may get, I liked this . . . I have discovered such and such. I am that much richer whatever the examiners may think." Marks have no doubt become the black juggernaut of his life. Do not try to be overoptimistic, because that will only make him lose trust in you. . . . Agree with him about the problem, even if it is dark. Start from the *bottom*. If he is not failing, tell him how good that is. If he likes *any* subject, tell him how important that is. If he gets despairing or frantic and thinks he can't work or think, give him some ritual phrase to repeat sternly to himself. Let him be gentle in his demands; tell himself he has as much right to work and be at Harvard as anyone . . .

Tell him . . . that I only want to share some of my own experience with him . . . that I thought . . . that my case was utterly hopeless.

Do ask him out alone and talk straight out with him. It is better he should break down and cry if he has to.

I think psychiatrists are often too busy to devote the right sort of care to this; they so seldom have time to get in deep and blither about father and mother relationships when some common sense, stern advice about practical things and simple human intuition can accomplish much.

. . . When he dies, his marks will not be written on his gravestone. If he has loved a book, been kind to someone, enjoyed a certain color in the sea—that is the thing that will show whether he has *lived*.

He probably feels something like a hypocrite, as I did—that he is

not *worth* the money and faith his parents have put in him . . .
Show him how much chance he still has . . . Help . . . his summer
plans . . . I wish you would give him as much time and energy as
you can through this time. Adopt him for my sake (as the Cantors did
me) . . . Show you love him and demand *nothing* of him but the
least that he can give.

*Sylvia returned to Smith in the second semester, taking only three
courses. She was not on scholarship at this time. I wanted her to be
free of any sense of obligation and cashed in an insurance policy to
meet her expenses. During the first few months in 1954, we telephoned frequently—more for my peace of mind than hers.*

*Sylvia was welcomed back by her classmates and the faculty.
Understanding and every possible kindness were given her. She
picked up an active "date life," which helped build up confidence, and
she said she enjoyed herself "in a casual, hedonistic way."*

*After Sylvia's return to college, she made me think of deep-sea
plants, the roots firmly grasping a rock, but the plant itself swaying
in one direction then another with the varying currents that pass over
and around. It was as though she absorbed for a while each new
personality she encountered and tried it on, later to discard it. I kept
saying to myself, "This is only a stage; it will pass."*

*Her memory grasped and held to discords and seemed to have lost
recollections of shared childhood and early girlhood joys. Kindnesses
and loving acts were now viewed cynically, analyzed for underlying
motives. We all strove to be patient, helpful, and understanding
through this very difficult period of self-rediscovery on her part.
Then, periodically, to our relief, her sunny optimism would reassert
itself and we would be once more showered with affection.*

SMITH COLLEGE
NORTHAMPTON, MASS.
[UNDATED; WRITTEN FEBRUARY 1954]

I have spent a good deal of time chatting in the rooms of various
girls in the evening and playing bridge, figuring that getting well
acquainted with some of the underclassmen is most important at first.
Am reading Hawthorne's short stories, *Crime and Punishment*, and
Sister Carrie by Theodore Dreiser.

Needless to say, it is simply wonderful to be back here, and I feel
no desire to graduate, amazingly enough, with the rest of my class.

Dear Mother,

The flight to New York was ecstasy. I kept my nose pressed to the window, watching the constellations of lights below as if I could read the riddle of the universe in the braille patterns of radiance . . .

. . . I spent the afternoon at the Museum of Modern Art, which I am getting to know better and better . . . I looked up a few paintings of modern American artists to describe for my long feature article for *Vogue*, which is going to take a heck of a lot of research. I stayed to see the late performance of the movie . . . and have never been so moved . . . It was a silent French version of the "Temptation of Saint Joan," with written titles and piano music going all the time . . . quite casually on its own, absorbing some of the powerful emotions aroused by the black-and-white counterpoint of faces—it was almost all faces—of Joan and her tormenters . . . a picture image of Joan on a wooden stool with a paper crown and stick scepter in her hand contained all the impact of Christ and all martyrs. The burning at the stake was incredibly artistic and powerful, but the very lack of sensationalism, just the realism of fire licking at sticks, of soldiers bringing wood, of peasant faces watching, conveyed by the enormity of understatement the whole torture of the saint.

After it was all over, I couldn't look at anyone. I was crying because it was like a purge, the buildup of unbelievable tension, then the release, as of the soul of Joan at the stake. I walked for an hour around Central Park in the dark, just thinking, and my date kindly took me for a ride in one of those horse cabs around the park, which was the slow-paced, black-and-white balance I needed to the picture. I fed the horse a lump of sugar I'd saved from lunch and felt much better.

[*Throughout her illness and this winter of 1954, Gordon Lameyer— one of her favorite boyfriends—wrote her faithfully, which gave her much support. Sylvia now found a good balance of work, play, and dating. Her self-discipline and confidence were steadily developing. Following the instructions of Dr. B., she charted each day, checking off as an item was accomplished—a practice she followed the rest of her life.*]

To: Dear Mummy   From: me

Subject: Odds and ends   Date: April 16, 1954

. . . Today I cut because I wrote my first poem, a sonnet, that I have written since last May! To be sure, I astringently revised several of my poems this past month (the second one I'm including has six new lines and six old revised and rearranged ones. I think it's my best so far for both thought content and sound—a union of both, not just a hyperdevelopment of one. Tell me what you think of them). But "Doom of Exiles" is All New . . .

DOOM OF EXILES

Now we, returning from the vaulted domes
Of our colossal sleep, come home to find
A tall metropolis of catacombs
Erected down the gangways of our mind.

Green alleys where we reveled have become
The infernal haunt of demon dangers;
Both seraph song and violins are dumb;
Each clock tick consecrates the death of strangers.

Backward we traveled to reclaim the day
Before we fell, like Icarus, undone;
All we find are altars in decay
And profane words scrawled black across the sun.

Still, stubbornly we try to crack the nut
In which the riddle of our race is shut.

While I have not got a paying Press Board job next year . . . I am the correspondent to the New York *Tribune*, which should be good experience, even if it doesn't pay money.

I am so happy about the prospect of my thesis on Dostoevsky, and also of my rooming with Nancy Hunter, who is now my dearest friend . . . Nancy is writing a thesis on "History of Ethical Culture," and I am so elated that with Marty and Clai [*Smith classmates*] gone that I have found such a beautiful, brilliant girl to be my confidante and belle amie!

April 19, 1954

Dearest Mother,

. . . Met Richard Sassoon (whose father is a cousin of Siegfried Sassoon)—a slender Parisian fellow who is a British subject and a delight to talk to . . .

. . . Am still chatting with Dr. Booth [*the college psychiatrist*] once a week—mostly friendly conversations as I really feel I am basically an extremely happy and well-adjusted buoyant person at heart—continually happy in a steady fashion, not ricocheting from depths to heights, although I do hit heights now and then.

Love, sivvy

{Telegram}

APRIL 30, 1954

SMITH JUST VOTED ME SCHOLARSHIP OF $1250. MORE BIRTHDAY GREETINGS. SYLVIA.

MAY 4, 1954

Just a note in the midst of a rigorously planned schedule from now till reading period and exams to say that I am fine. Had a good Saturday with Sassoon up here—most unique—another bottle of exquisite Bordeaux wine and a picnic of chicken sandwiches in a lovely green meadow. Strange and enchanting evening spent in farmhouse while waiting for Sassoon and tow truck to get his car out of quagmire on rutted dirt road. Four intriguing people who were evidently captivated by my peculiar arrival in the dark of night, hair damp with rain. They called me "Cinderella" and treated me like a queen till Sassoon came back with the reclaimed Volkswagen—a unifying episode of crisis!

Wonderful letter from Gordon, who is gradually changing to favor teaching (!)—my letters, subtle as they are, seem to be exerting influence. Also, I hope to know him on deeper, more mature levels than I was capable of last summer. See you Sat. the 15th.

x x sivvy

UNDATED; ARRIVED IN EARLY MAY 1954

HAPPY MOTHER'S DAY! . . . I'm going to New Haven to see Sassoon for a final party . . . should be absorbing as both Sassoon and his roommate . . . claim to be intensely in love with me. It's a bit disconcerting to get passionate, metaphysical love letters from the same mailbox and two antagonistic roommates. To top it off, Nancy Hunter and the third roommate have been "partners" for years.

Anyhow Sassoon and I are driving to NYC to celebrate our farewell party (Sassoon leaves for Europe in a short while).

. . . Nancy is coming [*for a visit in our home*] from June 1 to 5. Her birthday is June 3, and I want to have a big steak dinner and cake surprise. I do love her!

x x x Sivvy

MAY 20, 1954

. . . Just a note in the appropriate midst of *Escape from Freedom* to let you know I won one poetry prize this year on the basis of my sonnet "Doom of Exiles," which I wrote this spring. Only $20, I think, but it will keep me in new shoes for Marty's wedding. Also, I just got elected president of the Alpha Phi Kappa Psi Society, honorary society of the arts, which has the advantage of being a very honorary post with a minimum of work and a solid gold, ruby-studded pin from Tiffany's, which is handed down from president to president each year—minor events compared to the splash last year, but events nevertheless. Tomorrow I have sherry with Mr. Gibian, my thesis advisor. Then the reign of terror: exams. See you in a week.

x x x Sivvy

This, too, was a very turbulent summer. Sylvia returned from Smith with her hair bleached. Although initially shocked, I had to admit it was becoming. It was more than a surface alteration; she was "trying out" a more daring, adventuresome personality, and one had to stand by and hope that neither she nor anyone else would be deeply hurt. She strove for (and achieved) competency in her various undertakings—domestic and scholarly. She would be disarmingly confiding, then withdraw, and I quickly learned that it was unwise to make any reference to the sharing that had taken place.

The duodenal ulcer I had developed during the strenuous years of my husband's illness (1936–1940), and which had caused internal hemorrhaging several times, had been quiescent for the most part in the 1950s—that is, until the time of Sylvia's breakdown in the summer of 1953. In 1954, in an attempt to recover again, I took the summer off and joined my parents in a rented cottage on Cape Cod.

Sylvia, after the academic year at Smith closed in May, visited with friends in New York, attended several weddings, then returned to our home in Wellesley to "keep house" until she would join her friends in a Cambridge apartment and attend summer school at Harvard.

Sylvia at the beach, summer 1954 (photo: Gordon Lameyer)

Dearest Mother,

Thought I'd sit down on this cold, clouded day to write you a note about affairs here since last I talked to you. Practically speaking, all has run off well. I've cooked meals for Gordon all weekend and learned a good deal.

We had a very lazy weekend, doing absolutely nothing except eating, talking, reading, sunning, and listening to records, and I again realized that it takes a few weeks of utter relaxation to put one in shape in between big pushes of work.

. . . We ended by driving to Dr. B.'s ourselves Friday—luckily, because my talk with her lasted longer than usual. I do love her; she is such a delightful woman, and I feel that I am learning so much from her.

. . . I was in a mood to pamper myself this weekend and so went to bed early and read J. D. Salinger and Carson McCullers' short story collections in the sun. I just didn't feel like disciplining myself to more difficult intellectual reading. This coming week, however, I hope to start Dostoevsky in Cambridge and pick up German again, which I dropped for this week after the B exam, as if I'd been burned. . . .

. . . I do want you to know how I appreciate time for a retreat of sorts here. Of course, the house is lonely without you, but I have been such a social being so continually since last winter (the month of June being an intensification, not a cessation, of my social obligations and contacts) that I really feel the need to be in a social vacuum by myself for a few days when I [can] move solely at my own lazy momentum with no people around. Naturally, it is only too easy to want company to alleviate the necessity for self-examination and planning, but I am at the point now where I have to fight for solitude, and it thus becomes a precious, if challenging, responsibility.

My main concern in the next year or two is to grow as much as possible, to find out, essentially, what my real capabilities are, especially in writing and studying, and then to play my future life in consistency with my abilities and capacities. This is a very important time for me, and I need as much space and concentrated solitude for working as possible. I feel that you will understand . . .

If I can learn to create lives, stories, and excitement out of myself without depending on external stimuli as shots-in-the-arm, but rather as provocative-yet-dispensable additions to a life already whole and rich in itself, then I will be surer that I am maturing in the direction I want to go.

Meanwhile, I want you to know that I love you really very much and have wished occasionally that I could just whisk on a magic carpet to the Cape to give you an impulsive bearhug, because you are, and always will be, so dear to my innermost heart.

Much love to all.

Sivvy

. . . My main bother this month is my Fulbright application. I've had numerous interviews with the head of the graduate office and all my former professors, all of which have at least resulted in most gratifying results: Elizabeth Drew, Newton Arvin, and Mary Ellen Chase have agreed to write my letters of recommendation, and as they are all very big names in their field internationally, I should have an advantage there that might compensate for my mental hospital record. I think I definitely am going to write Dr. B. for my personal reference as I have to tell about McLean anyway, and a letter from her would serve the double purpose of eloquent recommendation and also of leaving no doubt as to the completeness of my cure. In addition to the fantastic red tape of the Fulbright, all of which is due in a month, I am applying separately to both Oxford and Cambridge, my two choices for university, through the American Association of University Women, since often Fulbright recipients are arbitrarily placed and I want either of these two erudite institutions—so that makes about 12 letters of recommendation, 3 health exams, 12 statements of purpose, etc. You can see how I'd love a private secretary! However, I hope to be able to have several photostats made of my three Big letters, so I can just send them out. Fortunately, my applications to Harvard, Yale, and Columbia don't have to be in till the middle of winter. (Harvard is the only place I really want to go!) . . .

. . . I'm busy making a bibliography for my reading, after which I'll plunge into skimming through all the works of Feodor D. in preparation of a detailed study of his Double characters. . . .

I hope to get over this cold soon, but my schedule is settling out well, so that I feel psychically happy if physically nasty. My brown-haired personality is most studious, charming, and earnest. I like it and have changed back to colorless nail polish for convenience and

Sylvia during "the platinum summer," 1954 (photo: Gordon Lameyer)

consistency. I am happy I dyed my hair back, even if it fades and I have to have it touched up once or twice more. I feel that this year, with my applying for scholarships, I would much rather look demure and discreet.

Your own sivvy

Dearest Mother,

. . . Now I think it is the time for me to concentrate on the hard year ahead, and I do so, although it means sacrificing the hours spent in pleasant frivolity over coffee and bridge—but I feel that the work I'm doing now is most important for the last push of my senior year—and I know how to have happy gay times when I really want to.

. . . I know that underneath the blazing jaunts in yellow convertibles to exquisite restaurants I am really regrettably unoriginal, conventional, and puritanical basically, but I needed to practice a certain healthy bohemianism for a while to swing away from the gray-clad, basically-dressed, brown-haired, clock-regulated, responsible, salad-eating, water-drinking, bed-going, economical, practical girl that I had become—and that's why I needed to associate with people who were very different from myself. My happiest times were those entertaining in the apartment [*the preceding summer, at Cambridge, Mass., while attending Harvard summer school*], where I could merrily create casseroles and conversation for small intimate groups of people I like very much and that served as a balance in the midst of the two extremes.

. . . I am a firm believer in learning to be inventive and independent the hard way—with little or no money, and I hope I can continue to investigate life's chances and try to be so even though inside I long for comforting security and someone to blow my nose for me, just the way most people do. I was proud of learning to cook and take care of bills this summer, but that is only the beginning. If only England would by some miracle come through, I would be forced shivering into a new, unfamiliar world, where I had to forge anew friends and a home for myself, and although such experiences are painful and awkward at first, I know, intellectually, that they are the best things to make one grow—always biting off just a slight bit more than you chewed before and finding to your amazement that you can, when it comes right down to it, chew that too!

. . . Right now it seems as if it is impossible that I [*will*] ever have a well-written thesis done, because now all reading is apparently unrelated (except that it is all about doubles and very exciting in itself) and thoughts are yet in embryo. The rough draft of my first chapter is due in a week from this Friday, and I am wondering if I can say anything original or potential in it, as I feel always that I have not enough incisive thinking ability—the best thing is that the topic itself intrigues me and that no matter how I work on it, I shall never tire of it. It is specific, detailed, and with a wealth of material; but, of course, I don't know yet what precise angle I'll handle it from. I'm taking the double in Dostoevsky's second novelette, *The Double*, and Ivan Karamazov (with his Smerdyakov and Devil) in "The Brothers" as cases in point and think I shall categorize the *type* of "double" minutely, contrasting and comparing the literary treatment as it corresponds to the intention of psychological presentation. In conjunction with this, I've been reading stories all about doubles, twins, mirror images, and shadow reflections. Your book gift, *The Golden Bough*, comes in handy, as it has an excellent chapter on "the soul as shadow and reflection."

. . . Do write often and give my love to all.

Your own sivvy

October 15, 1954

. . . Went up to have a talk with Miss Mensel yesterday, and she was just dear. I was beginning to feel concerned about senior expenses and all the college and house dues coming up, so decided to get a few little jobs to cover some of my spending money. I am now going to spend 1½ hours each Monday afternoon reading aloud to a blind man, starting next week. I also am going baby-sitting twice next week and spent two hours today proofreading copy for the college directory. Miss Mensel said that I was slated for a gift of $10 from the "riotous living" fund, which I was most interested to learn about. I decided, inwardly, that when I start earning money, I'd like to send at least $10 a year for Miss Mensel to give some scholarship girl to spend on a play, or put toward a weekend away, or something impractical like silver dance slippers—they have been so wonderful to me! She also said that I shouldn't leave my $50 deposit for scholarships as they will ask me to, but that I will need it to cover my senior expenses, which is a help.

Mary Ellen Chase has been just wonderful about my Fulbright application. She is going to write both to Oxford and Cambridge for me with Miss Drew, and from what she says, she seems to have no doubts about my getting in! She says the English universities will give me time to write, travel, and are nowhere as rigid with planning time as America's enormous grad schools, and from her accounts of Cambridge, England, I just languished with wishful thinking.

. . . In connection with this [*thesis*] topic, I'm reading several stories by E. T. A. Hoffmann; *Dorian Gray*, by Oscar Wilde; *Dr. Jekyll and Mr. Hyde*; Poe's *William Wilson*; Freud, Frazer, Jung, and others—all fascinating stuff about the ego as symbolized in reflections (mirror and water), shadows, twins—dividing off and becoming an enemy, or omen of death, or a warning conscience, or a means by which one denies the power of death (e.g., by creating the idea of the soul as the deathless double of the mortal body). My thesis, as I see it now, will only mention the philosophic and psychological theories (there are thousands) and will deal specifically with the *type* of Double in these two novels of D. and the literary methods of presenting them.

Needless to say, this year will be just hard work. But, except for my treading water precariously in German, I Love to Study! I am so happy with my brown hair and my studious self! I really can concentrate for hours on end and am hoping that I can justify my topic by doing it well.

Be good to yourself, dear mother, and know how much I look forward to seeing you well and happy when I come home Thanksgiving—I hope *this* year will be an unclouded Thanksgiving for all of us!

Best love to all—
sivvy

OCTOBER 25, 1954

. . . Really, mother, I am so happy and fortunate in my topic: it lends itself to writing and is so fascinating that my interest will never become dulled no matter how [*much*] I work on it continually. Except for a brilliant long essay on "the double" by Otto Rank, no book has been devoted to it, and Mr. Gibian says he thinks it would be a good topic for a graduate thesis or even for a book! I have fallen in love with it and feel reasonably sure that if I revise and rethink, I can write a good thesis.

One very nice thing has happened this week. I don't know if I told you, but the brilliant young Jewish writer and critic Alfred Kazin (wrote *On Native Grounds* and *A Walker in the City*) has a chair here for a year, and I felt badly, since he was in the English department, that I'd have no chance of coming in contact with him. Then the *Alumnae Quarterly* conveniently assigned me an interview with him. He is notoriously hard to see and even more impossible to interview, but after about 20 phone calls, I finally persuaded him to give me 5 minutes. At first he was very brusque, and then he asked me a few direct questions about myself. As soon as he found out that I was working my way through college and had a few things published and wanted to teach and write, he became charming and said he'd thought I was just another pampered Smith baby like the rest. He offered to criticize my writing, invited me to audit a class Friday, and told me to come back and talk to him again because he thought I was interesting!

Well, when I went to his writing class of ten, I was delighted with him, but appalled at the weak, mealy-mouthed apathy of the girls, who either were just too scared or just too stupid to have opinions. As an auditor, I found it hard to keep quiet. Finally, at the end of the class, Mr. Kazin turned to me and said, "Well, what do *you* think?" I told him, and he said, "Why don't you join the class. I think we need you!" I was really thrilled. The chance to write for a semester under such a man and to have him "invite" me, while countless other girls have wanted to get into his small course, seemed rare and wonderful. I thought it over carefully and decided that it is much more developing for my character to maybe get two B's in my other courses while grinding my rusty writing gears into motion under Mr. Kazin than it would be to rigidly strive for A's and sacrifice the rare opportunities of life. Mr. Kazin will not happen again, and it will be good for me to have the impetus of his criticism while starting out again. I can apply it to the things I want to write this coming summer.

The thing about writing is not to talk, but to do it; no matter how bad or even mediocre it is, the process and production is the thing, not the sitting and theorizing about how one should write ideally, or how well one could write if one really wanted to or had the time. As Mr. Kazin told me: "You don't write to support yourself; you work to support your writing."

Mr. Gibian is the best kind of thesis adviser I could have. Went over to talk to him yesterday and sat happily holding one of his twin baby boys on my lap while he held the other and discussed Dostoevsky while the baby gurgled happily and pulled my hair. It is amusing that I'm writing on the double, while my adviser has twins!

Dear Mother,

Kazin's course is delightful as ever. Our last meeting was held at his home this Friday, over coffee and lovely pastry. I read my last story aloud, and everybody analyzed it. It was the incident about Paula Brown's Snowsuit, remember? This course is the best thing for getting me in the habit of writing. Every time one sits down to the blank page, there is that fresh horror, which must be overcome by practice and practice. I stayed afterwards to help with the dishes and talked to the beautiful, blond Mrs. Kazin, whose second novel is coming out this winter.

. . . I have still not heard from the *Atlantic Monthly*, by the way, which is very tantalizing—it's been over two months now, which is so similar to *Harper's* treatment. I love building up my hopes, even though nothing comes of it. It's such fun to live in suspense. I am also trying out for *Vogue's* Prix de Paris contest for college seniors. The first prize is $1,000 (!) and so amply worth the time. I have already completed one assignment. The second is four articles which I shall write over Christmas. These two assignments will make me eligible for the final long thesis upon which the prize is judged. Last year two Smith girls were among the winners, so I should have some chance!

If only I get accepted at Cambridge! My whole life would explode in a rainbow. Imagine the wealth of material the experience of Europe would give me for stories and poems—the local color, the people, the fresh backgrounds! I really think that if I keep working, I shall be a good minor writer some day, and this would open such doors! One thing, if I get accepted in England, no mere $2,000 will stop me from going! It is the *acceptance* over there that I'm worried about. Oxford never likes people with any physical or mental ills in the past. Mary Ellen Chase and Miss Duckett may make Cambridge a possibility. I shall earn $500 next summer, at least, I think, and get something from Smith, I hope, and piece the rest together somehow.

I look so forward to the year ahead. There is much work always, but it is happy work, and I am loved, and I love, and everything is sweet and sensible. Much love to you all. See you soon.

Sivvy

Dear Mother,

The story looks just exquisite! I am so pleased . . .

I acted immediately upon your suggestion and sent the story off to

Woman's Day. You are right about its being too short for most magazines. I had thought to send it to *The New Yorker,* which accepts small sketches (it's really not a "story" in the strict sense, but rather a "slice of life") but *WD* might be more inclined to consider something with more pathos. Anyhow, I love having things "out," whether they are accepted or not. [*At this point, her aim was to have twenty things "out" at all times.*] I enjoy living in perpetual suspense.

. . . For our German unit tonight we had to translate and explicate a poem apiece by Rainer Maria Rilke, a really stimulating assignment because a bit beyond our complete grasp. I got so interested in mine, "Ein Prophet," that I made a stab at translating in verse with rhyme scheme and rhythm exactly like Rilke, and except for a few places I have to rework, it came out rather well, if I do say so!

Kazin has invited me out to an informal lunch next week for a long talk, and naturally I look forward to it more than anything else in the world. He has gladly accepted writing a recommendation for me for a Woodrow Wilson fellowship (the one Mrs. Cantor wrote for) and I know his name means a lot. If anything, this year has exposed me to the most magnificent of men! He is an inspiration which comes seldom in a lifetime. And it is so wonderful to know he admires me in return! Oh, yes, I do worship him.

. . . The *Smith Review* comes out this week with my story and poem in it. Look forward to bringing it home to you!

Looking forward to Christmas—

Much love, sivvy

P.S. Guess what! *Adlai Stevenson* is going to be our Commencement speaker! You should enjoy it doubly!

<{*Written on Street & Smith Publications memorandum paper*}>

DECEMBER 13, 1954

To: Mother   FROM: Daughter

SUBJECT: Cabbages and Kings   DATE: Monday [DECEMBER 13, 1954]

. . . This morning a happy thing happened: my second semester schedule, which has hitherto been a mess, is settling out miraculously. Had a conference with Alfred Fisher about my most recent poems and he offered to give me a private course one hour a week of special studies in poetics! He is a very strict man, and a brilliant professor, and this is a signal honor! Also, I'll be writing poetry!

The nasty requirement for a unit this semester, for which I have no desire or need, will probably be changed by the Honors Committee to include this course in special studies, so that my program will cohere beautifully. I must be very quiet about it all, because Fisher is terribly strict about taking on anyone to be tutored, and the waiving of the unit requirement (as yet to be done) is highly irregular! But it will mean my being able to take Kazin's Modern American Lit course and poetry (plus my Shakespeare and German courses which continue) and a review class which is required. So I am very excited and must write both prose and poetry over vacation with a big "Do Not Disturb" sign on my door.

In eager anticipation,

Your loving daughter,
Sivvy

Dear Mother,

. . . HANDED IN MY THESIS TODAY! . . . I was so excited that I cut classes to proofread it. It is 60 pages of straight writing, with 10 more for notes and bibliography. . . . It is an excellent thesis, I know it in my bones, and already two girls have told me that Mr. Gibian thinks it's something of a masterpiece! I am really pleased with it.

Another note: I hoped I could save it till I was sure one way or the other, but it's too exciting to keep, so I'll let you in on it. The *Journal* rejected my "The Smoky Blue Piano" story, but with the following wonderful personal letter: ". . . We feel the diary method of narration, certainly for this story, is awkward and makes the telling too limping. If you should ever decide to rewrite it as a straight story, keeping the nice sparkle it now has, we will be glad to see it again. Congratulations, anyhow, on a *good* first try."

Well, usually they say they'd like to see your *next* story or poem, but this offer to consider a rewrite stimulated me to my typewriter today, and I was amazed at the validity of their criticism. I did the story over in direct form (I knew inside the diary wasn't right), and the whole thing drew together and incandesced! Naturally, I took them up on their offer and sent it back immediately, tonight, after spending a whole day typing the 20 pages. It is the best short story I have ever written of its kind (the kind is the "Initiation" kind, written to meet certain specifications, while being true to my own humor and ideas). I knew it in my bones again and somehow felt that their letter to me would be exactly this, only I never expected them to say they'd consider it again after I rewrote it! I thought, like *The New Yorker*, they'd just criticize, so I could profit by it and then sell to *Harper's*, or something! But even if they don't take it rewritten, I know now, in my intuition, that it will SELL somewhere! . . .

Mr. Fisher has been having unofficial classes with me already for my Poetics course! We get along admirably, now that we are getting acquainted, and he is the most brilliant, enchanting man I've ever known, reminding me very much, in his way, of Gordon as he may be 30 years from now, who knows. Anyhow Mr. Fisher is exactly what I need for poetry criticism, and my first two "Batches" of about ten poems he went over so thoroughly, I find myself just flying home to rewrite them, which is a rare drive for any writer, I think! I have polished the two long ones I wrote over vacation, and he is very pleased.

I am now in the finals for the *Vogue* Prix de Paris and must write a "thesis" of over 10 pages (at least) on "Americana"; "on my discoveries in the arts this year, what I've found most exciting in the American theatre, books, music, etc." I'd really appreciate any advice you have on bird's eye reading I could do. I feel that you would be much more aware of current trends than I, what with your *Monitor* and *Saturday Review of Literature!* I hope to see more theater in NYC after next weekend and also take in the latest additions to the NYC art galleries in preparation for this essay, which I am hoping to get done mostly before second semester begins—plan to do a research job on it in NYC . . .

Love to all.

P.S. Am planning to rewrite a really good (if awfully naked and depressing) story for *Mlle* contest between semesters! It has possibilities and is in the nature of Ilona Karmel's "Fru Holm," only more subjective—more fun!

JANUARY 27, 1955

[*Written on back of envelope:*] P.S. . . . Sorry for the discouraging facts in this letter, but they are, unfortunately, facts.

x x x S.

Dear Mother,

I always hate being a harbinger of bad news, but I am really pretty miserable this morning. Evidently my interview decided the committee against me, and this is the first time I have been really rejected after having all the chances, and I have been terribly sad all morning. Perhaps at last those four little men will stop arguing and asking me sarcastic questions in my head. It simply doesn't do any good to say: "Don't worry, it's only one scholarship." It is, unfortunately, everything. Letters from Kazin, Phi Beta Kappa, all that did absolutely no good: my interview canceled all that.

The worst thing is that they told me it was practically impossible to get a Fulbright to Oxford or Cambridge (and they *know*, having been over there) and that Dean Rogers is now merrily receiving my Radcliffe applications for admission and scholarship no doubt with a preconceived rejection all ready in his mind. Obviously, if this American Regional Committee refused me, I have no chance for a Fulbright in national competition with countless PhD's. And also, obviously, if Rogers says in his letter to apply to a grad school with no overcrowding in the Department, he doesn't mean Radcliffe, where only a few make the grade every year. Even if I got admitted, that would be something, but I honestly am dubious about even that last hope, which was the very bottom one on my list, after the Fulbright, England admission, Woodrow Wilson, Radcliffe Scholarship. On this one simple fact of admission hangs my whole future. They can quite easily cut off my whole chance to expand my intellectual horizons with one little: "We regret to inform you."

Oh, I really will have to fight with myself to weather the repeated discouragements of this. I've borne the tens of rejections I've gotten for my writing this year with a gay philosophy, but this, after all, is my life. You were only too right when you challenged me about my ability to be an English teacher on the college level. I don't think I'm organized or positive or well informed enough to teach anybody a damn thing. I'll be lucky if I can teach myself to be a practical file clerk or waitress.

. . . Well, at least my thesis is all right, and my work here these last months of what may be my only academic experience seems to look promising . . . At least Smith loves me and I love Smith. It's so discouraging, because it implies a rejection of personality and potentiality as well as just "a superfluous applicant."

I'm enclosing a letter to Dean Rogers, in addition to his depressing refusal, for your opinion. I think the letter to him is all right and doesn't sound bitter, which was very hard for me, but I *must* have some idea about my failings, because they are inextricably involved with my Radcliffe chances. Dean Rogers only needs to say to a wavering committee at Radcliffe: "She is too risky. I saw her for an interview and she had no grasp of questions, was too cocky, or too nervous, or too God knows what—" and I'm done. The thing I'm worried most about now is being *admitted* even. I never thought I'd fall to such a level!

One fortunate thing is that after I've stopped crying about this and deluging my typewriter, I shall plunge into my work here, a little defiantly to be sure, but with renewed vigor.

. . . If only I *knew* what they disliked about me! I think it's only fair for him to give me some inkling, where my application to Radcliffe is so related to his decisions and so I won't go through life repeating that half hour interview and wondering what I said or did wrong. It's appalling to think that my application and letters were good enough to get me there and that something about my personality was so bad that it canceled all the rest.

Well, I sat and wrote ten back letters yesterday, Mrs. Prouty's among them, and am caught up there. This morning I wrote one short story for the Christophers and will write the other this afternoon. [*The Christopher Movement, founded in 1945, emphasized the importance of personal responsibility and individual initiative in raising the standards of government, education, literature, and labor relations.*] If even *one* of my three big contest prizes came through, I might be able to earn enough waitressing this summer to go to Graduate School without financial scholarship. But now I am really scared about even being admitted. If admitted, I will go, of course, but at present I hate Dean Rogers, which is not exactly charitable, but rather easy to do at this point.

Today this refusal, a *SatEvePost* rejection, my 2nd semester bill, and your forwarding of my check balance all came, and it is enough to make Vanderbilt wince.

Hello again. It is now after lunch, and I am beginning to think a little. I shall write immediately to Columbia and ask if it is too late to apply for a scholarship there (the due date is February 20, but they said to send for applications before January 15). I do not think they require the Graduate Record Exam at Columbia as they do at Yale (which is why I am ineligible for Yale, on top of the fact that New Haven leaves me totally cold and the department there is stricter than Harvard about languages). Columbia, at least, evidently has a huge graduate department and may be more generous about admission than Radcliffe. It is where Pat O'Neil wanted to apply next year and certainly has a good name, even if it is a huge machine. But I am old enough to adjust to a huge machine where the graduate department in English is as large as our senior class at Smith. In fact, I am beginning to think that Harvard is too small to hold both Dean Rogers and myself. Even if it is too late to apply for scholarship blanks at Columbia, I can still apply for admission, and I trust they do not know Dean Rogers. I would rather go there, now that I think of it, than be a waitress in Florida. I never could get orders straight.

. . . I was foolish to assume that Harvard would be panting to have me and put all my eggs in one basket. It is just that sometimes when all your chickens come home to roost at the same time, broken and bloody, it is a little discouraging.

Forgive me for spilling all this over to you, but if you have any pertinent advice, I'd be glad to have it. You seem to be more of a realist than I about my future prospects. I'd appreciate it if you'd send off the letter to Rogers immediately upon checking it for subtle malice. Keep the refusal for my grandchildren: "See what a brilliant career mother had in spite of Woodrow Wilson, Dean Rogers and various hard-hearted professors!" And they will look admiringly at a picture of me, just elected most popular waitress at Howard Johnson's.

Oh well, something will work out. I'll keep fighting.

Lots of love,
Your rejected offspring, Sivvy

JANUARY 29, 1955

Dear Mother,

Just thought I'd sit down and write you a little note on this bright sunny day. I hope you are much better and am sure that a good part of your attack (which you are so careful not to elaborate upon) was due to worry and brooding . . . I don't know whether it is an hereditary characteristic, but our little family is altogether *too* prone to lie awake at nights hating ourselves for stupidities—technical or verbal or whatever—and to let careless, cruel remarks fester until they blossom in something like ulcer attacks—I know that during these last days I've been fighting an enormous battle with myself.

But beyond a point, fighting only wears one out and one has to *shut off* that nagging part of the mind and go on without it with bravo and philosophy.

. . . Your *present* life is the important thing, and it must be relaxed and happy—not becoming so only after countless postponements. . . .

. . . I've decided to rewrite the "In the Mountains" . . . so it will be suitable for *Seventeen* in spring vacation. It is not suitable now and needs much more development of the inner struggle of the girl. It was an attempt to be understated and cryptic as Hemingway, which is fine for a lit. course, but not for 17.

Then, too, I am not sending the Mary Ventura story to the Christophers [*contest*]. I think it is much too fantastic and symbolic for what they want. They want warm, simple stories that will inspire people to go out and do likewise, and I don't think they want everyone in the U.S.A. jumping off speeding trains in the subway!

These last three days, I have done up some very good stories if I do say so. I wrote two for the Christophers, tailored for specifications, both based on a Bible quote, very plotted and noble, but not preaching. One is about a housewife ("Home Is Where the Heart Is"), who comes to mental crisis, faced by a family that seems to be seeking life outside the home. She manages creatively to bring them all back together. The other is even more dramatic—set in a hospital waiting room with flashbacks (I've read up on TV requirements and limitations and been realistic in my sets, main characters, and immediate interest angle), called "Tomorrow Begins Today," about what one teenager can do in channeling energies of high school students from destructive to creative channels. Both are under 10 pages, very decisive and forthright, and I think I have a much better chance than possible with a vague symbolic tale like "The Ninth Kingdom."

Also have rewritten my two best Kazin stories and am sending both off to *Mlle*'s short story contest, answering Cyrilly Abels recent letter that she is looking forward to see my new stories "eagerly." I am very proud of both of these stories—have digested thoroughly and rewritten critically (as you suggested, there has been a cooling time lapse since the first copy).

They seem to like a balance in their two winning stories, so one of mine, "The Day Mr. Prescott Died," is a sassily told humorous one (with real human interest, seriously, under it) in the first person. The other, a very dark story, is the best work of "art" I've ever done, I think. It is called "Tongues of Stone" (my favorite title yet) and is all very bleak and beautifully written, with a crisis and turn for the better at the immediate end. This was the one Mr. Kazin wrote his lovely letter to me about—saying that, thank God, I was a writer, but that writing was invented to give more joy than that story—so I took his advice and changed it from life to art—gave it a conclusion of dawn, instead of eternal night, which to me just makes it right.

I have a feeling that I may be destined to be more successful in writing than I thought at first. If any of these come through, I may well be able to go to Europe in spite of Dean Rogers, write there, learn French and German, and come back a better person. The reason why Miss Chase advised England is the free time to write there, which I long for. If either Oxford or Cambridge should accept me, I will go without a Fulbright. That I know. I shall get $2,000 somehow if I have the chance to go!

The Columbia application came today, so with fast work at the beginning of the week, before classes start for me Wednesday night, thank God, I should be able to get the necessary letters under way. They ask for thesis or other academic work, and bless Miss Page for having me make an extra carbon! . . . At Columbia you have to write an MA thesis, as you don't at Harvard, so my writing time would be almost nil. And writing is the first love of my life. I have to live well and rich and far to write, so that is all good. I could never be a narrow introvert writer, the way many are, for my writing depends so much on my life.

Chin up, mother, and get well for me! Do all you can to put me at ease about that! Love to all.

Your very own Sivvy

FEBRUARY 2, 1955

Dearest Mother,

. . . Snow has come here, and the bleak, black winter sets in, all of which provide many metaphors for poetry. Nothing more, I'm convinced of it, could happen in a discouraging way. The *Journal* sent my story back, saying that the narrative improved the writing, but it lacked an "indefinable something" that made a *Journal* piece. At present, I begin to feel that *I* lack that "indefinable something" that makes a winner.

Fortunately, I'm happier in the midst of these refusals than I was two years ago on the crest of my success wave. Which just shows what a positive philosophy can do. I'd be scared if I just kept on winning things. I do deserve a streak of rejection . . .

. . . I have felt great advances in my poetry, the main one being a growing victory over word nuances and a superfluity of adjectives. On the risk of your considering "Temper of Time" "depressing," I am sending you the 3 latest examples of my lyrics. Read aloud for word tones, for full effect. Understand that "Temper of Time," while ominous, is done tongue in cheek, after a collection of vivid metaphors of omen from the thesaurus, which I am rapidly wearing out. It is a kind of pun on the first page of the NY *Times*, which has news much like this every morning.

Some day Phyllis McGinley will hear from me. They can't shut me up.

The Christophers wrote a nice letter about receiving the stories, saying "God Bless You" and 'Sincerely in Christ," which struck me as rather ironic in the midst of all this flurry of rejections, literary and academic.

However, my typewriter won't be still. This summer I am going to write a pack of stories, read magazines religiously (as every Writer's Manual advises) and capitalize on my growing powers of neat articulation. And I am going to SELL "The Smoky Blue Piano" *somewhere*.

Now I can see the advantage of an agent—she keeps you from the little deaths every writer goes through whenever a manuscript comes back home. It's like having your child refused admittance to public school. You love it, and often can't see why. Read one encouraging story about a successful writer who wrote 10 stories in 10 months, and her agent collected 81 (!) rejections and not one acceptance. But the author gaily began her 11th story. Very encouraging!

Much love to my favorite mummy, and keep well for me. That's the one thing you can do for me and for Warren! We love you so much.

A kiss for the tip of your Grecian nose!

Love, Sivvy

APPAREL FOR APRIL

Hills sport tweed for
    april's back,
world parades her
    birthday frock.

Clouds don laces
    and white linen,
all the sky is
    light blue denim.

Air is clear as
    honeydew,
in pink tiaras
    daisies blow.

Daffodil puts
    on frilled yellow,
fringe of veil suits
    greening willow.

Crocus struts in
    amethyst,
robins button
    scarlet vest.

Squirrel brushes
    silver fur,
river flashes
    jeweled hair.

Sunlight gilds fair
    boy and girl,
apparels them for
    pastoral.

Tricked with clover
    is the land,
with leaf and lover
    wreathed around.

Lest spring bequeath me
    nakedness,
o sweet one, clothe me
    with a kiss.

TEMPER OF TIME

An ill wind is stalking while
    Evil stars whir
And all the gold apples go
    Bad to the core.

Black birds of omen now
    Prowl on the bough
And the forest is littered with
    Bills that we owe.

Through closets of copses tall
    Skeletons walk
While nightshade and nettles
    Tangle the track.

In the ramshackle meadow where
  Kilroy would pass
Lurks the sickle-shaped shadow of
  Snake in the grass.

Approaching his cottage by
  Crooked detour
He hears the gruff knocking of
  Wolf at the door.

His wife and his children hang
  Riddled with shot,
There's a hex on the cradle and
  Death in the pot.

WINTER WORDS

In the pale prologue
  of daybreak
tongues of intrigue
  cease to speak.

Moonshine splinters
  as birds hush;
transfixed the antlers
  in the bush.

With fur and feather,
  buck and cock
softly author
  icebound book.

No chinese painter's
  brown and buff
could quill a quainter
  calligraph.

On stilted legs the
  bluejays go
their minor leagues a-
  cross the snow,

inscribing cryptic
  anagrams
on their skeptic
  search for crumbs.

Chipmunks enter
  stripes of black
in the winter
  almanac.

A scribbling squirrel
    makes a blot
of gray apparel,
    hides a nut.

On chastely figured
    trees and stones
fate is augured
    in bleak lines

With shorthand scratches
    on white scroll
bark of birches
    tells a tale.

Ice like parchment
    shrouds the pond,
marred by misprint
    of north wind.

Windowpane wears
    gloss of frost
till dawnlight blurs
    and all's erased.

Before palaver
    of the sun
learn from this graver
    lexicon:

Read godly fiction
    in rare flake,
spell king's direction
    from deer track.

-{Postcard}-

FEBRUARY 5, 1955

Dear Mother,

Got the first really encouraging note from Dean of Radcliffe today (Rogers sent her my letter), saying my not winning the Woodrow Wilson "would in *no way weaken*" my chances for a grant at Radcliffe and the WW's were given mostly for *men* who might otherwise go into business, law, medicine, etc. Obviously, Rogers wrote her why I didn't get a WW, and it no doubt was not for character blots *only*, as I had thought.

Poems come better and better, and my courses, if demanding, are fiery and delightful. I feel much better about my prospects now that I have spread my applications out to include interesting job and Columbia (although my roster of choice goes [1] Fulbright to England, [2] teaching in Morocco, [3] Radcliffe and Columbia). Keep all your fingers crossed.

FEBRUARY 11, 1955

Dear Mother,

Happy Valentine's Day . . . Life here is in that nasty, fickle stage between winter and spring, and I have written several very good poems which I think you will like . . .

I am very proud of my brother but am afraid I cannot boast as much about marks. My Shakespeare wavers toward a B+ and my German is also only a B−. But I like both courses very much and feel that my writing deserves what it is getting by way of time.

Now for the money. The only way I would accept your kind offer of a monthly loan is that it was unequivocally understood it was a *loan* and that I would pay it back by graduation . . . quite frankly, I have used up all my 2nd semester funds already and have been forced to sell some of my old clothes and possessions to keep myself in postage stamps. [*Actually, as I learned recently from Warren, this poignant story of selling her clothes was a coverup for a secret trip to New York with Sassoon—apparently her suitcase had been stolen from the car in the city.*] In spite of strict budget and absolutely no amusements (I depend on my dates for food, plays, and wine), I would need, after your first $25 check, about $10–$15 a month, I think. I do appreciate this, as I refuse to borrow from authorities and was fully expecting to be hauled into court for my 2nd semester book bills!

Now, about the Morocco job. I thought I would wait until my interview with Mr. Robert Shea, head of the American School in Tangier, today before countering all your arguments, which I now feel very justified in doing.

I was sorry that you jumped to hasty conclusions about both the job and my future plans before waiting to hear the facts.

. . . I would be expected to do nothing more than learn from the expert teacher who shared my grade and to teach the whole grade, all courses, which would be a remarkably versatile training for me. I believe that in America much too much emphasis is put on courses, with the idea that anything from cooking to writing can be mastered if a course certificate is had.

. . . I do not want state certification or more years sitting at a desk learning how to teach when I can live and learn from the best international community. This is the beginning of my professional training. The "veteran" teachers in Tangier are, if anything, more skilled and versatile than those here . . . A lively love and general education and creative outlook are what they want. They will train themselves.

. . . Sue [Weller] and I would live in an apartment (the most luxurious, with patio and five or six rooms is $50 a month!) and do our own cooking (food is abundant, especially fruit and vegetables). We would have a maid to purchase for us because her salary would cost no more than what we would be cheated out of as foreigners at the public markets.

. . . The international outlook is the coming world view, and I hope to be a part of that community with all I have in me. I am young enough to learn languages by living and not the artificial acceleration or plodding of "book" courses. I want people opposite me at tables, at desks, not merely books.

. . . Mr. Shea is like the intelligent, loving, liberal father I have always longed for, and I can think of no man except Mr. Crockett who so much made me think that there are saints on earth, with a radiance and love of service and helping others to grow which is almost superhuman. The easy-going, sunny nature of this man attracted me from the first. . . . He is an international Mr. Crockett and he gave up an international job as diplomat in Persia because he loved the project of this school so much.

During my divine poetry hour with Mr. Fisher today, I discussed all this in detail, and he said, after approving heartily (he, too, was dubious about it last week when the complete facts weren't known), "Do you really want this job?" I assented earnestly, and he left the room a moment. When he came back, he said he'd just called the man, who was in the middle of interviews, and given me the highest recommendation he could think of. Such dearness I can hardly believe!

Mr. Fisher is the ideal reader and professor for me, for my particular poetry. Week by week I can feel the growth and heightened sensitivity sprouting up inside me . . . and I believe I am experiencing the most stimulating, creative process of two minds meeting and growing—I learn so much from him, and in turn I feel I am giving all that is in me, and he is happy with it.

. . . I have always wanted to combine my creative urges with a kind of service to the world. I am not a missionary in the narrow sense, but I do believe I can counteract McCarthy and much adverse opinion about the U.S. by living a life of honesty and love amidst these people for a short time. It is, in a way, serving my religion, which is that of humanism, and a belief in the potential of each man to learn and love and grow: these children, their underdeveloped lands, their malnutrition—all these factors are not the neat rigid American ideals, but I believe the new races are going to influence the world in turn, much as America did in her day, and, however small my part, I want a share in giving to them.

I know what my professors have done for me. . . . Even if my level is only making a Mexican get excited about history or dramatizing a government problem simply to recreate an abstract idea vividly, this is what I would like. This is for now. For perhaps only one year. I hope after that to be a much more linguistic and experienced woman. Maybe I'll be a reporter. Or a poet living in Italy. Or a student at Radcliffe. The important thing is that the choice grows naturally out of my life and is not imposed on it by well-meaning friends. Do consider what I say seriously. I hope you understand.

x x sivvy

‹{Postcard}›

FEBRUARY 15, 1955

Dear Mother,
. . . You'll be happy to hear of an ecstatic coffee hour spent at the home of my dearest friend, Mary Ellen Chase, discussing my plans for next year, which have suddenly taken a bright turn. Cambridge University accepted me as a foreign affiliate for 2-year program for honors B.A.—M.A. is automatic, and all colleges in America will hold out arms to me as teacher. Whole English department here is behind me and against machine-made American grad degrees. If Fulbright doesn't come, will get money somehow. *Don't tell anyone* except grandparents and Warren, but it looks like what I've always wanted in my secret heart.

sivvy

P.S. English men are great!

MARCH 2, 1955

. . . Thursday and Friday is an enormous 3-session symposium on "The Mid-Century Novel," starring among others, Alfred Kazin, Saul Bellow, and Brendan Gill, chaired by Miss Chase. Cyrilly Abels just sent me a lovely telegram offering me $10–$50 (depending on fulness of material) to cover this thing, so must spend almost 3 solid days concentrating to do a good job on this.

. . . Cross your fingers for me during these crowded days!

x x S.

MARCH 13, 1955

Dearest Mother,

. . . I have written three or four little poems, partly humorous, about the sculpture and paintings I saw at the Whitney Museum in NYC when I went there for the 1955 American exhibit.

. . . In spite of the fact that this is my worst week of exams and papers, I am very happy, probably because Sue Weller and I spent the morning today playing tennis for the first time in the season . . . I never felt so lively as today for months, and I am determined to keep up this exercise and to go out for crew again this spring the way I did last fall. I am not bad if I practice, and I love the feeling of being up early in the morning and having my muscles tightening. Basically, I think, I am an "outdoor" girl, as well as a contemplative sedentary writer.

Mlle just sent my lovely pink check, which will pay my book bill at least. Somehow, with the coming of the spring, nothing really bothers me, and I feel very happy and optimistic. I am turning out five poems a week, and they get better and better. I hope to write a lot this summer and try to get a little book of them into print in about a year: think I'll try out for the Yale Series of Younger Poets. Just for fun.

. . . Don't want to get your hopes up, but I can't help telling you that my fates seem to be brewing up something quite good. The Fulbright Adviser here just got a letter from the agent in Oxford, saying I'd been recommended for one, nothing more, and mentioning that if I could be sure of providing for the second year that Lady Margaret Hall at Oxford would admit me! Naturally, this is all very hush-hush, and I'm not even supposed to know, as my grant is apparently so indeterminate, but to know that Oxford also accepted me, without even the aid of a Mary Ellen Chase, on the testimony of my record, a long Chaucer paper done for Mr. Patch, and an interview with the wife of the President of Kenyon College, is a rather beautiful thing to contemplate. Especially after that smug obviously-Oxford professor at my Harvard interview told me it was impossible to get a Fulbright to either Oxford or Cambridge! Oh, even if I don't get one, I know somehow that I will go! Imagine having a *choice!* Of course, if I get a Fulbright, they will probably assign me to a particular one, but I hardly can worry about that!

Cross all your fingers for me this coming crucial month.

Your puddle-jumping daughter,
Sylvia

MARCH 24, 1955

Dearest Mother,

. . . When I come back, I shall again be ready to do the fantastic reading and writing program I have over spring vacation. I really need a respite from the daily round of classes and waitressing, and stoic living. It will be good to read and write in peace at home.

There are only a few people I want to see: Mrs. Prouty, Mr. Crockett, Patsy [*Patricia O'Neil*], and Dr. B., of course. And I do hope Warren will be around. I miss him very much and am hungry for talking with him again, as I am for living with you all. There is nothing like an alternation of work and play to keep one fresh and spirited. Fortunately, I am building up a list of outlets and tonics for my periodic slackening times. In the summer, it will be tennis, swimming, sunning and sailing. In the winter, New York is a help, and I hope to add skiing in the Alps next year!

The Harcourt & Brace editor, a charming young man of 26 (!), graduate of Harvard and recent recipient of a Fulbright to Cambridge University, came up Wednesday on his quarterly trip to bookshops in our environs. We had a charming long lunch and talk at Rahar's, after which we drove over to the bookshop at Holyoke and I browsed while he talked to the owner. The ride was a treat, and if he drops by in June on his visit to Hathaway House, I hope you have a chance to meet him: Peter Davison is his name; his father is an English teacher at Hunter College, a visiting British poet. . . .

Lots of love to all,
Sivvy

Sylvia's graduation photo from Smith

Sylvia typing in the backyard, Wellesley, 1954

Dearest Mother,

Well, all things come to those who wait, and my waiting seems to be extended for two weeks until the judges decide, after reading our poems over in the quiet of their boudoirs, which of the six of us deserves the coveted prize (won in the last 32 years by an amazing number of now well-known poets). [*She had entered the Glascock Poetry Contest, an intercollegiate competition held annually at Mt. Holyoke College.*]

Suffice it to say that I don't know when I've had such a lovely time in my life. I took to Marianne Moore immediately and was so glad to have bought her book and read up about her, for I could honestly discuss my favorite poems. She must be in her late seventies and is as vital and humorous as someone's fairy godmother incognito. Interestingly enough, she asked about you and said she hopes to meet you some day, and also said you should be proud of me, which I thought I'd tell you in case you didn't already know!

Took the train to Holyoke Friday afternoon, was picked up at the station and taken to a palatial guest room in one of the dorms where I met attractive Lynne Lawner, the contestant from Wellesley and a charming girl whom I enjoyed very much. We were interviewed by the *Monitor*, had our pictures taken again and again, clustered around Miss Moore, interviewed by the reporter from *Mademoiselle*, a Smith graduate whom I am also very fond of, and went to dinner of lamb chops, very good, if a little stilted at first, with everybody very new and still unacquainted.

Then came the reading: a magnificent audience (about 200) packed into a charming small room with dark walls, plush chairs, leaded windows, and a very literary atmosphere. The six of us sat facing the audience at a sort of seminar table, and the response was most rewarding.

All the contestants were amazingly attractive, charming people (from Holyoke, Smith, Columbia, Wellesley, Wesleyan, and Dartmouth), and read very well. The girls, I felt, were much superior to the boys—the only one I felt was serious competition was the one from Dartmouth whom I would bet on for winning. The other two girls were often excellent, but very uneven. All of us got most vociferous applause, and it was a real pleasure to see such an enthusiastic group—there were all sorts of other events going on, too, and no attempt was made to drum up an audience.

The reading went excellently, and I loved doing my poems, because they all sounded pretty polished and the audience was immensely responsive, laughed in some of the witty places, even, which made me feel tremendously happy. I think I'd love being a humorous public speaker. It's such fun to be able to make people laugh.

After the reading, we had a "party" to which selected Holyoke girls were invited, and I had a chance to talk to John Ciardi and Wallace Fowlie, the other two critics, poets and judges, both delightful, also teachers and translators, the former having translated Dante and the latter, Rimbaud and the French poets. I loved them both, and they grew on me more and more as the time went on.

This morning Lynne and I were brought a sumptuous breakfast in bed and had our voices recorded at the radio station. I hope they will send us records of them, as they said they might. Then we had a marvelous forum by the three judges on translations which I found delightful. The whole affair was culminated by a delightful luncheon at which everyone was very intimate and cozy, and Marianne Moore signed a dear autograph in my book of her poems. I really loved them all . . .

Love to all,
Sylvia

APRIL 21, 1955

Dear Mother,

Every now and then there comes a difficult spell where little discrepancies pile up and look enormous, or rather gray, and this week has been one of those. I just feel like writing you about it, although I usually am in a more cheerful mood, and I've been hoping that not hearing from you since Saturday doesn't mean that anything is wrong at home [*I had suffered another gastric hemorrhage*]. Did you see the spread [*of photos of the chief poets in the Glascock Contest*] in the *Monitor?* I don't know what day it came out, but I would like to have you save a copy or two and send one to me if you could. I think they did a generally good job except for that out-of-context quote which had me making the prize moron remark: "I think reading is important."

If I get through this week, I shall feel much better, but everything has piled up so that I know how a bank feels when all the people decide to go to the window the same day and withdraw their money just to be sure it's been there all along.

. . . I was very happy, however, to be given the Alpha award for creative writing (chosen by the English department), which is non-remunerative, just a gold A and an impressive note from the office of the President. I enclose the clipping. I think you would have been pleased to see how the tea came out. It was for the 50 members of Alpha in the very bright red-and-white Dutch room of the Alumnae House. I poured for the whole hour, a feat which I decided to learn in a dash of bravado, and there were sandwiches and a lot of good conversation. Nancy Hunter and Lynne Fisher were among the new members (Nan for her sonnets this semester) and I was most glad for them both. It went off very well, my first experience at presiding at anything, and I really had fun.

I have signed papers accepting the $1,000 Smith scholarship, which they will kindly let me renounce if I get the Fulbright. The next four weeks will be spent plunged in review for the 3 final comprehensives on May 21, 23, and 25, after which I shall be ready for a long, long respite. I have reached my limit of "giving out" this year and feel that my peace of mind is more important than bringing up my two high B's in Shakespeare and German, and God knows what I'll get on the Kazin paper, which is my whole mark for the semester. I am just ready for three months of long, leisurely living with no schedule to meet, plenty of sleep and less pressure than most people, and teaching is the one kind of job I can envision (in the near future) which would support me with these qualifications and which I think I honestly might enjoy.

The most difficult choice I have ever had to make happened today. Editor Weeks on the *Atlantic* sent me a letter with a $25 check for your favorite "Circus in Three Rings," BUT with a really thorny string attached. They liked the second stanza much better than the first and third and challenged me to do a revision around the second stanza with a new title (suggested by them), "Lion Tamer." Well, I was a kaleidoscope of mixed emotions and had a long talk about it all with Mr. Fisher. The top of my head said excitedly: this is your chance to get through the golden doors (they mentioned wanting to have me represented in the young poets' section of the August issue). Review, revise. Quick. The inside part looked at the poem, which sprang out of a certain idea of a trilogy, admittedly poorer in the third stanza than the others, frothy, not bad but light. I thought of their paternalistic letter and felt a little sick and disillusioned. I just can't tailor-make it over again. Another poem, yes, but the dangers of contrivance, of lack of spontaneity, are legion if I revise this. I'd have to live with it the year out and still I'm afraid a revision would sound artificial. I did resent this attempt at butchering to fit their idea of it.

Prose, I wouldn't mind, but a poem is like a rare little watch: alter the delicate juxtaposition of cogs, and it just may not tick.

So I think I'll sleep on it the weekend out, and if a revision comes, I'll send it, but I doubt it. If not, I think I'll send four of my best latest poems which are "consistent" (a lack they felt in the batch I sent last September) and ask Mr. Weeks to please seriously consider these alternates. Of course, I'll have to send back the check, too, which is a hard thing, and they certainly put me in a very awkward position. I battle between desperate Machiavellian opportunism and uncompromising artistic ethics. The ethics seem to have won, but what a hell! They should have accepted it completely, with the 2nd stanza recommending the others, or not at all. This limbo is definitely difficult! So much dreaming, and then this problem!

Well, do send me an infusion of energy. It will do me more good than thyroid. I really miss hearing from you, and your letters always cheer me up.

Your almost-but-not-quite, -try-us-again daughter,
Sylvia

APRIL 23, 1955

Dear Mother,

Along with love and best wishes for your birthday, I thought you'd like to know I tied for first prize at the Holyoke Contest with the boy, William Whitman, from Wesleyan. That means a check of $50 for me, plus a pleasant glow.

Best of all was a eulogistic letter from John Ciardi, my favorite of the judges, who called me "a real discovery," saying: "She's a poet. I am sure that she will go on writing poems, and I would gamble on the fact that she will get better and better at it. She certainly has everything to do it with. Praise be—" All of which made me so happy I could cry— He also wants to help my publishing and sent a list of quarterlies he wants me to send specific poems to with his recommendations—so it's not a completely indifferent world, after all!

Love,
Sivvy

APRIL 25, 1955

Dear Mother,

It was good to get your letter today; I am so sensitive to mail and really enjoy it. . . . Yesterday and today I spent getting off various letters and finishing typing up my manuscript for Mr. Fisher of poems: there are about 60 poems in the book titled "Circus in Three Rings" (poof to the *Atlantic*), and it does look like a good bit of work to have produced in one semester. I included all my poems, some bad, some good, some still needing revision, and dedicated it to "My favorite Maestro, Alfred Young Fisher." I also made a carbon of the manuscript so I can have it to work from this summer. I want to write at least ten good new poems to substitute for the inferior or slight ones and turn 30 in for a Borestone Mountain book competition this July and then the Yale Series next year. Of course, I really don't think I have a chance, as most are in that limbo between experimental art of the poetry little magazines and the sophisticated wit of *The New Yorker*, too much of the other for either. But I shall try.

Needless to say, the next four weeks are rather crucial, and I should find out a good deal of concrete information: Fulbright, *Atlantic*, *Vogue*, *Mlle*, Christophers, and several Smith prizes to be announced in assembly May 18. Now I shall just read relentlessly away, reviewing four years of notes and books and creating a correlation question. I feel much better about the German [*she dropped that course*] now, as I am in my cycle of ebbed energy and know that at these times I must pare my demands to a bare minimum. I feel this is more sensible than stubbornly trying to juggle too many balls at once. I look enormously forward to a summer of rest and slow-paced creative work and outdoor relaxation.

Don't worry about me at all. You see that I can cope with my limitations, even though it would be much nicer if I didn't have any. I do need at least 10 hours of sleep a night [*a family characteristic*], a minimum of pressure (most of the time) and a life that allows for cycles of energy (I wrote my thesis in two months, in great spurts of energy, much before any other senior finished) and corresponding complete relaxes. Teaching or marriage combined with free-lance writing would be ideal for this, I think. At any rate, be at ease about me these next weeks and wish me luck.

I hope your birthday finds you feeling much better and do give my love to all.

Sivvy

{Her phone call the next day, to wish me a happy birthday ended with "Thank you, Mother, for giving me life."}

Dearest Mother,

. . . By the way, amusingly enough, I just found out this morning that I won $100, one of the 34 prizes in the student contest for the Christophers! . . . I was interested to note that I was the only winner from a big Eastern college. . . . I am probably the only Unitarian that won a prize! . . . As you see, my frugality prevents me from calling home for anything less than a *definite Atlantic* acceptance, a Fulbright, or $500 or more. As yet nothing from these last.

Also I am enclosing the latest and last copy of the *Smith Review*, which I hope you will save for me, in which I have a story and poem. I'll be interested to know what you think of the story. I'm also sending Mrs. Prouty a copy with news about the Alpha award, the Glascock Contest, and this latest one.

. . . Do keep getting well and strong and give my love to all.

Sivvy

[*Sylvia was invited to judge a high school literary contest held at a writers' festival in the Catskill Mountains of New York.*]

Dearest Mother,

The hunter being home from the Catskills, she will take up her porcupine quill to add a supplement to this card, wishing you best luck and love on your day. After ten hours of sleep last night (got back to Smith at midnight), I feel much more human and scarcely able to believe that I lived so fantastically much in a mere 24 hours. Words can hardly convey the packed experience I've had.

Armed with my *Writer's Digest*, I boarded the Greyhound bus for Albany on Wednesday morning, was driven through lovely green hills and apple orchard country, and took another bus to Kingston, New York, where I was met by a fat, well-tempered, hot . . . farmish woman who introduced herself as Mrs. Thornell. At this point, I decided to be my country self and wondered what on earth Mr. Thornell would be like, the general chairman of the whole festival. Well, I learned a lot in a few hours. On the drive to their home, Mrs. Thornell, obviously deferent to my New York City appearance and "literary reputation," told me that her youngest daughter of three had just had her tonsils out unexpectedly that morning, that her aunt had died the week before, and that the house was in the midst of being redecorated. At this point I expected Mr. Thornell would be tied up in the pasture, cropping grass, and that the school would be held in a barn. On the contrary.

Bob Thornell was home cooking steaks, a charming, virile, 34-year-old chap, like a kind of woodland Mr. Crockett, a wonderful grin and easy-going disposition. I liked him immediately . . . Well, after dinner they [*he and his wife*] left for the hospital to visit their little girl and told me sternly to read or walk in their apple orchard and not touch the chaotic kitchen till they came back. I figured they would be worn out, what with all the confusion, and so spent an hour doing the enormous day's stack of dishes with the bright, talkative help of the oldest girl, red-haired Colleen. We must have heated five kettles of water in the course of our work, but I felt really proud when everything was all straightened up and went out to play baseball with Russell, the 8-year-old boy.

When the Thornells came back, Bob asked me if I wanted to go up to the school with him as he supervised the students who were fixing up the displays and signs for the next day, so he could show me around. I was glad for the chance to talk to him alone about the program . . .

. . . Bob took me for a long drive up through Woodstock, the artists' colony, and to the enormous reservoir, which was like an ocean of silver in the moonlight. I saw my first porcupine and countless rabbits . . .

The day itself was a revelation. Seven hundred students came from all over New York State. I spent the morning reading about 20 stories and 20 poems for the two contests I was judging, and out of the general collection of vague echoes and lilied spiritualists, was excited to find two excellent poems and several original stories, and learned a great deal in my reading and analyzing the subjects and form. No names were on the entries, only numbers, so I didn't know till the end of the day that my choice for 1st in poetry went to my favorite boy, Wallace Klitgaard, son of a now-dead Danish author, with a famous artist for a mother.

. . . They asked me to read aloud my own poetry and discussed it, and also two of the student poems. I was so stimulated by the groups, and several came up afterward, including a dear little man teacher from Middletown, to say how they enjoyed the discussion. I was really amazed by my diplomacy, my sudden ability to remember quotes to illustrate points, and to smooth differences into an acceptance of paradox. We had excellent discussions, and I realized that a moderator can guide a class to make conclusions and draw the whole thing together. I was happiest to see how they responded to challenge, humor, and figured that I would really like teaching after this session which elated me no end.

Met several publishers, artists, etc., either from NYC or Woodstock, also Mickey Spillane, a friend of Bob Thornell's, up from Florida, looking like a dear, tan, innocent kid, rather than the author of countless best-seller murder mysteries . . .

Bye for now,
Your own Sivvy

[At this time, I was in the Newton-Wellesley Hospital, getting intravenous feedings to build me up for a subtotal gastrectomy later. Sylvia telephoned, telling the nurse that the news she wished to impart would help me more than anything else could. The nurse wheeled me to the telephone in the corridor, and Sylvia told me she had been awarded a Fulbright grant to study at Cambridge University. Such joy!]

MAY 21, 1955

Dearest of Mothers,

I am up here on the sun roof in halter and shorts, basking in the pure blue air under a tall, waving tree of white dogwood and green leaves, while the leaves of the beech tree are coppery dark red. You have *no idea* how wonderful and reassuring it was to talk to you yesterday! That, plus the Fulbright, has made me able to face exams with equanimity, and now MORE GOOD NEWS! (if that seems possible!) I just got a wonderful letter from Editor Weeks of the *Atlantic Monthly* after my first exam of three (four hours long) this morning.

He said they all *agreed* with me that my original poem "Circus in Three Rings" was better than the revision they asked for and so it will *definitely* appear in the August issue of the *Atlantic* as you read it and liked it—what good fortune for the title poem of my embryonic book!

Best of all, he said they were "charmed" by my long 3-page poem "The Princess and the Goblins" (whose length deterred them at this time) and asked me to send it back with some *new work* this summer! Such bliss! That fortress of Bostonian conservative respectability has been "charmed" by your tight-rope-walking daughter! Do tell Mr. Crockett and Mrs. Prouty about this and the Fulbright.

. . . I am so happy, so encouraged. . . . I hope to visit [*Sarah Elizabeth Rodgers*] sometime this summer early for advice about plotting—I'd love to get that "indefinable *Journal* quality"!

Now, just so you can remember it all, I'll give you a list of prizes and writing awards for this year:

$30	Dylan Thomas honorable mention for "Parallax," *Mlle*
$30	For cover of novel symposium, *Mlle*
$5	*Alumnae Quarterly* article on Alfred Kazin
$100	Academy of American Poets Prize (10 poems)
$50	Glascock Prize (tie)
$40	Ethel Olin Corbin Prize (sonnet)
$50	Marjorie Hope Nicholson Prize (tie) for thesis
$25	*Vogue* Prix de Paris (one of 12 winners)
$25	*Atlantic* for "Circus in Three Rings"
$100	Christophers (one of 34 winners)
$15	*Mlle* for "Two Lovers and a Beachcomber by Real Sea"
$470	TOTAL, plus much joy!

Now can pay all debts and work toward coats and luggage. Get well *fast*—can't wait to see you Wednesday.

All my love,
Sivvy

[*I had permission to leave the hospital to attend Sylvia's commencement, and made the trip flat on a mattress in a friend's station wagon. Adlai Stevenson gave the commencement address, Marianne Moore was one of the honorary-degree recipients, and Alfred Kazin waved to Sylvia as she returned from receiving her degree. I was in full accord with her as she later whispered in my ear, "My cup runneth over!"*]

[WELLESLEY, MASS.]
TUESDAY NIGHT
JULY 19, 1955

Dearest Mother,

. . . Saturday, best of all, I'm going out to dinner and a play in Cambridge with Peter Davison, who is in town for good and called tonight . . .

I'd really forgotten how nice and Britishy and tweedy his voice sounded. When I said I had hundreds of questions to ask him, he promised to be a Mr. Anthony and answer them all . . .

I am working in the daytime now at my typewriter. Today I finished the Prouty article, about seven pages, and will send it off. [Reader's Digest *turned this down with a routine rejection slip. It was sent in to be considered for the* Digest's *"First Person" story*.]

Tomorrow I begin my story "Platinum Summer" (I changed it from "Peroxide," and think the tone is better) and hope to have it done by the time I see you next Tuesday [*I was convalescing on Cape Cod*]. Once I get rid of my inhibitions with the typewriter, I'm golden.

Signing off for now with much love to you all.

Sivvy

P.S. What news from Warren?

July 28, 1955

Dear Warren,

 . . . You know how I am: always get homesick before I go anywhere. Well, evidently before a two years' siege, my attacks set in early, and I have been wandering around with a blue streak of incredible nostalgia for *je ne sais quoi*. Paradoxically, I feel the desire to be intensely close to my friends . . . however, the closer I get, the sadder I feel to go away and leave them. Once I get on the ship, I will be fine, as I'll have something tangible to work with, but already I feel sort of rootless and floating, with nothing actual to bite my teeth into. Intellectually, I know the Fulbright is the best and only thing for me; staying in New England or even New York would suffocate me completely at this point. My wings need to be tried. O Icarus . . .

But listen: I want you to have some idea of your potential. It is great. Like me, when you're good (as a person, versatilely), you're very very good, and when you're bad, you need rehabilitation; ergo: we both have a great deal of growing (maturing) to do, and it is by our relationships with other people (after all, what is life but people) that we will grow to ripe stature. In other words, the self-examinations that are induced by our problems and disappointments in relation to others are paradoxically the best incentives to growth and change we have. And it does take guts to grow and change, especially when your horizon is lighted up by what looks like the very best of good things . . .

. . . It is rare to parallel someone else's growth and meet needs for a sustained period when we are so flexible.

What I am rambling around and trying to say is, How Much I think you have to work with and how much I want you to have the sure, positive, creative feeling of the one or two *men* I'm lucky enough to know: that your security and love of life don't depend on the presence of another, but only on yourself, your chosen work, and your developing identity. *Then* you can safely choose to enrich your life by marrying another person, and not, as e e cummings says, until.

I sure hope you take all this talk the way it's meant and maybe drop me a line sometime to let me know you don't think I'm talking through the top of my sun-bleached head. I want you to grow to a certainty of your identity (which I think is the most important thing in life) which will never ask for another court of appeal but your own conscience. That often means sacrificing the tempting urge to spill over All (blues, defeats, insecurities) to another person, hoping for advice, sympathy, or sometimes even scolding as punishment. It means knowing when to go off for a Socratic talk to yourself; sometimes it's a help to have one with someone who knows you and will always love you no matter what whenever; such as me . . .

. . . a much-looked-forward-to evening over Peter Davison's, reading aloud and talking. He's a Harvard man, good friend of Howard Mumford Jones, once had Fulbright to Cambridge, and is delightfully in the midst of publishing, authors, and poets and editors. His father is a Scotch poet, too. A pleasant person. Remember, there will be a lot more pleasant women in the world, Warren, intelligent, beautiful, sometimes both together, sometimes not. But it is all living, preparation for the final intelligent, beautiful one you will someday marry. I'll write again soon. Meanwhile, my best love to my favorite brother.

Your own Sivvy

PART THREE

September 25, 1955–April 29, 1956

The two Fulbright years stand out as the most exciting and colorful of Sylvia's life. In a fairly short time, she adjusted to the multiple changes and challenges of the university environment in Cambridge, England, where she found an active social life and again set herself high scholastic goals. It was at this time, however, that she decided the specialized concentration essential for a Ph.D. was not for her and reasoned that a life of "reading widely, talking deeply with all types of people and living fully" would give her the background necessary to enrich her creative writing. Two visits to the Continent whetted her appetite for more travel. The intense anxiety she had felt over her courses at Smith disappeared at Cambridge, and she plunged into her work with confidence and a new maturity.

She was now seriously searching for an extraordinary male counterpart with whom she could share all the emerging facets of herself; in February 1956 she found him in the poet Ted Hughes. The two had read each other's poetry before they met, each admiring the work of the other. The immediate effect of this encounter was mirrored in a flow of ecstatic poems.

[LONDON, ENGLAND]
SUNDAY AFTERNOON
SEPTEMBER 25, 1955

Dearest Mother,

. . . Where to begin! I feel almost smothered when I start to write this, my first letter! I feel that I am walking in a dream. Perhaps I shall start at London and go backwards. This is really the first day on my own, and since Sunday mornings in any strange city are a bit sad, I took a walk and sat in one of the little green squares to read a bit from the *London* magazine. . . .

London is simply fantastic. . . .

To go on—once I begin, it is almost impossible to stop, as memories keep crowding into my head.

The saddest reception was the one for English Lit. students, as I had no way of knowing the illustrious men who were there as guests until afterward (the hostessing was atrocious, and none of us had any idea of the nature of the visitors—they all looked like respectable professors). I only met David Daiches, who will be lecturing at Cambridge and is a well-known critic. Imagine my chagrin when I found out that Stephen Spender (the poet), John Lehmann (brilliant head of BBC and editor of the *London* magazine, a literary review) and C. P. Snow himself (!) had been in the crowd! It was terribly frustrating not to have been introduced to them, but I swallowed my anger at the inefficiency of the hostess and determined to meet them after I'd begun writing at Cambridge. It might be better that way, anyhow. Even T. S. Eliot had been invited, but couldn't make it at the last moment. . . .

Oh, mother, every alleyway is crowded with tradition, antiquity, and I can feel a peace, reserve, lack of hurry here which has centuries behind it. . . .

. . . The days are generally gray, with a misty light, and land-scapes are green-leaved in silver mist, like Constable's paintings.

The ship was wonderful, made more so by Carl [*a new acquain-tance*], who had tea with me and long bull sessions on deck. Weather was half-and-half, but I took no [*seasickness*] pills, danced every night in the midst of great tilts and rocks, and communed with the sea, by sun, rain and stars. Hot broth on deck every morning; after-noon tea (after one cold rainy day in London, I became an ad-dict), roast beef, cold, for breakfast, an hysterically funny Cockney waiter . . .

Best of all: my first land was France! We docked at Cherbourg, and Carl and I went ashore for the most enchanting afternoon of my life. I can see why the French produce painters: all was pink and turquoise, quaint and warm with life. Bicycles everywhere, workers really drink-ing wine, precocious children, tiny individual shops, outdoor cafes, gray filigree churches. I felt I'd come home.

We wandered in a park full of rare green trees, fountains, flowers and hundreds of children feeding goldfish and rolling hoops. Babies everywhere. I even got up courage and stammered out a bit of French to several vibrant, humorous old ladies on a bench and fell in love with all the children. My first vacation I shall fly to France! Such warmth and love of life. Such color and idiosyncrasy. Everything is very small and beautiful and individual. What a joy to be away from eight-lane highways and mass markets, where streets are made for bicycles and young lovers, with flowers on the handlebars and around the traffic lights.

It was good to get your letter. I do feel so cut off from home, especially since I am not at my final address yet. But if I am happy now, at the most disoriented stage of my journey, I imagine once I put down roots at Cambridge, there will be no end to joy. Do write, and I shall, piece by piece, write all my thank-you notes. Will write from Cambridge. Much love to you, Warrie, and the grandparents.

Sivvy

WHITSTEAD, BARTON ROAD
CAMBRIDGE, ENGLAND
OCTOBER 2, 1955
SUNDAY AFTERNOON

Dearest Mother,

I don't know how I can begin to tell you what it is like here in Cambridge! It is the most beautiful spot in the world, I think, and from my window in Whitstead [*students' residence*] on the third floor I can see out into the Whitstead garden to trees where large black rooks (ravens) fly over quaint red-tiled rooftops with their chimney pots.

My room is one of three on the third floor, and while it is at present bare of pictures and needs a bit of decorating, I love it dearly. The roof slants in an atticish way, and I have a gas fireplace which demands a shilling each time I want to warm up the room (wonderful for drying my washed hair by, which I did last night) and a gas ring on the hearth where I can warm up water for tea or coffee. I shall draw you a little map so you can see the layout. My books overflow everywhere and give me the feeling of color and being home . . . Small, but capable of warmth and color after I buy a teaset and a few prints for the bare walls. I love the window-sofa—just big enough for two to sit on, or for one (me) to curl up in and read with a fine view of treetops. . . .

I can't describe how lovely it is. I walked through countless green college courts where the lawns are elegantly groomed . . . formal gardens, King's Chapel with the lace-like ceiling and intricate stained glass windows, the Bridge of Sighs, the Backs, where countless punts, canoes and scows were pushing up and down the narrow River Cam, and the shops on the narrowest streets imaginable where bikes and motorcycles tangled with the little cars. Best fun of all was the open marketplace in the square where fresh fruit, flowers, vegetables, books, clothes and antiques are sold side by side in open-air stalls. . . .

Love,
Sivvy

Opus 2,
October 3, 1955

Dearest Mother,

. . . Here all is to begin again, and probably will be a bit slow and creaky at first due to the very lack of restraints and organization which will make it possible for me eventually to have a rich private, social, and intellectual life.

. . . I feel that after I put down roots here, I shall be happier than ever before, since a kind of golden promise hovers in the air along the Cam and in the quaint crooked streets. I must make my own Cambridge, and I feel that once I start thinking and studying again (although I'll probably be a novice compared to the specialized students here), my inner life will grow rich enough to nourish and sustain me.

I was glad to leave the American group in London and discovered the bohemian section of England with an old beau of Sue Weller's in my last days. Had rum and cold meat sandwiches in a fascinating Dickensian pub, called "The Doves," at night in a court overlooking the dark, low-tide Thames, where in the moonlight, pale swans floated in sluggish streams that laced the mudflats. It was a mystical evening. . . .

I appreciate your considerate news about the multitude of rejection slips and will be glad to get back the poems so I can reassemble them and try to get leads on the British literary magazines. Can't wait till I get established and can really start writing again. I feel this spring should be most fruitful. An acceptance now, of course, would be most kind to my morale. I've been living, acting, and being so much lately that it will be pleasant to grow contemplative and gestate again, "recollecting in tranquillity." . . .

. . . I would welcome any cookies . . . to remind me of home. I shall probably sound quite homesick these first few weeks; I always enjoy giving love, and it is slightly painful to have it shut up in one until deep friendships develop with fruitful, reciprocal confidences involved. Do bear with me. It really helps to write you and will be nice to establish a regular correspondence where we answer each other instead of talking in a sort of vacuum.

I have to begin life on *all* fronts at once again, as I did two years ago, but I have all that experience behind me . . . Remember, I love you very, very much, and give my dearest love to my favorite brother and the grandparents.

Your own Sivvy

OCTOBER 5, 1955

. . . Thought I'd follow up my rather tristful Sunday letter with news of the cheerful days following. Honestly, I love it here. . . .

. . . I can't wait to start meeting the British men, instead of all these familiar Americans. Imagine, the ratio here is 10 men to each woman! Evidently, as this vivid Margaret Robarts (the S. African with the motorcycle) told me, you could spend all your time doing nothing but seeing men socially, once you begin meeting them. I bought the *Varsity Handbook*, which tells about absolutely everything here and is quite witty. Extracurric life makes organizations at home look like child's play. There is a club for everything from Esperanto to wine-tasting to Gepettos (puppetry) to tiddleywinks! Clubs for each Faculty, social clubs, talent clubs, and hundreds of musical and theatrical societies.

Writing is evidently "in the doldrums." I gather the University magazines rise and rapidly wither, and from the one I glimpsed on the stands, poetry is fast fading from galloping consumption. I'm going to try finding out the British lit. magazines and pounding at them. My first poem published here officially will make me feel honestly a literary citizen.

Today I see my Director of Studies: don't know *how* I can ever choose between the miraculous smorgasbord of lecturers: *much* more tantalizing even than Smith! Bye for now. Love to all.

Your own happy Sivvy

OCTOBER 9, 1955

. . . Today is the anniversary of my first week in Cambridge, and as yet, all is poised on the threshold, expectant, tantalizing, about to begin. Lectures started Friday, and I have already been to four, but I have yet to establish the regular schedule of my days. I am most excited about my program, which I arranged with my director of studies, Miss Burton . . . who is to be my supervisor of studies this term (e.g., I meet with her and another student once a week and do papers on Tragedy) and [my] practical composition and criticism tutor (also one hour a week). This is apparently the only regular work I will be asked to produce, as there are no exams until a year from this coming June! I have chosen the exams I will "read for" and am at present wondering how two years will ever be enough! My lectures are chosen to lead into the subjects I've picked for exams.

There are six exams in all, three required. Of these, two are on composition and criticism (general) and one enormous one on Tragedy! This is marvelous for me, because over the next two years I'll be reading tragedy from the classics up to the modern French playwrights, Pirandello, Cocteau, etc., which includes enormous hunks of literature I've never seen before. (This term I'm attending lectures in the history of tragic theory, tragedy from Racine to the present, and Elizabethan and Jacobean tragedy.)

. . . The other exam is on the English Moralists in relation to the history of moral thought, which is a fat exam with a huge reading list, and I picked it not only because I know nothing about it, but because I'll have a chance to read a great deal in philosophy and ethics: from Aristotle to D. H. Lawrence! The third paper I chose was the history of literary criticism, with reference to English literature. This again seems excellent, because I'll have to read both criticism *and* the literature.

For the first time, I'm taking a program which should slowly spread pathways and bridges over the whistling voids of my ignorance. My lecture schedule is about 11 hours (morning) during the week with men whose books are beginning to fill my shelves: F. R. Leavis on criticism: a magnificent, acid, malevolently humorous little man who looks exactly like a bandy-legged leprechaun; Basil Willey on the moralists (he's written enormous, readable books on the 17th, 18th, and 19th century backgrounds); and, if I have time next term, David Daiches on the Modern English Novel. (*Really* "modern," I think, instead of the usual concept of "modern" here: e.g., "modern poets" are considered to be Wordsworth, Arnold, and Coleridge!) I must admit, my enormous ignorances appall me (all I seem to have read is Chaucer, Shakespeare, Milton, the 19th and 20th century writers!), but instead of feeling frustrated, I am slowly, slowly going to remedy the situation by reading and reading (most work here is independent reading) from the lists until my awareness grows green and extensive as my philodendron at home!

. . . Daily life here is at last becoming usual, so before everything becomes natural, I'll tell you a few details that struck me as unique at first. Our rooms are cool enough to keep butter and milk in (!) and I can see why there are so few iceboxes here. Imagine, in the morning when I get up to wash in the bathroom, my breath hangs white in the air in frosty clouds! . . .

. . . In lectures, women are very much the minority, which is a pleasant change, and I imagine much the way it is at Harvard and Radcliffe.

. . . I'm going to investigate a Dramatic Society today, and if there is no room for amateur beginners like me, I'll try the college news-paper. I hope to submit to the little pamphlet magazines here "free lance" and perhaps shall join the Labour Club, as I really want to become informed on politics, and it seems to have an excellent program. I am definitely not a Conservative, and the Liberals are too vague and close to the latter. I shall also investigate the Socialists, and may, just for fun, go to a meeting or two of the Communist Party (!) here later on. Anyhow, I hope to join a group where I can meet people socially who share my interests, instead of just viewing them from afar at lectures. . . .

Newnham is to be honored on October 20th by a visit from the Queen herself and the Duke (their first visit to Cambridge) and so the place is already in preparation for her coming. I can't believe I shall actually see her in the flesh. Imagine, she's coming to open a new veterinary laboratory: how poetic!

. . . When I am acclimated here, to the work, first of all, and the people, I want to try to do a few articles on the atmosphere here, and if I am ambitious, a sketch or two, to try out for the *Monitor*. As yet, I feel too much an initiate to hold forth. The same holds true of writing. We're allowed only three weeks by the Fulbright abroad each of the small vacations (December and April, roughly) so I think I shall stay in Whitstead for a week or two in each of the 5-week Cambridge vacs to write and catch up on my reading, as it is less than $2 a day to stay on for board and room. Lord knows what I will finally do in my vacations. I would like to ski in the Tyrolean Alps and go to southern France and Italy, but it remains to be seen when and with whom. As yet I do not know if Sassoon is going to be at the Sorbonne, which I sincerely hope he will be, because it would be ideal to have such a connoisseur escort me around Paris. But that is still a vague dream.

. . . Much love to all—Sivvy

Dearest Mother,

Hello again! I've told you the grimmer side of the week [*she'd been ill*], let me tell you the lovely part. To begin with, I went with some of the girls at Newnham to a Labour Party Dance Monday night. It reminded me a little of the old dancing school days, but once I got out on the floor, I didn't lack for partners. In particular, one tall, rather handsome, dark-haired chap, named Mallory Wober, caught my interest. He is a Londoner and has lived nine years in India (where his father is an executive of some sort), is reading for Natural Sciences, and seems extremely versatile, with a nice kind of humor . . . I think he "goes with" another girl here, but he invited me to tea with her and another boy Thursday (sufficient reason to make me recover and leap out of the Newnham hospital) in his "digs." It is the habit here, I gather, to write notes of invitation (which he did) and for the girls to go to the boy's place for tea or coffee . . . Seeing young men make tea is still a source of silent mirth to me!

Anyhow, Mallory has his own piano in his rooms and evidently is a brilliant pianist (he had Scarlatti's Sonatas out and the [*a*] Brandenburg Concerto, and much else that made me regret my own lack of musical knowledge and understanding). The other girl, Elizabeth somebody, was British and had just come in from "beagling" (hunting animals with beagles, I think) and was the kind of fair-skinned, rather hysterical and breathless type of English girl I've met so far. I must say, I am happy living in Whitstead where the girls are mature and well-rounded. I love this vital South African girl, Margaret Robarts, and the lovely blonde Marshall scholar, Jane Baltzell, from Rhode Island, who is reading English with me.

. . . Best news of all is the next. I decided to go out systematically for several activities I was interested in, so that I would have a chance to meet people socially this way. Well, I made a mental list: theater groups, newspaper, political clubs, and decided to try from the top. I had my audition (with about 100 other people at least) for the A.D.C. (Amateur Dramatic Club) here, which is the top of the several acting groups here and is the only one to have its own theater, where all the student productions are played out. I was scared to death as we all sat in the theater together, and I watched about 20 people have auditions before me, which was a bit gruelling. Also, I still had the end of my sinus cold and felt a bit giddy.

Well, once I got up there on stage, the natural ham in me came out, and so I did a bit of Rosalind in *As You Like It* (we could choose from ten set Shakespearean pieces) and the part of Camille in Tennessee Williams' play *Camino Real*. I also made a few remarks in between, describing a stage set which made them all have a siege of laughter, and this was most gratifying. Anyhow, I had no idea how I did, but one nice, ugly little boy came up to me later on the street and told me admiringly what a wonderful voice I had, that it filled the whole auditorium! Such joy!

The pleasant upshot of all this is that I am one of the nine girls to become a member of the Amateur Dramatic Club this term.

This coming Saturday night, we are putting on three 1-act plays in a "nursery" production to which influential people will be invited to see the "new talent" A.D.C. offers. All of the new members have [a] part in a play; mine happens to be not the feminine lead, but a rather dramatic character part in a farce by Pope about cuckoldry (!) in which I play a verbose niece who has high-flown and very funny ambitions to write plays and poetry. I come in about four times and have a short part (as do most of the players), so it is just enough to be stimulating . . .

Well, I just had to spill over my little triumph. Cross your fingers for me. I think I'll have a really good time in this Dramatic Club . . .

Best love to all,
Your loving daughter, Katherine Cornell

P.S. Your letters are a constant joy! They really capture the spirit of home. I love hearing news about everyone and the "little things" count most!

Sivvy

OCTOBER 18, 1955

Dearest Licensed Mother!!!

[*I had finally received my driver's license.*]

. . . I am in a marvelous mood. I feel as if I had planted a tree in new soil and were watching a few blossoms open slowly, lovely things, but, best of all, promising the most delectable fruit to come in the maturing sun. Such wild metaphors! It is probably the influence of my absurdly verbose appearances in our coming one-act play.

Instead of being snowed by the enormous amount of work and reading I must do to gain the full benefit of my academic life here, I am sturdily doing a little at a time and feeling most happy. . . .

I have been going to lectures and enjoying them immensely and am quite loving wearing my black gown, which makes me feel so wonderfully a part of this magnificent place. Sort of like sacramental robes! Best of all, my dear, adorable play director gave me the ultimate laurel today by saying my performance was "excruciatingly funny" and doubling up with laughter. I was so happy, because the part of this mad poetess, Phoebe Clinkett, is rather absurd farce and depends on a kind of double entendre slanting of words and gestures which I tried today, having just learned my part, 15 flighty, rather verbose speeches . . . I just hope that I can audition for some of the larger productions after this. My voice is the main thing in my favor. I have, of course, never *moved about* on stage except in the ancient *Admirable Crichton* [*high school play*] . . .

A tall, skinny, rather sweet chap came over yesterday and took me on an exquisite walk to Granchester for tea. I can't describe how beautiful it was to go down the little cobbled streets in the pink twilight with the mists rising from the willows along the river and white horses and black cows grazing in the pastures. Remember Rupert Brooke's poem? Well, we had tea by a roaring fire at "the orchard" (where they serve tea under flowering trees in spring) and the "clock was set at ten of three" and there was the most delectable dark clover honey and scones! . . .

Much love to all,
Your happy Sivvy

MONDAY NIGHT
OCTOBER 24, 1955

Dearest Mother,

"Why, Emmaline! Where have you been?" "To see the Queen!" Yes, I stood about a yard from the gracious Queen Saturday morning, speechless with excitement. It rained and rained all morning, and the royal party was scheduled to visit Newnham (for sherry and a few presentations) on their way to open a veterinary lab. All of us gathered in the dining room in our black gowns on either side of the aisle up which the Queen and Duke were going to walk. I stood right at the foot of the little platform on which the ceremonies were to take place and felt an eagerness which surprised me.

After many false alarms, there was a hush; then we all cheered as the royal couple walked into our humble dining hall with its white wedding-cake ceiling. The Queen looked quietly radiant in a Kelly-green princess-style coat and hat, and the Duke was most talkative and humorous, with a smile that passed all believing; he was enchanting! They stopped at random and chatted with girls down the line, the Duke making many amusing observations. Then four of the top students of Newnham were "presented" to the Queen and Duke. It was all quite lovely, and I ran out in the rain afterwards to see them go off in the royal car (again feeling unaccountably elated to be within touching distance of the handsome pair). Camera bulbs flashed, more cheers, and they were off for lunch at Trinity College.

A rather amusing sequel occurred in the afternoon. I was biking in the rain to the ADC theater for a last rehearsal before the performance that night and saw crowds of people lining the long road down which I had to hurry to reach my destination. I asked a policeman when the royal car was coming, and he laughed and said, "In a couple of minutes; hurry up." So the policemen (in their best white slickers) beckoned me on, and I flew down the street in my red mackintosh on my bicycle, feeling that I should be scattering rose petals or something, while a ripple of laughter ran through the waiting crowds. If I'd had the courage, I would have bowed right and left as I went by, but didn't want to create a mob scene. I must say the royal couple is most genial and attractive, with a kind of radiance which appeals to me. I do, however, envy them not at all the daily round of functions which must be their lot. Apparently, they enjoy it no end, though, and the people certainly all turned out to cheer their Queen in the pouring rain! . . .

. . . I had the loveliest time last night with the boy I met at the Labour Club dance and went to tea with last week—Mallory Wober. He gets more and more dimension each time I see him. First of all, he is extremely handsome in a rugged way, quite different from the pale, delicately made Englishman. He is tall, strong, with coal-black hair and vivid red cheeks and boldly cut features. He is a Natural Sciences major, and imagine my delight when yesterday afternoon, a gray rainy time, he settled me in a large, comfortable chair with a glass of sherry and played the piano for me for over an hour: Beethoven, Scarlatti, Haydn, with comments now and then. He plays excellently and has a sense of humor in his interpretations about it which helps me understand the music. Then we dropped in at the ADC party; then to the most magnificent Sunday night concert in the King's College dining hall, where the architecture looked like a lace of shadows and light, and we heard Hindemith (oboe and piano), Bartok (two violins) and Schubert's songs for five of Heine's poems! Then the Taj Mahal, an Indian restaurant, where Mallory spoke Hindustani and introduced me to mangoes and bindhi quaht (he's lived in Darjeeling for nine years) and the waiters. Biked home after a perfect evening. Do hope to see more of him. Must work hard this week. Very happy—

Sivvy

Dearest Mother,

Greetings from your happily aged daughter! [*October 27 was her twenty-third birthday.*] It was so lovely to get your telegram and the wonderful birthday gifts and letters from Warren, you and Dotty [*my sister*] and dear Grammy and Grampy. I must say the best present anyone can give me is a fat typed letter: all the news from home, even the tiniest daily details, are most welcome. Strange, but true, I feel so close to you all, as if I were only a short drive away. Probably it is that the language is native to me (even if the accent isn't!) and that from my childhood I built up by reading a feeling for England (I'd forgotten how many British writers I must have read, but so much here seems dearly loved already because I've met it before in my reading: the rooks and tea time from *The Cuckoo Clock*, the poetry about Granchester and the Cam, crumpets and scones from T. S. Eliot). . . .

. . . Whew! Best of all (if there can be any best—everything is so lovely) I have at last met Nathaniel LaMar, that boy from Exeter and Harvard who wrote the story "Creole Love Song" in the *Atlantic!* When I heard he was at Cambridge, I begged some boys at Pembroke to introduce me to him, so last night, Richard [*Mansfield*] and I caught him on the walk, and I have a tea-date with him next Sunday. He is a lovely, light-skinned Negro, and I look most forward to talking to him about writing, etc. . . .

. . . My favorite, tall, dark, handsome fellow, Mallory Wober, has just invited me to meet some of his friends at a sherry party before dinner. My project for meeting as large a cross-section of people possible this first term is certainly working out most pleasantly. I have simply been treated like a queen! . . .

Your joyous birthday girl,
Sivvy

OCTOBER 29, 1955

Dear Mrs. Prouty,

At last I am beginning to feel a native of Cambridge and want to take time in the midst of this pleasant carousel of activity on a multitude of new fronts to tell you a little about how happy I am here! . . .

I am most interested in acting now, and my ambition is to audition again and again until I get a part in one of the big plays. There is a companionship and fervor in producing a play which is equalled by nothing else: by the opening night, one feels a great rapport with everybody from the leading man to the electrician and wardrobe mistress!

Next, I want to begin writing again in December, when I am not so intensely involved in the immediate prospect of discovering all that Cambridge has to offer by way of people, books, scenes, and events. Plans for vacation are still very tentative, but I hope dreamily for Paris, the Mediterranean (The Sun), and perhaps a bit of skiing in the Alps.

Instead of wishing rather frantically, as I once did, to be brilliant, creative, and successful all at once, I now have a steadier, more practical approach which admits my various limitations and blind spots and works a little day by day to overcome them slowly without expecting immediate, or even eventual, perfection. Life is rich, full, and I am discovering more about it by living here every challenging day.

I'll write again soon. Meanwhile, much much love to you.

Sylvia

NOVEMBER 7, 1955

Dearest Mother,

It is a wet, warm, gray November day, and the yellow-green trees are letting go their leaves in the sodden wind. The week has been crowded with books and people, and I am slowly learning by experience the kind of life I want most to live here. With so many challenges on all fronts, academic, social, and extracurricular, I have to be firmly disciplined in choosing.

To sum up the past days: I saw a good bit of that outgoing, creative Negro boy, Nathaniel LaMar . . . and went to coffee with him Monday at the bohemian coffee house here where I had the first really good, open "bull session" I've had since I've been here. Temperamentally, Nat is very much like me, enthusiastic, demonstrative, and perhaps trusting and credulous to the point of naiveté. A strong contrast to the Englishmen, who have a kind of brittle, formal rigidity and, many of them, a calculated sophisticate pose. . . .

Also went out to dinner at the Union (the one place in Cambridge where women are not allowed unless escorted: the Debate Club) and saw a rather good production of my favorite *I Am a Camera* . . . which made me want to turn immediately to writing again. Acting simply takes up too much time. I was really glad I didn't get a part in the coming production of *Bartholomew Fair* (although, of course, it injured my ego slightly) because I have so much reading to do, and I would rather be a mediocre writer than a bad actress.

. . . One of the Cambridge "little magazines" has accepted two of my poems and I'm meeting the editor this afternoon. I feel about increasing my scope of reading much as I did about my thesis: I *know* it will take place eventually, but am irritated sometimes at the slowness.

Love to all—
Sivvy

NOVEMBER 14, 1955

Dearest Mother,

. . . There are several frustrations in my work, which, although I allowed for them abstractly, nevertheless bother me still, while I do my best to take them easily. In the first place, the girls in my practical criticism hour have a much broader background than I in the *periods* of literature, and so I am utterly left out when they have to "date" bits of prose and poetry from 16th, 17th, and 18th centuries. Naturally, none of the selections are from Chaucer, Shakespeare, Milton, the Russians, and only very rarely from the 19th or 20th, so I feel very ignorant. There is no preparation I can do for this class, except to read, very slowly, as I am doing, through the poetry of these centuries. Also, in my "supervision" in tragedy, with the same woman, Miss Burton, I again feel enormous handicaps reading, as it were, in a vacuum where I have had no background . . . in Restoration Tragedy. I've done only one paper for her so far on Corneille, which, in spite of the fact I read the plays in my still rusty French, seemed to be acceptable, although we get no marks and just discuss them with our tutor. These are my two most painful hours in the week . . . the kind of reading I have to do slowly to remedy this too-early over-specialization of mine is exactly what I wanted to come here to do, but it is still often difficult, in face of some of these glib girls, to compete on levels where my own lack of reading stands in my way. Occasionally, I would just like to catch them off guard with our early American Literature!

. . . I could read all day every day for the rest of my life and still be behind, so I do balance my mornings of lectures (which I do love) and reading with a kind of cultural and social life. People are still infinitely more important to me than books, so I will never be an academic scholar. I know this and know also that my kind of vital intellectual curiosity could never be happy in the grubbing detail of a PhD thesis. I simply don't believe that kind of specialization is for me. I like to read widely, in art, psychology, philosophy, French, and literature, and to live and see the world and talk deeply with people in it and to write my own poetry and prose, rather than becoming a pedantic expert on some minor writer of 200 years back, simply because he has not been written about yet. Ideally, I would like to write in at least half of my vacations here and publish enough to get some sort of writing fellowship, Saxton or Guggenheim, which would let me live without academic obligations (which I can make up myself after these two years) and write steadily, which is impossible here during the packed term. This is all rather private musing, and I would rather you kept it in the family and shared the more extroverted passages with other people.

Perhaps what I *do* miss most here is the lack of my friends who have known me in my past. I can't explain fully how much it means to have people who have shared years of one's life and with whom you can assume a deep understanding and common experience . . .

While I am very happy here and have many too many invitations to accept even half, all my acquaintances are at the same "historical stage" in knowing, and it takes only much time to achieve anything like the deep and vital friendships I left behind me at home. Everyone here is so "new" and untried. I am glad that I am outgoing and open and intense now, because I can slice into the depths of people more quickly and more rewardingly than if I were superficial and formal.

To continue: It is a lovely blue and gold day. When it is nice here it is "very very nice, and when it is bad, it is horrid." I have become used to clouds of frosted air surrounding me as I breathe in the bathtub and to concentrating on the cloud formations outside the dining room windows as I eat my soggy, sludgy mass of daily starch foods. My room is more and more a delight, and I now have my big earthenware plate heaped with a pyramid of fruit: apples, oranges, pineapples, bananas, grapes, and a large vase of bright yellow dahlias, which bring the sun inside to worship. . . .

Dick Wertz, Sassoon's roommate at Yale . . . dropped over . . . and we had the first good talk we've ever had. I have been constantly surprised how much I miss Sassoon, who is now at the Sorbonne, and spent hours talking about him with Dick. Ironically enough, the boys here are Sassoon's age, but in maturity and integration they are babies compared to him. Having created such vivid, brilliant worlds of talk and people and plays and art exhibits and all those many minute and important things that make up shared experience, I find fragments of the things I so admired and appreciated in him scattered here and there among other chaps, but naturally miss not having them all together. . . .

Friday, I had a lovely time with the first English boy I've met who is temperamentally like me: David Buck. He played the lead in one of the ADC nurseries (Dr. Triceps in Mirbeau's *Epidemic*), and I have admired him ever since. He is reading English in his first year, after serving two years in the Army in Germany, and is very strong and versatile. He is a champion swimmer and has a large role in *Bartholomew Fair*, where I have five lines as a rather screaming bawdy woman who gets into a fight. I think I will do it, even if it is so little a part, because it will give me a kind of stage presence and keep me active in the ADC. . . . Anyway, David and I had sherry at his room in Christ's (I still can't get over the way people casually talk about: "Come on over to Jesus" or "I live in Christ's"!)

Saturday, we went to visit the editor of the "big" magazine at Cambridge where, at David's recommendation, I left a few stories and poems. David writes for them, too. We lunched at The Eagle, one of the arty buffet pubs in town, which was lots of fun.

Saturday afternoon, Mallory took me punting on the Cam, which was lovely, as he looks like a dark-haired, red-cheeked Jewish Greek god (if that is possible), standing at the helm and poling along perfectly straight (a feat) under the bridges where people leaned over and stared and took pictures; and he told me about the Cambridge architecture we could see. Afterwards, he came back for tea at my place (I had fixed up the room with fruit and flowers and gotten all kinds of breads and cakes—I love to have people in for a change, after going out so much). I had refused another date for the evening, as I figured it would be anticlimactic, so I just sat and mused nostalgically on the paradoxes of life.

Yesterday was most amazing. I was, as I said, to have gone to Ely with John [*another boyfriend*], but Mallory had invited me to lunch, and it was a bad day, so I left a note on my door, telling whoever read it to come to tea; and Mallory delivered a note to John, postponing [*my*] seeing him. Well, Mallory took me and some of his Jewish friends from Israel around King's and the chapel, which was exquisite at dusk with all the colored stained-glass windows (which Mallory explained the stories of and the history and architecture) and myriads of candles and lacy fan-vaulted ceiling.

Then Mallory played the "Emperor Concerto" on his vic and "Greensleeves" and some other favorite ballads on his piano for me. We were biking back to my place with sandwiches for tea-lunch when John pulled up on his motorcycle, having read the note on my door and not having got my letter. Well, nothing remained but to have them both for tea, which bothered me a bit as they are very different, John being most shy and sensitive and retiring and Mallory being outwardly very witty and amusing. Believe it or not, they both stayed from 4 till 10 at night, talking about everything from "Is there a purpose to the universe" to the Belgian Congo—no mention of supper! John left only after I invited him to tea today, and Mallory took me to a lovely late steak dinner at the Taj. My first "salon," and most stimulating.

x x x Sivvy

TUESDAY MORNING
NOVEMBER 22, 1955

Dearest Mother,

Your Saturday letter arrived today, and I felt the impulse to sit down and answer it, even though I've told you most of the relevant news in yesterday's note. I must admit that now that Christmas draws near, I, too, feel occasional waves of deep homesickness flood over me which makes me want to go about and announce publicly from the cobbled corners in Cambridge just what a wonderful mother and brother and grandparents and friends I have and how noble and tragic and self-denying a figure I am to be away from all those I love so much for so long. No matter how old one is, there is so often the need to "let down" and spill over to those of one's own flesh and blood, who accept one simply for oneself, without making any demands.

When you think of it, it is so little of our lives we really spend with those we love. I . . . resent being away from Warren so much while he is growing and becoming a man, and I long to spend time with him and learn to know him and have him know me as I am growing to be, too. . . .

I shall be happy to carry your Christmas present with me wherever I go, and, probably in a cold and snowy Paris, open it on The Day. Perhaps the most difficult thing for me to keep up is writing letters to other people, who have been most wonderful about writing me. I get a large satisfaction about writing you, and also my brilliant and sympathetic Richard [Sassoon] who, from Paris, makes me feel I have a strong partisan just over the channel. . . .

. . . I see in Cambridge, particularly among the women dons, a series of such grotesques! It is almost like a caricature series from Dickens to see our head table at Newnham. Daily we rather merciless and merry Americans, South Africans, and Scottish students remark the types at the dons' table, which range from a tall, cadaverous woman with purple hair (really!) to a midget Charles Addams fat creature who has to stand on a stool to get into the soup tureen. They are all very brilliant or learned (quite a different thing) in their specialized ways, but I feel that all their experience is *secondary* [second-hand?] and this to me is tantamount to a kind of living death. I want to force myself again and again to leave the warmth and security of static situations and move into the world of growth and suffering where the real books are people's minds and souls. I am blessed with great desires to give of love and time, and find that people respond to this. It *is* often tempting to hide from the blood and guts of life in a neat special subject on paper where one can become an unchallenged expert, but I, like Yeats, would rather say: "It was my glory that I had such friends," when I finally leave the world.

. . . I have a feeling that I love dear Mallory primarily because he is a kind of substitute . . . for Warren: strong, handsome, with a kind of integrity and strange dearness which is so tempting to help mold.

I really feel that I could be a fine creator of children's souls. Preferably my own children, where intense love could be involved, as well as the teaching part!

I do enjoy your advice and feel very close to you in your letters. Shall talk to Miss Burton after December 3 when I give her my renewal application to fill out and the hectic term is over and I can prepare a serious discussion. I do love you all so very dearly.

Much love,
Sivvy

NOVEMBER 26, 1955

. . . Received your wonderful packed envelope of articles yesterday and enjoyed it no end. You have no idea how I love such juicy collections of items: I understand how important it was to send letters and news of art and incidental home affairs to the soldiers overseas: it keeps the image of home alive and vital, for it is by specific details that we recreate the atmosphere of family and love.

. . . *Bartholomew Fair* began this last Thursday night and will continue until Saturday, December 3, so all my evenings are taken up. Our opening night was cold (many critics from London were there, and we got a long, if rather critical, review in the London *Times*), and I must admit that the play's production is a herculean task, even for pro companies . . . Our costumes come from the wardrobe at Stratford-on-Avon, and I have a long-sleeved gown of vivid yellow satin, which is much fun. Unless I get something like the part of Cassandra in *Troilus and Cressida*, I shall let this stage and grease-paint part of my life go and become a more private person. I must say, though, that instead of frittering my time on small teas or avant garde movies, all very nice in themselves, I enjoy *working* with these boys and girls to create something and not just sitting around to talk and gossip and be passive. The ADC is my extracurricular life, and I am too much a part of this world to become a passive beholder. I want to be out on the stage, too, and create in any way, no matter how small.

. . . I am just finishing with the dregs of a very undermining sinus cold and fever which kept me confined to quarters for the last three days . . . I must tell you what an absolute Rock of Gibraltar Mallory has been to me! To begin with, I had an Ibsen paper to write, French to do, and classes, and the nightly appearances seemed endless. Well, Mallory called for me every night at the stage door of the theater and biked home with me . . . always bringing a ritual apple which we ate by the garden gate at Whitstead. . . .

Last Sunday, before the deluge of this week, I shared the most magnificent experience with him: Advent service at the King's Chapel. Since Mallory belongs to King's College, he got two tickets. Honestly, mother, I never have been so moved in my life. It was evening, and the tall chapel, with its cobweb lace of fan-vaulting, was lit with myriads of flickering candles, which made fantastic shadows play on the walls, carved with crowns and roses. The King's choir boys processed down through the chapel singing in that clear bell-like way children have: utterly pure and crystal notes.

I remembered all the lovely Christmas times we've had as a family, caroling with our dear friends, and the tears just streamed down my face in a kind of poignant joy. The organ pealed out and the hymn was that magnificent one "Wachet Auf" ("Now Let Every Tongue Adore Thee") which was so beautifully familiar . . .

DECEMBER 10, 1955

Dearest Mother,

My wonderful Christmas box came yesterday, and I can't tell you how lovely it was! . . . I immediately devoured a large number of the fresh, delicious hazelnuss [*hazelnut*] cookies and that unique flavor, which I have never encountered anywhere except at home around Christmas, brought back a flood of memories, much the way a certain song or scent can evoke whole portions of the past. . . .

This week has been both pleasant and difficult. I realize now that it parallels that "unfolding" period I always go through when first I come home on vacation: I plan lots of work for every day and then just drift about, sleeping, playing the piano, eating and assimilating— lying fallow, in preparation for beginning to be creative again. It is always hard, though, for me not to demand that I show a profitable work schedule for every spare minute. Well, I can work harder and better this coming week here for having rested and relaxed in this one . . .

My dear Mallory has stayed on to work (and will go home to London tomorrow) and has come over every day for tea and the evening. I haven't had such a healthy "co-ed" life since high school, really. Instead of going off on gay tangents of plays, wine and extravagant holidays on weekends as I used to at college, I live very simply, and much of my time with Mallory is spent placidly listening to music, reading aloud, making tea, biking, and just talking . . . Wednesday, I had dear, lovable Nat LaMar over for tea with Mallory and the three of us had a most pleasant time. Nat has already left for Paris and promised to get me some really cheap hotel reservations on the Left Bank, which should be a relief to have on arrival.

. . . I wish you could meet him [*Mallory*]. His mother would like me to come and stay with them in London . . . I shall probably visit them next Sunday . . . and stay there a few days on my return from Paris. Evidently Mallory's relatives are all gathering around to see me, too, for it is an Event to have a "Christian" girl accepted, I gather. Ironically enough, I am not really a Christian in the true sense of the word, but more of an ethical culturist: labels don't matter, but I am close to the Jewish beliefs in many ways. This family should be fascinating: the English Jews are a contradiction in terms—the vivid warmth and love in their personalities I find very close to home.

. . . Paris is a tremendous challenge, and I'm glad I won't be facing it alone . . . Nat and Sassoon should be a blessing at escorting me through the blazing lights and wonders of this city that never sleeps (not like London, which shuts up shop promptly at 11!). Know that I am thinking of you with much much love and rather a bit of wistfulness this Christmas.

Your own loving
Sylvia

DECEMBER 13, 1955

Dear dear Mrs. Prouty!

. . . I didn't realize how much I had been longing to talk to you until I actually began! Again, I have decided that I would like to combine writing (which I hope to be doing in my long vacation, & especially this summer) of simple short stories about people I know and problems I have met in life with a home & children. I love cooking and "homemaking" a great deal, and am neither destined to be a scholar (only vividly interested in books, not research, as they stimulate my thoughts about people and life) nor a career girl, and I really begin to think I might grow to be quite a good mother, and that I would learn such an enormous lot by extending my experience of life this way!

Perhaps the hardest thing I have to accept in life is "not being perfect" in any way, but only striving in several directions for expression: in living (with people and in the world), and writing, both of which activities paradoxically limit and enrich each other. Gone is the simple college cycle of winning prizes, and here is the more complex, less clear-cut arena of life, where there is no single definite aim, but a complex degree of aims, with no prizes to tell you you've done well. Only the sudden flashes of joy that come when you commune deeply with another person, or see a particularly golden mist at sunrise, or recognize on paper a crystal expression of a thought that you never expected to write down.

The constant struggle in mature life, I think, is to accept the necessity of tragedy and conflict, and not to try to escape to some falsely simple solution which does not include these more somber complexities. Sometimes, I wonder if I am strong enough to meet this challenge, and I sincerely hope I will grow to be responsible not only for myself, but for those I love most. These thoughts are some of the intangibles I've been working out here, in the midst of the outer active, stimulating life. One doesn't get prizes for this increasing awareness, which sometimes comes with an intensity indistinguishable from pain.

I wanted to share my inmost thoughts with you as well as the bright texture of my active days. Do you know how very much I think of you: how I remember our wonderful long discussions over tea and sherry in your living room (which has become a second home to me) and at the Brookline Country Club that lovely evening last summer!

Christmas has always been for me the time of reunion with those dearest people one carries in one's heart through the separation and work of the year. At this time, I want you to know that in spirit I am very close to you, loving you dearly, more than words can tell. . . .

. . . my very best love to you. . . .

Your loving
Sylvia

DECEMBER 14, 1955

Dearest Mother,

. . . I am making out my re-application for a Fulbright this week and feel sorry that it will be judged completely on what I have done this term, as I just feel my head above water now, and my roots taking firm grip. All this term has been "living," experiencing life widely so I can select a disciplined program for the rest of this year without that tantalizing distracting sense of the "untried." I am giving up the ADC for writing regularly a few hours a day, cutting my class schedule so I can do more reading and meditating, and narrowing my social life down to Mallory and one or two good friends, but I had to try everything to be able to choose with such sureness: "You can never know enough without knowing more than enough," as Blake says: "The road to excess leads to the palace of wisdom."

I am really sure the Fulbright won't be renewed . . . I will probably be able to live and travel abroad in these two long winter and spring vacations, but lord knows what about the three-month summer. My one hope is that in my writing later this vac (I'm coming back here ten days early before term) and during next term something salable may turn up. But I am rather pessimistic about it. With the return of my Borestone Mountain manuscript, all my pigeons are home to roost. Gone are the days where I got prizes for everything. This mature-market competition demands constant writing, so instead of waiting for a whole bulk of time, which I come to rusty and paralytic, I am going to do an hour or two every day, like Czerny exercises on the piano. I want to get enough written so I can have several things out and get rid of this sense of a financial deadend— even intangible hope is a better state! . . .

{Postcard}

NICE, FRANCE
JANUARY 7, 1956

Dear Mother,
Yesterday was about the most lovely in my life. Started out on motor scooter along famous wide "promenade des anglais" of Nice, with its out-door cafés, splendid baroque facades, rows of palms, strolling musicians—and headed inland to Vence, where I planned to see the beautiful recent Matisse cathedral of my art magazine, which I've loved via pictures for years.

How can I describe the beauty of the country? Everything is so small, close, exquisite and fertile. Terraced gardens on steep slopes of rich red earth, orange and lemon trees, olive orchards, tiny pink and peach houses. To Vence—small, on a sun-warmed hill, uncommercial, slow, peaceful. Walked to Matisse cathedral—small, pure, clean-cut. White, with blue tile roof sparkling in the sun. But shut! Only open to public two days a week. A kindly talkative peasant told me stories of how rich people came daily in large cars from Italy, Germany,

Dear mother... yesterday was about the most Saturday - con lovely in my life - started out on motor- scooter along famous wide "prom- enade des anglais" of nice, with its out- door cafes, splendid baroque facades, rows of palms, strolling musicians - and headed inland to Vence, where I planned to see the beautiful recent Matisse cathedral of my art magazine which I've loved via pic- ture for years. How can I describe the beauty of the country? everything so small, close, ex- quisite - + fertile - terraced gardens on steep slopes of rich red earth, orange + lemon trees, olive orchards - tiny pink + peach houses - to Vence: small, on a sun-warm hill, uncommercial, slow, peaceful. Walked to Matisse cathedral - small, pure, clean- cut, white, with blue-tile roof, sparkling in sun. But shut! only open to public 2 days a week. A kindly talkative peasant told me stories of how rich people came daily in large cars from Italy, Germany, Sweden, etc., + were not admitted, even for large sums of money. I was desolate, + wandered to the back of the walled nunnery where I could see a corner of the chapel, + sketched it, feeling like alice outside the garden, watching the white doves + orange trees. Then I went back to the front + stared with my face through the barred gate. I began to cry. I knew it was so lovely inside, pure white, with the sun through blue, yellow + green stained windows. Then I heard a voice "Ne pleurez plus, entrez" + the mother superior let me in, after denying all the wealthy people in cars, I just knelt in the heart of sun + the colors of sky, sea + sun, in the pure white heart of the chapel. "vous êtes si gentille" I stammered. The nun smiled "C'est la miséricorde de Dieu." It was.

love
Sylvie

Mrs. Aurelia S. Plath
26 Elmwood Road
Wellesley, Mass.
U.S.A

A handwritten postcard, 1956

Sweden, etc., and were not admitted, even for large sums of money. I was desolate and wandered to the back of the walled nunnery, where I could see a corner of the Chapel and sketched it, feeling like Alice outside the garden, watching the white doves and orange trees. Then I went back to the front and stared with my face through the barred gate. I began to cry. I knew it was so lovely inside, pure white with the sun through blue, yellow, and green stained windows.

Then I heard a voice, "Ne pleurez plus, entrez," and the Mother Superior let me in, after denying all the wealthy people in cars.

I just knelt in the heart of sun and the colors of sky, sea, and sun, in the pure white heart of the Chapel. "Vous êtes si gentille," I stammered. The nun smiled. "C'est la miséricorde de Dieu." It was.

Love,
Sylvia

WHITSTEAD, BARTON ROAD
CAMBRIDGE, ENGLAND
JANUARY 10, 1956

Dearest of Mothers,

Happy New Year! It seems almost impossible to be sitting back in my lovely room at Whitstead again, with three magnificent packed weeks in France behind me. So much to tell! I feel unbelievably refreshed, seething with ideas, rested, ready to write and work hard and deeply for the next three months. The academic year is ideal for my system, which works in large cycles, needing frequent alternations between intense periods of work and play. My New Year mood is so different from the rather lonely, weary, depressed and slightly fearful state in which I left Cambridge a mere three weeks ago. Coming "back" here for this first time made me feel *this* is truly home, and my vacation has given me an invaluable perspective on my life, work and purpose here which I had lost in the complex overstimulation of the first semester. I now feel strong and sure. There is nothing like experience to give one widened horizons and confidence! . . .

I must admit that my heart is with the French! The contrast coming back to England was really painful. . . .

. . . I am going to study French like mad this term to crystallize verbs and idioms (the hardest). My ear is excellent, and all the French say my pronunciation is perfect. So now I have to work on correct details and the eternal vocabulary building. Could hardly understand the harsh Cockney of London, the bored, impersonal, dissatisfied faces of the working class, the cold walls between people in train compartments.

But Cambridge is selling daffodils and tulips in the snow, and I bought an armful of bananas, apples, grapes, and oranges at market today. Am looking forward to a term of writing and work.

Love to all,
Sivvy

<small>JANUARY 16, 1956</small>

Dearest of Mothers,

. . . Oh, mummy, I am so happy that you are coming, there are tears in my eyes! I would love to show you London, too, as I can get around rather well now, and perhaps together we could take a trip to the parts of England you want most to see, as I have seen nothing but Cambridge and London and have been saving the rest for the summer, which will be fairer to England than any other time! Your trip plans make me glow with joy. If Warren gets his Experiment in Living Fellowship, all will be perfect. What a cosmopolitan, international family we shall become!

. . . Now, blessedly, my fears of traveling are gone, vanished completely. I was so scared, really, when I started out. It is one thing to *dream* a panorama of international travel and another to be faced with limited time and money and practical problems of choice and selectivity. . . .

Gradually . . . my plans for spring emerge. I think I will devote it to Italy: Venice, Florence, Milan and Rome. I would much rather live in *one* country for my brief 3-week vacation and know it well, from the heart (which is the way I feel about France, even though I haven't spent any time in the château country). It is amazing how plans take shape. This summer is a large question mark; but if Warren is in Germany, I would like to settle at least a week or so in his town and see him as much as possible, too. Also want very much to see Spain and Greece. Dear Elly Friedman [*Smith classmate*] writes she is coming in summer, so perhaps we can go together a bit; two is so much cheaper than one!

Felt extremely moved and homesick when I saw a magnificent German-Jugoslav movie, *Die Letzte Brücke*, Saturday night. Understood more of the German than I thought; missed Warren and you terribly. While being temperamentally a good deal more French and *southern*, I instinctively love German as my "mother and father" tongue and cursed myself for dropping it over the summer and this last busy term. I want so much to pick it up again and go on reading. It is the *daily* process of a little reading that keeps a language alive, not monumental future projects. I do want to *live* in German-speaking countries this summer, too, with books, and study it the ideal way—speaking, reading, going to plays, and being surrounded with German.

Here: I found it both home and hard, coming back to the atrocious food, the damp cold, and the unsimpatico people (compared with the loving French, who are kindred spirits). You ask about girl friends: well, the English girls are impossible: intellectually brilliant in their own fields of zoology or math, but emotionally and socially like nervous, fluttery adolescent teen-agers (probably a result of being kept apart from boys in school all during adolescence). A beautiful blonde Marshall Scholar is as close to a "best" friend as I have (she is in English and writing, too, in Whitstead) but she goes around with a Scotch girl most of the time, and there is, somehow, a subtle sense of rivalry between us. I do miss my dear Sue Weller. Close girl friends are difficult here because of the intensely individual and concentrated nature of our separate studies, but I do like [*her*] very much.

Am beginning to write slowly, painfully. Just finished two 8-page reportorial essays, one on Cambridge, one on Paris and Nice from which stories will grow (the Vence-Matisse-Cathedral one has several possibilities as article, story and essay). . . . But I *can* live on the golden fat of these past rich three months like a bear hibernating through the Russian winter and write now.

Love—

Sivvy

JANUARY 17, 1956

. . . I found myself feeling rather desperate during *Bartholomew Fair*, at having no inner life to speak of. "Muteness is sickness" for me, as Richard Wilbur says, and I felt a growing horror at my inarticulateness; each day of not-writing made me feel more scared. Fortunately, I have, two years ago, been through the Worst and have the reassurance that if I work slowly and wait, something will happen. In spite of my occasional spells of resentment at my own blindness and limitation (I would really like to get something in *The New Yorker* before I die, I do so admire that particular, polished, rich, brilliant style), I go slowly on, with little flashes of delight, for example, at the sliver of new moon this week outside my window, the sudden gentler blue air today, the sight of a red-cheeked blonde baby—little things; but as Sassoon says so rightly, "The important thing is to love this world; if a man has loved so much as a grapefruit and found it beautiful, God will save him." The hardest thing, I think, is to live richly in the present, without letting it be tainted and spoiled out of fear for the future or regret for a badly managed past.

This term, then, I plan to devote to reading for my supervisions and writing at least two hours every day, no matter what, no matter how bad it comes out. I am starting with these reported descriptions of people and places, trying for precise details, and today did the outline for a version of the Matisse-Cathedral story, which I am going to try in *New Yorker* style first, then perhaps *Ladies' Home Journal* style, and then as a feature article. I want to "lay in" reading and introspection this term and feel that my health should improve with good hours, plenty of fruit and biking, and a developing spiritual calm, which comes as soon as I am writing and sending out things. I would smother if I didn't write.

I honestly feel that if I work every day, in a few years I will have begun publishing again. Writing sharpens life; life enriches writing. Ironically enough, I write best when I am happy, because I then have that saving sense of objectivity which is humor and artistic perspective. When I am sad, it becomes a one-dimensional diary. So a full, rich life is essential.

Don't worry that I am a "career woman," either. I sometimes think that I might get married just to have children if I don't meet someone in these two years. Mrs. Prouty needn't worry either, the dear. France gave me perspective on Mallory, who is fine, but *so* young. I do need to meet older men. These young ones are so fluid, uncertain, tentative, that I become a mother to them. I miss a mature humor and savor and love of career which older men have. I feel that I am certainly ready for that. The only man I have ever really loved (that is, accepting the faults and working with them) is Sassoon, of course. And I fear for his particular nervous . . . health when I think of children. Oh, well, so much meandering. But I am definitely *meant* to be married and have children and a home and write like these women I admire: Mrs. Moore [*Sarah-Elizabeth Rodgers*], Jean Stafford, Hortense Calisher, Phyllis McGinley.

Wish me luck.

Love,
Sivvy

Dearest Grammy and Grampy,

. . . I am starting a rather more serious and solitary life this term, giving up the very demanding, if stimulating, acting in the theater and writing at least two hours a day . . . I am building up creativity from the inside out. Even though writing is difficult, often stilted at first, or rough, I firmly believe that if I work hard enough, long enough, some stories rising out of my rapidly growing perspective about people and places may be published. Somehow stories interest me much more now than the narrower, more perfect form of poems.

I can refer with authority now to much of England, France, and America, and the texture of my writing gets richer as I live more fully. I want most of all to be able to publish some of my transformed experiences, to share them with others.

. . . I am making slow progress in the wide fields of my ignorance, going on with French, reading modern tragedy (Strindberg, now), which is sheer delight, and going to study classical tragedy (Aeschylus, Sophocles, and Euripides), which I have, shockingly enough, never touched.

I can't believe that in June mother will be sitting here, and the windows will be opened over a spring garden! I am living for spring, really.

I am so *sorry* to hear you had that miserable gastritis [*Grammy was ill now with what turned out to be terminal cancer*] and only hope that by the time this letter reaches you, you will be feeling much, much better. Know that I am thinking of you and wishing you healthy and well again.

So many times I think of my grammy and grampy, and how nobody in the world could have dearer grandparents than I do! One takes so much for granted when one is living at home, and I want you to know now how often I think back with love at all the dear things that mean home to me: gramp's whistling and gardening, grammy's marvelous cooking, and sour cream sauces, and fish chowder, and those feathery, light pastry crescents filled with hot apricot jam—our wonderful lobster dinner under the pines at the Cape last summer— all these things we have shared. I feel unusually rich having such a dear family. Give my love to everybody. . . .

Love to all,
Sivvy

Sylvia's maternal grandparents, 1953

Dearest Mother,

. . . Do keep me informed of grammy's progress. I only hope it is nothing serious, but as you have always understood, I would *much* rather know what is going on than be surprised later; so please don't keep anything from me, thinking I might worry. I have the right to be *concerned*, which is different from worry.

. . . I am writing at least a few hours every day . . . have written the first draft of a 25-page story about the Matisse Chapel in Vence; you have no idea how happy it makes me to get it *out* on paper where I can work on it, even though the actual story never lives up to the dream. When I say I *must* write, I don't mean I *must* publish. There is a great difference. The important thing is the aesthetic form given to my chaotic experience, which is, as it was for James Joyce, my kind of religion, and as necessary for me . . . as the confession and absolution for a Catholic in church.

I have no illusions about my writing any more; I think I *can* be competent and publish occasionally if I work. But I am dependent on the process of writing, not on the acceptance; and if I have a dry spell, the way I did last term, I wait and live harder, eyes, ears, and heart open, and when the productive time comes, it is that much richer. This Vence story has my heart and love, and I am going to polish and polish now.

About the marriage question, please don't worry that I will marry some idiot, or even anyone I don't love. I simply couldn't. Naturally, I am sorry that none of the "nice" boys who've wanted to marry me have been *right* . . . I shudder to think how many men would accept only a small part of me as the whole and be quite content. Naturally, all of us want the most complete, richest, best parts of us brought out, and in turn will do this for another. Actually, as you probably know, Richard Sassoon is the only boy I have ever loved so far; he is so much more brilliant, intuitive and alive than anyone I've ever known. Yet he pays for this with spells of black depression and shaky health which means living in daily uncertainty and would be hard over any long time. But he is the most honest, holy person I know. And, in a sense, I suppose I will always love him . . . Ironically enough, he "looks" not at all like the kind of man I could be fond of; but he is, and that's that.

My dearest friend in Cambridge is Nat LaMar. I had a wonderful coffee session with him Sunday and met a stimulating married friend of his who works for *Time* and gave me a lead on some lucrative summer jobs, which I shall write for. Nat is a blessing; the true friend, warm, dear, and emotionally very much like me: sunny and extroverted, but with a profoundly serious, creative side. He had Archibald MacLeish; I, Alfred Kazin. We both have to write and live richly. So I rejoice in knowing he lives in Cambridge and love seeing him.

Tell Warren I have always envied *his* ability to work and do so much. I have always felt inferior in this way. Funny, how things *sound* so much easier than they ever are.

Love,
Sivvy

JANUARY 29, 1956

Dear Mother,

. . . It was such a relief to meet Nat's married friend . . . It is this rich, active kind of life I miss in the vague, abstract, immature boys surrounding me. I must always have my fingers in the world's pie and be *doing* as well as talking; *creating*, as well as analyzing. It is so true what you said about the relief of engaged girls. I am too weary of wasting time to run around to parties any more for "opportunity"; I have a greater faith that if I work and write now, I will have a rich, inner life which will make me worth fine, intelligent men, like Sassoon, and Nat, and his friends, rather than only an empty hectic fear of being alone. I believe one has to be able to live alone creatively before being ready to live with anyone else. I *do* hope someday I meet a stimulating, intelligent man with whom I can create a good life, because I am definitely not meant for a single life.

You have no idea how exciting it is to live here on the brink of the Continent. Even when I am not thinking directly of my coming travels, I feel that latent joy of possibility. All lies over the Channel; all the variety of the western world is so close. I can study Italian in Italy; German, in Germany, and find, at such close range, a rich variety of temperaments and settings. I actually feel smothered at the idea of going back to the States! Cambridge, wet, cold, abstract, formal as it is, is an excellent place to write, read and work—near the theaters of London and the vital, moving currents of people and art in Europe. I don't know how I can bear to go back to the States unless I am married. Here there is the chance to meet people living "on the edge" of the world's politics and art; there is so much more choice. I really think I would do anything to stay here. If only I could get a few things published in this next year, I would like so much to apply for a Saxton Fellowship (or even a Guggenheim) and go to live in Italy and write for a year, combining it with some kind of reporting job part time . . . I have finished rewriting my Vence story and look forward to typing it and sending it off this coming weekend. . . .

If you only knew how hard it is to *know* I'm not a career woman or going to be more than a competent small-time writer (which will make me happy enough) and to have *so* much love and strength to give to someone and not have yet met anyone I can honestly marry. It would be easier if I either wanted a career or had no great love for people; but waiting is so hard. Enough of this. . . .

Love from your own
Sivvy

FEBRUARY 2, 1956

Dearest Mother,

Naturally I was very moved when I read your letter this morning about Grammy. I only wish I could be there to take the double load of work off your shoulders, to do driving and take care of dear grammy. I can't believe anything could happen to her so I mightn't see her again. I love that dear woman so, I feel saddest that I, too, can't be there to help her feel that she is loved and joyously cared for. Please, every day, let her know how much she has meant to me; her strength and simple faith and presence have always been so much a part of my life: always meeting me when I came home, driving me, feeding me, all those family things. I can't imagine our home without her presence. . . .

Please, please, dear mummy, don't tense up and strain yourself (as is so easy to do in crisis), because no matter what happens, I want *you* to remain strong and well. Tell me if I can write to grammy or do anything. I would love to send her frequent little cards and notes if it would make her days brighter . . . I think of her with such tenderness. . . .

. . . (My two poems in the Cambridge magazine got lousy reviews; there are 10 critics to each poem, and although I think they are bad critics, using clever devastating turns of phrase to show off their own brilliance, I still was sorry, but the deep parts of me are not affected, and I cheerfully go on writing) . . .

I got a nice letter from Gordon [*Lameyer*] this morning. It seems he is coming over to Germany around the first of April to look for a university at which to study, and I hope to see him and maybe travel about a bit in Germany with him then. Anyone from home will look quite angelic to me. I shall perhaps spend the last of March in Italy and then maybe go up to see him in Germany. He would be lots of fun to travel with, I think . . . I do wish I could take some kind of short trip with Warren next summer. Let me know whatever happens about his Experiment [*in International Living*] applications.

I had a nice tea yesterday with Chris Levenson, editor of one of the Cambridge little magazines and "Cambridge poet," although his poems get scathing reviews, too. It seems this is an age of clever critics who keep bewailing the fact that there are no works worthy of criticism. They abhor polished wit and neat forms, which, of course, is exactly what I purpose to write, and when they criticize something for being "quaintly artful" or "merely amusing," it is all I can do not to shout, "That's all I meant it to be!"

. . . Also enjoy my lectures by David Daiches on the modern novel (Virginia Woolf and James Joyce), which are sheer pleasure. (He wrote a very bad article for the latest *New Yorker* called "The Queen in Cambridge," which infuriated me, because I could have done better. It was all secondary reporting, from posters and news-papers, and I had so much first hand. Well, I'll learn better next time.) England can be exploited for merely being England, and I want to do a few humorous skits about college characters, especially the grotesque Victorian dons.

Well, dear mummy, keep well and strong, and remember I think of you always with much much love and only hope dear grammy re-covers and that you will come over here this June . . .

Your own
Sivvy

FEBRUARY 6, 1956

Dearest of Mothers,

. . . In the last two years, we have certainly had our number of great tests (first my breakdown, then your operation, then grammy's), and we have yet been extraordinarily lucky that they were timed in such a way that we could meet them.

I am most grateful and glad that I banged up all at once (although I am naturally sorry for all the trouble I caused everyone else), for I can't tell you how my whole attitude to life has changed! I would have run into trouble sooner or later with my very rigid, brittle, almost hysterical tensions which split me down the middle, between inclination and inhibition, ideal and reality. My whole session with Dr. B. is responsible for making me a rich, well-balanced, humorous, easy-going person, with a joy in the daily life, including all its imperfections: sinus, weariness, frustration, and all those other niggling things that we all have to bear. I am occasionally depressed now, or discouraged, especially when I wonder about the future, but instead of fearing these low spots as the beginning of a bottomless whirlpool, I know I have already faced The Worst (total negation of self) and that, having lived through that blackness, like Peer Gynt . . . I can enjoy life simply for what it is: a continuous job, but most worth it. My existence now rests on solid ground; I may be depressed now and then, but never desperate. I know how to wait. . . .

My best love to all of you; keep well and happy for me!

Your own loving
Sylvia

FEBRUARY 10, 1956

Dearest Mother,

I am so happy and bubbly today that I just had to share some of it with you! Guess what! Just heard by telegram from Sue Weller that she has been awarded a Marshall scholarship for Oxford next year! I am overcome with joy. That means we shall go to London on weekends, to see plays, go skiing in the Alps, travel together: all so perfect, because she is the ideal companion. That girl really deserves this and has a marvelous career ahead of her, I'm sure.

Another, more tentative bit of news, which I want you to keep strictly to the family, is that I heard from the Fulbright Commission that my application for renewal has passed the first stage and I'll hear finally in mid-April.

So I wait! . . .

Love, Sivvy

FEBRUARY 18, 1956

Hello again, dearest Mother,

. . . Chris Levenson and I took the train to London late in the afternoon . . . and dashed off to the Arts Theatre of which we're both members to see W. S. Merwin's verse play, *Darkling Child*, something that Christopher Fry's experiments made possible, no doubt, about the Puritans and witches, with an intriguing play on the double theme, which I enjoyed (plus lots of contrast of light and dark in the verse, flame and sun, versus dark and grave metaphors). As always, in verse, it is difficult to make it "move" (the way Shakespeare's did) and Christopher Fry often makes his blazing language take the place of action, but here there was a certain fluidity of action, seasoned humor, and an interesting movement through ideas of Puritanism, love, and darkness which must be accepted on this earth.

Sometimes I come conscious of living here, in England, with a sharp jolt. Life goes so fast and there is so much to do here from week to week that, out of simple practicality, one becomes dulled to all those little detailed differences that made the first adjustment so challenging and even exhausting. I accept the cold, the perpetual shivering, the bad coffee and starchy food with a stoic amusement and walk through historic arches with familiarity and a certain regrettable ignorance about their background in time. However, I get thrills of delight every time I pass the spires of King's Chapel or go by the fruit and flower stands in market hill, or cross the Bridge of Sighs to climb the circular stone staircase to a cocktail party in St. John's. I enjoy walking and looking alone, and thinking. Already I am planning about walks we will take and all the things I want to show you when you come!

Occasionally, I am chastened and a little sad, partly because of the uncertainty of the coming years and the cold whispers of fear when I think of the enormous question mark after next year (which is still not finally financed). . . . The political frontiers here are most interesting, and I wish I could think of some angle which would result in a job which would challenge me to learn and keep intellectually awake. I am just about through with the academic community and beginning to itch for the practicality of work. I would like so much to work for a paper like the *Monitor*, but, of course, don't know how to break in. Ah, well, if you have any ideas, let me know. Meanwhile, love to all, and I hope grammy is getting much better and that you are keeping well.

Your own
Sivvy

FEBRUARY 24, 1956

Dearest Mother,

I am being very naughty and self-pitying in writing you a letter which is very private and which will have no point but the very immediate one of making me feel a little better. Every now and then I feel like being "babied," and most especially now in the midst of a most wet and sloppy cold, which deprived me of a whole night's sleep last night and has utterly ruined today, making me feel aching and powerless, too miserable even to take a nap and too exhausted to read the lightest literature. I am so sick of having a cold every month; like this time, it generally combines with my period, which is enough to make me really distracted, simply gutted of all strength and energy. I wear about five sweaters and wool pants and knee socks and *still* I can't stop my teeth chattering. The gas fire eats up the shillings and scalds one side and the other freezes like the other half of the moon. I was simply not made for this kind of weather. I have had enough of their sickbay and hospitals to make me think it is better to perish in one's own home of frostbite than to go through their stupid, stupid System. How I miss the Smith infirmary . . . ! Here, the people have such an absurd inertia. They go around dying with flu and just plodding on and on. . . .

Even while I write, I know this too shall pass and some day, eons hence, it may possibly be spring. But I long so much for some sustaining hand, someone to bring me hot broth and tell me they love me even though my nose is ugly and red and I look like hell . . . All the nagging frustrations and disappointments that one bears in the normal course of days are maliciously blown up out of all proportion simply because I am not strong enough to cope or be humorous or philosophical: my Vence story came back from *The New Yorker* (and now looks very absurd and sentimental to me). I can't smell, taste, or breathe, or even hear, and these blunted senses shut me off in a little distant island of impotence . . . I am being sorry for myself, because there isn't anyone here I can be deeply close to . . . Richard [Sassoon] will be going back to America this year to serve in the Army, and heaven knows when I'll ever see him again. I sometimes despair of ever finding anyone who is so strong in soul and so utterly honest and careful of me. Having known him, in spite of his limitations, makes it so much more difficult to accept the companionship of these much much lesser beings.

. . . I am so appreciative of the family environment, where, no matter what, one rejoices with the success of one's kindred and helps them through the hard places. I would take such delight in feeding and caring for my husband or children when they were sick or sad; human beings need each other so; they need love and tender care. I was so lucky to have such a bright, strong constellation of friends at home. I have friends here, too, but so much time is spent reading and studying that all we share is occasional plays and teas or a walk now and then; nothing that approaches that depth of experience when you work or live side by side with someone, sharing the daily texture of life. It is so hard not to have anyone *care* whether one writes or not; I miss that very subtle atmosphere of faith and understanding at home where you all knew what I was working at and appreciated it, whether it got published or not. It is the articulation of experience which is so necessary to me; even if I never publish again, I shall still have to write, because it is the main way I give order to this flux which is life. I have written one or two poems this week which I shall copy out in my next letter.

Please don't worry that I am sad; it is normal, I think, when one feels physically shot and lousy, to feel helpless. But I am stoic, even though I feel very much like being petted and loved, and I shall weather this long, barren winter. At least it makes me feel I deserve joy and pleasure and clement weather! This summer I shall follow the sun and participate in the primary joys of life, which are all frozen up now. Do bear with me and forgive me for overflowing; but I really needed to talk to you and spew out those thoughts which are like the blocked putridity in my head. . . . Love to grammy and grampy and my dear Warrie, too.

Your own Sivvy

February 25, 1956

Dearest Mother,

I felt that after the wailing blast of the last letter, I owed you a quick follow-up to tell you that it is a new day; bright, with sun, and a milder aspect, and my intense physical misery is gone, and with it, my rather profound despair. . . .

I had a complete physical exam last week (having had a chest x-ray) and was pronounced fine, but they suggested that I might see their psychiatrist to fill in the details of my breakdown, and so I would know him in case the stress of completely new circumstances made me feel I wanted to talk to him. Well, I went over to see him this morning and really enjoyed talking to him. He is a pleasant, keen middle-aged man, and I felt a certain relief in telling someone here a little about my past. In a way, it makes me feel a certain continuity. Well, I found myself telling him about my opinions of life and people in Cambridge, and as I went on, I realized that what I miss most is the rich intellectual and emotional contact I had with *older* people at home and at college. I am literally *starved* for friends who are older, wiser, rich with experience, to whom I can look up, from whom I can learn.

. . . I know there are, no doubt, brilliant dons here at Cambridge, and many men who are mature and integrated emotionally and intellectually, but I just haven't met them. The best ones we get on the lecture platform, but our women supervisors in Newnham are, as I have so often said, bluestocking grotesques, who know about life second-hand. As a woman, my position is probably more difficult, for it seems the Victorian age of emancipation is yet dominant here: there isn't a woman professor I have that I admire personally! I am not brilliant enough to invade the professors at the men's colleges (the biggest ones only teach research students, and the dons supervise the men in their own colleges), but there is no medium for the *kind* of rapport I had at Smith. I realized with a shock this morning that there isn't one person among my friends here or in Europe who is more mature than I! All the girls and boys I know are younger or barely equal (however brilliant they may be in their subjects), and I am constantly being sister or mother. Only when I am sick, it seems . . . can I be the dependent one. . . .

I feel that while I am ignorant and untutored in much, I *can* give some of my native joy of life to older people and balance our relation this way. I also am going to look up that couple whose address Dr. B. gave me. I've put it off and off . . . I really need deep contact with the mellowness and perspective of older people which the orientals do so well to reverence . . .

Tonight I am going to a party celebrating the publication of a new literary review, which is really a brilliant counteraction to the dead, uneven, poorly written two literary magazines already going here, which run on prejudice and whim . . . This new one is run by a combination of Americans and Britons, and the poetry is really brilliant, and the prose, taut, reportorial, and expert. . . . I must admit I feel a certain sense of inferiority, because what I have done so far seems so small, smug and *little*. I keep telling myself that I have a vivid, vital, good life, and that it is simply that I haven't learned to be tough and disciplined enough with the form I give it in words which limits me, not the life itself.

. . . I could never be either a complete scholar or a complete housewife or a complete writer: I must combine a little of all, and thereby be imperfect in all. Although I would like to concentrate on writing in intense spurts when I feel like it. . . . Do know that I am really happy, and it is not a contradiction to say that at the same time I am debating inwardly with problems. That is just life, and I am ready to take it and wrestle with it to the end of my days. I love you very much, and hope you will understand my present frankness and know that it has made me feel much better just to know that you are listening.

Your own loving Sivvy

SATURDAY MORNING
MARCH 3, 1956

Dearest Mother,

. . . Already the grounds of Newnham are purple and gold with crocuses and white with snowdrops!

I do want to tell you now how much your letters mean to me. Last Monday those phrases you copied from Max Ehrmann came like milk-and-honey to my weary spirit; I've read them again and again. Isn't it amazing what the power of words can do? I also loved your two letters which came today. I don't know if you've felt how much more mellowed and chastened I've become in the last half year, but I certainly have gotten beyond that stage of "not listening" to advice and feel that I have been confiding in you through letters more than ever before in my life and welcome all you think wise to tell me. Perhaps you still don't realize (why is it we are so much more articulate about our fault-findings than our praises, which we so often take for granted?) how very much I have admired you: for your work, your teaching, your strength and your creation of our exquisite home in Wellesley, and your seeing that Warren and I went to the Best colleges in the United States (best for each of us, respectively, I'm sure of it!). All this is your work, your encouragement, your produce, and as a family, we have weathered the blackest of situations, fighting for growth and new life. Perhaps I most especially admire your resilience and flexibility symbolized by your driving, which seems to open new possibilities for a richer, wider life in many other ways, too. I want you to know all this in words, for while I have been most verbal about all the limits in our lives, I don't think I've ever specifically told you all that I love and revere, and it is a great, great deal!

. . . I have made a sharp alteration in that radical treatment of men I've been giving hitherto . . . instead of cursing them all for not being Richard . . . I am casually accepting friends and dates merely for the present companionship and asking for nothing more than human company. I am also being much more generous and kind and tolerant, and taking life easier. There is no reason why I can't enjoy plays and movies and a little talk with boys who are nice and personable, just because I think I am made for a "great love."

. . . Had sherry at Chris Levenson's Thursday with Stephen Spender and others. When I get a few more recent (and more sociological) poems ready, I'll send them to his magazine. One thing, British literary circles are so *inbred*; every writer ends up in London, knowing everything about the work, mistresses and personal idiosyncrasies of everyone else, and talks and analyzes the others continually. Blessed be America for its catholic *bigness!*

Met, by the way, a brilliant ex-Cambridge poet at the wild *St. Botolph's Review* party last week; will probably never see him again (he works for J. Arthur Rank in London), but wrote my best poem about him afterwards—the only man I've met yet here who'd be strong enough to be equal with—such is life. [*The man was Ted Hughes.*] Will send a few poems in my next letter so you can see what I'm doing.

Much, much love,
sivvy

TUESDAY MORNING
MARCH 5, 1956

. . . The "J —— myth" has at last been dealt with, too, thank goodness. The explosion came when she wrote and underlined in pencil all over five new books I'd just loaned her. She evidently felt that since I underlined my own books in black ink, nothing further could damage them. Well, we had a real session, both of us agreeing to get all our troubles out in the open, and I feel much better. Actually, we are too much alike to be friends, and this "overlapping of identity" has bothered us both in different ways: we are both "American girls who write," with similar humor and used to being "queens" among our men . . . together we puzzled this odd situation out. Very simply, we will never be at all close (as we might have been in America) ironically, because one of us here is enough in any situation, and both of us dominate social affairs. She admitted that in my presence she suddenly became very clumsy (as I felt obtuse, I suppose) and we came to a positive working agreement which got rid of all suspicion and resentment and makes a healthier "laissez faire" situation. So I go on facing my private dragons and finding a rather powerful satisfac-

tion in wrestling with angels. So don't worry. I'll use your coming
check for a weekend in London after term is over. Meanwhile, love to
all from your own

Sivvy

Dearest of Mothers,

It is a beauteous morning, and I have my windows thrown wide
open to let the crisp, clear air and pale sunlight flood into my room.
Song sparrows are twittering and chirping in the gutters under my
windows, and the orange-tile rooftops are all sparkling in the light,
which reminds me so of the chilled champagne air of Vence, Nice and
the January Riviera. I felt especially desirous of just hugging you and
sharing this lovely morning, so, in substitute, I am writing this letter
before I set out to the laundromat and my weekly shopping, and also
sending you my two most recent, and, I think, best poems which I
have written in the last weeks. . . .

I'll be so eager to hear what you think of these: for myself, they
show a rather encouraging growth. "Channel Crossing" is one of the
first I've written in a "new line"; turning away from the small, coy
love lyric (I am most scornful of the small preciousness of much of
my past work) and bringing the larger, social world of other people
into my poems. I have been terribly limited hitherto, and my growing
strong concepts of the universe have been excluded from my poetry
(coming out, I think, most interestingly in my series of *Seventeen*
stories about social problems: Jewish question, sororities, etc., which I
still admire!). Now, I am making a shift. The world and the problems
of an individual in this particular civilization are going to be forged
into my discipline, which is still there, but, if you will read the poem
out loud (it's meant to be), you will, I hope, not be conscious of
rhymes and end-stopped lines, but of the conversational quality of
the verse.

"The Pursuit" is more in my old style, but larger, influenced a bit
by Blake, I think (tiger, tiger), and more powerful than any of my
other "metaphysical" poems; read aloud also. It is, of course, a symbol of the terrible beauty of death, and the paradox that the more
intensely one lives, the more one burns and consumes oneself; death,
here, includes the concept of love, and is larger and richer than mere
love, which is part of it. The quotation is from Racine's *Phèdre*, where
passion as destiny is magnificently expressed. I am hypnotized by this

poem and wonder if the simple, seductive beauty of the words will come across to you if you read it slowly and deliberately aloud. Another epigraph could have been from my beloved Yeats: "Whatever flames upon the night, Man's own resinous heart has fed." The painter's brush consumes his dreams, and all that.

Oh, mother, if only you knew how I am forging a soul! How fortunate to have these two years! I am fighting, fighting, and I am making a self, in great pain, often, as for a birth, but it is right that it should be so, and I am being refined in the fires of pain and love. You know, I have loved Richard above and beyond all thought; that boy's soul is the most furious and saintly I have met in this world; all my conventional doubts about his health, his frail body, his lack of that "athletic" physique which I possess and admire, all pales to nothing at the voice of his soul, which speaks to me in such words as the gods would envy. I shall perhaps read you his last letter when you come.

Well, overcome as he is by an intense, almost Platonic scrupulosity, he feels he must conquer the phenomenal world, serve two years in the Army, find a profession and become self-supporting and then and only then found a home and all the rest. So with all these large things, he leaves me, consecrated to silence, and a kind of abstract understanding in our own particular world of devils and angels. It would be a good thing if someone from this world could overcome his image and win me, but I seriously doubt that, however I seek, I will find someone that strong. And I will settle for nothing less than a great soul; it would be sinful to compromise, when I have known this. I feel like the princess on the glass hill; what possible knight could overcome this image? This dynamic holy soul which we share?

Well, the essence of my difficulty and torment this past term has been to realize that no matter how I wanted to escape the commitment, I cannot deny that I am captive to a powerful love which passes all the surface considerations of this world and reaches to what we can know of the eternal.

. . . I have changed in my attitudes: I parcel out the love I have, the enormous desire to give (which is my problem, not "being loved" so much: I just have to "give out" and feel smothered when there is no being strong enough for my intensity), in homeopathic doses to those around me: the little woman in the subway lavatory whom I changed from a machine into a person for a minute and hugged her; the crooked man selling malt bread; the little boy running his black dog which urinated over a pool of white swans: and all those around me. I am, essentially, living in two worlds: one, where my love is gone with Richard; the other, this world of books, market, and nice people.

If I could meet anyone this summer, or next year, or next, I would be most happy to learn to love again. I am always open to this. But until someone can create worlds with me the way Richard can, I am essentially unavailable.

I hope you understand that all this is very private, and I am sharing it with you as I would the deepest secrets of my soul, because I want you to understand that my battles are intricate and complex, and that I am, without despair, facing them, wrestling with angels, and learning to tolerate that inevitable conflict which is our portion as long as we are truly alive. I am growing strong by practice. All the growing visions of beauty and new world which I am experiencing are paid for by birth pangs. The idea of perfect happiness and adjustment was exploded in *Brave New World;* what I am fighting for is the strength to claim the "right to be unhappy" together with the joy of creative affirmation. . . .

. . . More practically . . . also, more seriously, how is grammy? I heard she was in the hospital again this week and am most concerned to hear how she is coming along. Please do let me count on your coming this June, unless she is in a critical state. In a sense, you have a debt to the young, to the living, and the future, you know. I'd love to be able to think you'd do everything possible to come; I've gotten to look so extremely forward to your sharing England with me!

More immediately still: will you please write to the Eugene Saxton Fellowship Fund (cf. that book in our library at home on scholarships) and ask for information about applications. I want very seriously to apply for a grant for the years 1957–58 for either writing a book of poems or a novel. I believe that my background of poetry prizes is a rather fine statement of promise: The Academy of American Poets, Lyric Young Poets, sharing the Irene Glascock, Smith prizes and publications. If, as I hope, I can write a good deal this spring and publish, I should be the "young writer" they seem to favor. Also, I feel the sproutings of a novel in me, which would have to be started in the form of short stories; but I am going to revolt from this critical world (which can dry one's blood, if one isn't careful; I see it in all the women around me) and want desperately to try spending a year writing, preferably in southern France, Italy or Spain, where the climate is "my air" all year round. I know I probably will have to apply sometime next fall early and want to be prepared with documents, etc.

Please, please, ask them about this in a letter, saying perhaps that your daughter is on a Fulbright. Better still, send me their address and a copy of their paragraph of purpose in the book, and I'll write—that would be best. I've had a new vision, partly because of this brilliant, analytical, critical boy I've met from Yale whose mind has clarified certain purposes in me which see dangers in the academic continuity. He's going back to be a professor at Yale and knows all the brilliant critics: Cleanth Brooks, E. M. Forster, David Daiches, C. S. Lewis, and so on. But the pedestrian, analytic mind, while tonic, appalls me. I fly to the saintly, religious, intuitive: the blend of both: Ivan Karamazov!

Love from a very happy Sivvy

PURSUIT

Dans le fond des forêts votre image me suit.
—Racine

There is a panther stalks me down:
    One day I'll have my death of him;
    His greed has set the woods aflame,
He prowls more lordly than the sun.
Most soft, most suavely glides that step,
    Advancing always at my back;
    From gaunt hemlock, rooks croak havoc:
The hunt is on, and sprung the trap.
Flayed by thorns I trek the rocks,
    Haggard through the hot white noon.
    Along red network of his veins
What fires run, what craving wakes?

Insatiate, he ransacks the land
    Condemned by our ancestral fault,
    Crying: blood, let blood be spilt;
Meat must glut his mouth's raw wound.
Keen the rending teeth and sweet
    The singeing fury of his fur;
    His kisses parch, each paw's a briar,
Doom consummates that appetite.
In the wake of this fierce cat,
    Kindled like torches for his joy,
    Charred and ravened women lie,
Become his starving body's bait.

Now hills hatch menace, spawning shade;
    Midnight cloaks the sultry grove;
    The black marauder, hauled by love
On fluent haunches, keeps my speed.
Behind snarled thickets of my eyes
    Lurks the lithe one; in dreams' ambush
    Bright those claws that mar the flesh
And hungry, hungry, those taut thighs.
His ardor snares me, lights the trees,

And I run flaring in my skin;
   What lull, what cool can lap me in
When burns and brands that yellow gaze?

I hurl my heart to halt his pace,
   To quench his thirst I squander blood;
   He eats, and still his need seeks food,
Compels a total sacrifice.
His voice waylays me, spells a trance,
   The gutted forest falls to ash;
   Appalled by secret want, I rush
From such assault of radiance.
Entering the tower of my fears,
   I shut my doors on that dark guilt,
   I bolt the door, each door I bolt.
Blood quickens, gonging in my ears:

The panther's tread is on the stairs,
Coming up and up the stairs.

CHANNEL CROSSING

On storm-struck deck, wind sirens caterwaul;
With each tilt, shock and shudder, our blunt ship
Cleaves forward into fury; dark as anger,
Waves wallop, assaulting the stubborn hull.
Flayed by spars, we take the challenge up,
Grip the rail, squint ahead, and wonder how much longer

Such force can last; but beyond, the neutral view
Shows, rank on rank, the hungry seas advancing.
Below, rocked havoc-sick, voyagers lie
Retching in bright orange basins; a refugee
Sprawls, hunched in black, among baggage, wincing
Under the strict mask of his agony.

Far from the sweet stench of that perilous air
In which our comrades are betrayed, we freeze
And marvel at the smashing nonchalance
Of nature: what better way to test taut fiber
Than against this onslaught, these casual blasts of ice
That wrestle with us like angels; the mere chance

Of making harbor through this racketing flux
Taunts us to valor. Blue sailors sang that our journey
Would be full of sun, white gulls, and waters drenched
With radiance, peacock-colored; instead, bleak rocks
Jutted early to mark our going, while sky
Curded over with clouds and chalk cliffs blanched

In sullen light of the inauspicious day.
Now, free, by hazard's quirk, from the common ill
Knocking our brothers down, we strike a stance

Most mock-heroic, to cloak our waking awe
At this rare rumpus which no man can control:
Meek and proud both fall; stark violence

Lays all walls waste; private estates are torn,
Ransacked in the public eye. We forsake
Our lone luck now, compelled by bond, by blood,
To keep some unsaid pact; perhaps concern
Is helpless here, quite extra, yet we must make
The gesture, bend and hold the prone man's head.

And so we sail toward cities, streets and homes
Of other men, where statues celebrate
Brave acts played out in peace, in war; all dangers
End: green shores appear; we assume our names,
Our luggage, as docks halt our brief epic; no debt
Survives arrival; we walk the plank with strangers.

MARCH 13, 1956

Dearest darling beautiful saintly Mother!!!

Hold on to your hat and brace yourself for a whistling hurricane of happiness! Spring has sprouted early this year, and all the cold doubts and dark fears of winter exploded in a mass of magnificent mail this morning:

MY FULBRIGHT HAS BEEN RENEWED!

Joy, bliss, and how wonderful it comes before my vacation! You must imagine what this does to my peace of mind. I've weighed myself and [*have been*] found wanting so often this hectic term (and often felt no matter how hard I read, I still would never make the grade) that this kind of consecration from the powers that be makes me feel that needed surge of strength to dare and drive through this next and last week of term, tired and discouraged as I've been, fighting for a stoic and creative attitude in spite of all frustrations and rejections and conflicts on every side. They are giving me a 12-month allowance to cover as much of the summer as I'm in England, so when you're here, I hope to be your hostess from the 13th to the 22nd of June! What joy to show you my London, my lovely Cambridge! And not have that worry of money over my head! I am sure my acting and writing has something to do with it, for my academic letters surely weren't anything more than businesslike; also, my statement of purpose was rather eloquent, and I luckily have the gift of an angel's tongue when I want to be persuasive! . . .

. . . I cannot draw well or write exceptionally, but I feel now so far beyond that perfectionist streak which would be flawless or nothing— now I go on in my happy-go-lucky way and make my little imperfect worlds in pen and on typewriter and share them with those I love. You have no idea how fresh courage came to me through your last letter and those who appreciated my article and drawing. I look ever upward and am in the midst of brilliant, beautiful, talented people. My accomplishments and abilities often seem so *small* in comparison. I often wonder—"Who am *I* to teach!" and must be helped to look back and see what a fine career I've really had and how far I've come in the academic world. I'm with real scholars and, of course, feel ignorant and untutored; but compared with high school, even college, I'm really becoming well read!

Other wonderful news came, too. I am meeting Gordon somewhere in Germany at the beginning of April and we are renting a car and driving through Germany, Austria, Switzerland, to Italy (Venice, Rome in spring, Capri!). Isn't it like a fairy tale! Mrs. Lameyer wrote me a dear letter, and I am happy, because Gordon and I are so compatible (in a *friendly* way) that it should be a fine trip! Then he may come to England to visit, too! My vacation plans had depressed me, for I didn't want to go to Italy alone, and now, I can be truly "alone" when I want, and Gordon, too, because of being together. (Single girls are always having to fight off men in Europe, and it is a bother to travel alone.)

Also I have the brilliant, attractive woman supervisor I wanted for the moralists next term, and if she likes, next year! The one woman I admire at Cambridge! I should grow amazingly by fighting her logically through Aristotle, Plato, through the British philosophers, up to D. H. Lawrence! I always wanted to take philosophy, and here's my chance! She is a fine woman, young and much admired by the most brilliant dons here. Also, I am probably going to be tutored in German, beginning next term, through the summer here. . . .

Another thing I must mention: you know I am very much in love with Richard. Well, we are both this way, and, knowing this, I can live through much sorrow and pain. I have never felt so celestially holy, for the fury which I have and the power is, for the first time, met with an equal soul. In a way, I must tell you that our community life in Wellesley, which I love and admire like an "Our Town," has bothered me a bit in this regard, for I feel they could well accept and admire a Gordon, who is physically beautiful and really my match outwardly, I think. But I still feel dubious about my Richard, because *I* see now through the boyish weakness of his frame and the delicate health and unathletic nature to a soul which is kingly and beautiful and strong. I see it so powerfully that I fear to expose him to the "conventional" world of judgment which I am so much a part of; he is a solitary soul, and I have given him life and faith. Do you understand my dilemma? Gordon has the body, but Richard has the soul. And I live in both worlds. It is hard; both fight now, and the perfectionist in me wants to combine them, but that seems impossible. Do write. Love to all.

Your happy Sivvy!

Sunday afternoon
March 18, 1956

Dearest Mother,

It has been a lovely cool spring day, and I walked slowly through green meadows and herds of grazing cows to Granchester for coffee with Gary Haupt, a sweet, if pedantic, Fulbright student from Yale whom I, no doubt, mentioned before, and who saw me through a rather traumatic experience yesterday at the casualty ward of Addenbrooke Hospital, where I seem to be spending a good deal of time lately. I'd gotten some cinder or splinter in my eye Monday and tried to bathe it out, but the itch and hurt got worse and worse. In the midst of the rush of last week's classes and final supervisions, I chalked it up to a cold in my eye and let it go till yesterday, when I couldn't eat or sleep because of the irritation. So Gary took me to the doctor. I spent a difficult hour, waiting in the casualty ward for my turn, listening to screams and seeing blood-stained people being wheeled by on stretchers. Finally the doctor examined me and said gravely, "Why didn't you come in before?" and announced they would have to operate on my eye. Well, you can imagine my horror. Fortunately, I was in such pain that I would have let them cut it out if only the hurt would stop. The doctor was very kind and gentle and gave me a local anesthetic via drops which made my eye hard as a rock, and then proceeded to take all sorts of gruesome knives and scrapers and cut the imbedded cinder out of the brown part of my eye, while I looked on (couldn't help it) and babbled about how Oedipus and Gloucester in *King Lear* got new vision through losing eyes, but I would just as soon keep my sight and get new vision, too. The operation was a success, and I went through the next 24 hours having to give myself eyedrops every hour to heal the hole, so couldn't sleep all night. Gary was a great help and consolation and stood by me through the long operation and fed me wine and sherry all day and read Thurber aloud while I went through a very painful time as the anesthetic wore off. I'm having a final checkup tomorrow at the hospital, but feel fine now, except for being tired, and the world looks shining as Eden through my healed eyes. . . .

I really had a scare, and, knowing my imagination, you can imagine how gruelling it was to be operated on fully conscious with both eyes open!

I wonder, by the way, if you'd consider being a literary agent for me? It would be so much easier than spending a fortune on postage for heavy Mss. over here. I'm thinking now of my story "The Christmas Heart," which you have at home and would be so grateful if you would start sending it off now (simply with stamped, self-addressed large manila envelope inside, no letters) to a series of magazines in the order mentioned: when it comes back, just quote me the rejection and send it to the next. I'm going to try writing commercially once again and might as well try the rounds on that story, which is not too bad. . . .

. . . I am just starting to feel out the markets here, but the slicks printed here are much too rose-colored and improbable to be published at home. I admire the slick market in NYC and find the stories muscular, pragmatic, fine technically and with a good sense of humor. This one [story] is probably too feminine and serious; but please, if it isn't asking too much, try . . .

This coming term, I'm going to write. I'd be happiest writing, I think, with a vital husband. If that doesn't happen for a while, I'll write while teaching. No more advanced degrees for me. I have no desire to be a critic or scholar.

Amusingly enough, all the scholarly boys I know here think of me as a second Virginia Woolf! Some of them are so idealistic! It's a wonderful world, and I want to live an active, creative life, giving of my joy and love to others. My love to you, and do let me know how dear grammy is and how Warren's plans are coming. His program sounds so esoteric! Love from your

bright-eyed Sivvy

TUESDAY NOON
MARCH 20, 1956

Dearest Mother,

I received your lovely letter this morning with the note about the Saxton Fund, which I am coming to believe is exactly the chance I want to devote a year to nothing but writing while living in southern France and Italy. It is possible to write while studying or teaching, but

I need an opportunity to concentrate on nothing but for a year to find my style, my voice. I do believe I have one! But the complex life here and the academic demands of my Fulbright make writing too incidental. . . .

Where, by the way, is the money for grammy's hospital care coming from? I am so lucky here under "the system" for I have to pay nothing for doctor's or hospital fees, while the British have to pay large weekly amounts [for] insurance. I must say, too, I am happier every day to be an American! For all the golden "atmosphere" of England, there is an oppressive ugliness about even the upper-middle-class homes, an ancient, threadbare dirtiness which at first shocked me. Our little white house is a gem of light and color compared to the dwellings here. . . .

Some day, maybe, I'll have a home in the Connecticut Valley, lots of children, stories, and Cape Cod summers! . . .

. . . Please give my dearest love to grammy; I think of her constantly and wish for her health. She is a saintly woman. Keep a large amount of love for yourself and take good care—I want a rosy, fat mummy to meet me in June!

Love to all,
Sivvy

PARIS, FRANCE
36 RUE DE LILLE
(HOTEL BEARN)
MARCH 26, 1956

Dearest Mother,

Oh, you would never believe it if you saw me now. I have the loveliest garret in Paris, overlooking the rooftops and gables and [an] artists' skylight! I was marvelously lucky to find a place during the Easter week, because every place is full, and I moved to this room this morning. It costs 520 francs a night, which is roughly $1.50 . . . I hear music now rising up in the courtyard; the people here are lovely in the hotel, and I am fortunate to have such genial characters running it. They gave me this cheapest room today because they knew I was a student. . . .

Perhaps the hardest and yet best thing for me is that Sassoon is not here; he is still down south on vacation, so except for a possible Cambridge boy I know is coming, I am on my own. As you may imagine, this is very different from being escorted everywhere as I was at Christmas, but I am getting most proud of my ability to maneuver alone. It is good for me, and I am beginning to enjoy it thoroughly. . . .

. . . Love to all from your Americaine à Paris!

Sylvia

Dearest of Mothers,

Eh bien, life gets better and better. I am sitting by my window with the fresh morning air blowing the starched white curtains and with my own special vista of rooftops and chimney pots which I draw daily—it has such good tilts and textures. To me, it is simply beautiful. There is a large green-eyed cat at the window opposite, a tiger cat, who stares at me when I work and plays games of hiding. I am getting to love this city like no other in the world. It is so intimate and warm and kind with its lacy gray stone buildings, hundreds of black wrought-iron balconies, marvelous gardens and parks and little shops, all pastels, and even the peeling walls and colored posters pasted over each other seem exquisite to me.

. . . I wrote a note to Anthony Gray, the British boy I just met before I left, and he surprised me by coming over that very night with his sister, Sally. I was napping (from about 6–8 p.m.) because I'd walked over ten miles and was weary. It was so nice to wake up and find them. We went out to dinner together and had a good talk. Tony is tall, blond and blue-eyed, and an Oxford man (his father teaches zoology at Cambridge) and very debonair and confident, much the most self-assured fellow, good for fun, but I am sure not for serious talk (so many Englishmen think women become unfeminine when they have ideas and opinions) . . .

I'm hoping to hear from Gordon any day about when I meet him [to travel in Europe together]. Should be here through Easter.

Love from Sylvia

Whitstead, Barton Road
Cambridge, England
April 17, 1956

Dearest of Mothers,

I am back at Whitstead at last, grateful to rest in peace, to see no more trains or hotel rooms, to stop running. I didn't get any of your letters all my vacation because of the imbecilic American Express and so felt terribly cut off from all communication for that time and was glad to get back to my calm, daffodil-starred, yet chilly, Cambridge and find mail.

It hurts terribly in my heart not to be home with you all, helping you through this hard hard time with grammy. I cannot believe that I will never see her again and wish that you would make as much effort as you can to give her some of the power of the love I have for her. I feel so cut off, and all my strength so futile here. I love that woman so, and all of you, and would give anything to share the sorrow and the adoration for dear grammy in the community of our family and our neighborhood.

Most of all, I am concerned for you. Will grampy live with [*Aunt*] Dot and [*Uncle*] Joe this summer? Because *you must come to England*. . . .

I have been having a rather strenuous time, myself, of late, and much to deal with. Richard went off to Spain for a month and was miserable alone and wrote long letters which I didn't receive till I got back here, too late, after feeling terribly deserted in Paris that last week. . . .

[*Traveling with*] Gordon was also a mistake. I should know by now that there is always bound to be a hidden rankling between the rejector and rejected. In spite of this I managed to enjoy much, although fighting a great sorrow and preferring to be alone . . .

We left Paris for Munich where I froze in a blizzard, and Gordon's utter lack of language ability . . . horrified me . . . We left the next morning . . . through Austria and the Tyrolean Alps. I sat with my nose pressed to the window and almost cried as we went through Innsbruck [*my cousin, Gregor Resch, lives there*].

Now back to recuperate, write, work. I am writing for the college newspaper and should have some sketches and an article on Paris in this week. God, it's *good* to get back to newsprint and an office! I think I'll get along fine; all very nice, honest guys.

The most shattering thing is that in the last two months I have fallen terribly in love, which can only lead to great hurt. I met the strongest man in the world, ex-Cambridge, brilliant poet whose work I loved before I met him, a large, hulking, healthy Adam, half French, half Irish [*and a good deal of Yorkshire farming stock, too*], with a voice like the thunder of God—a singer, story-teller, lion and world-wanderer, a vagabond who will never stop. . . Forgive my own talk of hurt and sorrow. I love you *so* and only wish I could be home to help you in yours.

All my love—
sivvy

Dearest Mother,

I have not heard from you in several days and wish with all my heart that these times are not trying beyond endurance. . . .

I shall tell you now about something most miraculous and thundering and terrifying and wish you to think on it and share some of it. It is this man, this poet, this Ted Hughes. I have never known anything like it. For the first time in my life I can use *all* my knowing and laughing and force and writing to the hilt all the time, everything, and you should see him, hear him! . . .

He has a health and hugeness . . . the more he writes poems, the more he writes poems. He knows all about the habits of animals and takes me amid cows and coots. I am writing poems, and they are better and stronger than anything I have ever done; here is a small one about one night we went into the moonlight to find owls:

METAMORPHOSIS

Haunched like a faun, he hooed
from grove of moon-glint and fen-frost
until all owls in the twigged forest
flapped black to look and brood
on the call this man made.

No sound but a drunken coot
lurching home along river bank;
stars hung water-sunk, so a rank
of double star-eyes lit
boughs where those owls sat.

An arena of yellow eyes
watched the changing shape he cut,
saw hoof harden from foot, saw sprout
goat horns; heard how god rose
and galloped woodward in that guise.

Daily I am full of poems; my joy whirls in tongues of words. . . . I feel a growing strength. I do not merely idolize, I see right into the core of him . . . I know myself, in vigor and prime and growing, and know I am strong enough to keep myself whole, no matter what. . . .

. . . I accept these days and these livings, for I am growing and shall be a woman beyond women for my strength. I have never been so exultant, the joy of using all my wit and womanly wisdom is a joy beyond words. What a huge humor we have, what running strength!

We had dinner last week at Luke Myers', a fine American boy-poet whose poems are [as] fine in their way as Ted's—no precocious hushed literary circles for us—we write, read, talk plain and straight and produce from the fiber of our hearts and bones. Luke's girl was an artist, and I fell in love with her right away. Ted knows music, so we listen to Beethoven and Bartok in record shops for free, and I'm making dinner for Ted and a mutual Jewish friend, Iko, next week, and we'll go listen to Iko's Beethoven. I am happy, in the midst of all jeopardy, and this spring in Cambridge, with Ted here even for a little before he goes off to Spain and then Australia, is utter joy. I am beyond jealousy, which is something I thought I'd never come to: because myself is fun enough and joy enough, even in sorrow, to make a life! Please think of me, accepting sorrow and pain, but living in the midst of a singing joy which is the best of Hopkins, Thomas, Chaucer, Shakespeare, Blake, Donne, and all the poets we love together.

Your own loving
Sivvy

APRIL 21, 1956

Dearest of Mothers,

I only hope the paradoxical joy of my being and intense sense of living as richly and deeply as ever in the world may shed some power and solace in the middle of your dark sad time. I shall tell you most amazing news.

The best thing is my joining *Varsity!* The Cambridge weekly paper! Here, enclosed, is my first feature and the two upper sketches are mine! The Fulbright commission should go wild with delight. Already I am assigned interviews, fashion stories, sketching at a horse race! I dearly love the boys on the paper, and as there are only two girl reporters, I feel like Marguerite Higgins—

Guess what: the feature editor has invited me to drive to London on Tuesday with him to a large reception for Bulganin and Khrushchev at the Claridge Hotel! I am drunk with amazement. Shall go wrapped in bunting of stars and stripes! Your daughter drinking in the same room with the heads of Russia!

All gathers in incredible joy. I cannot stop writing poems! They come better and better. They come from the vocabulary of woods and animals and earth that Ted is teaching me. We walked 15 miles yesterday through woods, field, and fen, and came home through moonlit Granchester and fields of sleeping cows.

I cook steaks, trout on my gas ring, and we eat well. We drink sherry in the garden and read poems; we quote on and on: he says a line of Thomas or Shakespeare and says: "Finish!" We romp through words. I learn new words and use them in poems. My god. Listen: here are two lyrics; they are meant to be said aloud, and they are from my joy in discovering a world I never knew: all nature.

VARSITY — Saturday, May 26th, 1956

Sylvia Plath tours the stores and fo

MAY WEEK FASHI

WITH May Week just around the corner like some fair Country of Cockaigne — but barely visible through the present smog of Tripos exams—we set out to discover what the well-dressed Newnhamite or Girtonian might wear for punting, cocktails and balls.

From large department stores to small specialty shops, Cambridge offers a fine, colourful selection of spring fashions which should enable our Cambridge undergraduates to rival the most chic and charming of imported London models.

We chose a different Cambridge shop to outfit us for each occasion and picked featured and favourite styles for photographs. While aware that our assignment was for a newspaper article rather than for private purchase, department managers kindly donated advice, information, and much time, treating us,

Strapless white cocktail dress.

indeed, like a Saturday Cinderella.

bathing suits

To begin with bathing suits, perfect for beach holidays and very safe punting. At Robert Sayle's on St. Andrew's Street we found this bright white one-piece (pictured right), peppered with black polka-dots, bow-tied over each hip, by Aqualine in elasticated rayon batiste (at 79/6). Also on the rack and worthy of note: a vivid red swimsuit by Slix in rayon lastex, bordered narrowly at bodice and hem by a woven cotton design of blue hearts and red rickrack on a white ground (67/9).

For the sleekest of black suits to set off a tan, we liked a rayon lastex model by Trulo, cut close with straight princess lines and two small darts sliced in the cuffed top (99/6).

Valuable beach accessories also at Robert Sayle's: a wide-brimmed raffia sun-hat, gaily beaded in red (27/9); a stylish Italian beachbag in black straw, embroidered with white raffia flowers, to carry every-

thing from picnic to sunglasses (12/6); a flamboyant red-and-white striped towelling stole with big pockets and black-tasseled fringe (24/9); and finally, to complete the whole ensemble, a white terrycloth beachcoat with attractive full circular yoke (73/6). Happy swimming, everyone!

cocktail dress

Our cocktail and dance dress featured at Joshua Taylor's (see picture) is a strapless white cotton by Jean Allen, patterned with pink rosebuds and green leaves; the marvellous pouf skirt billows most bouffant over its triple crinoline petticoats (£10 12s. 6d.). Draped from the front to a pert bow in back, this gala outfit sports its own cover-up bolero and so becomes suitable for afternoon garden parties or champagne soirées overlooking Great Court, Trinity.

Runners-up: A poppy-red button-down jumper dress in French cotton put out by Continentals (at £4 7s. 6d.), with square open neck and cool, clean-cut flared skirt; also, a green-and-white striped cotton dress by Estrava, fresh as a mint julep, with off-the-shoulder boat neck, cuffed pockets at hip (£4 10s.).

Rembrandt Originals are showing a versatile tan cotton dress, its skirt printed in a stunning black design; definitely to be seen in motion, the accordian pleated skirt flares out, changing the pattern with every walking step; sleeveless, buttoned neatly down the front and trimmed by a slim black belt, this dress is fitted for casual afternoons

Wh

about

For quisite Vogue's posite b strapless in fle sketche

Strapless Frank Usher ball gown.

FASHION NOTE

ne-piece, with black polka dots,
bow tied over each hip.

25 19s. 6d.).
timate in ex-
wns, we visited
t shop just op-
uel and chose a
k Usher model
white nylon
lightly with a

delicate black pattern and
banded once about the bodice,
twice about the full skirt, with
black lace and velvet ribbon
(17 guineas).

Pick your partners, men; we
propose a toast to the best
May Week yet.

**Bought your May Week
outfit yet? Sylvia
Plath, American Ful-
bright Scholar at
Newnham, reviews May
Week fashions on the
centre page.**

*Newspaper clipping of Sylvia
modeling for the Cambridge* Varsity

ODE FOR TED

From under crunch of my man's boot
green oat-sprouts jut;
he names a lapwing, starts rabbits in a rout,
lagging it most nimble
to sprigged hedge of bramble,
stalks red fox, shrewd stoat.

Loam-humps, he says, moles shunt
up from delved worm-haunt;
blue fur, moles have; hafting chalk-hulled flint
he with rock splits open
knobbed quartz; flayed colors ripen
rich, brown, sudden in sunglint.

For his least look, scent acres yield:
each finger-furrowed field
heaves forth stalk, leaf, fruit-nubbed emerald;
bright grain sprung so rarely
he hauls to his will early;
at his hand's staunch hest, birds build.
Ringdoves roost well within his wood,
shirr songs to suit which mood
he saunters in; how but most glad
could be this adam's woman
when all earth his words do summon
leaps to laud such man's blood!

SONG

Through fen and farmland walking
with my high mighty love
I saw slow flocked cows move
white hulks on their day's cruising;
milk-sap sprang for their grazing.

Spruce air was bright for looking:
most far in blue, aloft,
clouds steered a burnished drift;
larks' nip and tuck arising
came in for my love's praising.

Sheen of the noon sun striking
took my heart as if
it were a green-tipped leaf
kindled by such rare seizing
into an ardent blazing.

In a nest of spiders plucking
silk of their frail trade
we made our proper bed;
under yellow willows' hazing
I lay for my love's pleasing.
No thought was there of tricking,
yet the artful spider spun
a web for my one man
till at the day's flawed closing
no call could work his rising.
Now far from that ransacking
I range in my unease
and my whole wonder is
that frost's felled all worth prizing
and the early year turned freezing
like the bleak shape of my losing.

And these are for you to say aloud on your birthday. And remember to buy a lovely suitcase! Please let me know you are coming, so I can start making reservations. This is Eden here, and the people are all shining, and I must show it to you!

All my love—
Your singing girl, Sivvy

APRIL 23, 1956

Dearest Mother,

Well, finally the blundering American Express sent me your letter from Rome . . . our minds certainly work on the same track!

. . . I have already planned to stay in London three nights and have written to reserve a room for us; we'll just eat and talk the day you come, but for the next two I'll get some theater tickets and we'll plan jaunts to flowering parks, Piccadilly, Trafalgar Square . . . walking, strolling, feeding pigeons and sunning ourselves like happy clams. Then, to Cambridge, where I have already reserved a room for you for two nights. . . . I have made a contract with one of my husky men to teach me how to manage a punt before you come, so you shall step one afternoon from your room at the beautiful Garden House Hotel right onto the Cam and be boated up to Granchester through weeping willows for tea in an orchard! Worry about nothing. Just let me know your predilections and it shall be accomplished. . . .

You, alone, of all, have had crosses that would cause many a stronger woman to break under the never-ceasing load. You have borne daddy's long, hard death and taken on a man's portion in your work; you have fought your own ulcer attacks, kept us children sheltered, happy, rich with art and music lessons, camp and play; you have seen me through that black night when the only word I knew was No and when I thought I could never write or think again; and, you have been brave through your own operation. Now, just as you begin to breathe, this terrible slow, dragging pain comes upon you, almost as if it would be too easy to free you so soon from the deepest, most exhausting care and giving of love.

. . . know with a certain knowing that *you* deserve, too, to be with the loved ones who can give you strength in your trouble: Warren and myself. Think of your trip here as a trip to the heart of strength in your daughter who loves you more dearly than words can say. I am waiting for you, and your trip shall be for your own soul's health and growing. You need . . . a context where all burdens are not on your shoulders, where some loving person comes to heft the hardest, to walk beside you. Know this, and know that it is right you should come. You need to imbibe power and health and serenity to return to your job . . .

I feel with all my joy and life that these are qualities I can give you, from the fulness and brimming of my heart. So come, and slowly we will walk through green gardens and marvel at this strange and sweet world.

Your own loving sivvy

APRIL 23, 1956

Dearest Warren,

This letter is only for you: I am asking you some things to help me in. First, I have hacked through a hard vacation, shared really only the best parts with mother, not the racking ones (it is so easy to give merely the impression of rich joy here and not the roots of sorrow and hurt from which it comes) and am now coming into the full of my power: I am writing poetry as I never have before; and it is the best, because I am strong in myself and in love with the only man in the world who is my match and whom I shall no doubt never see after this summer as he is going to Australia. He is worth you, the very first one, and worth me and all the strength and health I have. Maybe mother will show you one or two poems I've sent her about him; his name is Ted Hughes . . .

. . . I hunger so to share some of my life with you, to learn of yours, even though the obligations of my philosophy course *are* now on my neck, I write: one has to *make* time. I love you beyond words.

You and mother are my whole family, and now you and I must give of ourselves to make her life rich and radiant, in the midst of her great sorrow. I so hope you can come to Europe this summer. My most proud love on your birthday and coming of age!

Sivvy

P.S. . . . I am living like mad and would like to find my voice in writing. I'm sketching again, too: stilted, stiff, but fun. Oh, Warren, how I long to see you again; we can teach each other so much by our respective lives; I am finding a growing self and soul of which I am becoming proud in a good, honest sense. The one sin in this world is exploiting other people or cheating and fooling oneself; it's a lifelong fight to forge a vital life; I wish us both the guts and grace to do it on your birthday and my half-birthday. I'll get Ted to read your horoscope! He does that, too!

Love again,
Sivvy

⊰April 26 was my fiftieth birthday; on that day our beloved Grammy lapsed into a coma, and she died three days later.⊱

APRIL 26, 1956

Dearest Mother,

Happy birthday! I am thinking of you at this very moment and hoping that in the midst of your present trial, you can spare the energy and moment to be glad, most utterly, that you were born to carry on grammy's spirit and flesh and to spread the blood and being of our line to Warren and me. We have had such joys in our lives that it is only fitting, somehow, we be chastened and strengthened by bearing sorrow. If anyone asked me what time of my life was most invaluable, I would say those six terrible months at McLean; for, by re-forging my soul, I am a woman now the like of which I could never have dreamed . . .

Last night, at the posh Claridge Hotel, with the hammer and sickle waving over the door, your daughter shook hands with Bulganin! Oh, mother, such a time! Read the April 24th write-ups in the papers! The biggest diplomatic crush of all time! I stayed the full two hours from 6:30 to 8:30 and gorged on more black caviar than I have ever seen in my life, drank Russia's health in vodka, and met the most amazing people . . . Rubbed elbows with Anthony Eden and Clement Attlee, was introduced as "Miss Plath" by red-clad major domo to Madame and Mr. Malik, Soviet ambassadors who threw the party. Met many mayors: by accident the Mayor of Northampton, England, who, by coincidence, was going to entertain the mayor from *my* Northampton in a few weeks; had picture taken with the lovely, red-fezzed Commissioner of Nigeria and his beautiful, laughing Negro wife: both spoke perfect English and understood my childlike delight at the whole affair. Saw Khrushchev and Bulganin from inches in a press of people that would have crushed them to death had it not been for muscular Russian bodyguards. Bulganin, a dear, white-bearded little man with clear blue eyes, went about like a small plump ship, waving two fingers, smiling, shaking hands and having his interpreters translate the good wishes of all who spoke to him. I found myself shaking his hand and begging, "Please do come to visit Cambridge," which words were repeated by his interpreters. The crowd broke into "For he's a jolly good fellow," and one wise-cracking British radio man hissed in my ear: "They'll never let you back in the States if you sing that!" Had several short, good talks with Russian officers who were learning English, even mentioned Dostoevsky and ended up toasting Russo-American relations in vodka with a charming blond chap working in commerce: both of us agreeing that if we could meet each other as simple people who wanted to have families and jobs and a good life, there would never be any wars, because we would make such friends.

Now, back in Cambridge, it seems impossible to settle down to work. Had my first supervision Tuesday morning with my brilliant woman (who reminds me so much of Dr. B.) and we had a fine, spirited hour, discussing Plato's Gorgias. My mind is whetted; I have never been so keen, so eager to learn. . . . Am also working on a book of poems which I shall submit just before you come in June to a board of judges (5), including the best poets and most congenial to my style: Louise Bogan, Richard Wilbur, Rolfe Humphries, May Sarton, and one other. If this does not pass, I shall write more in the summer and turn it in for the Yale Series of Younger Poets next winter.

Ted is teaching me about horoscopes, how to cook herring roes, and we are going to the world's biggest circus tonight. God, such a life! . . .

. . . If you have a chance, could you send over my *Joy of Cooking*? It's the one book I really miss!

Love and joy from your caviar-ful daughter,

Sivvy

Dearest most wonderful of mothers,

I'm so struck full of joy and love I can scarcely stop a minute from dancing, writing poems, cooking and living. I sleep a bare eight hours a night and wake springing up merry with the sun. Outside my window now is our green garden with a pink cherry tree right under my window in full bloom, thick with thrushes caroling.

. . . I have written the seven best poems of my life which make the rest look like baby-talk. I am learning and mastering new words each day, and drunker than Dylan, harder than Hopkins, younger than Yeats in my saying. Ted reads in his strong voice; is my best critic, as I am his.

My philosophy supervisor, Doctor Krook, is more than a miracle! She took me on an extra half hour last week, and I'm in medias res of Plato, marveling at the dialectic method, whetting my mind like a blue-bladed knife. Such joy.

Bodily, I've never been healthier: radiance and love just surge out of me like a sun. I can't wait to set you down in its rays. Think, I shall devote two whole weeks of my life to taking utter care and very special tendering of you. I've already reserved London and Cambridge rooms . . . We'll leave about the 22nd . . . for Paris, where I'll see you through your first two or three days and get all set up for you so you'll know what you want there, and then I'll take off for a month of writing in Spain on the south coast . . . [getting] tan, doing nothing but writing, sunning and cooking. Maybe even learning to catch fish!

Ted is up here this week, and I have become a woman to make you proud. It came over me while we were listening to Beethoven, the sudden shock and knowledge that although this is the one man in the world for me, although I am using every fiber of my being to love him, even so, I am true to the essence of myself, and I know who that self is . . . and will live with her through sorrow and pain, singing all the way, even in anguish and grief, the triumph of life over death and sickness and war and all the flaws of my dear world. . . .

I know this with a sure strong knowing to the tips of my toes, and having been on the other side of life like Lazarus, I know that my whole being shall be one song of affirmation and love all my life long. I shall praise the Lord and the crooked creatures He has made. My life shall be a constant finding of new ways and words in which to do this.

Ted is incredible, mother . . . wears always the same black sweater and corduroy jacket with pockets full of poems, fresh trout and horoscopes. In his horoscope book, imagine, it says people born in Scorpio have "squashed" noses!

. . . How I cook on one gas ring! Ted is the first man who really has a love of food . . . He stalked in the door yesterday with a packet of little pink shrimp and four fresh trout. I made a nectar of Shrimp Newburg with essence of butter, cream, sherry and cheese; had it on rice with the trout. It took us three hours to peel all the little tiny shrimp, and Ted just lay groaning by the hearth after the meal with utter delight, like a huge Goliath.

His humor is the salt of the earth; I've never laughed as hard and long in my life. He tells me fairy stories, and stories of kings and green knights, and has made up a marvelous fable of his own about a little wizard named Snatchcraftington, who looks like a stalk of rhubarb. He tells me dreams, marvelous colored dreams, about certain red foxes . . .

The reason why you must be at ease and not worry about my proud growing this time is because I have learned to make a life growing through toleration of conflict, sorrow, and hurt. I fear none of these things and turn myself to whatever trial with an utter faith that life is good and a song of joy on my lips. I feel like Job and will rejoice in the deadly blasts of whatever comes. I love others, the girls in the house, the boys on the newspaper, and I am flocked about by people who bask in my sun. I give and give; my whole life will be a saying of poems and a loving of people and giving of my best fiber to them.

This faith comes from the earth and sun; it is pagan in a way; it comes from the heart of man after the fall.

I know that within a year I shall publish a book of 33 poems which will hit the critics violently in some way or another. My voice is taking shape, coming strong. Ted says he never read poems by a woman like mine; they are strong and full and rich—not quailing and whining like Teasdale or simple lyrics like Millay; they are working, sweating, heaving poems born out of the way words should be said. . . .

Oh, mother, rejoice with me and fear not. I love you, and Warren, and my dear suffering grammy and dear loving grampy with all my heart and shall spend my life making you strong and proud of me!

Enclosed, a poem or two ["*Firesong*," "*Strumpet Song*," and "*Complaint of the Crazed Queen*"]. I don't remember whether I sent you these.

Your loving
Sivvy

PART FOUR

May 3, 1956–June 17, 1957

These are radiant letters, when love and a complete sharing of hope and dreams acknowledge no limits. Sylvia and Ted were eager to dedicate themselves to a life of discipline for their mutual creativity.

Sylvia modeled and wrote for Varsity, *the collegiate magazine; her studies and writing flourished.*

To my complete surprise, three days after landing at South-ampton on June 13, 1956, I found myself the sole family at-tendant at Sylvia's and Ted's secret wedding in the Church of St. George the Martyr, London. From Paris I saw them off for "a writing honeymoon on a shoestring" in Spain. Sylvia produced many articles, sketches, and poems in spite of having to cope with primitive living conditions. In her writing only the affirmative, strong, maturing voice was evident at this time.

In the fall the return to student life and separation from her husband was traumatic. Therefore, the two decided to risk everything and announced their marriage, a situation finally accepted by both the college and the Fulbright Commission. They found a small flat and set up housekeeping on an extremely modest scale. Sylvia completed her courses for her Cambridge degree, while Ted taught in a school for young boys. Their plans for coming to America in June buoyed their spirits through this strenuous period.

In spring news that Ted's first book of poetry had been ac-cepted was followed by the welcome announcement that Sylvia had been appointed to teach Freshman English at Smith College for the academic year 1957–1958.

WHITSTEAD, BARTON ROAD
CAMBRIDGE, ENGLAND
MAY 3, 1956

Dearest of Mothers,

No doubt this is the most difficult of times for you; know that I feel this; and that from the sorrow at one end of your scale, I want you to turn to the joy and love growing day by day at this young green end. I really must share with you the miracles of the last days.

I am coming into my own; I am becoming at one with myself, growing toward the best in me . . . how best I can be for a woman, even with my past wastes and squanderings of energy. . . .

For the first time in my life, mother, I am at peace. Never before, even with Richard, did I cease to have little opportunist law courts in session in my head, whispering, look at this flaw, that weakness; how about a new man, a better man? For the first time, I am free. I have, ironically, been exposed this term to the handsomest, most creative and intelligent men in Cambridge (writers, artists, etc.) and in the midst of this, I am at peace, able to enjoy them as people, but utterly invulnerable. Even with Richard I had my eye out for a strong, healthy man. This is gone for the first time.

I feel that all my life, all my pain and work has been for this one thing. All the blood spilt, the words written, the people loved, have been a work to fit me for loving . . . I see the power and voice in him that will shake the world alive. Even as he sees into my poems and will work with me to make me a woman poet like the world will gape at; even as he sees into my character and will tolerate no fallings away from my best right self.

. . . I have no fear, only a faith: I am calm, joyous, and peaceful as I have never known peace. And, fantastically, I am keen mentally as I have never been; my supervisor is delighted, I can tell. I told her this week, at the best supervision yet on Plato, that I was not taking this as a "course" but as a fight to earn my humanism through the centuries of philosophy and religion in this world. It is a voyage of the mind, to true knowledge and not just opinion and belief. She, in turn, said she had been so stimulated by my questions last week that she had revised some lecture notes.

Oh, mother, on May Day Ted and I went up a green river in a punt and, miraculously, there was not another boat on the river! I learned to punt, so I can take you the same way, and saw baby owls, cows, and even a water-rat. We had tea, honey, and sandwiches under the apple tree in Granchester. . . . Ted has written many virile, deep banging poems. . . . We love the flesh of the earth and the spirit of that thin, exacting air which blows beyond the farthest planets. All is learning, discovering, and speaking in a strong voice out of the heart of sorrow and joy. Oh, mother, I shall be so happy to have you come. I have never had so much love to give before. Do be strong, bear what is to be borne at home, and come to me to be loved and cared for.

Your own loving sivvy

Dearest Mother,

It was with a sense of rest and peace at last that I received your letter yesterday telling me of Grammy. Strangely enough, I have been living in tense wait long distance, and often, every day, talked with Ted about grammy and grampy and my home. He was with me when I read your letter, and we felt we sort of consecrated our May Day to grammy. Before I got your letter yesterday, we were shopping together for mushrooms and steak and wine for dinner and had the impulse to go into a cool, lovely little 15th century church in the heart of Cambridge and just sit together in peace and silence and love. I gave a prayer in my heart then for grammy, and for my own family, and for my dear Ted. We are so very happy together.

I can't tell you with what joy I read of Warren's Experiment [in International Living] fellowship to Austria! I am as proud as proud; if any boy deserves it, he does. I want very much for Ted to meet him as Ted, at last, is a man worthy of my brother, and I want Warren to know Ted. I hope you will have the chance to meet Ted in Paris where his older sister is living and working.

. . . I have the most blazing idea of all now. Out of the many vital, funny, and profound experiences as an American girl in Cambridge, I am going to write a series of tight, packed, perfect short stories which I shall make into a novel, and this is what I shall apply to the Saxton Fund for money to do. I shall begin it in Spain this summer and hope to finish it at the end of the year following graduation. All the notes I've taken on socialized medicine, British men, characters, etc., will come in. Ted is with me all the way, and we are rather excited about this. It is "my own corner" and his criticism as it is in progress, from the British slant, with his infallible eye, will be invaluable. What a product of the Fulbright! My work on Varsity next year will take me into the heart of Cambridge, and I can really make a fine thing of this: starting with the voyage over and having about a year's time covered. Will try to sell the stories separately in The New Yorker and Mademoiselle.

Yesterday I discovered another wonderful thing about Ted and me together: he sat on the couch all afternoon and read my copy of Salinger's Catcher in the Rye while I wrote a bright, witty 10-page article on the Bulganin reception which I'm sending, on a long chance, to The New Yorker, and I rewrote my Paris article and sent it with sketches to the *Monitor*. Never before have I composed and worked with a man around. . . .

You will definitely meet him this summer. He may shock you at first, unless you imagine a big, unruly Huckleberry Finn. He hasn't even a suit of clothes, . . . and wears new dungarees and an old black sweater which I must mend at the elbows this week. . . .

The hardest thing for me now is not to share all this with a rich community of friends; I hope Sue will be able to help me take a little pressure off next year. It is like having discovered the one only biggest diamond mine in the world and having to sit inside alone full of radiance and not tell anyone. But I can tell you, if you will sit tight on it, that within a year, after I graduate, I can think of nothing I'd rather do than be married to Ted. . . . He is signed up to go [*to Australia*] on a kind of British program which pays the way of the men who will work over there. . . .

Statistically, by the way, he will be twenty-six this August; served in the RAF as radio mechanic two years before Cambridge, graduated from Cambridge in 1954, and has worked at everything from grafting roses to reading for a movie studio. Now, this summer, he will be writing and waiting for his ship to leave for Australia.

Oh, mother, take this to your own secret heart and share it with me. . . .

Much love from your own sivvy

SUNDAY NOON
MAY 6, 1956

Dearest Mother,

. . . From despairing of ever being able to use our whole selves, our whole strengths, without terrifying other people, we have turned into the most happy, magnanimous, creative pair in the world. . . . I have new power by pouring all my love and care in one direction to someone strong enough to take me in my fullest joy. (It is interesting to know that most Cambridge boys preferred me when I was sick with sinus and they could take care of me, because that was the only time they were stronger.) . . . I am utterly at peace and joyously my best when with him.

I do hope you can meet him in Paris, mother; he is the dearest, kindest, most honest man that ever lived. . . .

Much much love, Sivvy

Dear Mother,

. . . Had a wonderful supervision with dear shining Doctor Krook yesterday morning on Plato again. I do a paper every week, read it and discuss violently. I know she has fun and feel that by the time I am through with this course in the middle of next year, we will be good friends. Already we are communicating about our own private feelings and opinions; everything relates. Had the most moving discussion of the idea of the Trinity with her, a revelation to me of the blind, stupid ignorance I had in not even *listening* to such conceptions. I am standing at the juncture of Greek and Christian thought now, and it is significant to see what the mind of man has made, the significance of the development from the dialectical inquiries of Socrates to the Epistle of St. Paul, which will be my next port after Aristotle. Never has my mind been so eager, so keen, so able to make leaps and sallies into new understanding!

. . . Ted is probably the most brilliant boy I know. I am constantly amazed at his vast fund of knowledge and understanding: not facts or quotes of second-hand knowledge, but an organic, digested comprehension which enriches his every word. . . . My most cherished dream, which you must think of only as a dream so far, is to bring him home with me next June for a sort of enormous barbeque in Wellesley to which I will invite all the neighbors, young couples, and dear people like Mrs. Prouty, Dr. B., et al., just to meet him before we set out on our world-wandering; not really wandering, but living and teaching English in country after country, writing, mastering languages and having many, many babies.

Oh, mummy, I have never been so calm and peaceful and happy in my life; if it is this way, with all the awkward limitations of our separate positions now, me studying, he having to work, it will be incredible to fight out a life side by side. We are both ripe and mature, sure, because of so much experience in the world, so much waste of our true energies, of our wish to have one undeviating faith and love our lives long and to commit every fiber and dream to forging this life: always growing straight in the light of each other.

I am so glad you and Warren are coming this summer, so you can meet him. If only you both will just take him for what he is, in his whole self, without wealth or a slick 10-year guarantee for a secure job, of a house and car—just for his native dearness, story-telling, poem-making, nature-loving, humorous, rugged self—I am sure you will be as drawn to him as I could wish. To find such a man, to make him into the best man the world has seen: such a life work!

. . . I know I was not meant to be a single woman, a career woman, and this is my reward for waiting and waiting and not accepting all the lesser tempting offers which would have betrayed my capacity for growing beyond thought into the fulness of my middle and late years.

I am beginning my novel in Spain this summer, working on it next year, and using *Varsity* to get in every nook and cranny of Cambridge. It is my corner and such a salable subject! I'll try to sell the stories to *Mlle* and *The New Yorker* and get some grant to finish it and rewrite it to unity the year following graduation, along with a book of poems. Honestly, my whole being just sings straight with purpose and projects. You must come and share this joy! You'll be a proud grandmother yet! Probably quadruplets when the time comes: statesmen, scientists, artists and discus throwers!

Much love from your own sivvy

Thursday morning
May 10, 1956

Dearest Mother,

You will no doubt think I have gone utterly potty to be writing you so many letters, but I am at that time when a girl wants to share all her joys and wonders at her man with those who will understand and be happy about it, and I miss your presence more now than I did in all the hard times during the winter when I was unhappy, uncreative and discouraged about the course my life was to take. Please bear with my volubility at this point! I have no girl here like Sue or Marty with whom I can share my happiness (without their feeling secretly jealous, as do all girls who do not have that strong singleness of purpose which love brings), and I really long for a woman confidante . . .

(Later Thursday) I've just come from the most marvelous 2-hour coffee session with dear Mary Ellen Chase, who came to Cambridge last weekend with her brilliant, classical-scholar companion, Eleanor Shipley Duckett (both of them making fabulous money on new books and articles and radio broadcasts!). It was absolute heaven to tell her all about my year, my writing, and to hear about my beloved Smith and all the people there. She strongly suggested that I would be asked back there to teach as soon as I graduate from Newnham. I would really like the chance to teach and get the experience of Smith, but could never imagine going back without a husband. Imagine living in that atmosphere of 2,000 young, attractive girls, without any social life of my own! I wouldn't want "social life" either, as I've known it. I just want my home and my one man. I feel most honored at this prospect of their asking me, though, and if Ted and I need money, maybe he could get a job at Amherst for a year, and we could write and teach and have a home, sometime. It's a thing to think of. But I'm so pleased about his not going to Australia but teaching in Spain next year and his apparent willingness to book passage back to America with me next June that I'm going to live the summer out before getting any more previous. If we got married (I don't know just where or when right now, but probably sometime after I graduate next year), do you suppose it would be possible for us both to get part-time or full-time summer jobs and a cottage down the Cape for the summer . . . so we could travel and write all over America the next year? This is just one of the little pots cooking in my head, but you might talk to the Cantors or anyone who has an "in" at the big hotels where we can make lots and lots of money . . . do think about it!

What a gala year with Warren graduating and me bringing my man home! Cross your fingers.

Much love, Sivvy

FRIDAY MORNING
MAY 18, 1956

Dearest Mother,

It was so wonderful to get your last happy letter and to think that in less than a month I shall be welcoming you at Waterloo Station! Just let me know whether it is morning, noon, or night, and I'll take my station in the waiting room with sandwiches and a camp stool! Our hotel, by the way, is Clifford's Inn, Fleet Street, London, in case you want to know.

I know you're fantastically busy, but have two small desperate requests: could you please possibly send my *Joy of Cooking* and *lots* more 3-cent stamps. I'm starting to send batches of Ted's poems out to American magazines because I want the editors to be crying for him when we come to America next June. He has commissioned me his official agent and writes prolifically as shooting stars in August. I have great faith in his promise; we are coming into our era of richness, both of us, late maturing, reaching beginning ripeness after twenty-five and going to be fabulous old people! . . .

I forget whether I wrote you or someone else about the Fulbright blast in London. I took Ted in his ancient gray 8-year-old suit and introduced him to the American Ambassador; then, after the Duke of Edinburgh spoke, he came down to chat, asking me where I was studying and what I was doing. When he asked Ted the same, Ted grinned and said he was "chaperoning Sylvia." "Ah," the Duke smiled and sighed, "the idle rich." So international protocol is taken care of. . . .

I am really longing for this summer in which to concentrate on writing. I feel such new power coming on me: I've been working up all kinds of things—poems, articles on everything from the woman-situation at Cambridge (my short, witty article on this came out verbatim today in the esoteric *Isis* magazine at Oxford! I'm going intercollegiate!). [*Wrote*] this week's Cambridge newsletter and spring and summer fashions for *Varsity*. (I'm doing a survey of the dress shops tomorrow morning.)

The New Yorker rejected my Bulganin article as too late, which, of course, crushed me as it was a damn good, neat, funny article.

. . . I was awfully pleased to get the Oxford assignment, as you may guess, for it is an honor to contribute, especially as representative of the women at Cambridge!

In your letter you didn't say where and from when to when Warren will be in Austria. I am dying of curiosity, for I want Ted to meet him very much. I think those two will get along fine.

Oh, mother, I only want you to have time to get to know Ted. In a few years the world will be marveling at us; we both have such strength and creativity and productive *discipline*. (Ted's poems are like controlled explosions of dynamite when he really writes full tilt.) . . . We are capable of the most scrupulous and utter faithfulness in the world, demanding the most from each other, caring intensely for bringing each other to full capacity and production . . . Our energy is something amazing. I only want you to come into the light of this and share our humor and love of life, which is almost impossible to convey the least speck [*of*] in words. We definitely want to get married in Wellesley next June after I graduate, and naturally I am just dying to talk over plans.

By the way, if you think it might help grampy to fix on something special for *him*, tell him . . . very privately as a secret that I want him to know he should begin preparing for his granddaughter's wedding, where there will be at least *one* bottle of champagne and one small dish of caviar [*for him*]! I want it to be . . . small and intimate, with all those I love and who know what life means to me: Cantors, Crocketts, Freemans, Mrs. Prouty, neighbors, Marty, Patsy— everyone I love.

I was so happy to hear about your plans to come to Italy in 1958; hope Ted and I might be working there that year. What fun to have you come visit us! We plan on seven children, after each of us has published a book and traveled some, so the seventh child of that child might be a rare white witch!

Cambridge is a lovely green Eden, and to have an English spring and the dearest, most brilliant, strong, tender man in the world is too much to keep alone; do come, share with us!

Much, much love, sivvy

SATURDAY
MAY 26, 1956

Dearest Mother,

May has turned chill and grey these last days, and I am writing from the midst of a wet, snuffly spring cold, but very happy. I'm enclosing the clippings from my latest article in *Varsity* on which I appeared as a cover-girl (!), showing how hard up they are! and my article inside, with more pictures. At least I look healthy, don't I? . . .

All this experience will be wonderful for my Cambridge novel. *Varsity* is my key to the town and all the people in it. Needless to say, Ted is very proud of me, especially [*of*] the poems I'm doing now. He just wants me to develop every talent I have, to do well in exams, and is very helpful and encouraging, and my best critic.

Most amazing is the way *all* my faculties are flourishing in my daily happiness and joy. I had the best philosophy supervision yesterday and neither Dr. Krook nor I could believe it when the bell rang for her next pupil. She told me to come again this morning for an extra hour as we "hadn't finished talking," and I am just blazing with intellectual joy and keenness. She is very very pleased with my work, especially my last papers on Plato, and she is going to become my mentor in the poetic and philosophic realm just as Dr. B. is in the personal and psychological. At last I have discovered a woman on the Cambridge faculty for whom I would sweat my brains out. This philosophic discipline will be invaluable for me, and I'm so happy I can continue it next year with her; she is just alight, and we are temperamentally most compatible.

Ted is staying with his poet-friend, E. Lucas Myers (my next favorite poet after Ted), through May Ball week, and I generally meet him after lunch for an afternoon of study while he writes, and cook dinner here (Cambridge food in restaurants is probably the worst in the world) and talk and read aloud. Our minds are just enraptured with words, ideas, languages. I took out my Rilke poems and my dear *Märchen der Brüder Grimm* to read aloud my favorite German pieces to him (he doesn't know German) and translated on the spot, getting very excited. I've definitely decided to take German all next year, concentrating on Rilke and Kafka, and some Thomas Mann. Ted likes hearing it, gets intrigued by my rough, impromptu translations. He is now applying for a job teaching English in Madrid . . . to earn us some money for next year.

We spent a whole day out in the Whitstead gardens in the sun, me typing first copies and carbons of about 25 of his best poems, and he editing, to send off to *The New Yorker, Atlantic, Harper's* and poetry magazines. . . . I can't wait to see how he is received in America. He is going to be a brilliant poet; I know it with every critical fiber in me. His imagination is unbelievably fertile; our children will have such fun!

Last night while I peeled mushrooms to go with our dinner of sweetbreads, he read me aloud from a book of Celtic tales we just bought and from Dylan Thomas' story book, *Portrait of the Artist as a Young Dog.* I can't tell you how wonderful it is to share so completely my greatest love of words and poems and fairy tales and languages . . . also, the world of nature and birds and animals and plants. I shall be one of the few women poets in the world who is fully a rejoicing woman, not a bitter or frustrated or warped man-imitator, which ruins most of them in the end. I am a woman and glad of it, and my songs will be of fertility of the earth and the people in it through waste, sorrow and death. I shall be a woman singer, and Ted and I shall make a fine life together. This year of work and discipline away from each other will probably be the hardest ever, but we can both be ascetics while we are working for something as magnificent as our whole creative lives; we plan to live for at least a hundred years.

. . . Both of us are old enough to have our own identities and self-knowledge quite firmly shaped, but, thank God, young enough to grow and change under the love and guidance of each other. . . .

. . . I want you to know him well, in all his talent and dearness; he will make us both really proud of him some day, not far off. Warren will be able to help me very subtly, I think, into weaning Ted into shopping for clothes for himself and giving him "man information" about America . . .

Much love, sivvy

*{Warren was now in Austria as a member of the
Experiment in International Living.}*

Dearest Warren,

My fingers are so full of amazing news to type that I hardly know where to begin. First of all, you better stop what you are doing and be very quiet and sit down with a tall glass of cool lager and be ready to keep a huge and miraculous secret: your sister, as of 1:30 p.m., June 16, in London at the 250-year-old church of St. George the Martyr is now a married woman! Mrs. Sylvia Hughes, Mrs. Ted Hughes, Mrs. Edward James Hughes, Mrs. E. J. Hughes (wife of the internationally known poet and genius); take your pick. It is really true, and it is a dead secret between you and mummy and Ted and me. Because I am going to have another wedding at the Unitarian Church in Wellesley next June with you (I hope, if you're willing) as Ted's best man, and Frankie [*Sylvia's uncle*] giving me away, and a huge reception for all our friends and relations who will be informed by mother this fall that Ted and I are engaged.

This all seems so logical and inevitable to me that I can hardly begin to answer the questions which I know will be flocking to your mind: Why two weddings? Why a secret wedding? Why anyhow? Well, it so happens that I have at last found the one man in the world for me, which mother saw immediately (she and Ted get along beautifully, and he loves her and cares for her very much) and after three months of seeing each other every day, doing everything from writing to reading aloud to hiking and cooking together, there was absolutely no shred of doubt in our minds. We are both poverty-stricken now, have no money, and are in no position to have people know we are married. Me at Newnham, where the Victorian virgins wouldn't see how I could concentrate on my studies with being married to such a handsome virile man, the Fulbright, etc., etc. Also, he is getting a job teaching English in Spain next year to earn money to come to America with me next June, so we'll have to be apart while I finish my degree for three long 8-week periods (I must do very well on my exams). I'll fly to be with him for the 5-week-long vacation at Christmas and

Easter. So this marriage is in keeping with our situation: private, personal, legal, true, but limited in its way. Neither of us will think of giving up the fullest ceremony, which will be a kind of folk festival in Wellesley when we proclaim our decision to the world in another ceremony, very simple, but with a wonderful reception: then, too, we can really start our life of living together forever. So this seems the best way.

I have never been through such fantastic strenuous living in my life! Mother and I are here in Cambridge now for five days, Ted having gone off to his home in Yorkshire for two days to take all his stuff from the condemned London slum where he lived (and, thank God, will never return to). The three of us leave for London early Thursday, the 21st, fly to Paris (I wouldn't risk mother on a channel crossing) the 22nd where we will stay for a week, Ted and I seeing mother off, after showing her Paris for a week, on her flight. Ted has been simply heavenly: mother came Wednesday (I haven't been able to eat or sleep for excitement at her coming) and Ted took us to supper at Schmidt's, a good cheap German restaurant, that night, and we decided to get married while mother was in London. Our only sorrow was that you weren't there. When Ted and I see you in Europe this summer, we'll tell you all the fantastic details of our struggle to get a license (from the Archbishop of Canterbury, no less), searching for the parish church where Ted belonged and had, by law, to be married, spotting a priest on the street, Ted pointing, "That's him!" and following him home and finding he was the right one.

We rushed about London, buying dear Ted shoes and trousers, the gold wedding rings (I never wanted an engagement ring) with the last of our money, and mummy supplying a lovely pink knitted suit dress she brought (intuitively never having worn) and me in that and a pink hair ribbon and a pink rose from Ted, standing with the rain pouring outside in the dim little church, saying the most beautiful words in the world as our vows, with the curate as second witness and the dear Reverend, an old, bright-eyed man (who lives right opposite Charles Dickens' house!) kissing my cheek, and the tears just falling down from my eyes like rain—I was so happy with my dear, lovely Ted. Oh, you will love him, too. He wants so to meet you. So to the world, we are engaged, and you must help us keep this an utter secret. After mother goes on June 29th, we will be alone together for the first time and go to Spain for the summer to rent a little house by the sea and write and learn Spanish.

We are meeting mother in London around August 5, and Ted is

taking her (and me) to his home in Yorkshire (he wants her to rest and is very concerned about her packed tour, trying to get her to stay longer in one place, Austria). . . . We'll no doubt see her off August 14. THEN, we'd like to see you, joining you wherever would be best (we'd love to see Vienna, but would have to hitchhike, so maybe nearer, Italy, France, or Rotterdam, wherever you'd be then). We MUST be with you at *least* a week. Preferably more. Tell us what day to meet where any time after the 14th and we'll try to arrange. Write me c/o Whitstead here till I write you our Spain address . . . I want you so to get to know my dear new husband. By the way, his first poem (about us in an allegorical way!) has been accepted by *Poetry* in Chicago (should bring $34 when published). Hope we'll both be teaching English in some college in New England in 1957!

Much love,
Sylvia Hughes

(P.S. Write c/o my maiden name!)

PARIS, FRANCE
JULY 4, 1956

Dearest Mother,

. . . Both of us are just slowly coming out of our great fatigue from the whirlwind plans and events of last month; and after meandering about Paris, sitting, writing and reading in the Tuileries, have produced a good poem apiece, which is a necessity to our personal self-esteem—not so much a good poem or story, but at least several hours work of solid writing a day. Something in both of us needs to write for a large period daily, or we get cold on paper, cross, or nervous. Ted is doing a large detailed story which he will soon whittle down . . . I have never been so entertained in my life, and if by faith and criticism and giving him the opportunity to write and write, I can help bring these stories into perfect being, I shall be completely happy. . . . My commercial flair has been much stimulated by reading the *McCall's* you left, and I have several ideas which I hope to write out in the next month. We are really happiest keeping to ourselves, and writing, writing, writing. I never thought I should grow so fast so far in my life; the whole secret for both of us, I think, is being utterly in love with each other, which frees our writing from being a merely egoistic mirror, but rather a powerful canvas on which other people live and move. . . .

Much love,
Sivvy

Sylvia and Warren in Paris, 1956

Dearest of Mothers!

If only you could see me now, sitting in halter and shorts seven stories high above the modern tooting city of Madrid on our large, private balcony with gay blue-and-yellow tiles on floor and wall shelves, pots of geranium and ivy, and across, baroque towers and a blazing blue sky, even now, going on 8 p.m. . . .

It is so wonderful that wherever Ted and I go people seem to love us. We are fantastically matched; both of us need the same amount of sleep and food and time for writing; both are inner-directed, almost anti-social in that we don't like functional parties and are happiest with simple, unpretentious working people, who adopt us immediately.

. . . Anyway, I have never felt so native to a country as I do to Spain. First of all, the colors we saw from the train window all the way down were brighter than I thought possible . . . blazing yellow, tan and light-green fields under a blue-white sky, green-black pine trees, white adobe houses with orange tile roofs, and all, bless it, utterly agricultural or sheep and bull country. . . .

Best of all, I have a light, clear head that I never knew was possible. I never knew what a load of weight I was carrying in my sinuses! For the first time in my *life* I feel clear-headed, vigorous and energetic in my own fashion . . . I am utterly delighted at the thought of coming back here for two 5-week periods during the year. Plan to learn Spanish cold this summer and study it on my own at Cambridge. It is so much faster here, in the center of Spain, where everyone is only too eager to teach us words and pronunciation. . . .

Spain is utter heaven . . . With Ted and me. . . , all is possible. We have such fun . . .

We both send best love to you, hoping your trip is as wonderful as it sounded from the first card . . .

Much much love,
Your own Sivvy

P.S. What a lovely family we are now! All of us opening wide, new horizons, and you right up with us!

Dearest, dearest Mother,

At last we have found our place, our home, after a hectic month of living out of suitcases and searching for cheap restaurants. You would hardly believe it if you saw where I am sitting now! What has happened in the last two days is like a fairy tale, and I can hardly believe myself that our summer dwelling has surpassed my wildest, most exotic dreams. I feel that our real honeymoon has at last begun, with our plan for simple living, writing and studying. . . .

As soon as I saw the tiny village . . . after an hour of driving through the red sand desert hills, dusty olive orchards and scrub grass that is so typical around here, and saw the blaze of blue sea, clean curve of beach, immaculate white houses and streets, like a small, sparkling dream town, I felt instinctively with Ted that this was our place. On the bus ride we'd become more and more skeptical about the feasibility of getting a furnished house with linens, cooking utensils, etc., and had almost regretfully decided a hotel room would be more likely a place for good plumbing, light, air, etc., when a little lively black-eyed woman on the bus seat in front of us turned to ask if we understood French. Whereupon she informed us that she had a lovely house on the sea front with a garden and big kitchen, where she was letting rooms for the summer. It sounded almost too good to be true, combining the advantages of a private house, which we couldn't afford, with the comfort of a hotel.

Well, she led us through the bright white streets where there were burro carts, open market with fresh fruit and vegetables, gay shops—a strange mixture of clean, colorful poverty, with large, pastel hotels—everything apparently just finished . . . utterly new, with the modern styles blending with the simple native architecture. Very strange, because while Benidorm is just being discovered by tourists, except for the hotels, it is utterly uncommercial, built along a mile curve of perfect beach, with glassy, clear waves breaking on shore, a large rock island out in the bay, and the most incredible azure sea, prussian blue toward the horizon and brilliant aqua nearer shore.

Her house was a large brown café-au-lait–colored studio closer to the sea than grammy's place in Winthrop, with a palm and a pine tree growing in the front yard, a back and side garden full of red geraniums, white daisies, roses, a fig tree . . . a backdrop of purple mountainous hills, incredibly lovely. She also had a huge, cool kitchen with all the cooking utensils one could wish. Of the four rooms for rent upstairs, Ted and I fell in love with the one we are living in now—a small pink-washed room just big enough for two new maple beds, which we pushed together facing the sea, a little dressing shelf and mirror, and a half-bookcase, half-wardrobe. The real glory, though, are the large French window-doors opening onto our balcony terrace! That's where I'm sitting now, drying my newly washed hair, facing the whole expanse of blazing blue Mediterranean . . . Ted is in the inner room on the bed, studying Spanish . . . Our life is incredibly wonderful, and we will stay here solidly till September 29 when we'll head back to leave me in Cambridge. There is so much to tell about our wonderful place here! . . .

. . . I am going to do a series of sketches with a local-color article which may be sent to the *Monitor*. This is The Place to write. We have just been resting the last two days, getting rid of the last months' tension and exhaustion. Both of us got sunstroke our first day, Ted burning an excruciating red, and me getting that terrible siege of dysentery, which leaves one utterly weak. Last night, however, he hypnotized me to sleep, and I woke up completely cured and feeling wonderful . . .

We are utterly happy . . . and I can't imagine how I ever lived without him. I think he is the handsomest, most brilliant, creative, dear man in the world. My whole thought is for him, how to please him, to make a comfortable place for him; and I am free . . . from that dread narrowness which comes from growing self-centeredness. He is kind and thoughtful, with a wonderful sense of humor . . .

We have figured that it would be good for me to write a series of stories for the women's magazines about Americans abroad, because I am very good at local color and also can write dramatic contrast plots where the native scene gives rise to a parallel in psychological conflict. I'm going to begin one on the Madrid bullfights this week. We went last Sunday evening, and I am glad that Ted and I both feel the same way: full of sympathy for the bull. I'd imagined that the matador danced around with the dangerous bull, then killed him neatly. Not so. The bull is utterly innocent, peaceful, taunted to run about by the many cape-wavers. Then a horrid picador on a horse with a straw-mat guard about it stabs a huge hole in the bull's neck with a pike from which gushed blood, and men run to stick little colored picks in it. The killing isn't even neat, and with all the chances against it, we felt disgusted and sickened by such brutality. The most satisfying moment for us was when one of the six beautiful doomed bulls managed to gore a fat, cruel picador, lift him off the horse; . . . he was carried out, spurting blood from his thigh. My last bullfight. But I'll now write a story with it as a background. We plan to write a good four to six hours a day in a rigid routine for the next two months—at last. Bliss.

Wish you could spend your last week here instead of England. . . . Do try, even if only for a few days. You'd love it and could swim and sun and I'd cook here. You could take a train to Madrid and fly from there to London. Ted says to take it easy, gaze at greenery; sends love.

x x x sivvy

Undated; postmarked July 14, 1956, from Benidorm

Dear Warren,

. . . It seems so natural for me now to write about Ted and me without describing him, for I can't imagine how I ever lived without him. . . . marrying a fine writer is the best thing I could have ever done. We are perfectly congenial, enjoying communicating with the natives, disliking parties and superficial cocktail affairs, loving the simple, rich, inward life, devoting most time to writing, loving good, simple cooking, reading and learning languages. Ted is the only man I've ever met whom I'd rather be with than alone; it is like living with the male counterpart of myself. He knows all about so many things: fishing, hunting, birds, animals, and is utterly dear.

We finished typing a manuscript of about 30 of his best poems and sent them off from Paris to a contest in America. . . .

. . . What a husband! You MUST come meet him. Write me, Mrs. Sylvia Hughes or Mrs. Ted Hughes, c/o the address on the letterhead. PLEASE COME.

July 25, 1956

Dearest Mother,

. . . I was so happy to get your wonderful letters about your trip and only wish that you could manage to turn the last week of it toward us in Spain. If only we could have foreseen the kind of establishment we'd be in! I wish you could see us now. . . .

How can I tell you how wonderful it is here? [*They had moved to another house.*] For the first time in a year, I have come to rest. Two [*potentially rich*] summer months still lie ahead. All the change and furor of this past year in which I don't think I've really ever rested, going from a tiring term to even more tiring traveling vacations, are melting into one. Our house is cool as a well, stone tiled, quiet, with a view of blue mountains and even a corner of the sea. Our front porch is shaded by a grape arbor, pungent with geraniums. Our furniture is dark, heavy walnut, which is pleasant against the white plaster walls. We don't see a tourist from morning till night.

Ted and I are just coming into our own. We have figured out a rigorous schedule which is at last beginning to be realized. Here is a day in the life of the writing Hugheses: We wake about seven in the morning, with a cool breeze blowing in the grape leaves outside our window. I get up, take the two litres of milk left daily on our doorstep in a can and heat it for my café-con-leche and Ted's brandy-milk . . . [*to accompany*] delectable wild bananas and sugar. Then we go early to market, first for fish . . . it is fascinating, because every day brings a different catch. There are mussels, crabs, shrimp, little baby octopuses, and sometimes a huge fish which they sell in steaks. I generally make egg and lemon mixture, dip them in that and flour and fry them to a golden brown. Then we price vegetables, buying our staples of eggs, potatoes, tomatoes and onions (see we each have an egg and a good portion of meat a day). If only you could see how fantastically we economize. We go to the one potato stand that sells a kilo for 1.50 instead of 1.75 pesetas and have found a place that charges a peseta less (about 2½ cents) for butter. I hope that never again in my life will I have to be so tight with money. We will one day have a great deal, I am sure of it . . .

. . . Ted and I write, he at the big oak table, I at the typewriter table by the window in the dining room (our writing room) from about 8:30 till 12. Then I make lunch and we go to the beach for two hours for a siesta and swim when the crowds are all gone home and have it completely to ourselves. Then two more hours of writing from 4 to 6, when I make supper. From 8 to 10 we study languages, me translating *Le Rouge et Le Noire* and planning to do all the French for my exams this summer; Ted working on Spanish. Then, if there is time, we walk through the moonlit almond groves toward the still purple mountains where we can see the Mediterranean sparkling silver far below.

I am just beginning to get the feel of prose again, going through that very painful period of writing much bad, uneven prose to get back in story form as I was when I was doing the "Mintons" and those [*stories*] for *Seventeen*. I am working on the bullfight one now and have a terrific idea for a humorous *Ladies' Home Journal* story called "The Hypnotizing Husband," which, alas, I won't be able to finish till this fall at Cambridge, because I want to read up on a lot of hypnotism stunts to make it ring true. It is a great idea and keeps coming at me while I'm cutting beans, etc. Ted is now doing the last chapter of the most enchanting children's book ever. Every day he reads me a new chapter or two . . . you would love them. They are so beautiful I just laugh and cry. I am sure it will become a children's classic. . . .

Ted and I have decided to go stay with his family for the week before I go back to Cambridge and tell them we are married. I have been feeling very badly about his writing them as if he were alone, and he was sorry he hadn't told them when we were married . . . so he is writing them, and I will go meet my new parents-in-law in September.

In spite of the discouraging rejections which arrive daily (we can't afford stamps to send stuff out Spanish airmail to America now, so are piling up manuscripts till this fall), Ted has had one more piece of good news: *The Nation* has enthusiastically accepted his poem "The Hag," so that is two poems, and we share one magazine! Next year will be most fruitful, I feel. I should write ten stories this summer, and Ted, two short books at least . . . We are very happy even in these lean times. How I look forward to America and my friends and the Cape next year! My life has been like the plot of a movie these past years: psychological, romance, and travel thriller. Such a plot. Do write and take care of yourself.

Love from us both—
Sivvy

AUGUST 2, 1956

Dearest Mother,

. . . Do let me know when you plan to announce my "engagement." Perhaps early in October would be best when I have been back in Cambridge and had time to write the Cantors, Marty Plumer, etc. If Uncle Frank gives me away and Warren is best man (I do hope dear Patsy can be a bridesmaid) all strain should be lifted, since everyone is in the family. I look more forward to this wedding than I can say, for it is the beginning of our real life . . . with the burdens of the present lifted.

I do hope we can get good teaching jobs at the same college. With Ted's poems in *The Nation* and *Poetry* . . . he should be helped a good deal. He is the most brilliant man I've ever met and so unassuming about his knowledge that I'll have to help his applications by making him put all his assets down. He literally knows Shakespeare by heart and is shocked that I have read only 13 plays. He is going to help me on dating literature (part of the Cambridge exams) at his home and is making me really think and write deeply. I could never get to be such a good person without his help. He is educating me daily, setting me exercises of concentration and observation. This bullfight story is the most difficult thing I've ever written with the action descriptions. It made me realize that his vision is really photographic, while mine is inclined to be an impressionist blur, which I am gradually clarifying by exercise and practice. . . . Do write soon.

Much love,
Sivvy

Hotel des Deux Continents
Paris, France
August 25, 1956

Dearest of Mothers,

It is now Saturday the 25th and Warren is sitting on our bed reading your letter while Ted is at the bowl scrubbing the last dirt out of his shirt, which only his hands are strong enough to get clean. Our trip up was really wearying, but much of it fun. I enjoyed the last week in Benidorm more than any yet, as if I were just coming awake to the town and went about with Ted doing detailed pen-and-ink sketches while he sat at my side and read, wrote, or just meditated. He loves to go with me while I sketch and is very pleased with my drawings and sudden return to sketching. Wait till you see these few of Benidorm—the best I've ever done in my life, very heavy stylized shading and lines; very difficult subjects, too: the peasant market (the peasants crowded around like curious children, and one little man who wanted me to get his stand in, too, hung a wreath of garlic over it artistically so I would draw that); a composition of three sardine boats on the bay with their elaborate lights, and a good one of the cliff-headland with the houses over the sea. I'm going to write an article for them and send them to the *Monitor*. I feel I'm developing a kind of primitive style of my own which I am very fond of. Wait till you see. The Cambridge sketch was nothing compared to these. Ted wants me to do more and more. . . .

The trip to Paris was exhausting, leaving at three in the afternoon and getting in at nine the next morning. We were stiff and cramped, but revived over breakfast on the train and had a delightful, gray morning sitting by the Seine, watching the fishermen on the bank and the women on the barges hanging out washing. Such a joy to have subtle, gray weather after the blank blazing sun. Life is so much heightened by contrasts. I am actually looking extremely forward to going up to Ted's wuthering-heights home next week. For all my love of the blazing sun, there is a lack of intellectual stimulus in countries as hot as Spain.

Warren arrived early yesterday morning, and we fed him breakfast and made him take a nap all afternoon. . . .

. . . Paris is not *French* Paris; the only language you hear is English, and I am glad that Ted and I can give Warren the atmosphere as we know it, not as the tourists find it. Hope we can live here a year some day (but not in July and August), because of the continuous fine movies, plays, and art exhibits. I really love this city above any I've ever been in; it is dear and graceful and elegant and what one makes it. I could never live in London or New York or Madrid, or even Rome, but here, yes. . . .

Hope your trip back was not full of mal de mer; rest before school. We all love you dearly . . .

Sivvy

Yorkshire, England
September 2, 1956

Dearest Mother,

I wish you could see your daughter now, a veritable convert to the Brontë clan, in warm woolen sweaters, slacks, knee socks, with a steaming mug of coffee, sitting upstairs in Ted's room, looking out of three huge windows over an incredible, wild, green landscape of bare hills, crisscrossed by innumerable black stone walls like a spider's web in which gray, woolly sheep graze, along with chickens and dappled brown-and-white cows. A wicked north wind is whipping a blowing rain against the little house, and coal fires are glowing. This is the most magnificent landscape . . . incredible hills, vivid green grass, with amazing deep-creviced valleys feathered with trees, at the bottom of which clear, peat-flavored streams run.

Climbing along the ridges of the hills, one has an airplane view of the towns in the valleys. Up here, it is like sitting on top of the world, and in the distance the purple moors curve away. I have never been so happy in my life; it is wild and lonely and a perfect place to work and read. I am basically, I think, a nature-loving recluse. Ted and I are at last "home." . . .

Ted's parents are dear, simple Yorkshire folk, and I love them both. We live upstairs in Ted's old room, which I have for my workroom, and he writes in the parlor downstairs. His father, a white-haired, spare, wiry fellow, has a little tobacconist's shop downtown, and his mother is plumpish, humorous, with marvelous, funny tales of neighbors and a vivid way of describing things. She has a tiny kitchen, and I cook for Ted and me. She loves pottering about, making us starchy little pottages and meat pies. (I'll be so happy to have an American kitchen . . . with orange juice and egg beater and all my lovely supplies for light cookies and cakes!)

I think they both like me . . . Ted's marvelous millionaire [*an exuberant exaggeration*] Uncle Walt . . . took us over to Wuthering Heights Friday in his car. He is a powerful, heavy man with a terrific, dramatic sense of humor, and we got along fine. We had a picnic in a field of purple heather; and the sun, by a miracle, was out among luminous white clouds in a blue sky. There is no way to Wuthering Heights except by foot for several miles over the moors. How can I tell you how wonderful it is. Imagine yourself on top of the world, with all the purplish hills curving away, and gray sheep grazing with horns curling and black demonic faces and yellow eyes . . . black walls of stone, clear streams from which we drank; and, at last, a lonely, deserted black-stone house, broken down, clinging to the windy side of a hill. I began a sketch of the sagging roof and stone walls. Will hike back the first nice day to finish it.

Last night Ted and I hiked out at sunset to stalk rabbits in a fairy-tale wood, falling almost perpendicularly to a river valley below. I swung over cascading brooks on tree branches, stared at the gold sky and clear light; stopped in a farm to pet three black new-born kittens, admired cows and chickens. Ted, a dead-eye marksman, shot a beautiful silken rabbit, but it was a doe with young, and I didn't have the heart to take it home to make a stew of it. . . .

Best news came yesterday morning. Guess what, at last! A marvelous letter and check for $50 from Editor Weeks of the *Atlantic* for my poem "Pursuit," which I sent you. And such a letter. I must quote: "We all think your poem 'Pursuit' a fine and handsome thing and look forward to the opportunity of publishing it on a page by itself in the *Atlantic*. Could you tell me about another poem of yours, not in this sheaf, 'Two Lovers and a Beachcomber by the Real Sea,' a copy of which was shown me by a mutual friend? It is really quite striking." . . . Too bad *Mlle* has already published the latter poem, but I was delirious with joy at such a lovely letter. I've been badly needing some acceptance this year, and this will keep me going for another year. Keep an eye out for the issue and buy up lots of copies—a *whole page* to myself! Like Dylan Thomas, and for the same price! It is the first poem I wrote after meeting Ted, and his "Bawdry Embraced" in *Poetry* was dedicated to me. . . . I adore you, and my love to Warren. Do write and say you survived your crossing.

Much much love,
Sivvy

SEPTEMBER 11, 1956

Dearest Mother,

. . . I never thought I could like any country as well as the ocean, but these moors are really even better, with the great luminous emerald lights changing always, and the animals and wildness. Read *Wuthering Heights* again here and really *felt* it this time more than ever.

. . . I can't for a minute think of him [*Ted*] as someone "other" than the male counterpart of myself, always just that many steps ahead of me intellectually and creatively so that I feel very feminine and admiring.

There is an animal farm across the street where we've been seeing baby pigs, calves, kittens and puppies. I really want my children to be brought up in the country, so you must get a little place, too, somewhere in the country or by the sea (we'll buy it when we are rich) where we can alternate leaving our . . . children with you and Mrs. Hughes while we take vacations or travel. Our life will be a constant adventure. . . . This year will be a tough discipline, but I need it and so does Ted. We've talked much about our wedding in June and both of us are determined to have it. We both long for a kind of symbolic "town" ceremony, and it may be the last time I see my friends and relatives together for many, many years. So plan on it definitely. . . .

. . . Want simple ceremony with gala reception for all, lots of food and plenty of drink. Ted wants that, too, very much. . . . Can't wait to get to America and cook for him.

Am sending three stories to *Mlle*, with fingers crossed—my stories. We are full of projects, plans and love. . . . VIVE THE 1957 WEDDING OF THE WRITING HUGHESES! All is perfectly quiet on the British front. Ted's family's dear. We both love you; can't wait to share our life and times with you in America. Life is work and joy.

Much much love to you and Warrie—

Sivvy

SEPTEMBER 21, 1956

Dearest, lovely Mother,

How we have loved your long, newsy pink letters! So much is happening, hanging fire, that I now, these last ten days before I return to Cambridge, feel rather torn. I am actually almost eager to be back and plunged in work, for as you know, I generally leave places [*mentally*] a week early and am going through my worst homesickness for Ted now.

Elly Friedman, the dear, is up here now, and Ted and I got her an exquisite room at the most magnificent, quaint old stone inn, low beamed, lined with books. Ted and I would love to buy it. She is the best visitor; perfectly independent and leaves us to work until late afternoon, and I've had some good long talks with her which have caught me up on Smith. Imagine, there was a rumor among the seniors that I was coming back to teach there this year! Probably one of my teachers confided to a student and this got around. I should think, if I do well at Cambridge this year, I should have no worry of a job there. But I have decided very definitely against applying for a job for Ted there too for many important reasons. First, I would have the responsibility for him, proving him, in a way, and my ties there are very emotional and deep with the place and professors both. In my first year of marriage and teaching, I don't want to stack the odds against me, and the girls at Smith are unscrupulous (witness the two professors, still on the faculty, who have married three Smith girls in succession). . . . I would be absurd to throw Ted into such hysterical, girlish adulation. I shouldn't have a minute's peace, because I know how college girls talk and romanticize endlessly and how they throw themselves at men professors, be they ancient or one-legged. So I shall apply for Ted at Amherst . . . If Ted doesn't get in Amherst, he's perfectly willing to take another kind of job on radio or TV station or whatever, and, if he is successful writing TV scripts, he could do that at home. But I refuse to give my married life and independence completely to Smith. I don't want *both* of us to be tied to the same faculty meetings, social life and Smith-girl gossip. . . .

. . . You can imagine how weary I am of living off Other People's kitchens and houses . . . I long for my own privacy and pantry more than anything . . . If I get through this hard year, I feel I deserve a wedding and gifts and reception and honeymoon for a summer the worst way; it has not always been easy. We will really begin our proper married life with our wedding next June.

. . . Ted has not a definite job yet in Spain, but will leave with his . . . uncle on October 1 or thereabouts . . .

Ted, by the way, has an audition for reading modern poetry at the BBC in London next week (they heard a tape recording of his reading of Gawain and the Green Knight which he made at a friend's and liked it). I am going down with him, fingers crossed that they'll want to broadcast it. I have great hopes for Ted in TV scripts, too. If only Amherst would accept him, it would be so great. Advise me about how to apply for applications. Much much love to you and Warren.

Sivvy

SEPTEMBER 28, 1956

Dearest Mummy,

. . . *So glad* you aren't renting [a] room. DON'T! I know from repeated experience that for sensitive persons like you and me for whom the home is the last refuge of rest, peace and privacy, it is impossible to live and share kitchens with strangers. One is always wondering, "Are they through with the bathroom now? Can I shove their stuff over in the icebox to make room for mine?" . . . Can't wait till I'm home and in the brief days Ted and I are in Wellesley, I'd love you to give me recipes of our favorite things you make so well— corn and fish chowders, apple pie, apricot-jam halfmoons, etc. . . .

Am sure I'll have earned enough money by spring to help considerably with wedding expenses—never felt so creative; so many projects out this year. I'm concentrating on my novel of Cambridge life and a book of poems for the Yale Younger Poets Series . . . We wait the news from six stories and sixty poems (half each) sent out. I'll be back in Cambridge hard at work Monday, October 1. Have passed the "blues" period and am now dying to get there and plunge into a stout year of study.

. . . We spent two days in London and just got back—very auspicious, Ted having audition reading modern poetry for the BBC. I was thrilled; I made him read one of his own poems stuck between Yeats and Hopkins. The dear man judging . . . sat with me in the listening room, saying, "Perfect, superb." . . . The man wants him to do a broadcast of Yeats if the committee approves, and perhaps they'll also approve his reading his own poems over the erudite Third Program . . . The pay is excellent for this, and we wait word of the committee's decision eagerly; it would be another feather to his letter of application for a teaching job. When we are famous enough, we want to make reading tours in America. My mind seethes with ideas for stories; my novel preoccupies me; and I am spending this year daily doing a detailed notebook of Cambridge with sketches, trying to sell chapters as stories, then [will] finish the writing of it next summer. I need this year badly to read, study, and write. What bliss not to have to consider any social life!

. . . We spent one athletic day hiking ten miles over the moors and swamps from Wuthering Heights, where I did [a] sketch in the freezing wind. Saw museum of Brontës, things in the old Parsonage— incredible miniature children's books of a magic kingdom they made up, in tiny print with exquisite, luminous watercolors—what creative children! Charlotte did the loveliest little watercolors. Will write article about it this week.

Have received proof for poem "Pursuit" from the *Atlantic*, so it should come out soon. Looks terrific, with French quote from Racine from "Phèdre," meaning, in case anyone asks you: "In the depths of the forests your image pursues me."

Hope I can get novel out within next two years. I'd like best to dedicate the novel to Mrs. Prouty, but wish to dedicate my *first book* to her, and it may be *poems*, which I'd rather dedicate to Dr. B.—those two women have been the greatest helps in my life and both, I think, deserve a book dedication. . . .

. . . If only we can teach at Amherst and Smith! . . . I'll write Mary Ellen Chase for advice in applying as soon as Ted has his job settled and some things published. She might be able to help me with names.

All goes well; Ted and I thrive and plan to work like mad this year to secure a writing Cape summer after a gala wedding and reception and get good twin teaching jobs. Wish us luck. Write often.

Love,
Sivvy

Dearest darling Mother,

Something very wonderful has happened. On my return to Whit-stead in rain, weariness, and general numb sadness yesterday, I received a lovely letter from *Poetry* magazine, Chicago, saying they found my poems admirable and are buying SIX (!) for publication! Do you know what this means! First, about $76 (they pay 50 cents a line) . . . then, they are all my *new* poems, written after "Pursuit" and glorifying love and Ted. They are obviously in the market for a new lyrical woman. And they are *happy* poems.

This also means that my manuscript of poetry which I am going to get ready to submit to the Yale Series of Younger Poets Contest this January will have a terrific list of introductory credits. Already, nine of my poems were published; add seven, this fall, and perhaps more this winter, and it's rather impressive. My manuscript should have much more chance; and, bless it, *Poetry* is a magazine of poets . . . That, combined with my commercial publications, is also fine . . . They are publishing "Two Sisters of Persephone," "Metamorphosis," "Wreath for a Bridal," "Strumpet Song," "Dream with Clam-Diggers," and "Epitaph for Fire and Flower," a longish one which I began on the beach in Benidorm, Spain! I'll enclose a copy.

Also got a lovely letter from Peter Davison, who is now associate editor of the Atlantic Monthly Press, saying he wants to encourage me from his new position and wouldn't it be nice if they could publish a novel by me some day? I wrote him a colossal letter, telling him of Ted's stuff and my novel plans, asking advice, etc. He can be a most valuable friend. Your little daughter will be a writer yet!

. . . I want to type up a poem-book Ms. for each of us. Ted is producing terrifically—the *Atlantic* has had his poems for four months; I have fingers crossed. You would be so touched—he wants to get his fables printed especially for you, so you would not worry that he can support me! He thinks you would be pleased. The dear one.

Naturally, it will be hard work here, but I am happy alone, want to see no one, but live in the spirit of Ted, writing daily. I'll see him in London before he leaves for Spain, so there is that to look forward to. He waits now word from the BBC.

You must tell Mrs. Prouty about my new poem acceptances! It shows what true love can produce!

If only you knew how happy I am with Ted. I have been with him every minute for over four months, and every day I love him more and more. We . . . never run out of growing conversation. We talked the whole day on our bus trip to London, and it is so exciting, both of us writing, producing something new every day, criticizing, dreaming, encouraging, mulling over common experiences. I am walking on air; I love him more than the world and would do anything for him . . . We want to work and work . . . success will never spoil either of us. We are not dependent on the social arty world, but scorn it, for those who are drinking and calling themselves "writers" at parties should be home writing and writing. Every day one has to *earn* the name of "writer" over again, with much wrestling.

Our last days at Ted's were lovely, even under the strain of coming parting. We listened to Beethoven after dinner by the light of the coal fire, the stars shining outside the big windows, and read in bed together quietly and happily. I finished my drawing of Wuthering Heights and will do a little article on it. . . .

Do write a lot this year.

Much love,
Your happy Sivvy

EPITAPH FOR FIRE AND FLOWER

You might as well string up
This wave's green peak on wire
To prevent fall, or anchor the fluent air
In quartz, as crack your skull to keep
These two most perishable lovers from the touch
That will kindle angels' envy, scorch and drop
Their fond hearts charred as any match.

Seek no stony camera-eye to fix
The passing dazzle of each face
In black and white, or put on ice
Mouth's instant flare for future looks;
Stars shoot their petals, and suns run to seed,
However you may sweat to hold such darling wrecks
Hived like honey in your head.

Now in the crux of their vows, hang your ear
Still as a shell: hear what an age of glass
These lovers prophesy to lock embrace
Secure in museum diamond for the stare
Of astounded generations; they wrestle
To conquer cinder's kingdom in the stroke of an hour
And hoard faith safe in a fossil.

But though they'd rivet sinews in rock
And have every weathercock kiss hang fire
As if to outflame a phoenix, the moment's spur
Drives nimble blood too quick
For a wish to tether: they ride night-long
In their heartbeats' blazing wake until red cock
Plucks bare that comet's flowering.

Dawn snuffs out star's spent wick
Even as love's dear fools cry evergreen,
And a languor of wax congeals the vein
No matter how fiercely lit: staunch contracts break
And recoil in the altering light: the radiant limb
Blows ash in each lover's eye; the ardent look
Blackens flesh to bone and devours them.

OCTOBER 8, 1956

Dearest of mothers,

Loved your letter this morning—love all your letters—so much to say. First, good news: the erudite Third Program of the BBC has accepted Ted's reading of Yeats and will make a recording. I am just exploding with pride; it was all I could do not to leap up at breakfast today and shout: MY HUSBAND IS A GENIUS AND WILL READ YEATS ON THE BBC! As soon as he finds [out] the date they want him to make the recording, he'll let me know and we'll meet in London. We hope more readings may come out of this. It means Ted has a certified enunciation and should be a big help in getting a teaching job, don't you think?

. . . Have been back here exactly a week and am going through the most terrible state, but stoically, and will somehow manage. It is the longest I have ever been away from Ted and somehow, in the course of this working and vital summer, we have mystically become one. I can appreciate the legend of Eve coming from Adam's rib as I never did before; the damn story's true! That's where I belong. Away from Ted, I feel as if I were living with one eyelash of myself only. It is really agony. We *are* different from most couples; for we share ourselves perhaps more intensely at every moment. Everything I do with and for Ted has a celestial radiance, be it only ironing and cooking, and this *increases* with custom, instead of growing less . . . Perhaps, most important, our writing is founded in the inspiration of the other and grows by the proper, inimitable criticism of the other, and publications are made with joy of the other. What wife shares her husband's dearest career as I do? . . . Actually, I never could stand Ted to have a nine to five job, because I love being with him and working in his presence so much. . . . I hope you will forgive me for blasting off about this; you must understand, as you have only Warren to talk to, that I have only you. I am living like a nun, sequestered completely in my study (it took me a whole week to be able to read: am reading Paul's Epistles and Augustine for philosophy; also Chaucer—bless Chaucer). Writing every morning, all morning. . . . I need no sorrow to write; I have had, and, no doubt, will have enough. My poems and stories I want to be the strongest female paean yet for the creative forces of nature, the joy of being a loved and loving woman; that is my song. I believe it is destructive to try to be an abstractionist man-imitator, or a bitter, sarcastic Dorothy Parker or Teasdale. Ted and I are both recluses; we want to work and read and stay out of NY circles and ego-flattering fan parties . . .

Love and more love to you and dear Warren,

Your own sivvy

P.S. Got terrific, lovely letter from Peter Davison in his new influential position as Associate Editor of the Atlantic [*Monthly*] Press. He is very interested in Ted and me; wants me to send Ted's children's fables to their small but receptive children's department. Wants me to enter their novel contest—probably in 1958—and will read all manuscripts gladly. What a wonderful help and friend he can be. He looked up Ted's poems still at the [Atlantic] *Monthly* offices; says no decision has yet been made, but they are definitely interested and Editor Weeks will see them soon. Cross your fingers—

x x xs.

OCTOBER 16, 1956

Dearest Mother,

. . . Our London weekend has given me a new calm and dispelled that first hectic suffocating wild depression I had away from my husband for the first time in our married life. It almost began with a nightmare. I'd arranged to have Ted meet me at King's Cross station about 7:30, but when I found he was getting into the bus station at 7, decided to take an early train to Liverpool Street and meet *him*. I wrote a letter to this effect which, if he didn't receive, I figured would be all right as I'd be at the bus terminal from 6 on and would have no chance of missing him. Well, I waited from 6 to 8 at the terminal and the bus he was supposed to take came; he wasn't on it. The bus terminal inspectors were all callous cretins, and the most I could get out of them was that all buses were in and no accidents reported. I was really frantic, unable to understand why Ted wasn't on one of these; he'd bought reservations: so, in a fury of tears, I fell sobbing into a taxi and for 20 minutes begged him to hurry to King's Cross to see if by some miracle Ted might be there. I was sick, not knowing what to do but yell, but yell . . . through the streets of London. Well, to shorten the trauma, I walked into King's Cross into Ted's arms. He'd made the bus driver drop him off early so he could get to me sooner and had been worried about my not arriving on the train, not having received my later letter. He looked like the most beautiful dear person in the world; everything began to shine, and the taxi driver sprouted wings, and all was fine.

For two blessed days we wandered about together, sitting in parks, browsing in bookshops, reading aloud, eating fruit, and just basking in each other's presence. For the first time now, I feel I can work and concentrate and manage this stoic year.

Ted makes his BBC recording on October 24, so I'll manage to get down on the 27th to celebrate my birthday with him; one more re-union before he goes off to Spain.

. . . Have written several of my best short stories this week, which he criticized in London. My best, "The Invisible Man," I have great hopes for—about this charming extroverted, versatile chap who is invisible to himself alone . . . and what happens. Maybe it'll be a classic, too, to add to Peter Schlemiel and Hoffmann's mirror-image-less man; I can't wait to send it off. Love your letters; only 8 months till we're Home. Bless Warren for me; love to Grampy.

Your own Sivvy

OCTOBER 22, 1956

Dearest Mother,

It is a rare blue and gold day—very rare. Walked out this after-noon to sit by the delicate yellow willows in a golden haze by the Cam, brooding over white swans, bobbing black water hens, and much else. I'm sending you by regular mail a copy of *Granta* (the *New Yorker* of Cambridge undergraduate life), which contains a story I believe you might have read, as I wrote it for Mr. Kazin ["*The Day Mr. Prescott Died*"]. Ben Nash, the nice editor, has done fine illustra-tions, I think.

Just received word that *The Nation* has accepted another one of

Ted's poems, a fine one about the violence of wind. I am with great difficulty saving this to tell him when I go to London on my birthday, as I can't bear not *seeing* his joy and being present at it. *The New Yorker* rejected his fables (yet we will try it till we're bloody), so I hope this will cheer him up: if only the *Atlantic* would buy one of the poems they've kept for five months now. Ted makes his recordings of Yeats and *two of his own poems* this Wednesday.

Which brings me to this great, enormous problem I must discuss with you or explode. More and more I doubt the wisdom of being apart from Ted in this tense, crucial year of our lives. At first, I thought I could study better away from him and domestic cares and that the Fulbright might cancel my grant if I were married and Newnham disown me. Also, I wanted a wedding, a gala social ceremony. However, one by one, these motives are exploding in front of my eyes. Both of us work and write immeasurably better when with each other. I, for one, waste more time away from Ted in dreaming about him, writing him, brooding on my absence from him than I'd ever use up cooking us three meals a day. I looked up the Fulbright lists, and they have three married women on grants. Dr. Krook, my philosophy professor, is most sympathetic about Ted's and my work together, and I am sure would testify to Newnham that I could do my work better while living and studying with my husband. All of this revolves around the question—to reveal my secret marriage and live with Ted in Cambridge for the next two terms or Not? . . . If we decided to reveal our marriage, we would decide it of necessity this week . . . Ted hates much about Cambridge and I don't know if he'd consider living and trying for a teaching job here or not. It would certainly be better qualification for teaching than in Spain—I am thinking of his teaching children or at an American Air Force base. We would save greatly if I didn't have to travel back and forth to Spain twice, not to mention how much more time and energy I would have to work at the library here during terms and long vacations. . . .

I have perfect reasons for both Fulbright and Newnham authorities —I can say we thought Ted would be working in Spain and the job fell through (which is true) and that he can't support me but must earn ship fare, so I should still keep my grant. Dr. Krook can testify, I'm sure, to my keeping up and increasing the quality of my work.

. . . I am living for Ted, and Ted before all else, and if he would think it good to reveal our marriage and go through the official red-tape, I would move out of Whitstead into no-matter-what lodging to work and write and study with him. I feel it is wrong to live apart for six of the best months of our lives; we are very miserable apart . . . also, even when together, the need for separation subtly blights our joy.

Now I would like to know how you feel about this. I will decide things with Ted this weekend. You could . . . say to friends, Ted got a job in Cambridge or London, and we felt it ridiculous not to get married here and now . . . Do help me through this with advice and opinions. I feel sure I could go through the difficulty of red tape here if you back me up.

All my love,
Sivvy

OCTOBER 23, 1956

Dearest Mother,

This will be an installment letter, coming so soon after the last. It is chiefly to tell you another bit of good news . . . I got a beautiful check for over £9 this morning (that's about $26) from guess who! THE CHRISTIAN SCIENCE MONITOR!!

At their pay-rates, this seems like a rather glorious sum. You will be awe-struck, I think, when you see what they bought: a short little article on Benidorm (that lovely little Spanish town where we spent five weeks on our honeymoon) and four of the best sketches in pen-and-ink I've ever done. I think that these drawings will also amaze you. It shows what I've done since going out with Ted. Every drawing has in my mind and heart a beautiful association of our sitting together in the hot sun, Ted reading, writing poems, or just talking with me. Please get lots and lots of copies of each article. The sketches are very important to me. The one of the sardine boats is the most difficult and unusual I've ever done. . . . The castle rock and houses for design is a favorite; the stairway is my least favorite, but not too bad. I hope you love them; send them to Mrs. Prouty, please; show her how creative Ted's made me! . . .

. . . When Ted and I begin living together we shall become a team better than Mr. and Mrs. Yeats—he being a competent astrologist, reading horoscopes, and me being a tarot-pack reader, and, when we have enough money, a crystal-gazer. Will let you know of our decision after this weekend . . . It is ridiculous for us to separate our forces when it is such a magnificently "aspected" year—I'm typing a book of his poems (an impressive 50 pages) for a contest at the end of November . . . I'd love Cambridge so if he were here. There's no question of his supporting me, either, since all he'll earn will have to go for ship fare to America. I write and think and study perfectly when with him; apart, I'm split and only can work properly in brief, stoic spells. . . .

Later: WELL, HERE IS THE LATEST BULLETIN: Ted came up from London tonight . . .

Both of us have been literally sick to death being apart, wasting all our time and force trying to cope with the huge, fierce sense of absence. SO: Spain is out. Ted is coming to live and work in Cambridge for the rest of the year. In the next two weeks we are going on a rigorous campaign of making our marriage public; first, to my philosophy supervisor; next, to the Fulbright; next, Newnham. We are married and it is impossible for either of us to be whole or healthy apart. . . . I can write and do good exams if my Teddy is with me. Do write and stand by. We will be so happy together from December 7 on. Wish us luck with the authorities.

Your own loving Sivvy

OCTOBER 28, 1956

Dearest Mother,

. . . Ted came up to Cambridge after his recordings at the BBC Thursday and has been here since. I wish you could see his pay rates! It is probably the most lucrative free-lance work there is; he gets paid again each time they rebroadcast. . . . They liked his recording of Yeats so much they are asking him back this Thursday to do some more. And these two days should amount to well over $150! I am so very proud. . . .

. . . Ted is amazingly struck by my "book" (all the poems I have together, very few "old" ones—only those which have previously been published, in fact) and claims that it will be a best-seller because it is all song, but also logic in music . . . We shall see.

We celebrated my birthday yesterday; he gave me a lovely pack of Tarot cards and a dear rhyme with it. So, after the obligations of this term are over, your daughter shall start her way on the road to becoming a seeress and will also learn how to do horoscopes, a very difficult art, which means reviving my elementary math . . .

x x x Sylvia

Dearest Mother,

Well, between my private crisis and the huge crisis aroused by Britain's incredible and insane bombing of Egypt, the universe is in a state of chaos! You have no idea what a shock this bombing caused us here. The *Manchester Guardian*, my favorite British paper, called this armed aggression by Britain "a disaster" and I cannot understand what Eden hopes to gain by it other than such a loss of face, aid and support among Britain's colonies, allies, and, of course, growing enemies as can never be remedied. The crass materialistic motives of this attack on the Suez are so apparent as to give Russia food for propaganda for years to come. I shall be eager to hear Cambridge student opinion about this. Letters of horror have deluged 10 Downing Street from all over Britain. The eloquence of Gaitskell in the Opposition is heartening. To think I literally rubbed elbows with Eden at that Claridge's reception! The British arrogance—that old, smug, commercial colonialism—alive still among the Tories, seems inexcusable to me. I think the British policy in Cyprus has been questionable enough. This is the last.

All the newspapers look to American foreign policy in a way which makes me hope fervently that Washington lives up to the U.N. and not its old loyalty to Britain. What joy there must be in Moscow at this flagrant nationalism and capitalism; this aggression by force, which has always been the cry of the Western Allies.

. . . Even Budapest has been thrust to the back page by this; the Russians are leaving. What a world! I remember that Persian diplomat who interviewed me about the job teaching in Africa saying that the western powers were like children in their ignorance about the immense force and manpower on tap in Arabia and Africa. The editorial in the *Manchester Guardian* was superb: this attack is a disaster from every angle—moral, military, political. Britain is dead; the literary and critical sterility and amorality which I long to take Ted away from is permeating everything. God Bless America. How I long to come home.

Now for the private crisis. What a week . . . I went to London yesterday to make my announcement of marriage to the Fulbright [*Commission*]. As I expected, they raised no question of continuing my grant. I did not expect, however, the royal welcome I got! Congratulations from the handsome young American head who told me my work, both social and scholastic, in Cambridge was so fine they wished they could publicize it (!) . . . One of their main qualifications of the grant, I discovered, is that you *take back* your cultural experience to America, and they were enchanted at my suggestion that I was taking back *double* in the form of Ted as a teacher and writer.

We had a rather gruelling day in London, me being very tired and feeling the usual blueness the day before my period; Ted being tense about his own prospects and ours. By a stroke of luck, we were accepted as tenants for a flat just 5 minutes away from Whitstead, nearer Granchester and the country, but still convenient to here. To my chastened eyes, it looks beautiful. We share a bathroom with a Canadian couple upstairs and have the whole first floor: living room, bedroom, large sort of dining room, antique but sturdy gas stove and pantry. I met the landlady today who, pleasantly, lives in another town. She assured us we could paint the walls (now a ghastly yellow) as long as we didn't choose purple or orange. No doubt, she'd be only too happy for free improvements; but what a change in my attitude. Nothing I'd rather do than paint it all a lovely blue-gray. Ted and I will really feel we "make" a home, then. The rent is 4 pounds a week, plus expenses for gas, light, phone, and coal. We'll keep the place extravagantly warm! It even has two apple trees in the ragged little back yard and a bay tree. It's got pots and pans, old kitchen silver and a few old sheets for the double bed. I'll make it like an ad out of *House and Garden* with Ted's help. . . .

. . . The hardest part, seeing my tutor at Newnham, came this afternoon. When I realize what ease I'd have had in arranging this, I'd never have contemplated keeping my wedding secret here—the secret part was hardest to explain. My tutor, whom I dreaded approaching, was heavenly. She scolded, of course, for not coming to her in the first place, and the one problem now is getting another affiliated student to come to Whitstead for the next two terms, but I think that will work out. She's invited Ted and me to sherry Sunday. I'm not going to tell anyone else until I actually move on December 7, the end of the term. Ted will start living in our new home tonight, and we'll fix it up gradually. . . . Only five weeks until we're officially living together in our own apartment.

. . . When I write Mrs. Prouty and Mary Ellen Chase, shall I tell them when I was married or just say I am? It will leak out anyhow—the day, I mean.

x x Sivvy

P.S. Who are you and Warren voting for this week??? I suppose your silence means Eisenhower!

Dearest Mother,

. . . I am so emotionally exhausted after this week, and the Hungarian and Suez affairs have depressed me terribly. After reading the last words from Hungary yesterday before the Russians took over, I was almost physically sick. Dear Ted took me for a walk in the still, empty Clare gardens by the Cam, with the late gold and green and the dewy freshness of Eden, with birds singing as they must have for centuries. We were both stunned and sick. The whole world . . . we felt was utterly mad, raving mad. How Britain's crazy hope for quick success (after which most nations would be too lazy to do anything about it) covers the real cry of the Hungarians is disgusting. It makes the West have no appeal against Russia in the Hungarian case. Eden is, in effect, helping murder the Hungarians. There have been riots in London. Even though a lot of commercially interested Tories uphold Eden, Oxford and Cambridge are sending delegations and petitions against him. The horror is that with time and enough propaganda yelling about the danger of America's becoming a bedfellow with Russia, America will, no doubt, support Eden, too—a prospect which will make it insupportable for me. If only we would act as the Suez situation demands and stop Britain and France, who are aggressors.

. . . We will come to work in America and then want to find some corner of the world . . . some island or other, if we can get money enough, and go there and try to live a creative, honest life. If every soldier refused to take arms . . . there would be no wars; but no one has the courage to be the first to live according to Christ and Socrates, because in a world of opportunists they would be martyred. Well, both of us are deeply sick. The creative forces of nature are the only forces which give me any peace now, and we want to become part of them; no war, after these mad incidents, has any meaning for us. All I think of are the mothers and children in Russia, in Egypt, and know they don't want men killed . . . I wish Warren would be a conscientious objector. It is wrong to kill; all the rationalizations of defense and making peace by killing and maiming for decades are crazy. . . .

. . . We have two depressing rejections: Ted's poems from *London* magazine and my story from *The New Yorker*. A Smith girl secretary there [*at the* New Yorker] . . . who admired my work told me they accept stories only from a very narrow clique of writers usually; better to send poems, which I did. BUT: one very bright note: this morning Ted got another poem, "The Drowned Woman," bought by *Poetry* (Chicago) and ONE BOUGHT BY the *Atlantic,* "The Hawk in the Storm"! I am so very proud.

. . . I love you; don't worry about us. Ted and I are together . . . He is wonderful and we'll face everything that comes with as much courage as we can. Much much love to you and Warren.

Your own Sivvy

November 13, 1956

Dearest Mother,

. . . I am rather blue today, all the meanness of fate falling on me over the weekend in the form of a nasty sinus cold and a very painful slipped disc in my back . . . also two rejections of poems and stories from the disdainful *New Yorker*. If people only knew the miseries one goes through and the discouragements, they would realize how much balances out the small successes. . . .

This last Saturday, by the way, the official council at Newnham met and decided I could go on working here. They had told me not to worry, but the ingrained English maxim that a woman cannot cook and think at the same time had me dubious enough. So my Fulbright continues and I continue.

I must say I am eager to get to America, and Ted and I can certainly do with a few parties and presents. The next two months will be very hard, having to pay bills at both Newnham and the 55 Eltisley Avenue place. Ted has not as yet got a job; he probably can get teaching jobs in January . . . but it is very difficult now. He may have to take a laboring job for these first months to cover coal, electricity, gas and food bills.

We have bought a huge, rather soiled but comfortable, second-hand sofa for our living room for £9.10s, which we'll sell next spring, and a can of paint for the dirty yellow walls. How I long to get away from the dirt here. Everything is so old and dirty; soot of centuries worked into every pore. However, I managed to turn out, by utter luck, a delicious roast beef dinner in our strange gas oven, our first dinner there—*rare* roast beef, buttery mashed potatoes, peas, raspberries and cream. I'll be glad to move there on December 7 . . . and forego this split existence. . . .

Tell anyone-who-wants-to-send-me-gifts of a bulky or house-furnishing nature to send them to 26 Elmwood Road . . . I want to have some nice things waiting when I come home. I've given up all

Sylvia at home in Cambridge after her marriage, winter 1956–57

the ceremony and presents belonging to a new bride and would like to feel we'd have it easy for once in the near future in America. I am sick of battling the cold and the dirt away from all my friends. America looks to me like the promised land. As long as we can stay out of the appalling competitive, commercial race, I'll be happy. I'd like New England teaching and writing years and leisurely Cape summers. Do tell Mrs. Prouty Ted has got a poem in the *Atlantic*, too. I love that woman so and look so forward to bringing Ted to meet her. . . .

. . . I can't believe it is only seven months till I come home. I feel like Rip van Winkle . . . Give my love to everybody and write a lot.

Love from Sivvy

November 21, 1956

Dearest Mother,

. . . Oddly enough, under all this pressure, I've written several very good poems and the more I write, the better. Yesterday I devoted to typing Ted's first book of poems (which makes the one we sent off last spring look like juvenilia); 40 magnificent poems, 51 pages (six poems out of that already accepted—two each by *Poetry* and *The Nation*; 1 *Atlantic*, 1 BBC). We're submitting it for a November deadline for a first-book-of-poems contest run by Harper's Publishing Company; Marianne Moore, Stephen Spender and W. H. Auden will judge. I don't see how they can help but accept this; it's the most rich, powerful work since Yeats and Dylan Thomas.

My own book of poems (now titled "Two Lovers and a Beach-comber") grows well, and I should have 50 good poems by the time I submit it to the Yale Series of Younger Poets in February.

Item: Do write "married recently" in our marriage announcement and say after December 7 "the couple will be at home at 55 Eltisley Avenue, Cambridge, *England*." I'd rather not even have a politic untruth in print about the date. . . .

Good news: Ted has, by the same miracle that got us a flat the day we wanted it at an impossible time of year, got a job starting this very Monday! He is too late for getting a Cambridge teaching diploma, and, as the work and people are very stuffy in that program, I'm just as glad. He'll be teaching from now till June at a day school in Cambridge for teen-age boys; they're not smart. . . . He will officially be teaching English, but also helping in athletics and drama productions and everything in general. The master told Ted a touching story about how these boys, . . . marking time till they get trade jobs, can be "shocked" into awareness that might make life a little richer for them. Once the master was talking about "treasure," and took out the things in his pocket, among them a colored pebble he'd picked up on a beach. That was, he said, *treasure;* he could, by looking at the pebble, recall the sun, the sea, the whole day. He told the boys to bring a "treasure" to class the next day. Among them, one boy brought a fossil. The master sent him over to the nature lab to learn about it and in no time the boy had taught himself to read (some can't even do that!) and soon had the best fossil collection in Cambridge.

The master said Ted can use any methods he wants in teaching, no matter how unconventional. The main thing is energy and enthusiasm: the boys will like what he likes. Ted is very happy about this as it has been a difficult time for both of us with no money coming in and the double expenses of Newnham and the new flat this December. Too, the job is just what he'll be terrific at. We'll manage all right now, I'm sure of it; as soon as he starts drawing a regular salary, the acceptances will begin coming in. . . .

Thanks for the money; we'll have a good picture taken this vacation, you may be sure. . . .

Olwyn, Ted's sister, stopped by this weekend on her way from a stay at home to her job in Paris. She is 28 and very startlingly beautiful with amber-gold hair and eyes. I cooked a big roast beef dinner, with red wine and strawberries and cream. She reminds me of a changeling, somehow, who will never get old. She is, however, quite selfish and squanders money on herself continually in extravagances of clothes and cigarettes, while she still owes Ted 50 pounds. But in spite of this, I do like her.

. . . Much much love to you and Warrie.

Your own Sivvy

NOVEMBER 29, 1956

Dearest Mother,

. . . I am so proud of Ted. He has just walked into this job, and the boys are evidently just fascinated by him. He says he terrifies them and then is nice. With his natural sense of the dramatic, he can interest them and have them eating out of his hand. He brings home their compositions and exams to correct and reads them aloud to me. I get such a touching picture of those individual, simple little minds. Ted says they loved some ballads by W. H. Auden he read to them, yelled for him to do them over, and then he told them to write eight lines of a story ballad. They did, and very enthusiastically. . . . Ted teaches math, social studies, English, dramatics, art, and just everything—on a very simple level, of course, but thus even more demanding for a brilliant intellect like his. He seems very happy about the job and will get paid over vacation. You should see him—he gets books on Russian history, on the Jews, on the Nazis out of the library. The boys are very interested in these topics, and Ted can absorb knowledge in no time. I am convinced he is a genius.

We have such lovely hours together . . . We read, discuss poems we discover, talk, analyze—we continually fascinate each other. It is heaven to have someone like Ted who is so kind and honest and brilliant—always stimulating me to study, think, draw and write. He is better than any teacher, even fills somehow that huge, sad hole I felt in having no father. I feel every day how wonderful he is and love him more and more. My whole life has suddenly a purpose. . . .

Much, much love—
Your own Sivvy

CAMBRIDGE, ENGLAND
JANUARY 9, 1957

Dearest, darling Mother,

. . . As I write, the living room is lovely and warm with the coal fire, which I've kept going all day. . . . It has been a very happy day–Ted got his first acceptance from a British magazine, *Nimbus,* this morning, of one or two poems—they haven't selected the exact titles yet. It has a very impressive format, like the *Atlantic,* but, the editor says, was on the brink of failure. Naturally, we hope and pray it sticks together long enough for Ted's poems to come out. But the very interested acceptance gave us both a gay mood. We work really hard, and the British magazines have hitherto ignored us both continually. However, the planets point to a magnificently successful year for us both, and we will work to make it come true.

Ted has me memorizing a poem a day, which is very good for me, and we are working out a schedule of going to bed at ten, getting up at six and writing two hours steadily before Ted bikes off to work. . . . This way we accomplish much, and Ted feels his job isn't taking all his writing time. We're both "early morning" people and need about the same amount of sleep. Term starts for me next week, so I am cramming, reading for it.

I didn't have a chance to write all last term, so am working on two love stories for the women's magazines; one set, I hope originally, in a laundromat; the other, a college-girl story. . . . I will slave and slave until I break into those slicks. My sense of humor should be good for something. This next week I hope to type the revision of Ted's children's fables, and my poems I will send off to the Yale Series of Younger Poets.

Sue Weller has been in Cambridge a week, just left today, so I have been feeding her cheese omelets, roast beef, sherry, etc., trying to cheer her up. She is very lugubrious . . . about her boyfriend's being on duty in the Navy this year and having had to postpone their intended marriage indefinitely. I feel so happy, I was almost feeling guilty talking to her. Ted and I sometimes have violent disagreements, to be sure, but we are so very joyous together and have such identical aims and expectations of our lives that we never have conflict over any serious issues. I really don't know how I existed before I met Ted. . . . he is so kind and loving and appreciative of my cooking that I delight in trying new things for him. He is also very strictly disciplining about my study and work. It couldn't be better. . .

Love,
Sivvy

JANUARY 19, 1957

Dearest Mother,

 . . . What you must understand is that Ted does not want to be a university professor for a career. He wants to write now and for the rest of his life. And in marrying a writer, I accept his life. For teaching, it is plainly necessary to have a Ph.D. to teach at a university level, unless you are rare, like Alfred Kazin, and have written a mountain of critical work. Ted has no desire to do any more academic work . . . he'll only teach if they'll take him on the basis of his publishing and his Cantab. [Cambridge] M.A. So the American dream of a secure sinecure writing on campus seems out for our future life. I find it best not to argue—Ted is so understanding about my need to get a self-respecting teaching job in America and "give out" and is eager to teach anywhere he can himself for a year or two . . . Writing comes first with both of us, and although Wilbur and other writers find their plums in the academic world, Ted just doesn't want to spend years getting necessary degree qualifications when he should be writing hardest. And my faith in him and the way we two want to live understands this . . . *I* know Ted's mind is magnificent, not hair-splitting or suavely politic, but employers may find Ph.D.'s more convincing. Whatever, we're together and that and writing makes our joy. . . .

Much love,
Sivvy

JANUARY 28, 1957

Dearest Mother,

It is just after 8:30. Ted's biked off to work, and I am preparing for a day of intense Chaucer reading. At 11 I have coffee with Mary Ellen Chase—the first chance I'll have had to talk with her since her arrival about two weeks ago, and I hope to get a reliable picture of teaching prospects, at least in New England. From the reception of the few letters I've sent off to Radcliffe, Tufts, and Brandeis, I don't believe America needs any teachers at all; they all "have no positions open next year," but will keep letters on active file, which, no doubt, means as penwipers or something equivalent . . . My hands are tied until I hear from you and get a list. I feel so cut off from everything—unable to arrange interviews, etc. I would rather be an office typist in New England than teach in Michigan . . . brilliant and rare as we are, how can we hope to compete either with the regulation Ph.D.-experienced people or the 10-books-of-poetry-published people? Heaven knows. I feel it would be a very great strain for me to try teaching at Smith this very first year, even if the miracle happened and they wanted to employ me . . . When you think of the years it takes to make a doctor, expecting success posthaste in writing "or I'll give it up" is ridiculous. Both Ted and I depend on writing and could never give it up, even if we never published another line all our lives. Ted is so magnificent and understanding about my writing and study and needs and I, too, feel so close to his, it is a blessing. . . . I am so gloriously glad to find a rugged, kind, magnificent man, who has no scrap of false vanity or tendency to toady to inferior strategic officials that I am only too willing to accept the attendant temporary uncertainties. Only I feel that in America, of all countries, there should be a place for us both. Our rejections make, by contrast, people like Editor Weeks and the editors of *Poetry* and *The Nation* seem like large, worthy guardian angels. . . .

Much love to you and dear Warren—
Sivvy

Dearest Mother,

. . . My coffee session with Miss Chase yesterday took several black loads off my mind. First, about my worries over competing with people who have doctorates. "You and Ted would be crazy to get doctorates," were her very words. She said they figured the grad school grind in America would kill me, so "they sent me to Cambridge." I gather "they" feel some control over my life, which explains Miss Chase's shock when I told her about my coming marriage last spring. "They" hadn't allowed for love, evidently . . . Well, she said I shouldn't ever think of getting a doctorate; I wasn't going to be a scholar or academic, nor Ted, either. Also, wives and husbands are often hired on the same faculty. They would rather have me have poems and essays published in the *Atlantic* than have a Ph.D. . . . My attitude about teaching there [*at Smith*] has changed. The Freshman English program is ideal—only three sections . . . Beginners' salaries are only about $3,000; but I could *write*, and it would be a terrific opportunity. They even said, Miss Chase did, that IF they offered me an appointment (still dubious, so don't mention it), Ted might very well get one the next year. This year will be hard for him as several interviews are necessary anywhere for a "foreigner." But she suggested various boys' prep schools. If Smith falls through, I'm relatively sure she will help us get jobs elsewhere, and her word wields tremendous influence.

Forget Babson, B.U., etc. They want *women* at Smith, amazingly enough; the faculty is overbalanced with men.

I want to dazzle the British here with my exams—my only real way of matching them—they ignore writing altogether, but still I'm turning in a book of poems as a supplement to my exams. Wish us luck and dream with us about this summer.

x x x Sivvy

Dearest Mother,

So happy to hear you liked our poems [*in* Poetry, *Chicago*]. We've garnered a huge batch of rejections this month—many "letters from the editor," but nonetheless causing chagrin, so it's pleasant to see even the revival of old things. . . .

. . . I love Teddy more and more each day and just can't imagine how I ever lived without him. Our lives fit together perfectly. He is so helpful and understanding about my studies and has made a huge chart of the English writers and their dates (dating and knowing style is necessary here and I had nothing of that, unfortunately, at home) and stuck it up all over one wall of the bedroom where I can learn it.

. . . In spite of the rejections, I am very happy and alive and writing better poems—a big one about a Sow, about 45 lines, and one about "The Lady and the Earthenware Head," which has the best verse I've ever written. Hope I can find a good berth for them somewhere.

It is often infuriating to read the trash published by the Old Guard, the flat, clever, colorless poets here (in America there is, with much bad, still much color, life and vigor). I have my fingers crossed that Ted will come to associate America with the growing acceptance and publishing of his writings. England is so stuffy, cliquey, and plain bad, bad . . .

Much much love from us both. Let us know as soon as anything comes through about dearest Warrie.

Your own Sivvy

FEBRUARY 8, 1957

Dearest Mother,

It is just 10:30 and I am fresh from a morning walk through the meadows to Granchester. The sun is flooding into our living room, the birds chirruping, and all is wet, melted, and spring smelling. We still have had no snow here. I wish I could describe the beautiful walk. I set off after Ted left and I had cleaned up the house, and met not a soul. I tramped over a mud-puddled path, through a creaky crooked wooden stile and strode along—meadows shining bright silver-wet in the sun, and the sky a seethe of grey clouds and egg-shell blue patches, the dark bare trees along the river framing brilliant green meadows. On my right was a knotty, gnarled hawthorn hedge, red haws bright; and behind the hedge, the allotment gardens of cabbages and onions rose to the horizon, giving way to bare plowed fields. I found a squirrel tree—I saw a bushy-tailed grey squirrel clamber up and vanish in a little hole. I startled flocks of great hook-beak black rooks wheeling and watched a glistening, slim, pinkish-purple worm stretch and contract its translucent coils into the grass. There was a sudden flurry of rain, and then the sun shed a silver light over everything. I caught a passing rainbow in a pastel arc over the tiny town of Cambridge, where the spires of King's Chapel looked like glistening pink sugar spikes on a little cake. I kept smelling the damp, sodden meadows and the wet hay and horses and filling my eyes with the sweeps of meadow rises and tree clumps. What a lovely walk to have at the end of the street! I felt myself building up a core of peace inside and was glad to be alone, taking it all in.

I went to visit my head, too! Remember, the model head M. B. Derr [*Smith roommate, junior year*] made of me? Well, it's been knocking about, and I didn't have the heart to throw it away because I've developed a strange fondness for the old thing with passing years. So Ted suggested we walk out into the meadows and climb up into a tree and ensconce it there so it could look over the cow pastures and river. I returned there for the first time today, and there it was, high up on a branch-platform in a gnarled willow, gazing out over the lovely green meadows with the peace that passes understanding. I like to think of leaving "my head" here, as it were. Ted was right: every time I think of it now, I feel leaves and ivy twining around it, like a monument at rest in the midst of nature. I even wrote a rather longish poem about it (only ending differently), which I'll type out in an adjoining letter and send you.

. . . Ted is so much happier about his teaching. I have never seen such a change. He doesn't come home utterly exhausted the way he used to and proudly tells me how he's learned to make his discipline work and how his psychology in treating them works out. He has become interested in one or two of the boys and given them extra reading, etc. I feel he is mastering his work now, not letting it sap all his energy and letting the boys run all over him. They must really admire him; he is such a strong, fascinating person, compared to the other sissy teachers they get. He told me how he had them shut their eyes and imagine a story he told them—very active and vivid—and when the bell to end school rang, they all groaned and wanted him to finish the story. So I am glad that he is literally making the best of a very hard job.

I do wish we could win the pools. Pan (our Ouija imp) has been getting better and better about it and tells us more and more accurately. Last week we got 20 points out of a possible 24 (which would be a fortune of 75,000 pounds, given out every week). We keep telling Pan we want it so we can have leisure to write and have lots of children, both . . . If we won, we could deposit the money and live off the interest and write when and wherever we wanted and not get desperate about jobs. I feel I could write a good novel if I had a year off. I need time and peace. Oh, well, it's a nice dream. Wish us luck, anyhow.

x x x Sivvy

Dear Mother—Here is a copy of the poem I said I'd send. It is called "The Lady and the Earthenware Head."

THE LADY AND THE EARTHENWARE HEAD

Fired in sanguine clay, the model head
Fit nowhere: thumbed out as a classroom exercise
By a casual friend, it stood
Obtrusive on the long bookshelf, stolidly propping
Thick volumes of prose—
Far too unlovely a conversation piece,
Her visitor claimed, for keeping.

And how unlike! In distaste he pointed at it:
Brickdust-complected, eyes under a dense lid
Half-blind, that derisive pout—
Rude image indeed, to ape with such sly treason
Her dear face: best rid
Hearthstone at once of the outrageous head.
With goodwill she heard his reason,

But she—whether from habit grown overfond
Of the dented caricature, or fearing some truth
In old wives' tales of a bond
Knitting to each original its coarse copy
(Woe if enemies, in wrath,
Take to sticking pins through wax!)—felt loath
To junk it. Scared, unhappy,

She watched the grim head swell mammoth, demanding a home
Suited to its high station: from a spectral dais
It menaced her in a dream—
Cousin perhaps to that vast stellar head
Housed in stark heavens, whose laws
Ordained now bland, now barbarous influences
Upon her purse, her bed.

No place, it seemed, for the effigy to fare
Free from annoy: if dump-discarded, rough boys
Spying a pate to spare
Glowering sullen and pompous from an ash-heap
Might well seize this prize
And maltreat the hostage head in shocking wise
Afflicting the owner's sleep—

At the mere thought her head ached. A murky tarn
She considered then, thick-silted, with weeds obscured,
To serve her exacting turn:
But out of the watery aspic, laurelled by fins
The simulacrum leered,
Lewdly beckoning. Her courage wavered:
She blenched, as one who drowns,

And resolved more ceremoniously to lodge
The mimic-head—in a crotched willow tree, green-
Vaulted by foliage:
Let bell-tongued birds descant in blackest feather
On the rendering, grain by grain,
Of that uncouth shape to simple sod again
Through drear and dulcet weather.

Yet, shrined on her shelf, the grisly visage endured,
Despite her wrung hands, her tears, her praying: Vanish!
Steadfast and evil-starred,
It ogled through rock-fault, wind-flaw and fisted wave—
An antique hag-head, too tough for knife to finish,
Refusing to diminish
By one jot its basilisk-look of love.

And that's that . . .

x x x Sivvy

SUNDAY AFTERNOON
FEBRUARY 24, 1957

Dearest Mother,

Hello, Hello! I realized after I had put the call through that it must not yet be 6 a.m. in the hamlet of Wellesley, but I thought you wouldn't mind being wakened up by such good news, and I simply couldn't keep it another minute. They had changed your phone number, so there was much delay and waiting, but finally you were roused and discovered.

We walked around in a trance all yesterday. Ted and I felt grumpy Saturday morning after a week of three letters-from-editors rejecting Ted's poems for spurious reasons. They talk about having "room" for poetry as if they only had visas for a special secret aristocracy and the visas were all taken. They are SO SORRY. Well, the idiots should Make Room for fine poetry, and that's Ted's.

The big judges—W. H. Auden, Stephen Spender, and Marianne Moore (all of whom I've met, interestingly enough)—are big enough to recognize new poetic genius and not be scared of it as small jealous poets and frightened poetry editors are.

The telegram came at about 10:30 yesterday morning. We gawped at it. At first we both thought that Ted's poem at the *Atlantic* had got some piddling prize. Then light dawned, and we both jumped about, yelling and roaring like mad seals. The telegram was from New York and said: "Our congratulations that *Hawk in the Rain* judged winning volume Poetry Center First Publication. Award letter will follow." Well, we await the letter in a fury of excitement to know details.

No money prize is offered—just publication—by Harper's, I believe. But under the auspices of these three fine judges, the three best living and practicing poets in the world today, I'm sure Ted's book will be a best-seller.

You know, it is, to the day, the anniversary of that fatal party where I met Ted! And I'd read his poems before and had a vision of how much I could do for him and with him. Genius will out. We are not letting it go to our heads, but working twice as hard. I only hope he gets his book of children's fables accepted somewhere. He has got a terrific idea for another children's book, and we could demand a really good illustrator if this one were a published success. The second one is about his demon-fairy, Snatchcraftington, taking a little boy, or boy and girl, on 26 adventures through the lands of each letter of the alphabet: from the Land of A to the Land of Z.

I am more happy than if it was my book published! I have worked so closely on these poems of Ted's and typed them so many countless times through revision after revision that I feel ecstatic about it all.

I am so happy *his* book is accepted *first*. It will make it so much easier for me when mine is accepted—if not by the Yale Series, then by some other place. I can rejoice then, much more, knowing Ted is ahead of me. There is no question of rivalry, but only mutual joy and a sense of us doubling our prize-winning and creative output.

You know how breathlessly *I* always waited for mail and prize telegrams. Well, imagine how marvelous it is to have Ted grown equally sensitive to the mailman's miraculous, potential footstep and wait as eagerly as I.*

* From the time Sylvia was a very little girl, she catered to the male of any age so as to bolster his sense of superiority. I recall her, when she was four years old, watching a boy of eleven demonstrating his prowess on a trapeze for her, clapping her hands, crying, "Juny [*Junior*], you are *wonderful!*"

In her diary, written when she was a seventh-grader, she described coming in second in the Junior High School spelling contest—a boy came in first. "I am so glad Don won," she wrote. "It is always nice to have a boy be *first*. And I am second-best speller in the whole Junior High!"

She did not pretend the male was superior; she sought out those who were, and her confidence in her husband's genius was unshakable.

A whole pot of milk burned black on the stove yesterday while we called you and danced about. We had to air the house; it was burnt down to a black crisp, the milk, I mean, and throw the pot away.

Then both of us wandered around town in the rain, shining with joy. We ate lunch at a lovely English bar—salad, bread and cheese, and ale. Bought an armful of books, had tea opposite King's and a delicious supper . . . We didn't have enough money for snails and venison, but are going back to eat them if I win any poetry money soon. . . .

We don't care really what reviews the book gets as long as it's bought and read. It's magnificent—far superior to Richard Wilbur, who never treats the powerful central emotions and incidents of life. . . . Ted writes with color, splendor and vigorous music about love, birth, war, death, animals, hags and vampires, martyrdom, and sophisticated intellectual problems, too. His book can't be typed. It has rugged, violent war poems like "Bayonet Charge" and "Griefs for Dead Soldiers," delicate, exquisite nature poems about "October Dawn," and "Horses"—powerful animal poems about Macaws, Jaguars, and the lovely Hawk one which appeared in the *Atlantic* and is the title poem of the book. He combines intellect and grace of complex form, with lyrical music, male vigor and vitality, and moral commitment and love and awe of the world.

O, he has everything.

And I am so happy with him. This year is hard for both of us. I should not have three jobs—writing, cooking and housekeeping, and studying for tough exams. I would like, after a year, maybe two, of teaching to satisfy my self-respect, to give up work and combine writing and being a wife and mother . . . but children only after I have a poetry book and a novel published, so my children fit into my work routine and don't overthrow mine with theirs. We are such late maturers, beginning our true lives at the average age of 25, that we don't want children for at least several years yet. Until we're well-off enough financially to afford a housekeeper . . . so I won't be torn between domestic chores and my writing fulfillment, which is my deepest health—being articulate in print.

We plan to stay in America probably two years, then apply for writing fellowships, both of us—Saxton and Guggenheim—and live for a year or two, writing solidly, in Italy in a villa near Rome. And then, if there are children, perhaps you would come over in the summer to live next door and help babysit now and then!

As Doctor Krook, who is "Doris" to me now, the dear woman, said so sweetly yesterday at my fine supervision on D. E. Lawrence: it seems to be nothing but delightful choices and prospects for us two! . . .

Write soon . . .

x x x Sivvy

Dearest Mother,

The most blissful thing is your two letters about the Spauldings' Cape cottage. You don't know the change that's come over Ted and me, just dreaming of it. For us, it's the most magnificent present in the world: a Time and a Place to write! And the Cape is my favorite place in the world. Just the *vision* of that little spick-and-span kitchen with the refrigerator and stove and the sun streaming in sustains me through the grim plodding of studying masses for exams. And to have a place I *know* will be such a rest. It is really exhausting to have to "discover" a new town—shops, quiet nooks, etc., and I think the seven weeks on the Cape will be the best start on my campaign to make Ted fall in love with America. He is getting really excited and glad about it now; and I, vicariously, am more than doubly glad to go back and open up its treasure chests to him. He loves to fish, so maybe you and I can accompany him and Warren deep-sea fishing some weekend.

We'd love a party on June 29 and should be marvelously rested from the boat trip. My exams finish about June 1, so I'll have leisure to pack while Ted goes on teaching right up to the sailing date.

By dint of much typing, I manage to keep 20 manuscripts out continuously from both of us. There was a dead lull for a week after the telegram. . . .

Miraculously, with the publication of a sumptuous new Cambridge-Oxford magazine (which contained two of my poems, right after an article by Stephen Spender, on request from the editor), our fame has spread around Cambridge among the students. Editors of *Granta*, the Cambridge "New Yorker," have humbly asked both Ted and me for stuff. I came home after my classes late yesterday afternoon and found a very sweet boy talking to Ted—editor for one of the spring issues. I made coffee and gave them a piece of orange chiffon pie, and we had a good talk. Ted is much more modest than I about his work, so I act as his agent. The next issue of *Gemini* (the new magazine) in May will carry three poems by Ted and a story and book review by me, and I think *Granta* may well produce us both. We do love to appear together. . . . The undergraduate magazines are read in London by editors—there are so few university writers—whereas in America, undergrad publications are legion and ignored by higher-ups. I've convinced Ted that his book will sell better if people get to read and hear and like his poems first; he is difficult, strong, and overpowering and needs to be read much. So he should publish everywhere he can. I have another little editor coming tomorrow, really a nice fellow, very brilliant, who went to Moscow this year on a student-visit and who translates Russian short stories, etc. (Shall try another Apfelkuchen; I love giving hospitality to intelligent people.) . . .

x x x Sivvy

MARCH 12, 1957

Dearest Mother,

It is with the maximum of self-control that I don't at this moment rush to call you up again over the phone and rouse you at what must be 4 a.m.! Hold on to your hat for some wonderful news:

I have just been offered a teaching job for next year!

AT SMITH!

I got the nicest little letter from blessed R. G. Davis this morning (I know dear, blessed Miss Chase is responsible for this and for my knowing so early). The salary sounds very fine to me: $4,200!!! . . .

Well! You can imagine how much indefinite, vague concern this sets at rest. I am just walking on air. Ted is so happy for me and is really excited. He will help me in every way. We are writing Amherst for him, and if there is nothing there, will try surrounding boys' schools. But with my good salary, I'd rather have him working part-time at a radio station or on a newspaper than have a killing program such as he has had this year.

As I see it, this means nine hours of teaching a week (three classes [*courses*] of three hours each) . . . I know they are the last stronghold of liberalism at Smith. Harvard, et al., are producing Ph.D. businessmen.

Did you see in the *Alumnae Quarterly* where President Wright stood up against the project to lengthen Ph.D. term of work and advised against the absurd requirement to have the Ph.D. thesis "add to the sum of knowledge" (as it made people spend years on ridiculous, worthless subjects). He said these requirements might be all right for the "plodder," the routine, stodgy type, but would discourage brilliant, young potential teachers with a creative gift. Imagine what pride I'll feel working under a President with such fine ideas!

I'm writing dear Mrs. Prouty at the same time, so you can share the news with her, feeling I've already told her firsthand. . . .

I know just what you mean about "winter doldrums." I've started taking thyroid again and feel much better. It got so I couldn't work after 2 p.m.; I felt so sleepy and uncaringly exhausted. But I feel suddenly as if I see light behind the grim advancing hydra of exams— beautiful light—writing furiously on the Cape, teaching and writing furiously at Smith in the lovely Pioneer Valley, among the people I admire most in the world. What an introduction for Ted!

We *still* wait for the letter about his book, but I imagine it will come out next fall, and then what fine publicity it will have in the center of these poetry-conscious university communities. So light your way through this gruelling run-down month with vision of a summer and an academic year within driving distance of us!

. . . Naturally, I'm humble and a little awed by this teaching job. I'll want advice from you and courage this summer. I want to make them work devilishly hard and love every minute of it. I can't think of anything I'd rather do than teach at Smith. I *know* it; of course, not the higher-up "ins and outs" of the Department, but what they do. I remember the dull . . . teacher I had for Freshman English and will do my best to fascinate the little girls and keep them gaping at dangling carrots. (I am thinking of having a suit or two tailor-made here.) I'll throw away my knee socks for good and be a grown woman. How wonderful not to be always receiving! If I'd been offered a writing fellowship, I'd have turned it down. I feel a deep need to develop my self-respect by teaching, by "giving out," and Ted understands this so well.

. . . I've been bogged down on the second of two stories I'm working on for the *Ladies' Home Journal* market (this last one based on the character of [*a Smith classmate*] and called "The Fabulous Roommate"). Well, he took me on a long evening walk, listened to me talk the whole plot out, showed me what I'd vaguely felt I should change about the end. Last night he read all 30 pages of it, word for word, unerringly pointing out awkwardness here or an unnecessary paragraph there. He is proud of the story, thinks it's exciting and valid as a character study (not an "art" story), but the sort of thing that takes up where I left off in *Seventeen*. . . .

Love to you and dear Warren,
Your happy Sivvy

Dearest, darling Mother,

It is about 10, and I am slightly groggy with sitting up last night to type my last paper of the term. I have two supervisions today, the last day of term, praises be, and shall grit my teeth and endure. I feel if I had one more minute of pressure I should explode. Actually, I feel I should be doing much more than I do, but small things come up. . . .

I got an interesting and rather pleasant letter from a London literary agency with offices in New York, saying they'd read my poems in *Gemini* (the new Oxford-Cambridge magazine) with admiration and would be interested in handling any stories or novels I wrote and would I care to come to lunch in London to talk this over. Ted and I may stop in; we keep planning this London trip to cover all our business . . . but I won't bother with agents until we get home and I get advice from friends like Peter Davison.

Tomorrow I'll feel wider awake and relaxed in the beginning of vacation. What bliss to study at random from a choice of 100 and more books and not to turn out any more blithery papers . . .

. . . My best love to you and Warren. I can't wait to run up my beloved Nauset beach in the sun!

Love,
Sivvy

Dearest Mother,

. . . Wendy Christie (that nice widow-friend of Doctor Krook's) burst in yesterday, waving a London *Sunday Times.* To my amazement, *Harold Hobson,* well-known theater critic, in his weekly column, devoted several lines to a very favorable review of "Spinster," one of my two poems in the new Oxford-Cambridge *Gemini!* I was astounded and overjoyed. Tried to get copies today, but couldn't, so I quote. (Look it up if you can. It's really a terrific honor—a poem reviewed in a theater column!) Mr. Hobson starts the top of his third column review of *As You Like It* (a Cambridge undergrad production) with the following words:

The young ladies of Cambridge, it appears, know all about love. On my way from Liverpool Street, I read in the new university magazine, *Gemini,* a poem "Spinster" by Sylvia Plath, twelve times, no less. Here, sharp-edged, memorable, precise, is a statement of the refusal of love, a firm, alarmed withdrawal of the skirts from the dangerous dews.

. . . Isn't that nice, though? Ted and I agreed the greatest joy a poet has is writing something a perfect stranger can want to read "twelve times"! Do share this with dear Mrs. Prouty. In THE LONDON SUNDAY TIMES! I still have to pinch myself.

I have just typed and sent off two stories to the *Ladies' Home Journal*—about 43 pages in all—"The Laundromat Affair" and "The Fabulous Roommate." Wish me luck . . . I still manage to keep 20 manuscripts between us out. Thanks for the cold pills, by the way. Hope they'll be a good charm to ward off any symptoms.

. . . Well, to try to make a rhubarb pie before Ted gets back, I'm off. Much love to you and Warren—

Sivvy

MARCH 19, 1957

Dearest Mother,

Such nice mail today, and I feel so much brighter after a good night's sleep that I thought I'd write a follow-up to my last letter written yesterday. I'm so glad you, too, are rejoicing about the Smith job. I will, no doubt, be scared blue the first few days, but from the keen way I enjoyed managing those round-table discussions on poetry at the English festival in New York State, I'm sure I'll love my work. The schedule is surely the freest anywhere, the girls intelligent and willing (at least the larger proportion of them), and since they're not lecture, but discussion, courses (every girl has to do an 8-page theme every two weeks), I should learn a lot, and where Ted and I are "young poets" and writers with strong integrity and critical views, I should have pride enough to feel that my viewpoint, growing as it is every day, may help them gain new insights at their stage of development. After all, they *are* seven years behind me!

The big, brown envelope came from Harper's today. Very exciting. A huge blue contract to sign with hundreds of little bylaws. Ted gets the chance to negotiate with a British publisher himself, so I think we'll write to Faber & Faber, T. S. Eliot's place. They should, I hope, jump at the chance. As I said before, the book is scheduled for publication in mid-August. We are going to have a decent picture taken of Ted Saturday. . . .

I am going to buy a huge scrapbook when I come home and paste up all Ted's acceptances and important letters (they have only dinky scrapbooks here). These are things our grandchildren should treasure. . . .

Imagine, the royalties on the book will be only 15 percent of 43 percent of the retail price (the 43 percent is the wholesale price!). On a $3 book this means the measly sum of about 10 cents a copy. To make the paltry sum of $100, you'd have to sell 1,000 books. I hope the reviewers make it a best-seller. They should! You see, selling the poems to magazines earns far far more. Poetry prizes, too. So the next book, we think, will be made up only after all the poems in it are already sold to magazines. I must find out about copyright laws. I think we both must get agents in New York now. Especially if I sell anything to the women's magazines. . . .

I accompany Ted to his play tonight and tomorrow—the first time I'll have been at his school. We are so glad it is getting over with. Ted has been so deadly exhausted, I am insisting he gives up teaching on June 1, the day I finish my exams. We shall both take a rest-trip to Yorkshire to bid good-by to his parents and then, perhaps, visit Scotland. I have seen next to nothing of England's natural beauty and feel I should. I am so prejudiced against it in everything else: politics, class-system, medical system, fawning literary cliques, mean-minded critics (the irate, nasty person-to-person letters the most respected critics—G. S. Fraser, Louis MacNeice, Spender, Leavis, et al.—throw back at each other in the weekly papers are shockingly mean and narrow). Of course, for official purposes, I have found England heavenly (and, for myself, I have): the one place in the world that offered me the husband of my whole life and love and work. . . . I feel more in love with him now than I ever did before we were married. And this marvelous chance of both of us beginning from scratch and working up together has been magnificent. . . .

x x x s.

TUESDAY NOON
MARCH 25, 1957

Dearest Mother,

This must be a gruelling time of year for everybody. Ted and I both were exhausted and blackly depressed this weekend as an aftermath of little sleep and a term's accumulation of fatigue and last-minute slaving by both of us—Ted on his play, me on my papers and articles. Sunday loomed blacker than pitch, and it seemed an intolerable effort to move to go to bed. We took a long night walk and felt much freer and with early bed this week and me "free" from the paper-producing routine, and Ted's play over, we improve rapidly. Both of us haven't written anything to please ourselves for months, it seems, but now, suddenly with the clearing spring air, we feel much more optimistic. But so much still hangs fire—15 manuscripts of poems and stories and our two books: my poems and Ted's animal fables.

Ted's play enchanted me. I haven't laughed so hard or enjoyed myself so much at a play since I've been here. . . . I never want Ted to have to undergo a year of strain like this again. I don't care if he only gets a part-time free-lance job this next year. I want him to write above all. Both of us feel literally sick when we're not writing. . . . Must read novels this summer: George Eliot, etc. Ted and I have read scarcely any novels. How we both look forward toward this summer! It hasn't been an easy year for either of us.

Ted was very impressed about the news of Wilbur's astounding fortunes. When I think that Wilbur was publishing his first book of poems at Ted's age, ten years ago, I don't feel we are so retarded. I am secretly hoping Ted will get a good college teaching job—maybe at Amherst the second year (if I'm asked back to Smith)—and will discover how unique the chance is for American poets, and even though we travel abroad, will want to come back. There is not a question of our living in England; both of us are eager to get out (although I am terribly fond of Cambridge). It's Europe and America. Ted is so eager to go; he feels the opportunity there more and more, I think. And if I manage this year right—giving him time, leisure and peace to write (the Cape is perfect—your most significant present!), maybe he'll want to center his life there. But one must never push him . . .

. . . I grind daily on the rough draft of my "novel"; I only know that it will cover nine months and be a soul-search, American-girl-in-Cambridge, European vacations, etc. If I do my daily stint, mere unrewritten blatting it out, I should have about 300 single-spaced pages by the time we sail for home—a ragged, rough hunk to work from this summer. Once I see what happens myself, I'll start careful rewriting; probably chuck this and rewrite the whole mess . . .

I get courage by reading Virginia Woolf's *Writer's Diary;* I feel very akin to her, although my book reads more like a slick best-seller. Her moods and neuroses are amazing. You must read this diary; most illuminating. . . .

x x x sivvy

Mrs. Prouty was, of course, delighted to learn of Sylvia's appointment to Smith, and wrote her a long congratulatory letter which concluded with these intuitive remarks:

Dear Sylvia,

. . . There is no end to the thrilling things happening. It frightens me a little.

I am very proud of you, Sylvia. I love telling your story. Someone remarked to me after reading your poem in the *Atlantic*, "How intense." Sometime write me a little poem that *isn't* intense. A lamp turned too high might shatter its chimney. Please just *glow* sometimes. Much love and to Ted, too.

Olive Prouty

MONDAY A.M.
APRIL 8, 1957

Dearest Mother,

. . . Am at last coming out of a "ghastly stretch of sterility" put upon me by writing countless essays last term, taking all my writing energy. I just yesterday finished one of my best, about 56 lines, called "All the Dead Dears."

I so appreciated your apropos quotes from Auden and Cronin; they help so much. Just to know it is *normal* to have cycles of feeling barren as hell sustains one. I am now growing more and more accustomed to it, but both Ted and I realize the fatality is to *stop* writing. We would go on, daily, writing a few pages of drivel until the juice came back, rather than stop, because the inertia built up is terrible to conquer. So, for our "health" we write at least two hours a day. I am plodding daily on my "novel" and have about 80 single-spaced pages ground out (actually 160 Ms. pages); my aim is 300 single-spaced pages by the time I come home. Then the blessed summer to ram it into shape.

I must say I have the most peculiar feeling about my book. I am grinding out a lot of tripe, having never written a novel, and, as Ted says, won't know what I'm saying till I've written the first draft. But it's a place to put everything in—a kind of repository for my thoughts and feelings and freeing them with this wonderful fluency. I have a feeling, in flashes, that I can make it a best-seller; but only with at least a year's work. I'd love to dedicate it to Mrs. Prouty and hope I can get her to approve when it's done. . . .

. . . Got up at 4:30 a.m. this day with Ted and went for a long walk to Granchester before settling down to writing. I never want to miss another sunrise. First, the luminous blue light, with big stars hanging; then pinkness, spreading, translucent, and the birds beginning to burble and twit from every bramble bush; owls flying home. We saw over fifteen rabbits feeding. I felt a peace and joy, being all alone in the most beautiful world with animals and birds. Little shrews twitted from the tall grass, and we saw two lovely brown-furred water rats (remember *The Wind in the Willows*) feeding on the bank, then skipping into the water and swimming. You'd laugh, but I'm going to put this scene into my novel. We began mooing at a pasture of cows, and they all looked up, and, as if hypnotized, began to follow us in a crowd of about twenty across the pasture to a wooden stile, staring, fascinated. I stood on the stile and, in a resonant voice, recited all I knew of Chaucer's *Canterbury Tales* for about twenty minutes. I never had such an intelligent, fascinated audience. You should have seen their expressions as they came flocking up around me. I'm sure they loved it! . . . Well, must be off to shop and laundry now. Am ripping through French translations of Baudelaire and Stendhal and feeling virtuous. What news of dear Warrie?

Love to you both, Sivvy

APRIL 13, 1957

Dearest, darling, adorable Mother,

It has been so lovely to get your happy letters this week. So glad Warren's thesis is done and am sure it is brilliant, although far over both our heads. . . .

We have had a rather taxing week, but with a nice climax today. Ted and I got four rejections between us on Tuesday (two each—our literary life is very symmetrical). Ted's book of children's fables (alas) they ultimately decided was "too sophisticated." I'm going to keep on trying the big companies like Macmillan; small ones don't take risks. If the Hobbit wasn't "sophisticated," what is? [*Rejected, also,*] some of Ted's poems from the *Saturday Review* (Ciardi is making a big mistake in rejecting us. He's "overstocked," I bet—with his own poems!); some of my poems from the *Paris Review*, with a very nice letter asking me to send more; and two stories from the posh *Sewanee Review* with a rather amazing letter from the editor to the effect that my stories showed a "spectacular talent," which from a conservative editor is rather encouraging.

Well, we weathered this news with typing and retyping sessions, sending five or six more Mss. out, and this morning got our reward— again, in a twin package—from, guess where—John Lehmann at the *London Magazine!* Our first real professional "British" acceptance, and it is the "Atlantic Monthly" of England! They accepted two of my poems: "Spinster" (the one favorably reviewed in the *Sunday Times*) and "Black Rook in Rainy Weather" (about to be published also in the *Antioch Review*). They accepted a longish one of Ted's, "Famous Poet," and obviously felt they could not resist the pressure of such about-to-be-world-celebrated poets. At last! The halls of British conservatism have recognized us.

Of my two poems, the impeccable Mr. Lehmann wrote, "Your outstanding gift seems to me a sharply focussed truth of feeling and observation, at its most effective in 'Spinster' and 'Black Rook.' " We aren't really bragging, but only childlikely happy our sweating and work-of-our-life is recognized. We still get on an average two rejections apiece to every acceptance.

The joy is, in these rejections, of people saying we have a gift. That's all we need to know, although we *do* know it deep in ourselves. All that a gift demands to be recognized is constant deep thinking and sweating, continuous work. No public literary-lion life for us; although, on the occasion of a book-publishing, we will modestly appear, gaunt-cheeked and prophet-eyed, to partake of free champagne and caviar!

Both of us feel we are very late maturers . . . our own personalities are still squeaking new and wonderful to us.

. . . What fun we'll have, clipping Ted's reviews . . . We are going to catapult to fame, I predict. Simply because it means so little to us and our writing and being HEARD and READ is everything. . . .

Much love, Sivvy

Sunday afternoon
April 28, 1957

Dearest Mother,

. . . I am living at the University library from morning to night . . . enjoying my work, really, steadily reading tragedy now, the Greeks, then on through 2,000 years up to Eliot, concentrating on several major figures: Corneille, Racine, Ibsen, Strindberg, Webster, Marlowe, Tourneur, Yeats, Eliot; there are so many. This tragedy paper (only a 3-hour exam for all that) is a fine help on my reading.

I'd never read any of the plays before, really. This summer I must devour crucial novels. Ted and I have read hardly any prose.

. . . We'll pack and get our stuff crated in the few days after we finish work and be off for the therapeutic Wuthering Heights country, when I hope to begin writing again. I feel seething when I'm not writing daily and am forced now to give it up for these next five weeks. But my novel becomes more and more exciting to me, and I hope to work on it all summer. We are already sending our manuscripts with the Wellesley address on return envelopes, so open anything that looks official to either of us and communicate the contents. . . .

Ted's visa seems to be for residence, with all that implies. I think he might be willing even to change citizenship, although I will not try to persuade him, because America is uniquely the country which gives its poets a kind of "patronage" at the universities . . . He has just written one of his best poems today (after a long dry spell) on the recent auto death of Roy Campbell.

. . . We plan, after two years, definitely to get writing fellowships to Rome. I hope you'll brave the seas on a bigger ship then and spend at least the summer with us in a nearby villa! Ted enjoys your letters so much and says he is so happy I have such a lovely mother. I do think his parents are dear and we both have in common coming from good, solid stock where the sole endowments are talent and intelligence and health; name and money we'll make ourselves, step by step, together.

x x x Your own Sivvy

MAY 7, 1957

Dearest, darling Mother,

How happy your letter made us this morning with the wonderful news of Warrie's Fulbright! I'm writing him a note this morning, too, before I go biking off for my routine day . . .

This is one of those clear, rare, champagne-aired mornings which make me feel like a sinner against creation when I go into the huge factory-stacked library, not to glimpse the sun again before it sets, but my dreams of the moors and the Cape sustain me. I will not feel at all "guilty" in indulging in sun and sea there.

You know, I think that through our years of family scraping to get money and scholarships, etc., we three developed an almost Puritan sense that being "lazy" and spending money on luxuries like meals

HAPPY BIRTHDAY TO YOU!

There was an invincible mother
(I defy you to show me another!)
Who in some magic way
Grew younger each day
And never found birthdays a bother.

Her feats are too great to be reckoned:
One summer the continent beckoned:
She mastered a car,
Said: "Big Ben's not so far!"
And whiz! she was there in a second.

Gay Paree and much vin did not wearia;
She thought Rembrandt's exhibit superia;
From bottom to top
Of the Alps she did hop---
Next year she'll be conquering Siberia!

At the green age of fifty-one, this is
A health to our venturesome missis!
May her next fifty springs
Bring new joys and jauntings!
From S & T here is love, hugs and kisses!

A handmade birthday card, 1957

out or theater or travel was slightly wicked; and I think all three of us are being given the rare chance of changing into people who can experience the joys of new adventures and experiences. You are the lesson to us all. I really think you have grown in the past year at least 25 years younger in the sense that you are so wonderfully open to experience! So few women manage this. Ted and I look forward to having such *fun* with you this summer and next year, simply picnicking on Nauset Beach and swimming and talking and taking long walks.

We live very simply by nature, in our favorite old clothes and with our cheap, red wine for dinner and (this year, at least) no theater, movies or extras. But every now and then we believe in going out to dinner, or dressing up, as we did this last Saturday night, and going to a party. The editor of *Gemini* gave a cocktail party to all The Literati of Cambridge, and as Ted and I had never met him, we went; I, in that lovely pink knit dress I wore for my wedding and new white heels (what a blessing to wear heels with Ted and still be "little") and a silver headband he'd bought me for a surprise at a time when I was depressed about exams. A most enlightening affair.

. . . Can't wait to write on my novel this summer. I really feel I am going to do a fine one. All my love to you and our wonderful Warren. After all these years of work, sickness, death, and bearing others' suffering, you must enjoy every minute of life with Warrie, Ted, and me.

x x x Sivvy

Dearest Warren,
. . . I live in dreams of the Cape and our summer . . . I'll be reading madly in preparation for my courses at Smith and writing on my novel, tentatively to be called "Hill of Leopards," about an American girl finding her soul in a year (or, rather, nine Fulbright months) at Cambridge and on the Continent. It will be very controversial as I intend to expose a lot of people and places. And start my new gospel, which is as old as native rituals, about the positive acceptance of conflict, uncertainty, and pain as the soil for true knowledge and life. How I long to begin it! Ted and I want to devote our lives to writing and travel and raising a family of at least four. He admires you very much and hopes you can take us both fishing on one of those ships on the Cape sometime. Ted loves to fish and is so marvelously restful to be with. How heavenly it will be.

I can't wait to get out of this dusty, dirty, gloomy coal-bin of a house (except for the front room in which I am now writing) to go to the moors, then the Atlantic, then home, then the Cape. Smith scares me, but only in a healthy way. I will gain the much-needed sense of "giving" and (for once) supporting myself, which I could not live without. I will work to really interest my students (I imagine I'll have close to 100 in all!) and feel it will be a perfect way to "share" my Fulbright experience and learning, as well as by writing.

. . . I hope to break into the women's slicks this summer. I just haven't had the time to rewrite. The *Ladies' Home Journal* liked my laundromat story (two people meet at a laundromat via a very funny 13-year-old girl, quiz-kid type, and fall in love finally) and said they'd look at it again if I rewrote the ending—no promises. Well, I sent it to *Good Housekeeping* and when it comes back will rewrite it. I think I should sell it somewhere, the setting is quite "original"; their motto is: LOVE LOVE LOVE: but not, please, in the same old setting—Love in jet-planes, Love on water-skis, Love in Sumner Tunnel (traffic jam, etc.), but never Love plain. So I put mustard, pepper and curry powder on it.

O the sun is so lovely, and I must bury my bleared eyes in 2,000 years of Tragedy. My life is just balancing till the end of the month. Then, whoopee! novels, stories, poems. I can feel them battering to get out. DO WRITE. We both send love and congratulations and an invisible rabbit's foot for your exams.

Love,
Sivvy

FRIDAY A.M.
MAY 10, 1957

Dearest Mother,

Couldn't resist sitting down and writing some more good news about my wonderful Ted which came this morning . . . FABER & FABER, *the* British publishing house, has just written to accept Ted's poetry book for publication in England. Not only that, but Mr. T. S. Eliot (who is on their staff) read the book, and the publisher writes: "Mr. Eliot has asked me to tell you how much he personally enjoyed the poems and to pass on to you his congratulations on them." . . .

. . . Since last June Ted has sold fourteen poems, a broadcast poem and a book to two countries. I guaranteed fifteen poems sold in a year if he let me be his agent when I first met him, and he's written his best since we've been working together . . . even as I have. I've had sixteen sales since August (just twice as many as I'd sold in the five years before meeting Ted) and many of these, like "Ella Mason and Her Eleven Cats," were assignments Ted gave me last spring. If only I can get my book accepted in the next few months, it will be perfect.

My two main ambitions this summer (apart from preparing my courses at Smith and writing poems, naturally) are my novel and breaking into the women's slicks finally. I feel years older than I was the summer I left and my stories which I wrote this year . . . are really much, much improved. If I devote my whole self and intelligence to it, I know I can make it, and five stories would be a year's salary. Ted wants to make children's books his other field . . . I am planning to try an article on Cambridge for *Harper's* and a story on Cambridge for the *Atlantic;* both editors said they would be interested in seeing my results . . . The doors are open; one only has to slave and work and live for the art of writing, as well as living with the utmost integrity and emotional sympathy. . . .

Much love,
Sivvy

MAY 24, 1957

Dearest Mother,

How lovely it was to get your letter this cold gray morning. Ted and I read it aloud over breakfast and both of us send congratulations and much love to our new Associate Professor! Really, though, you have long deserved it, I should think. . . .

We were stunned this week to get the proofs of Ted's book, not from Harper's, but from Faber & Faber, one week after they'd accepted it! We've gone through and through it with a little, but incomplete, handbook page on proofreading marks and put in endless commas. Ted has made some alterations, which I've limited. He would rewrite a poem to eternity and stop the presses. I don't mind retyping constantly, but we realize we must be much more strict in checking the typed Mss. we send. You need to review us on punctuation rules and Ms. correcting. You must remember all this from doing Daddy's book, and we need you as a third, impartial proofreader. What fun it should be, though. I don't count it as work at all; we'll always be having something to proofread, I hope. . . .

We heard dear, shrewd, funny, lovable Robert Frost read yesterday afternoon to a packed enthusiastic hall. He's getting an honorary degree from Cambridge this spring. Ted loved him, and I feel the two of them have much in common. Well, I must gossip no longer but STUDY. I take exams at night in my dreams, alas, as well as next week. I'll do my best, but as Ted says, I have an education and the marks can't alter that.

We both send much love to you and Warren. In 32 days we'll be with you.

x x x Sivvy

WEDNESDAY A.M.
MAY 29, 1957

Dearest Mother,

I am taking time early this sunny morning to limber up my stiff fingers in preparation for my Tragedy exam this afternoon and write you so you will know I'm still extant. Just. I have honestly never undergone such physical torture as writing furiously from 6 to 7 hours a day (for the last two days) with my unpracticed pen-hand. Every night I come home and lie in a hot tub, massaging it back to action. Ted says I'm a victim of evolution and have adapted to the higher stage of typing and am at a disadvantage when forced to compete on a lower stage of handwriting!

My exams Monday (another American girl and I went with knees shaking) were quite pleasant. French translation and notes, fair and simple, and the afternoon Essay topics varied and interesting—a marked change from papers of other years.

I took "Stylization," and, I think, wrote a very clever essay ostensibly in praise of style in all its forms as a religious devotee of style, defining it as that order, line, form, and rhythm in everything from the sonnet to the whalebone corset which renders the unruly natural world into becoming bearable. I made up a fable of God as the Supreme Stylizer and the Fall, and an allegory of the history of man—a bloody pageant in search of the Ultimate Style of thought, ritual, etc., bringing in Yeats and Eliot, etc. . . . Anyway, I was elated Monday, but the exams yesterday were worse than anything I had imagined. Dating, that black terror of Americans who have no sense of the history of language, was compulsory, and it took half an hour simply to read the exam through. . . .

. . . for D. H. Lawrence I had read most of the novels and memorized passages on moral theory only to be *forbidden* to speak of his novels and requested to analyze his life *development* (a favorite word) from either his short stories or nonfiction and verse. I was so furious at this that I got back by writing on his fable, "The Man Who Died," about Jesus, under the question on fable and moral . . . All the questions bore no reference to the *moral* work of the writers, but were large, general relations to politics, law, the "thought of the century," etc. A mean, vague, fly-catching mind behind it all. As one person said to me on going out: "It took me an hour to find how I could fit what I knew into the questions." Well, I wrote on Hobbes, Lawrence, Blake and Plato with references to my reading, which has certainly been wider than any of the other people's. It's disgusting to think that two years of work and excellent, articulate, thoughtful papers should be judged on the basis of these exams and *nothing else*. I have been so wound up by the enormity of disgorging such amounts of knowledge morning and afternoon that I am just going to spend my time on the moors (after the colossal job of packing this weekend), lying in the sun, hiking and unwinding. I'll deserve it! . . .

. . . I . . . got a note from the Yale Press, saying my book had been chosen among the finalists for the publication prize, but Auden wouldn't have judged them [*it*] till some time in early summer. My heart sank as I remember his judgments on my early Smith poems [*Auden called them facile*], but I do hope my book, "Two Lovers and a Beachcomber," shows growth and would give anything to have it win; Auden would have to write a foreword to it then. . . .

x x x Sivvy

P.S. Wednesday, 6 p.m. Tragedy exam all over; *very* stimulating and fair to make up for yesterday's two horrors. Only *one* to go Friday a.m.—blessed Chaucer and a whole day (!) to study for it. Luck and love to Warren.

x x x Siv.

HEBDEN BRIDGE
YORKSHIRE, ENGLAND
SATURDAY NOON
JUNE 8, 1957

Dearest Mother,

How lovely to get your letter here at what I feel is the beginning of my new life. I am sitting comfortably ensconced in one of the great armchairs in the little living room with big picture windows overlook-

Sylvia in Yorkshire, 1956

ing a rainy landscape of green moortops and fields of cows; toasting my toes in front of the coal fire, browsing in James' short stories while Ted reads Chaucer nearby and his older sister, Olwyn, recovers by sleeping late from her trip up from Paris yesterday for a 10-day vacation. As for me, I am just beginning to feel reborn.

. . . We had not a moment of respite, and I felt as if a brand had been stamped on my head after exams . . . which prevented me from absorbing anything, but only pessimistically rewriting the exams in my mind. A very nasty young don took this opportune moment for making a devastating and absolutely destructive attack on one of my poems by showing how "hollow" it was compared to—guess who?—John Donne! Very typical of Cambridge criticism (all the other little "creative" writers were similarly dismissed, but I was singled out for particularly vicious abuse) and this coming at a time of nonwriting was especially trying.

Instead of bothering to stay around for the plethora of teas, dinners and sherries of the literary magazines and dons, we left the first day I could do so legally. I never parted from a house with more joy and feeling of good riddance . . . packing our things and knowing that we wouldn't see them again for a month but could go free to the moors. . . .

We walk for miles and meet not a soul—just larks and swallows and green, green hills and valleys. I never would have sensed the complete rest and freedom from "preparing a face to meet a face" that one must around Cambridge. Ted's mother has fixed up our room, and we read in bed and lounge about, and by the time we come home, we should be rested and raring to write and work and be happy to see people at home. Every step now is an advance. This has been in many ways the hardest drudging year of our lives. I can scarcely believe we've been married a year, come June 16. We counted days till now all through the long, dingy winter, and America looks like the Promised Land. Both of us are delighted to leave the mean, mealy-mouthed literary world of England. The only person I shall miss is my dear moralist supervisor, Doris Krook, who is as close to a genius saint as I've ever met. . . .

Only seventeen days [to their sailing date]! How incredible and wonderful it seems. We'll call you from NYC right away.

x x x Sivvy

Monday morning
June 17, 1957

Dearest Mother,

Well, your daughter has been married a year and a day, as the fairy stories say, and hopes to be married a hundred more. I can't actually remember what it was like not being married to Ted; but, as our horoscopes read, when Leo and Scorpio marry, they feel they've known each other forever in a former life.

We took yesterday off from relatives and spent it together on a shady hillside overlooking all the moors, reminiscing about our wedding day and the tough times past and good times to come. I woke to see Ted lugging into the room a huge vase of pink roses. We packed chicken and steak and books and set off.

The weather up here this past week has been exquisite; it is the one place in the world where I don't miss the sea. The air is like clear sea water, thirst-quenching and cool, and the view of spaces, unlike anything I've seen in my life—you would love it; there are magnificent walks to take. . . .

Ted's book proofs from Harper's, which we corrected up here, were elegant, so much more professional than Faber's, and their rearranged order of the poems (which Faber is not following), infinitely better. I am thrilled that the book is dedicated to me! My first dedication! I am so proud of the poems; each time I read them I get shivers. . . .

I just got my first term syllabus for my English 11 course this morning—fascinating. I can't wait to prove myself teaching. I am ashamed I haven't read half the novels on the list myself, but I'll get the ones we don't have at home and take them to the Cape this summer so that I'll have read them all and naturally pick the ones I am best in—a marvellous choice is given us.

. . . I want to get so well on in my novel that I can rewrite it during the academic [year] and have it ready for publication in the spring. I think it will be called "Falcon Yard." After many trials and errors in titles, this came to me and Ted at the same minute. It is the name of the yard where we met and thus the central episode of the book.

There is a good chance Ted may get a teaching job at Amherst the second year in America, and if I am only asked back to Smith, it would be perfect. Then we would both apply for fellowships to write for a year in Italy. Me, I hope, on my second novel by that time. By that time, I shall be 27 with enough books and money behind me to start having our projected three or four children. It is very important for us to have them later in life, in the late 20's, because both of us are slow, late maturers and must get our writing personae established well before our personalities are challenged by new arrivals. Doesn't it all sound heavenly and exciting? Work, work, that is the secret, with someone you love more than anything. . . .

. . . We loved your anniversary card, which arrived Saturday. Had a lovely tea out here with Ted's relatives and his amazing Dickensian-Falstaffian uncle (my favorite relative) who . . . gave us £50, which is a big help.

. . . See you in a week!

x x x Sivvy

PART FIVE

July 1957–October 28, 1959

Sylvia sailing into New York harbor, June 1957

Sylvia and Ted arrived in Wellesley the last week in June 1957, and were given a catered reception held in a large tent in the rear of our small house, attended by more than seventy people. Sylvia was radiant as she proudly introduced her poet husband.

A few days later her brother drove them to the Cape (their two bicycles on top of the car), to a small cottage in Eastham. Here Sylvia prepared her work for the fall semester at Smith College.

In Northampton the two found themselves again in cramped quarters in an attic apartment near the college. It was another rugged beginning. Sylvia, frustrated because teaching left her no time for writing, feared her talent would become hopelessly rusty. However, Ted's appointment in January as instructor of English and creative writing at the University of Massachusetts enabled them to chart a new and daring plan for their writing future. By keeping themselves on a strict budget, they were able to save enough to give up teaching the following June and rent a two-room apartment on Beacon Hill in Boston, planning to devote the remainder of 1958 and 1959 to writing. This decision had been a very difficult one for Sylvia, for she felt deeply indebted to such good friends as Mary Ellen Chase, Alfred Young Fisher, and Alfred Kazin, who had recommended her highly for both the Fulbright grant and the teaching post at Smith.

In Boston Sylvia and Ted set up a program of daily study and writing. In addition, Sylvia worked part-time at the Massachusetts General Hospital, writing up case histories, and audited Robert Lowell's course in poetry at Boston University. There are no letters home during this period; we were close enough to visit often, and used the telephone instead of the mails.

By spring 1959 both writers had published a number of poems and Ted was awarded a Guggenheim grant. They now planned to have a child, whom Ted wished to be English-born. Sylvia concurred in this decision; however, before leaving the United States, she wanted them both to see the country from coast to coast. So, in the summer of 1959, they borrowed my car for a cross-country camping tour. In California they would meet my husband's sister, Frieda.

On their return East they accepted an invitation to spend two months at Yaddo, Saratoga Springs, New York, a writers' colony. There they wrote daily, and many of Sylvia's poems produced in this period appeared in 1960 in her first book of poetry, The Colossus.

Before Thanksgiving, Sylvia and Ted returned to Wellesley, and in mid-December they embarked for England.

EASTHAM, MASS.
JULY 18 [?], 1957

Dearest Mother,

I have just finished the dishes and am sitting down to write the last few of my thank-you notes before turning to Virginia Woolf's next novel. I miss hearing from you, except for that brief pink note, and hope you will write us little things, gossip and all. Now that I am home and you are so near, I miss you more than I did in England, where I stoically knew you and Warren were far beyond easy commuting distance. We look forward to seeing you here a week from tomorrow. Do let us know roughly what time. . . .

The weather here has been beautiful. Ted and I are just getting into a routine, and the beginning writing is, as usual, awkward and painful. We will never get in this rusty state again, for writing is the prime condition of both our lives and our happiness. If that goes well, the sky can fall in. It is heavenly to write here: quiet, with no distractions or social duties. We try to get four hours of writing done by noon, bike to Nauset Light Beach for the afternoon of swimming and running, and read books in the evening. I shall only have to go shopping once a week, which is fine. . . .

I am a bit grumpy about not hearing [about] that poetry manuscript. By the time you get this, it will probably have come back and you will have sent it down here. It would actually be a relief to stop wavering between hope and despair and learn its fate definitely. Do send it right on if it comes; and call up, of course, if it should be accepted . . .

Both of us are getting deeply rested at last and losing the exhausting Cambridge scars. You could have done nothing more wonderful than giving us these seven weeks. . . .

Much love,
Sylvia

SUNDAY EVENING
JULY 21, 1957

Dearest Mother and Warren,

It was lovely getting the long letter yesterday. I am feeling very happy and complete now, because today, at last, at last, I began making progress writing a story I'm really deeply fascinated by, with "real" characters, a good problem-plot and deft description. After bumbling about on the first five pages of it Friday, I really got back most of my old fluency and have much richer thoughts and experience to work with. My mind (my creative mind) had been completely crammed by hour by hour exam-reading and endless practical details and concerns for the last six months. And within a week, I am in the middle of a story, with two more acting themselves out in my head, and knowing that the more I write, the better, much better, I'll be. So my dull gloom and rusty fingers and head are all gone, and all the rest of life—meals, beach, reading—becomes utter delight.

Ted has some more wonderful news: good fortune really draws more good fortune like a magnet. Imagine, the slick, austere *New Yorker* has just accepted one of his poems, "The Thought Fox," for publication in early September!!! We heard via the Harper grapevine . . . that they'd shown *The New Yorker* his poems and we should be hearing from them. Ironically enough, a year ago, we sent the same poem to *The New Yorker* and it was rejected. What reputation does! In the same mail he got the proofs of two poems and simultaneous acceptance from the *Spectator,* a witty London weekly. So we should have a steady income of small checks for the next few months—15 of his poems are scheduled to come out in August and September, no less! He is writing on some Yorkshire tales now and has done a lovely bullfrog poem and is looking tan, wonderfully rested, and enjoying my meals.

We are really unfolding and getting into our stride. I suppose a week is very little time to get adjusted in, after a year of slavery, to freedom writing, but it's seemed an age to us, and now we're happy as chipmunks, our cheeks chockful of ideas. . . .

. . . Have read three Virginia Woolf novels this week and find them excellent stimulation for my own writing. Bless you a thousand times for making this possible for us—a perfect place for reestablishing our writing. Who knows, we may earn next summer here all by ourselves this summer if we work hard enough. . . .

. . . I hope to get two stories off to the *Saturday Evening Post* by the time you come and begin on my novel after warming up.

. . . Do write more; we love to get your letters . . .

x x x Sivvy

AUGUST 6, 1957

Dear Mother,

. . . I am at last writing my first poem for about six months, a more ambitious topic: a short verse dialogue which is supposed to sound just like conversation but is written in strict 7-line stanzas, rhyming ababcbc. It frees me from my writer's cramp and is at last a good subject—a dialogue over a Ouija board, which is both dramatic and philosophical.

I really think I would like to write a verse play, now. If I practice enough on getting color into speech, I can write in quite elaborate rhymed and alliterative forms without sounding like self-conscious poetry, but rather like conversation. So I am much happier. I mailed

Sylvia and Ted at Eastham, Cape Cod, 1958

my baby-sitter (or, rather, my mother's-helper) story to the *Ladies' Home Journal* yesterday, along with a revised version of my laundromat story. Both are very light and frothy, as they say, with much funny dialogue, but the mother's-helper story is richer in many ways than the earlier one. I am as yet most pleased, however, about the one I sent off to the *Saturday Evening Post* just before you came, which is the most dramatically tight story I've ever written, starting at the peak of a crisis in the morning, with very tightly knit . . . flashbacks and four rich characters, even five, and a surprise and climax in the evening. I am really hoping to sell it somewhere as it is a central problem, yet not a trite situation. . . .

. . . Will write more later. Love to you and Warrie.

x x x Sivvy

SEPTEMBER 23, 1957

Dearest Mother,

Got your nice long letter today. Much appreciated the advice about deep breaths [*I had advised yoga breathing exercises*], etc. I ricochet between chills and fever but am working on a rather devil-may-care attitude which seems to be best for me, as I am so overconscientious. I will never be anything less than conscientious at least. My first class is on Wednesday at 3 p.m. . . . Thus, in effect, my 3 p.m. class will be a test for the next day's two morning classes, and I can revise mistakes in between. I have three office hours "by appointment" and am supposed to see all my 65 students for conferences as often as possible, which I see now will take much of my time, but I want to be very conscientious about this, too. . . .

This next week is full of meetings: oaths of allegiance, department and faculty meetings, buffet supper and president's reception next Wednesday. How I long to be busy! This brooding and isolation is something I must avoid. As soon as I am busy, with a hundred things to do, read, forms to fill out, I function very happily and efficiently. I am sure that once I get into a daily routine, I'll find that I don't have to spend all my time on class preparation and correcting papers, and it will be a relief to know we are discussing only two stories for tomorrow, say, instead of feeling, as I do now, the abstract simultaneous pressure of the term challenging me all at once. Ted is wonderful: so understanding, and cooks me breakfast and cleans up the dishes. . . .

The head of the Hampshire Bookshop, an ex-Smith woman, very

nice, sent Ted two little bottles of American champagne on his publication day, last Wednesday, and *Harper's* sent a telegram. We drank one bottle then by candlelight and will drink the other (about a glass each) when I've finished my first week of teaching on Saturday.

My first day of class is very routine. I'll introduce myself, as you say, talk about the course and assign the term's books and the week's assignments and ask them to write out a questionnaire I'll make up—about themselves, their interests, their reading, so I'll have a profile of each one to help me get to know them and to aid in filling out my own information. I'm free to tell them (and encouraged) to come around to my office just to "get acquainted," so will give my best to this, seat them alphabetically, etc. My second class day I'll begin really teaching—the most difficult book of the course—two chapters from William James. The classes are not lectures, but discussions, so I can only prepare the main points to cover and perhaps a little background material and must learn what I can draw from them. I also want to learn how to explain grammatical errors. I have an editorial eye and *know* something's wrong when I see it, but must learn the rules. . . .

Must run to my office now, where I plan to read all afternoon. Do call Wednesday evening at supper if you can get over to the Aldriches [*our good neighbors, who had unlimited phone service and invited me to do this once a week. Sylvia, however, kept me on the line so long, it was an abuse of generosity, and I had to discontinue the practice after a while*]. After six, I plan to spend the evenings at home. We are scheduled to go to NYC Sunday, October 20, for a reception and a half hour's reading for Ted. Much love. Bless me on Wednesday, Thursday, Friday, and Saturday!

Your own Sivvy

UNDATED; NOVEMBER 1957

Dearest Mother,

. . . I wish we could get to know more people outside the faculty and gradually develop an outside life. It is a rest to be away from my job, which I wasn't at all until yesterday afternoon. I find it little relaxation to have evenings with the people in the department—the specter of my questions hovers always in the background, and they don't want to talk shop any more than I do. But, of course, I can't be really frank with them or say how I begrudge not sitting and working at my real trade, writing, which would certainly improve rapidly if I gave it the nervous energy I squander on my classes . . .

Ted and I looked so longingly at the farms on the hilltops here. We would like a spreading house, with a couple of apple trees, fields, a cow, and a vegetable garden, because we can't stand city living and don't enjoy suburbs where neighbors' children and radios impinge on the air. We are really country people, and there must be a sunny hilltop place we could buy sometime in the next ten years. I like the hills in Hadley and Easthampton, on the other side of the river, very much.

I hope, as soon as my job ends this year, to apprentice myself to writing in earnest. Part-time dallying never got a beginner anywhere, and now I don't even have time for that and feel my talent rusting, and it is very painful to me.

We love this apartment and will probably stay here all summer no matter what we are doing next year.

Much love,
Sivvy

NOVEMBER 5, 1957

Dearest Warren,

I have been very wicked not to write sooner, and we loved your letters. But I've been in a black mood and haven't felt like writing anybody, because I haven't had anything particularly cheerful to share.

I've just now finished correcting a set of 66 papers on two Hawthorne stories I assigned and am faced with cramming for my preparation for this week's classes, which begin for me tomorrow. This coming weekend will be the first where I haven't had a set of papers or exams to exhaust me and put me off preparing anything much for class, so I hope I can face my problems squarely and get some idea of what the hell I'm teaching. I keep feeling I *could* make up some good stuff out of my head to teach them about symbolism or style, but have so little time as yet, and so am always deathly nervous. I must make up little brief 5-minute lectures on topics, for I am a hopeless extempore speaker. If I only *knew* my "subject" or was an expert, but I am struggling enough to review mere grammar and term paper forms, which bore me, alas. This week, too, I'm being "visited" by other professors, which is enough to throw me into a cold twitch. I wish I were more conceited, it would be a big help.

Ted's reviews are really amusing: every reviewer praises him in some way, although one or two British ones are reluctant. They are really grotesque: each seizes one or two or three poems and raves about them, passes off one or two others, but each raves about different poems. Some say he is all music but has nothing to say (a very stupid review); some say he is all profundity but has slack lines of rhythm. They are all rather batty.

. . . As you may imagine, I feel very clairvoyant. I saw all this would happen; I also saw no critic would have my omniscient appreciation, but that all would rave about the poem or poems that fitted their view: war poems, or lyric poems, or rhymed poems, or nature poems. Edwin Muir in the *New Statesman & The Nation* said Ted's Jaguar poem is better than Rilke's panther poem! How's that! Did we tell you Ted has got two new poems accepted in the *Sewanee Review?*

I sometimes wonder if I can live out the grim looming aspect of this year without despairing. I miss not cooking and keeping up the house—Ted is an angel and makes my breakfast and lunch, but I only get a chance to make a dessert on the Saturday afternoon after classes when I have one breath of freedom. I envision myself as writing in the morning and reading widely and being a writing-wife. I am simply not a career woman, and the sacrifice of energy and lifeblood I'm making for this job is all out of proportion to the good I'm doing in it. My ideal of being a good teacher, writing a book on the side, and being an entertaining homemaker, cook and wife is rapidly evaporating. I want to write first, and being kept apart from writing, from giving myself a chance to really devote myself to developing this "spectacular promise" that the literary editors write me about when they reject my stories, is really very hard.

Also, I don't like meeting only students and teachers. That is the life here, and it is, in a way, airless. Ted and I have been hashing this over and over. We need the stimulation of people, people from various jobs and backgrounds, for writing material. And I can't write about academics. We cast about for a place to live that wasn't New York and thought next year of living in Boston. Ted would get a job, not anything to do with a university, and I would write in the mornings and work part-time at odd jobs which would get me into meeting queer people and give me time to sketch and really work at writing. I would like to be anonymous for a while, not the returned and inadequate heroine of the Smith campus. There is nothing worse than going back to a place where you were a success and being miserable. But I may feel better when I get more rested. At least, I am able to sleep now and eat heartily on weekends. But this life is not the life for a writer. After I have written 20 stories and a book or two of poems, I might be able to keep up writing with work or a family, but I am needing to apprentice myself to my real trade, which I hope to do next year.

I'm really wicked to run on about my problems like this, but it helps somehow to get them talked out. Every time you make a choice you have to sacrifice something, and I am sacrificing my energy, writing and versatile intellectual life for grubbing over 66 Hawthorne papers a week and trying to be articulate in front of a rough class of spoiled bitches. If I knew *how* to teach a short story, or a novel, or a poem I'd at least have that joy. But I'm making it up as I go along, through trial and error, mostly error. And our classes are going to be visited by professors off and on from now on, so I shall probably be dismissed with a sigh of relief at the end of the year.

. . . It's easier for the men, I think, because the Smith girls respect them more, and the older women have experience and a kind of authority and expertness which carries them through. It's Ted who really saves me. He is sorry I'm so enmeshed in this and wants me to write starting this June: being writers, not established, is difficult because you don't just want to take routine jobs with no future for money, but professional jobs take too much training and sacrifice to make writing possible. . . .

How I long to write on my own again! When I'm describing Henry James' use of metaphor to make emotional states vivid and concrete, I'm dying to be making up my own metaphors. When I hear a professor saying: "Yes, the wood is shady, but it's a *green* shade—connotations of sickness, death, etc.," I feel like throwing up my books and writing my own bad poems and bad stories and living outside the neat, gray secondary air of the university. I don't like talking *about* D. H. Lawrence and about critics' views of him. I like reading him selfishly for an influence on my own life and my own writing.

Ted is working on a children's book and some poems, but I feel he'll do better when I'm through this and happy again. I can be a good writer and an intelligent wife without being a good teacher. But the ironic thing about teaching like this is that I don't have time to be intelligent in a fluid, versatile way. I'm too nose-to-the-grindstone. The girls know I'm new at teaching and young and probably much more, and they take advantage of it, which they wouldn't if I were really good. *Eh bien.*

Do write me soon. I love to hear from you. So does Ted. Forgive this rather drear letter. Unlike mother, I am a writer, not a teacher, and must work at my trade in order to be worthy of the name.

x x x Sivvy

Dear Warren,

. . . I have heard unofficially that I will probably be asked back for next year and would have "good chances of promotion," but have chosen to get out while the getting's good. I see too well the security and prestige of academic life, but it is Death to writing. Vacations, as I'm finding out, are an illusion, and you must spend summers preparing new courses, etc. Writing is obviously my Vocation, which I am finding out the hard way, but Ted and I are fermenting good plans for this June 1, hoping to rent a little apartment on the slummy side of Beacon Hill, which we love, and work, me part time and Ted full time, at unresponsible, unhomeworked jobs (for money, bread and experience with unacademic people) and write for a solid year, then try for a grant to Italy on the basis of a year's manuscripts. Such vision keeps me going. Had a fine time recording at Steven Fassett's studios on Beacon Hill where all the poets record for Harvard . . .

I love that part of town and can't wait to find a place there, become unacademic, anonymous, and write. . . .

Grampy was dear and loaned Ted a watch till Christmas as Ted's trying to set up a radio station for a couple of hours in Amherst for the WHMP station manager: just a gamble at a part-time job which might make him feel better. He needs to see people and work some, as I do, but Northampton isn't a good place at all for the kind of queer, offbeat, interesting job he'd like, so we tried this, instead of selling in shoestores. If he can get sponsors, he will get a wage. Ted has, by the way, fractured his fifth metatarsal in his right foot to complicate matters—he did it by jumping out of an armchair while his foot was asleep!

. . . I want to finish my poetry book this summer, write a series of short stories and begin a novel, without anything such as a teaching job and preparation hanging over my head; so mother will teach me to use a dictating machine and I'll hire out at part-time jobs to give my life variety and contact with people, which every writer, or most, need as a balance to complete solitude at the typewriter.

Mother, Ted, and I had a really hysterical evening and dinner with Mrs. Prouty last night. She's obsessed with Ted, as she was with you, and really plays up to him, calling him handsome, trying to get him on TV, etc. She has an "ant farm," which she watches constantly, and it's very strange and absorbing. Must close now.

Much love,
Sivvy

Dearest Mother,

This letter should by now greet you at Dotty's, and how happy I am to know you'll be out of the hospital [*another operation*] today and on the road to recovery. It was wonderful getting your cheery letter and hearing about your rapid improvement. Our family must really be pretty tough and resilient. You've been through so much hospital treatment and are coming out better than ever! . . .

. . . somehow, I've felt more philosophical this last week in spite of my deep exhaustion. The year doesn't look quite endless. I also got a rather grim satisfaction that those 700 pages of papers didn't floor me . . . Too, I am taking things which would earlier have floored me—occasional sassiness, poor preparation for class by some girls, difficult office-hour conferences—more in my stride. I had a hard problem with a very nasty case of plagiarism in my last set of papers, so obvious as to be impossible as "a mistake," and had to send the girl to Honor Board. She is a very shifty character and wavering between a D plus and C minus, not preparing for class discussions and, unfortunately, just the sort who'd do something like this. She claimed it was all a mistake, she just "didn't know how it happened," and I probably got much sicker over it than she did. But I sent her to Honor Board.

Although it is extremely painful for me not to write, knowing how even more painful it will be when I start to write in June, I've decided to make the best of a bad job and make them sorry to lose me. I have had several teachers say to me they've "heard" from students and visiting teachers to my classes that I'm a "brilliant teacher," so in spite of my obvious faults, I can't be bad. One thing, I'm hardly ever dull, and since it's my first year, I think I'm doing about all I could ask of my ignorant self. I'm getting a little more realistic about it. If I can just get my preparation done a week ahead, instead of this last-minute rush, I'll feel even better.

Ted, at last, is writing wonderful poems again. He's gone through a dry spell and been unhappy with his bad luck about his leg, his missing driving lessons, his not being able to get a job (there's no work there at all, really!), and his feeling of isolation. Now, after Thanksgiving vacation (which seemed to break the jinx of depression on us and get us rested and refreshed, thanks to your luxurious treatment), he's just turned out six beautiful poems, which give me at least a vicarious pleasure, and a delightful short fairy story.

I am so lucky to be married to Ted: we read poems aloud and

discuss people and magic and everything, always interested and happy when not tired. If only we can get into our stride, our own writing life, then no weariness or worry will get at the deep part of us. I feel terribly vulnerable and "not-myself" when I'm not writing and now know I can never combine teaching and writing, nor can Ted. So, only six more months!

Evidently I'm not alone in feeling exhausted about teaching! It seems to take much more out of the women than out of the men. Probably the men get a certain physical satisfaction out of teaching the opposite sex. Some of the old-maid women teachers treat the girls like daughters, but they all get tired. Marie Boroff . . . said she felt "great psychic exhaustion" with her two jobs, and that there was absolutely not energy left after a teaching day for creative work. Old Miss Williams, another teacher, told me the same thing yesterday about her exhaustion after office hours. These people, however, can bear the tiredness because teaching is their Vocation, but it's not mine, even though I could be a good one if I had the scholarship and inclination to work with other writers' work and not produce my own. But it relieves me to think that even the seasoned ones have the same problems I do, doubts, etc. . . . .

I must close now, so want to say how happy we'll be to see you in only two weeks. We are eating royally and are caught up on sleep. So don't you worry.

Much, much love also to grampy, Dot and Joe, and Bobby and Nancy.

Love,
Your own Sivvy

Sylvia and Ted arrived in Wellesley five days ahead of schedule; I had just returned home from a week's convalescence at my sister's house. Ted was still limping badly, having but recently recovered from the broken bone in his foot. Sylvia was rosy—we thought from the cold wind—and evidently delighted to be home.

After a few minutes' conversation, however, I realized this early arrival had a purpose behind it other than just our mutual pleasure. I placed my hand on Sylvia's forehead in the old maternal gesture; it was burning hot, so I took her temperature. (No protest on her part, which was unusual.) It was well over 102°, and Ted admitted that she had been feeling poorly for several days to the point where he had become very concerned about her condition. I immediately called our family physician and had Sylvia in bed before the doctor arrived. It was viral pneumonia plus physical exhaustion, and he started her on antibiotics.

Despite all our physical disabilities, by Christmas Eve a little tree was trimmed, and we enjoyed a quiet celebration and the comfort of being together.

MONDAY NIGHT
JANUARY 13, 1958

Dearest Mother,

I suppose the two of us have had rather rough weeks. I managed my full amount of classes and a faculty meeting last week, but it really took a lot of energy out of me as I had no reserve of voltage to spare. Also, I had to prepare my work for the next day every night, so by the time Saturday came, I was really beat. But we slept till noon on Sunday, which was a lovely, icy blue day, and went for a 5-mile walk which cheered us no end. I am still inclined to be rather depressed, a kind of backwash of convalescence from the pneumonia, I guess, but should have a chance to rest up after this week while preparing for the second semester before the exams come in. . . .

I recently had a two-hour talk with one of my worst problem children, a girl who refused to talk in class and objected to being called on. She came in prepared to be very much on the defensive (she would whisper in class and make fun of other girls), but we got along immediately. I was very proud of my psychology, and I think she left feeling excellently treated, although I told her several unpleasant things, such as that she had chosen to get an E in classwork and that I'd like her to move into another section. Selfishly, I just wanted to get rid of her as she distracted the other girls, but I made a completely different point of it. We had also a good talk on religion and the course books, and I felt, ironically enough, that she was a kindred spirit of sorts. She wanted, ironically also, to stay in my class, but I managed to get around that, too.

I do feel I am building up a pretty good relation with most of my students and am feeling some rather well-placed conceit as one of the more favored of the freshman English teachers. They are really *good* girls. . . .

Do drop us a line when you can. Keep well and don't take on any extra work too soon.

x x x sivvy

Dearest Mother,

. . . Ted hasn't heard yet whether he'll be teaching half time or full time. We rather hope it's full time now. His classes begin in ten days, so I hope we'll find out soon. One of his scheduled books is *Crime and Punishment,* and I've just finished two weeks of lectures on it, so he can use my notes. Very convenient . . .

Saturday night we drove over to meet some people on the University of Massachusetts faculty. Very different people. Somehow pathetic, wistful, or just pedantic and cranky. At least Ted was relieved, and the prospect of work doesn't worry him now, as these people are hardly genii . . . Anyhow, he has some really good books to teach and the recommendation will be very helpful in teaching jobs in Europe.

. . . Halfway through! And my whole attitude to teaching is changed. Simply knowing that I'm leaving in June has freed me to enjoy it and have a casual attitude, which is evidently catching in a good way. My three o'clock class, in particular, is more enjoyable, and I have a good feeling of general class sympathy, with the exception, of course, of a few bored or stubborn ones. If I can just get ahead of myself in preparation, things should ease up. But how I long to get at writing. To break into the pain of beginning again and get over the hump into something rich—my old life of poems and stories and articles, so once again I can look for the mails with some reason for eagerness.

Perhaps Monday, March 31, and Tuesday, April 1, Ted and I can come down to look at houses or apartments on Beacon Hill. We could move in on the first of June, I think, or the first of July, if necessary . . . We want to know Boston like the back of our hand before we're through.

. . . Do write.

Much love,
Sivvy

Dear Warren,

. . . I have received a letter from a New York magazine, *Art News,* offering me from $50 to $75 for a poem on a work of art, so I'm hoping to go to the Art Museum and meditate on Gauguin and Rousseau and produce something this week—it's so tantalizing to have the outright assignment, I just hope I'm not all dried up . . .

xxxS.

{Written on Smith College memorandum paper}

DATE: MARCH 22, 1958
From: Sivvy

To: Mother

Just a note to say that I have at last burst into a spell of writing. I was rather stunned Thursday morning, my first real day off after a week of correcting 70 papers, averaging midterm grades and writing a report on another senior thesis, but I had about seven or eight paintings and etchings I wanted to write on as poem-subjects and bang! After the first one, "Virgin in a Tree," after an early etching by Paul Klee, I ripped into another, probably the biggest and best poem I've ever written, on a magnificent etching by Klee titled "Perseus, or the Triumph of Wit over Suffering." A total of about 90 lines written in one day.

Friday went just as well: with a little lyric fantasy on a lovely painting by Klee on the comic opera *The Seafarer,* a long and big one on his painting "The Departure of the Ghost," and a little lyric on a cat with a bird-stigma between its eyebrows, a really mammoth magic cat-head. These are easily the best poems I've written and open up new material and a new voice. I've discovered my deepest source of inspiration, which is art: the art of primitives like Henri Rousseau, Gauguin, Paul Klee, and De Chirico. I have got out piles of wonderful books from the Art Library (suggested by this fine Modern Art Course I'm auditing each week) and am overflowing with ideas and inspirations, as if I've been bottling up a geyser for a year. Once I start writing, it comes and comes.

I am enclosing two of the poems . . . sending the two poems on the etchings to the sumptuous illustrated magazine, *Art News,* which asked me to write one or several poems for their series of poems on art . . .

Today I had a reaction, feeling miserable and exhausted with my period and drugging myself to a stupor with aspirin for lack of anything stronger. But after chicken broth, I revived and am looking forward to writing another 90 lines tomorrow. If I can write, I don't care what happens. I feel like an idiot who has been obediently digging up pieces of coal in an immense mine and has just realized that there is no need to do this, but that one can fly all day and night on great wings in clear blue air through brightly colored magic and weird worlds. Even used the dregs of my inspiration to write about six of those Dole Pineapple Jingles! We could use a car, or $5, or $15,000!

Hope you like these little poems.

Love,
Sivvy

BATTLE-SCENE FROM THE COMIC OPERATIC FANTASY
The Seafarer

It beguiles—
This little Odyssey
In pink and lavender
Over a surface of gently
Graded turquoise tiles
That represent a sea
With chequered waves and gaily
Bear up the seafarer
Gaily, gaily
In his pink plume and armor.

A fairy tale
Gondola of paper
Ferries the fishpond Sinbad
Who poises his pastel spear
Toward three pinky-purple
Monsters which uprear
Off the ocean floor
With fanged and dreadful head.
Beware, beware
The whale, the shark, the squid.

But fins and scales
Of each scrolled sea-beast
Troll no slime, no weed.
They are polished for the joust,
They gleam like Easter-eggshells,
Rose and amethyst.
Ahab, fulfill your boast:
Bring home each storied head.
One thrust, one thrust,
One thrust: and they are dead.

So fables go.
And so all children sing
Their bathtub battles deep,
Hazardous and long,
But oh, sage grownups know

Sea-dragon for sofa, fang
For pasteboard, and siren-song
For fever in a sleep.
Laughing, laughing
Of greybeards wakes us up.

DEPARTURE OF THE GHOST
(After Paul Klee)

Enter the chilly no-man's land of precisely
Five o'clock in the morning, the no-color void
Where the waking head rubbishes out the draggled lot
Of sulphurous dreamscapes and obscure lunar conundrums
Which seemed, when dreamed, to mean so profoundly much,

Gets ready to face the ready-made creation
Of chairs and bureaus and sleep-twisted sheets.
This is the kingdom of the fading apparition,
The oracular ghost who dwindles on pin-legs
To a knot of laundry, with a classic bunch of sheets

Upraised, as a hand, emblematic of farewell.
At this joint between two worlds and two entirely
Incompatible modes of time, the raw material
Of our meat-and-potato thoughts assumes the nimbus
Of ambrosial revelation. And so departs.

But as chair and bureau are the hieroglyphs
Of some godly utterance wakened heads ignore,
So these posed sheets, before they thin to nothing,
Speak in sign language of a lost otherworld,
A world we lose by merely waking up

Into sanity: the common ghost's crowed out,
Worms riddling its tongue, or walks for Hamlet
All day on the printed page, or bodies itself
For dowagers in drafty castles at twelve,
Or inhabits the crystal of the sick man's eye—

Trailing its telltale tatters only at the outermost
Fringe of mundane vision. But this ghost goes,
Hand aloft, goodbye, goodbye, not down
Into the rocky gizzard of the earth,
But toward the point where our thick atmosphere

Diminishes, and god knows what is there:
A point of exclamation marks that sky
In ringing orange like a stellar carrot;
Its round period, displaced and green,
Suspends beside it the first point, the starting

Point of Eden, next the new moon's curve.
Go, ghost of our mother and father, ghost of us,
And ghost of our dreams' children, in those sheets
Which signify our origin and end,
To the cloud-cuckoo land of color wheels

And pristine alphabets and cows that moo
And moo as they jump over moons as new
As that crisp cusp toward which you voyage now.
Hail and farewell. Hello, goodbye. O keeper
Of the profane grail, the dreaming skull.

APRIL 22, 1958

Dearest Warren,

. . . In spite of the appalling weather, Ted had a loyal audience
[*for a poetry reading at Harvard University*]—among them . . . dear
Mrs. Prouty (who said in loud, clear tones: "Isn't Ted *wonderful!*"). He
was—a very good hour of poems, old and new—talk in between.

I met the young poet Philip Booth (who just received a Guggen-
heim), and we had a lovely dinner at Felicia's Café near Hanover (?)
Street with Jack Sweeney (whom we dearly love—he remembers your
A's in some humanities course) and his lovely Irish wife and (at last)
Adrienne Cecile Rich and her husband (she's the girl whose poetry
I've followed from her first publication). The excitement tolled the
end of my cold, and I feel much better . . .

Do try to look up Ted's beautiful, blonde sister in Paris. She is
golden-eyed, golden-haired and very delicate and tall as I am—looks
about 18, although 28. She works for NATO . . .

Love,
Sivvy

TUESDAY
JUNE 10, 1958

Dearest Mother,

. . . We were very tired but managed an amazing lot of fun, meetings, and walking for miles in our five days [*in New York*]. We just
caught Ted's two publishers before they sailed and had a posh pink-
table-clothed dinner with them at the Biltmore. . . . Went to two
parties . . . one, a rich Fifth Avenue party where we rode up in the
elevator with Lionel and Diana Trilling. The place was full of publishers, editors and Columbia professors; the novelist Ralph Ellison;

old Farrar of Farrar, Straus, Cudahy; the editor of the *Hudson Review*, and suchlike. Then a late and sumptuous buffet at the home of Hy Sobiloff, owner of Sloane's Fifth Avenue Furniture Store, and very dull, wealthy business people, but a fine negro cook whose food and artistry in table arrangement of cakes, strawberries and melons we praised to her pleasure. . . .

I didn't tell anybody, but I thought you'd be amused at the coincidence that dogs my steps: coming down in the subway afterwards, I almost ran into Dick Wertz, Nancy Hunter's old flame, who was at Cambridge when I was and is marrying a Smith girl from my class who is teaching with me this year. I was about to speak to him, as his back was turned to me, when, talking to him, I saw Richard Sassoon. I kept quiet and passed by and probably only I of all the five people knew about it. Of all the people in NYC!

We walked miles, lunched with our editor friend at World Publishing Company, and they are still interested in seeing my poetry book as it is early this fall. We strolled through Central Park, Harlem, Fifth Avenue and took Ted up to the top of the Empire State Building and had my fortune told by a subway gypsy whose card, ironically enough, showed a picture of a mailman and said I'd get a wonderful letter soon that would change my life for the better.

We saw the Bowery "bums" and the Harlem negroes and the Fifth Avenue tycoons, and, best of all, Marianne Moore, who was lovely at her home in Brooklyn and admires Ted very much and served us strawberries, sesame-seed biscuits and milk and talked a blue streak. Can we reserve tickets and take you to see her this Sunday? Our last night after Marianne Moore was lovely, too: two experimental Ionesco plays and a good dinner in the Village.

We hope to come home for supper Thursday. My reading-recording is Friday afternoon, and we'll go to dinner with Jack Sweeney that night. Mrs. Prouty has asked us (Ted and me) for dinner Sunday noon, but I thought maybe you and grampy and Ted and I could have a special dinner Monday the 16th to celebrate our second anniversary. How about it? And then we must return to Hamp and get to work . . .

Much love,
Sivvy

Dearest Warren,

. . . I realize, as I start to write, how many letters I've written you in my head and how much I've missed you. There are so very few people in the world I really care about, and I guess you and Ted are the closest of all. Perhaps we can go for picnic and swim at the Cape to celebrate your return. I want so much, over the course of the next year, when I hope we'll be very close and you coming over to dinner often (we're going to look for a Boston apartment this weekend) and visiting us much, to hear, bit by bit, about your ideas and experiences in Europe and of your work at Harvard. You know I've always had a secret desire to go to Harvard, and the next best thing is your going. I have that horrid habit mothers get of being secretly determined all my sons will go to Harvard.

I finished teaching on May 22 and felt honestly sorry to say goodbye to my girls. I was amused at my last day of classes to get applause in the exact volume of my own feelings toward every class: a spatter at 9, a thunderous ovation at 11 which saw me down two flights of stairs, and a medium burst at 3. Now that it is over, I can't believe I've taught 20 stories, 2 novels, 10 plays, and countless poems, including *The Waste Land*. But I have. And I've done more than I thought or hoped for those first black weeks of teaching which upset me very much: I think I have chosen excellent works, won over my most difficult pupils and taught them a good deal.

On the whole, my colleagues have depressed me: it is disillusioning to find the people you admired as a student are weak and jealous and petty and vain as people, which many of them are. And the faculty gossip, especially among the men, over morning coffee, afternoon tea, and evening cocktails is very boring: all about the latest gossip, possible appointments, firings, grants, students, literary criticism—all secondary, it seems—an airtight, secure community, with those on tenure getting pot-bellies. Writers especially are suspect if they don't place academic life first, and we have seen one or two of our writing acquaintances given very raw and nasty deals. Of course, we have been at an advantage, both having resigned in face of requests to stay. But it has been impossible for either of us to get any work done, and we feel that if we drifted into this well-paid security, we would curse ourselves in ten years' time for what might have been.

I am sure, for example, that Ted has the makings of a great poet, and he already has some loyal supporters like Marianne Moore and T. S. Eliot, whom we hope to see when we go to England. Ted is better than any poet I can think of ten years his senior, and I feel as a wife the best I can do is demand nothing but that we find workable schemes whereby we both can write and live lives which are dictated by inner needs for creative expansion and experience.

Of course, there are very few people who can understand this. There is something suspect, especially in America, about people who don't have ten-year plans for a career or at least a regular job. We found this out when trying to establish credit at a local general store. We fitted, amusingly enough, into none of the form categories of "The Young American Couple"; I had a job, Ted didn't; we owned no car, were buying no furniture on the installment plan, had no TV, had no charge accounts, came as if literally dropped from foreign parts. The poor secretary was very perplexed. Anyhow, I can talk to you freely about our plans, if not to mother. She worries so that the most we can do is put up an illusion of security—security to us is in ourselves, and no job, or even money, can give us what we have to develop: faith in our work, and hard hard work which is Spartan in many ways. Ted is especially good for me because he doesn't demand Immediate Success and Publication and is training me not to. We feel the next five years are as important to our writing as medical school is to a prospective surgeon. Ted says simply to produce, work, produce, read not novels or poems only, but books on folklore, fiddler crabs and meteorites—this is what the imagination thrives on. The horror of the academic writer is that he lives on air and other people's second-hand accounts of other people's writing . . .

Well, you see what I mean: the writer is cut off from life and begins to *think* as he analyzes stories in class—very differently from the way a writer *feels* reality, which, according to many teachers, is too simple as such and needs symbols, irony, archetypal images and all that. Well, we will try to get along without such conscious and contrived machinery. We write and wake up with symbols on our pages, but do not begin with them. . . .

Ted and I left for New York City immediately after my last papers . . . Oscar Williams was a queer, birdlike little man, obviously very at-odds since his best friend, Dylan Thomas, and his beloved poet-painter wife, Gene Derwood, died in the same year. He lives in a tiny rooftop studio painted light blue, with a skylight, covered with oil paintings by his wife, bright-colored animals and portraits, photographs of his dead loves, brick homemade bookcases full of poetry books, tables, floors and bathtub covered and full of unwashed glasses, and a fine little tar-roof porch overlooking the gulls and boats and ringed with potted rosebushes and mint plants. He served us Drambuie and we got along well. . . .

. . . We also visited Babette Deutsch, a . . . poet and critic, who is married to the Russian scholar Avrahm Yarmolinsky; she'd written in admiration of Ted's poems. And lunched with Dave Keightley, [a] friend of ours . . . his publishing company editors, World Pub., are interested in seeing a manuscript of my poetry book (now provisionally titled "Full Fathom Five") this fall. They've never published poetry before, but are interested in "genuine fresh talent," which I hope I have. I've been changing, I think much for the better, in my writing style. Ironically, of the 35 or so poems I've published in my career, I've rejected about 20 of these from my book manuscript as too romantic, sentimental and frivolous and immature. My main difficulty has been overcoming a clever, too brittle and glossy feminine tone, and I am gradually getting to speak "straight out" and of real experience, not just in metaphorical conceits. I'll enclose a recent poem which I hope you may like . . .

One thing which we haven't told mother for obvious reasons is that Ted applied for a Saxton writing fellowship for this year, and we were sure of getting it for him as Marianne Moore, et al., volunteered to write, and he had a magnificent project for a poetry book. It was the only fellowship, as a Briton, he was eligible for. Ironically, we learned this week that the fellowship is run by trustees from Harper's and as he is published by them, his project can't be considered on merit; if it had been so considered, he obviously would have got a grant. So, with supreme and rather distressing irony, the very qualification of his worth, publishing a book, is his one flaw, rendering him ineligible. So I shall apply for the same grant (don't tell mother about this either), and Ted will apply for a Guggenheim for next year . . .

God feeds the ravens. I hope you understand this better than mother does. When we are both wealthy and famous, our work will justify our lives, but now our lives and faith must justify themselves. We live very simply and happily and walk each day in Our Park, which is next door and which no one else frequents. There are several brown rabbits, two magnificent black frogs who swim like suave purple-bellied Martians and return our stares for hours, innumerable squirrels, bright yellow birds, red-headed woodpeckers and fruit trees and a garden which is mysteriously replanted as the flowers die: first tulips and daffodils, then hyacinths; then one day we came back to find these gone and beds of geraniums and white petunias in their place. The little rose garden is just coming out, and about once a week we make off with a red or yellow rose.

We met the mad and very nice poet Robert Lowell (the only one, 40-ish, whom we both admire, who comes from the Boston Lowells and is periodically carted off as a manic depressive) when he came to give a reading at the University of Massachusetts. He is quiet, soft-spoken, and we liked him very much. I drove him around Northampton, looking for relics of his ancestors, and to the Historical Society and the graveyard. We hope to see him in Boston when we move down . . .

Ted and I plan to celebrate our second anniversary at home with mother this Monday, June 16. It seems impossible I've been married for two whole years, and much more impossible that I ever *wasn't* married to Ted! Oh, we have rousing battles every so often in which I come out with sprained thumbs and Ted with missing earlobes, but we feel so perfectly at one with our work and reactions to life and people that we make our own world to work in, which isn't dependent on anyone else's love or admiration, but self-contained. Our best pleasure is writing at home, eating and talking and walking in woods to look for animals and birds. Money would be very helpful, but we have everything except this . . .

Well, I must close now, or I will be typing into tomorrow and next week. Here is a poem ["*Mussel-Hunter at Rock Harbor*"] I made about the fiddler crabs we found at Rock Harbor when we went to get mussels last summer for fish bait. I hope you like it. If you find anything inaccurate about the crabs, do tell me about it. Read it aloud for the sounds of it. This is written in what's known as "syllabic verse," measuring lines not by heavy and light stresses, but by the *number* of syllables, which here is 7. I find this form satisfactorily strict (a pattern varying the number of syllables in each line can be set up, as M. Moore does it) and yet it has a speaking illusion of freedom (which the measured stress doesn't have) as stresses vary freely. Don't follow my example. Write soon! And I promise to answer.

Much love—
Sivvy

To: You   DATE: JUNE 25, 1958
IN RE: ODDS AND ENDS   FROM: Me

. . . VERY GOOD NEWS: In the mail I just got my FIRST acceptance from *The New Yorker!* And not of a short little poem but of
two very fat and amazingly long ones: "Mussel-Hunter at Rock Harbor" and "Nocturne," [*published in* The New Yorker *under the title
"Night Walk," this appeared in* The Colossus *as "Hardcastle Crags"*]
the first 91 lines; the last, 45 lines! In our materialistic way, Ted and I
figured, amid much jumping up and down, this should mean close to
$350, or three full months of Boston rent! For two poems! They wrote
a glowing letter, very generous for *The New Yorker.* . . .

How's that for a good beginning to a summer of work! You see
what happens the minute one worships one's own god of vocation
and doesn't slight it for grubbing under the illusion of duty to Everybody's-Way-Of-Life! This is well over three times as much money as
I got for half a year of drudgery in correcting exams for the professor
of that American Lit. course and well over a month's salary for a
week's work of pure joy. "The Mussel-Hunters" may not come out
till next summer, as they're very crowded with summer poems, but I
should get the check in a few days. What a nice anniversary gift for
our coming to America!

                                                    x x x Sivvy

You see—the gypsy fortune teller with her card depicting the mailman was very right!

To: You   DATE: JULY 5, 1958
IN RE: BITS & PIECES   FROM: Me

. . . I am becoming more and more desirous of being an amateur
naturalist. Do you remember if we have any little books on recogniz-
ing wild flowers, birds, or animals in Northern America? I am reading
some Penguin books about "Man and the Vertebrates" and "The
Personality of Animals" and also the delightful book *The Sea Around
Us,* by Rachel Carson. Ted's reading her *Under the Sea Wind,* which
he says is also fine. Do read these if you haven't already; they are
poetically written and magnificently informative. I am going back to
the ocean as my poetic heritage and hope to revisit all the places I

remember in Winthrop with Ted this summer; Johnson Avenue, a certain meadow on it, our beach and grammy's. Even rundown as it now is, the town has the exciting appeal of my childhood, and I am writing some good poems about it, I think. I'll enclose that poem "Night-Walk," the other one *The New Yorker* accepted, which I think you've read. . . . In the years of our marriage, writing only a total of a few weeks, Ted and I have made about $2,000 (not counting *The New Yorker* money, which we are beginning our third year with).

We did our Ouija board for the first time in America, and it was magnificent fun—responsive, humorous, and very helpful. It seems to have grown up and claims it is quite happy in America, that it likes "life in freedom," that it uses its freedom for "making poems," that poetry is made better by "practice." Thinking we might make use of it, we asked him (*Pan* is his signature) for poem subjects (this is always the problem: a good poem needs a good "deep" subject). Pan told me to write about "Lorelei." When asked, "Why the Lorelei," he said they were my "own kin." I was quite amazed. This had never occurred to me consciously as a subject, and it seemed a good one: the Germanic legend background, the water images, the death-wish, and so on. So the next day I began a poem about them, and Pan was right; it is one of my favorites. What is that lovely song you used to play on the piano and sing to us about the Lorelei? . . .

I hope Warren will be agreeable to exchanging a dinner at our place about once a week for an hour or two of German reading out loud. I am painfully beginning to review my German again by reading one by one the Grimm's Fairy Tales in that handsome book you gave me, which I just love, and making vocabulary lists from each tale, trying to review one grammar lesson a day. I suppose as one grows older one has a desire to learn all about one's roots, family, and country. I feel extremely moved by memories of my Austrian and German background and also my ocean-childhood, which is probably the foundation of my consciousness . . .

The Ouija board also told Ted to write about "Otters," so he is doing so, and the beginnings sound quite good. Pan claims his family god, "kolossus," tells him much of his information. . . .

Well, that's all the news for now. Try to get to the Aldriches next week and call us again. I get up about seven each morning now as it's cooler . . . Ted also sends love—

Sylvia

JULY 9, 1958

Dear Warren,

. . . I haven't been out in the sun at all this summer—the first time in my life I'm not tan, but have been working hard at poems for my book. I've discarded all that I wrote before two years ago and am tempted to publish a book of juvenilia under a pseudonym as about 20 published poems have been ditched. I hope to get my poetry book together in early September or October and send it the round of publishers this winter. It should be a good collection. I feel I've got rid of most of my old rigidity and glassy glossiness and am well on the way to writing about the real world, its animals, people, and scenery.

Ted and I are recovering from a sad and traumatic experience. We picked up a baby bird that looked in its last death throes, fallen from a tree, and brought it home. We had it for a week, feeding it raw ground steak, worms, milk (probably a very bad diet), and got enormously fond of the plucky little thing, which looked like a baby starling, with funny furry eyebrows. But when it ran, it fell, and looked to be badly injured. Its leg stiffened then (its pelvis must have been broken, or something), and it sickened, choking and pathetically chirping. We couldn't sleep or write for days, nursing it and hunting vainly for worms, identifying with it until it became gruesome. Finally, we figured it would be [a] mercy to put it out of its misery, so we gassed it in a little box. It went to sleep very quietly. But it was a shattering experience. Such a plucky little bit of bird. I can't forget it . . .

x x x Sivvy

{Written on Smith College memorandum paper.}

To: Mummy
In re: ODDS & ENDS

DATE: AUGUST 1, 1958
From: Sivvy

. . . I have thought much and wouldn't have Ted change his citizenship for the world. It is part of his identity, I feel, and will always be so.

I've thought very carefully about that Stenotype folder . . . I would be only interested in learning how to Stenotype if I could learn *very* quickly and start work this winter so it would do me some good. Thus I'd be interested in hearing about the hours, practice time, and span of learning needed for the daily course. Perhaps you could find out these things for me. I would enjoy having a practical skill that would take me into jobs "above average" or "queer," not just business routine. My appearance and education should help me if I had the practical skill. BUT if I *should* get this Saxton grant for writing, I would have to give up the idea. I probably won't get the grant (which would pay for ten months' writing) and thus would like to have the facts about Stenotyping lined up. How heavy is the machine? Is the roll of tape expensive? I particularly want to get into *court reporting.* That's what I'd like to work for. Would I need any other kind of experience? Would I be hired over people with shorthand? Could you investigate this? The two main things: how long to learn the fastest way? Could I get into court reporting and other jobs equivalently interesting? [*A mutual friend helped Sylvia by lending her Speedwriting books, which Sylvia mastered on her own. She made use of that skill along with her fast, accurate typing by working periodically throughout 1958–59 at the Massachusetts General Hospital, writing up case histories of patients.*]

Love, Sivvy

The following is from a page of my diary, Sunday, August 3, 1958. Ted, Sylvia, and I had visited the home of Ruth Freeman Geissler (Sylvia had been maid of honor at Ruth's wedding in 1955).

We visited Ruth on Thursday. She had come home with her five-day-old son, a wee, red-faced infant. Her two daughters were entrancing, especially the lively two-year-old, who immediately captured Ted, enslaving him for the duration of our visit.

I thought the golden, curly-haired one-year-old, a Cover-Girl baby, would attract Sivvy most; but, no, it was the newest one, the wizened little boy (believe I felt Ted withdraw from him—a very young baby can be so raw and weird looking). Sylvia, however, opened the curled hand and stretched out the exquisitely finished little fingers; examined the wrinkled petal of a foot—each toe a dot, yet complete with a speck of pearly nail—the whole foot shorter than the length of her little finger. There was such warmth, such yearning in Sivvy's face, my heart ached for her. I'd love to be a fairy godmother, to wave a wand and say, "Here, my darling, is a little house; here is a good woman to help you each morning. Now have your baby; spend your mornings writing, then belong to your family the rest of the time."

In early July 1959 Ted and Sylvia set out on the cross-country tour.

Dear Mother and Warren,

. . . At the blue moonlit hour of quarter of three, I was wakened
from a dream where the car blew to pieces with a great rending crash
[and] by a *very* similar crash and falling jangle. My immediate
thought was that a bear had with one cuff demolished the car and was
eating the engine out. I woke Ted and we lay for a few moments,
listening to the unique sounds of a bear rooting through our belong-
ings. Grunts, snuffles, clattering can lids. We thought he might have
somehow broken off the trunk door and got into our tinned supplies,
divining food by a seventh sense. Then there was a bumpity, falling
noise as the bear bowled a tin past our tent, and I sat up quaking to
peer out the tent screen.

There in the blue weird light of the moon, not 10 feet away, a huge,
dark bear-shape hunched, guzzling at a tin. I found in the morning
that it was the black-and-gilt figured cookie tin we took the date-nut
bars in; it had been in the back seat of the car in my red bag, shut,
full of Ritz crackers and Hydrox cookies, and some postcards. The
bear must have lifted out the bag after smashing the window, rolled
the can about till the lid came off, undone the wax paper and eaten
every last crumb. I found the postcards the next day, lying among the
rubble, the top card of moose antlers turned down and *face-up* the
card of a large bear with an actual bear paw-print on it.

We lay there for what seemed years, wondering if the bear would
eat us, since it found our crackers so interesting. Just as we were
relaxing and felt the dawn starting to lighten, we heard a heavy
shuffling tread. The bear, back from its rounds, had returned to the
car. Ted stood up to look out the back window—it was all I could do
to keep him from going out before to check on the damage—and
reported that the bear was at the back of the car, halfway in the left
rear window. It had discovered our oranges. From then until sunup,
we lay listening to the bear squeeze the oranges open and slurp up the
juice. It was interrupted only by a car which drove by and scared the
bear to run toward the front door of our tent. It tripped on the guy
ropes anchoring our porch and for a moment the whole tent shook so
we thought it had decided to come in. Then there was a long silence.
Then more orange-squeezing. We got up, rather shaken. The car window had been shattered to the root, and wiry brown bear hairs stuck
all along the edge of it.

Amazingly, the story got around camp. An old regular came up to advise us that bears hated kerosene and to smear all our window frames with that. Another said bears hated red pepper. Well, we felt we had the daylight hours to build a fortress against our enemy, who would indubitably return. So we moved some sites up, which cheered us. Then we packed everything of value and all food in the trunk. We reported the accident to the ranger, who recorded it, so it's there if the insurance people need it, and he was very noncommittal.

I mentioned the incident to a woman up early in the lavatory, and she seemed very disquieted by my report of the broken window. It turned out she had just moved from West Thumb, another camp, where a woman had been killed by a bear Sunday, the night we came. That woman, hearing the bear at her food at night, had gone out with a flashlight to shoo it away, and it turned on her and downed her with one vicious cuff. Naturally, the story was hushed up by the rangers, but this woman who had been "sleeping under the stars" with her husband felt concerned, especially since a bear growled them into flight when they hesitated about sharing their breakfast with it.

Well, this story put proper concern into us, too. By twilight we had the car kerosened, flung red pepper everywhere, sprayed Fly-Ded all about, drank Ovaltine and took a tranquilizer each—which I had been saving for the Donner Pass—and went to bed at 9 p.m. to the usual shouts, "There it is," "Up there, a bear!" That night everybody banged the bear away with pans, for they run at noise; our story had got around. We slept the sleep of the blessed, and the bear did not touch our kerosene-soaked poncho sealing the broken window. . . .

Well, we are fine and both of us tanned and having the experience of our lives. We hope to try some deep-sea fishing if we can . . .

Love to you both and to Sappho [*their cat*].

Sivvy and Ted

Pasadena, California
Sunday, August 2, 1959

Dear Mother,

. . . PLEASE don't worry about my poetry book, but send it off. I know about summer editors, but want to send it to as many places as I can. I also have gone over it very carefully and am not going to try to change it to fit some vague, abstract criticism. If an editor wants to accept it and make a few changes, then, all right. You need to develop a little of our callousness and brazenness to be a proper sender-out of

Sylvia and catch, summer 1959

manuscripts. I have a good list of publishers and haven't begun to eat into it. The biggest places are often best because they can afford to publish a few new people each year. . . .

Aunt Frieda [*her father's sister*] had a wonderful cold chicken lunch, string beans, potato salad, tomato and lettuce salad, hot rolls, fresh pineapple, coffee cake and tea ready for us yesterday when we came. Both she and Uncle Walter are handsome, fun, and so young in spirit. They have a little green Eden of a house, surrounded by pink and red and white oleander bushes, with *two* avocado trees loaded down with (alas) not-yet-ripe fruit, a peach tree, a guava tree, a persimmon tree, a fig tree and others.

Aunt Frieda has had some wonderful adventures and is a great storyteller. Ted gets on magnificently with Walter; we simply love them both. It is amazing how Frieda resembles daddy—the same clear, piercing, intelligent bright blue eyes and shape of face. Ted and I plan to be home about the 28th or maybe even before if we have no setbacks. Love to you, Warren, and Sappho.

Sivvy

Sylvia and Ted returned home according to schedule, both looking very tan and well. Nevertheless, I sensed a great weariness in Sylvia; at times, a tremulous quality as she spoke of the two-month stay they were planning in the writers' colony at Yaddo, Saratoga Springs, New York, and the return to England—this time to make their home there—which would take place in mid-December. Was it her old "homesickness-just-before-leaving-home" or something more? I felt it was a combination of both, and so it proved to be, for Sylvia had become pregnant just before she and Ted started their cross-country trip.

However, as she told me two months later, she was not sure she was pregnant until she had arrived at Yaddo. She wanted this pregnancy; she had seen a gynecologist in the spring and had "her tubes blown out," as she put it.

She made no allowances for herself during these beginning months, but packed and unpacked and packed again, and pushed herself to write each day. It was not until her return to Wellesley from Yaddo, when she was five months along in her pregnancy, that she had a medical checkup.

I think the interim at Yaddo was very good for her; she had no responsibility in regard to meals or housework; she could do what she enjoyed most—write. Even though the very privilege of being a "guest" there made her feel a sort of compulsion to be creative—which was at times frustrating in itself, building up a feeling of guilt if she did not produce each day—some good poems did emerge (most of them appeared in her first book, The Colossus) *during the stay there, and she looked back upon it as an oasis in a year of change.*

Yaddo
Saratoga Springs, New York
September 10, 1959

To: Warren and Mother   From: Me
In re: OUR ARRIVAL

. . . I am sitting in my "studio" on the third (top) floor of West House (where, on the first floor, we have our large bedroom, bathroom and closet—the combination about twice as big as our Boston apartment). The house is lovely, all nooks and angles, with several studios in it. The libraries and living rooms and music rooms are like those in a castle, all old plush, curios, leather bindings, oil paintings on the walls, dark woodwork, carvings on all the furniture. Very quiet and sumptuous.

I am the only person on the top floor, and my study is low-ceilinged, painted white, with a cot, a rug, a huge, heavy dark-wood table that I use as a typing and writing table with piles of room for papers and books. It has a skylight and four windows on the east side that open out onto a little porch looking over gables and into tall, dense, green pines. The only sound is from the birds, and, at night, the distant dreamlike calling of the announcer at the Saratoga racetrack.

I have never in my life felt so peaceful and as if I can read and think and write for about seven hours a day.

Ted has a marvelous studio out in the woods, a regular little house to himself, all glassed in and surrounded by pines, with a wood stove for the winter, a cot, and huge desk. I am so happy we can work apart, for that is what we've really needed.

The food so far seems to be very good. Two cups of fine coffee for breakfast, a coffee roll, eggs done to order, toast, jam, orange juice, served in a great dining room. We can eat any time from eight to nine. Then we pick up box lunches, two little thermoses with milk and coffee, so we won't be interrupted all day, and go off to work. Usually in the summer there are about 30 people here, but now there are only about 10 or 12, mostly artists and composers (who seem very nice) and a couple of poets we have never heard of. A magazine room has all the reviews we like and the British magazines. There seem to be lakes full of bass, a famous rose garden, and long wood-walks, all of which we look forward to exploring. . . .

. . . One thing: I would like some information about Austria, especially the Tyrol, for something I'm working on and would love it if you'd write me a descriptive letter about those places you visited— materials of the houses, furnishings, how old-fashioned are they? Sort of stove, animals, colors and types of scenery, occupations, how children help with chores—little colored details like that—the clothes they wear and so on.

Do write us.

Love,
Sivvy

SEPTEMBER 23, 1959

Dear Mother,

. . . I read some of my poems here the other night with a professor from the University of Chicago who read from a novel-in-progress. Several people are leaving today, among them a very fine young Chinese composer of whom we are very fond, on his second Guggenheim this year. Women come here, I learned, who have families. They leave their children in camp or with relatives: a great rest for them.

We get on well with the director and her secretary, and she wrote a little note that she hopes we come again before long for an even longer stay. So it is pleasant, indeed, to feel that this place will always be open to us. I imagine the MacDowell Colony will be, too, since they sent us their application blanks, but this is obviously the finest of the three such institutions in America. I particularly love the scenic beauty of the estate: the rose gardens, goldfish pools, marble statuary everywhere, woodland walks, little lakes. Ted and I took out the estate rowboat in a very weedy little lake and caught a bass apiece Sunday, about ¾ of a pound each—enough for a lunch; yet we threw them back. The food here is so fine we had no real need of fish to eat.

We had severe cold here, with frosts, but now it is warm enough to walk coatless again. We miss Sappho. We feed some of our milk to a white-pawed tiger cat here that jumped out at us from the woods, but no cat can compare to Sappho's delicacy and breeding.

Wish you might drive up here to spend an afternoon with us.

With love to you and Warren—

Sivvy

To Mother and Warren,

Thanks for your good letter . . . We really don't have any news
—our life here is so secluded. We simply eat breakfast, go to our
respective studios with a picnic lunch and write, read, and study, then
have tea, chat a bit, have dinner and read before bed. . . .

Ted has finished his play—a symbolic drama based on the Euripides play *The Bacchae,* only set in a modern industrial community
under a paternalistic ruler. I hope the Poets' Theater will give it at
least a reading. We have yet to type it.

I do rather miss Boston and don't think I could ever settle for living
far from a big city full of museums and theaters. Now Mrs. Ames, the
elderly Mother of Yaddo, has left for Europe, there are only her
poetess secretary Polly, a very nice woman, two painters and a composer on a Guggenheim here. From what we hear, certain artists live
on these colonies almost all year, spending four months in the winter
at Yaddo, then moving on to the MacDowell Colony. I could never do
that myself—too much like living in a vacuum. But it is nice to know
that practically any time we could invite ourselves back here . . .
Ted loves it and is getting a lot of work done. . . .

Lots of love to you both—

Sivvy

To Mummy and Warren,

Greetings! As usual our main news is that we are well fed. Every
dinner seems bound to outdo the last . . . After a week of solid,
steaming rain, we are at last having crisp, clear weather—the Green
Mountains blue in the distance, the newly fallen pine needles a resilient carpet underfoot.

Ted's proofs for his *Harper's* story ["*The Rain Horse*"] have
come—very exciting, and it reads marvelously. It will have black-and-
white drawings with it, I gather. Tentatively, it is scheduled for the
December issue. We are very proud of it . . . I hope I can hypnotize
him to finish up one or two others.

The New Yorker, at last, bought the poem you sent me, "A
Winter's Tale," for their December 26th issue, which is pleasant.
There is a lot more competition for special seasonal occasions like
that, and I wrote the poem as a light piece after that pleasant walk
you and Warren and Ted and I took last Christmas time around
Beacon Hill. . . .

Am very painstakingly studying German two hours a day: a few grammar lessons, then translating a Goethe lyric or a page or two from the Kafka stories Warren brought me from Germany—listing all the vocabulary and learning it. Hope to speed up after a few weeks at it.

Do write!

Much love,
S.

Dear Mother,

. . . I am growing very pleased with the idea of living in England. The speed and expense of America is just about 50 years ahead of me. I could be as fond of London as of any other city in the world, and plays, books, and all these things are so much much more within one's means. Travel, too. You must never take a ship again, but fly over to visit us.

Last night Polly, the very sweet woman from Brookline (a cousin of Wallace Fowlie) . . . had two bottles of vin rosé for dinner and a birthday cake with candles in honor of my day, which touched me very much.

I want Ted to take me on a trip around England, especially to Wales and to little fishing villages. When you come, we should go on a jaunt of some sort, staying at old inns and taking country walks. . . .

Much love,
Sivvy

Sylvia and Ted returned to our Wellesley home just before Thanksgiving—Sylvia very noticeably pregnant.

Ted worked away in the upstairs bedroom, while Sylvia sorted and packed the huge trunk which we had set up in the breezeway. There were painful choices to make—what to take, what to leave behind. This was really leaving home—apartment hunting in London lay ahead, as well as making arrangements for the baby, due at the end of March.

On the day they left, Sylvia was wearing her hair in a long braid down her back with a little red wool cap on her head, and looked like a high school student.

As the train pulled out, Ted called, "We'll be back in two years!"

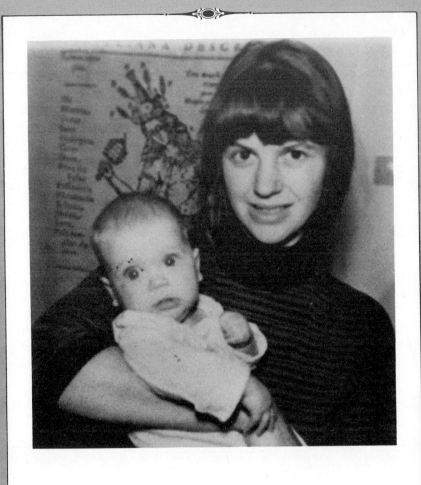

PART SIX

December 13, 1959–August 25, 1961

With the help of friends, Sylvia and Ted found a tiny third-floor flat in London near Primrose Hill and Regent's Park.

In February 1960, Sylvia signed a contract for her first volume, The Colossus and Other Poems. *The haunting memories of emotional terror voiced in some of the poems were in direct contrast to the strong, affirmative voice she gave forth in her letters and conversations with her family.*

When, on April 1, 1960, Sylvia gave birth at home to Frieda Rebecca she was attended only by an Indian midwife. The joyous advent of her little daughter touched off another spate of writing. By now Ted had the use of a friend's study where he could work in quiet, and Sylvia worked there, too, drafting The Bell Jar—*unknown to me. In their writing, they stimulated and supported each other: after all their hard work, the harvest was just beginning.*

In the winter of 1961 Sylvia had to undergo an appendectomy and soon after suffered a miscarriage.

In July 1961 I visited them, staying with Frieda while Sylvia and Ted went on a holiday to France. Before I left for the States, they had decided to purchase an old rectory in Devon. Sylvia was again pregnant, and they were longing to establish a home of their own.

YORKSHIRE, ENGLAND
[TED'S HOME]
DECEMBER 26, 1959

Dearest Mother,

I am sitting, about to go to bed, in the little second parlor down-stairs by a roaring coal fire with the rain swatting against the triple window in front of me, very comfortable, after a light supper of creamed turkey and mushrooms on toast I made. Olwyn is out for dinner; Ted's parents are dozing in the front parlor after admiring the lovely book on America you sent them (you couldn't have chosen better), and Ted is upstairs in our bedroom at his desk . . .

It scarcely seems possible we have been here two weeks. I have spent most of my time typing some things for Ted and the new manuscript of my poetry book (about 86 pages). It has rained and blown almost constantly (reread Ted's poem "Wind"; it's perfect), but we have gone out for brief walks. Now we are pretty much rested up and in very good health. Next Sunday . . . we go to London to stay a few days, as long as we need, to locate a good, comfortable apartment within easy walking distance of a big park, shops, a laundromat, etc., in Central London. We look forward to the trip and hope to spend our evenings going to plays. We have had tea at each of Ted's relatives: an Aunt Hilda and an Uncle Walter (the wealthy one), and taught Ted's sister and Hilda's daughter Vicky (21, an art teacher in grammar school and very nice) how to play Tarock [*the Viennese version of the Italian game*], and we play a great deal. I would like a refresher course with you experts, however, as I am sure there are many conventions we do not know—various ways to reveal yourself to your partner, etc. Anyway, your Tarock pack is in good use. . . .

. . . When my big poetry manuscript comes back from Farrar, Straus (they must have sent it by now), just keep it for scrap paper; I've typed up my large and new version of the book here.

. . . Olwyn is very nice, a beautiful blond, slim girl, my height and size, with yellow-green eyes and delicate, graceful bone structure; looks 21, not 31. I get along with her much better now that she's really accepted me as Ted's wife and like her immensely. She has a long vacation from her job as secretary-translator for a French theater agency in Paris; her most interesting job yet.

. . . No [*Christmas*] tree, which I missed. But Ted and I will have a little one next year for our Nicholas/Katharine (do you like Katharine Frieda Hughes as a name?). DO WRITE. I miss you and Warren and Sappho immensely and look for letters. Ted joins in sending love.

Sivvy

RUGBY STREET
LONDON, ENGLAND
JANUARY 10, 1960

Dear Mother,

I have no idea when I last wrote you, but it was a long time back. Ted and I have been in London for just a week now and out of touch with everything in Yorkshire, including mail, so I don't know what's waiting for us there.

The search for an apartment has been very tiring: London is so enormous in area and very expensive by American standards. . . . Now we are considering unfurnished flats and, thanks to an industrious and influential British lady, wife of a young American poet [W. S. Merwin], will look at some tomorrow that have hot water, central heating, a fridge—about a 10-minute walk from Regent's Park and very good shops. We'd invest in a new double bed and get tables and chairs in second-hand shops—a small start toward furnishing a home; but that's tomorrow. Junk and second-hand shops here are good for sturdy furniture and china.

We started out living in a cold, cheerless room-and-breakfast place for $5 a day, but hunting for the other two meals was a bore and inconvenient, so now we are much more comfortable and have moved into a spare room here [on] Rugby Street with Helga and Daniel Huws. Now we can easily cook our meals and that is very restful. Helga is a real German Hausfrau—scrubs, polishes, so although they live in a condemned district, her two floors are clean and colorful; her German cooking is delightful and makes me feel at home. . . .

. . . Thanks to Dido Merwin (the British woman) and her husband Bill, I got an appointment with their doctor yesterday, whom I liked immediately. He examined me, weighed me (I'm 145, only 10 pounds more than usual) and referred me to his partner, who is an obstetrician. I shall go to his prenatal clinic Thursday. The procedure here is radically different from that in America, and I'm not sure but that I shall like it better. Hospital beds are spoken for at least eight months ahead of time, and, except in special cases, all childbirth is "natural," without anesthesia (because this is less expensive, I imagine), and the hospitals keep you twelve days. Midwives do most of the deliveries. . . . My doctor said that at this date I could only be entered in a hospital as an "emergency" patient—or I could be delivered at home by him or his partner if I preferred them to a midwife and be given care and advice by a trained nurse . . . most deliveries here are home deliveries. This sounded *much* the best thing to me and if one of these unfurnished flats comes through (they are just around the corner from the M.D.'s office), I shall be all set and very glad to escape the crowded labor wards and hospital food. Ted will cook and care for me; I shall get good sleep and not feel lonely and cut off . . . The best care here is under the System . . . and so the baby should be perfectly free. . . .

. . . Once we get a foothold in London, life will become much easier and pleasanter, and I think I shall like it better than anywhere else; but I have gone through a very homesick and weary period. . . .

Love to you and Warren.

Sivvy

Dearest Mother,

Ted and I arrived back at the Beacon [*Ted's home*] last night after two gruelling weeks in London to find three good letters waiting from you; you have no idea how much mail from you means, especially now, when I most miss having you with us. . . .

Now I am sitting in the big warm bathrobe Mrs. Hughes made me, with a crackling coal fire at my back, overlooking a sunny (for the first time in a month) landscape of dazzling snow-covered moortops and a raft of billowing clouds racing under a blue sky—our first snow. I had a hot bath last night, my first in two weeks (Helga puts up with the lack of a bathroom in their London flat and a public toilet three flights down in a dirty open cellar with a Germanic stoicism), and I am just waiting till the water heats to wash my grubby hair.

. . . Faber . . . sent us a copy of the paper jacket of Ted's [*second*] book which amazed and delighted us—a triumph as covers go . . . The book should come out here in late March or early spring, and we'll send you a copy right away. . . .

After traveling endlessly on busses, subways and taxis . . . and seeing ugly, dirty, too expensive furnished and unfurnished flats and getting more and more cold and tired, we ended up with two possibilities practically next door to my doctor. One was an unbelievably big and beautiful furnished ground floor flat overlooking a road and Primrose Hill (a green park across the street from Regent's Park) from the big front room; a charming garden from the mammoth bedroom and glassed-in kitchen and dining area, at 9 guineas ($27) a week, to be heated by electric fires (extra). We could have afforded this on Ted's Guggenheim [*awarded Ted in 1959*] for a year, and it would have been available right away, but the owner, who lived downstairs and was presently away doing his decorating work in the Bahamas, has said NO CHILDREN. We telegrammed to see if a crib-size baby would be all right for a year, but there is, as yet, no answer.

The other alternative (and a rare one) is a third floor [fourth *floor in the United States*] unfurnished flat in a 5-story house in a quiet square, overlooking a little green with benches and fence for mothers and children, in 5 minutes' walking distance from Primrose Hill and beautiful Regent's Park (with a zoo, swings, sandboxes, swans, flowers, etc.), a laundromat, shops, my doctors, too. The whole house is in the stage of being all done over—painted, papered, bathrooms put in, which will mean our starting in on buying our own things. The flat is really too small . . . and lacks a study for Ted, but it is only 6 guineas ($18) a week (gas and electricity extra) on a 3-year lease, which is sublettable or assignable. . . .

Our marvelous friends, the Merwins, have tables, chairs, and rugs to loan us until we pick up our own here and there in the excellent second-hand shops in London. *So we signed the lease this Friday . . .* At least we'll have our own things and can hang our own pictures, etc. It's an ideal location, like living in a village, ten minutes from the center of London. Getting a foot in is the hard part. . . .

I'm going to see if London has diaper service. Will go down there at the end of next week to shop and get blood and urine test results from the doctor, whom I saw again this week. Why do they ask if any relative has had diabetes? How hereditary is it? Forward all mail *here.*

x x x Sivvy

JANUARY 27, 1960

Dearest Mother,

. . . I made a mushroom omelette for breakfast and have been having a very pleasant and relaxing day, our trunks being packed and sent off to London at last. Ted has constructed a bird-feeding station and a clothes line wrapped with bacon rinds just outside the picture window, so against a backdrop of blue-misty green fields and blurred trees, I have been watching the marvelous little birds come: tiny robins, round, with a patch of warm orange like a bib; blue tits, smaller-than-sparrow-sized versions of our jays; and the lovely multicolored chaffinches.

I feel in very good health . . . I am taking iron pills and every so often sleeping pills (not barbiturates) like those you gave me, for the baby kicks so much at night (it seems to wake up then) that it keeps me awake. So this way I can assure myself of a good night's sleep, which is really the foundation of my health. When I am as rested as I am now, I feel I can cope with anything; while when I allow myself to get tired, I feel very homesick and blue. I really look forward to next week, settling in, having time just to rock back and forth, looking happily ahead to the baby! I have been rushing about so much I hardly notice being pregnant at all. I am an impressive size now. . . . My only actual symptoms are a tendency to backache after standing or typing (walking doesn't tire me; I manage two or three, even five miles a day) and occasional heartburn, which is evidently natural—I haven't much room for a stomach and have a very good appetite . . . Can you get used to Frieda Rebecca as a girl's name? I think I'll write Aunt Frieda about it, as I'm sure it would please her to know I want to name my first girl after her (even if *this* is a Nicholas Farrar, as I'm sure it will be). Isn't it wonderful to have a children's book [*Ted's* Meet My Folks] ready to be dedicated to whomever it is!

x x x Sivvy

7 CHALCOT SQUARE
LONDON, ENGLAND
FEBRUARY 2, 1960

Dearest Mother, Warren, and Sappho,

This is the first piece of mail to go out from our new residence. I am typing at an old, unpainted table loaned us by our friends, the Merwins . . . listening to hammers, clanking chisels, and the cries of children in the "Chalcot Square Gardens," as the sign says below.

. . . Yesterday they installed the stove, which is the most beautiful I have ever seen or worked on . . . I loved putting out my beautiful pots and pans, Warren, and always think of you when I use them, which is often each day.

The bed came yesterday, too. Six feet six inches long and five feet wide . . . We had a wonderful sleep on it last night, exhausted to the bone as we were from workmen arriving all day yesterday and all our trunks, suitcases to be unpacked downstairs and carried up by armloads . . . Ted did all that lugging of all our books and clothes. . . .

Our friends, the Merwins, are going to their farm in France at the end of April and for the summer and are going to let Ted use Bill's study—the quietest place in London—and we use their garden while they're gone! Isn't that lovely? Dido said all we have to do in return (she always makes some little task, she says, so that people won't feel they're imposing) is to keep their marvelous Siamese cat company . . . and mow the little lawn. They live 5 minutes away from us, so it will be heavenly. The widowed woman who lives in the Russian-novel antique attic upstairs came here twenty years ago and is a French interpreter for the telephone company. She lives surrounded by hyacinths—all sorts of flowering plants—very warmhearted; says you can hear the lions and seals and foreign birds roaring and cawing in the distance from the Regent's Park Zoo when the windows are open in the summer! I just wish we could buy a house around here someday.

My prize is very simple and small—about $20 for a poem that tied for first place in a British critical magazine. Poems were sent in from all over, but it made me cheered those dreary first weeks in London. . . .

Lots of love from us both,
Sivvy

SUNDAY EVENING
FEBRUARY 7, 1960

Dearest Mother and Warren,

Well, here I am, sitting at my little enamel table in the warm, cheerful kitchen, my Olivetti open before me, the timer (yours) ticking away, an apfelkuchen in the oven and a chicken stew gently simmering on top of the stove. . . .

. . . Ted . . . has just finished painting the living room walls white over the nice rough-textured liner paper, which looks wonderful . . . We are going to have a lovely engraving of Isis from one of Ted's astrological books blown up to cover one of the side-wall panels . . . and, of course, Ted's "Pike" and our Baskins [*the artist Leonard Baskin, a member of the Smith faculty who was close to both Sylvia and Ted*] . . .

. . . My midwife, Sister Hannaway, should come to the house to see me sometime this week, and I shall go to her relaxation classes in Bloomsbury Square as soon as I make arrangements with her. Now that the strain of looking for a place is over and the apartment responding so rapidly to our work, I feel happy as I have ever been in my life; both of us eagerly anticipating Nicholas/Rebecca. . . .

Love to Warren and more congratulations on his wonderful midterm marks.

x x x Sivvy

FEBRUARY 11, 1960

Dearest Mother and Warren,

A little middle-of-the-week letter to pass on some very pleasant news: picture (yesterday) your daughter/sister, resplendent in black wool suit, black cashmere coat, fawn kidskin gloves from Paris (Olwyn's Christmas present) and matching calfskin bag (from Italy) . . . and of enormous and impressive size, sailing into the notorious York Minster pub on Dean Street in Soho, just off Shaftesbury Avenue, about 12:15 and up to the bar to meet a pleasant half-American, half-Scots young editor for the well-known British publishers, William Heinemann (publishers of Somerset Maugham, Evelyn Waugh, D. H. Lawrence, Erskine Caldwell, etc.), and taking out a pen thereupon and signing on the counter the contract for her first book of poems; namely, *The Colossus.*

Which is to say, the first British publisher I sent my new collection of poems to (almost one-third written at Yaddo; 48 poems in all, after countless weedings and reweedings) wrote back within the week accepting them! Amaze of amaze. I was so hardened to rejections that I waited till I actually signed the contract (with the usual 10 percent royalties, which, of course, will amount to nothing) before writing you. They do very few, very few poets at Heinemann and will do a nice book. It should come out late next fall or at New Year's. It is dedicated to that paragon who has encouraged me through all my glooms about it, Ted. That means in our small family of soon-to-be three every member will have a book dedicated to him/her and written by some other member! Maybe the baby itself will inspire a children's book, or several!

The Colossus and Other Poems, by Sylvia Plath. For Ted. That is what the book is, named after the title of the ninth poem in it, one written at Yaddo.

Ted waited in a pub next door for me to come in after seeing my editor (who now becomes my agent for America and will work on getting the book published there, if it doesn't get the Yale prize this year), and we went to a pleasant, second-floor Soho Italian restaurant for veal and mushrooms to celebrate, having sat in the same restaurant in misery a month back, homeless and cold and very grim. Of course, I shall write Mrs. Prouty about it. . . .

Much love to both of you . . .

Your new authoress,
Sivvy

FEBRUARY 18, 1960

Dear Mother and Warren,

. . . Just back from my doctor. I am in fine health and sleeping nine hours a night, plus a rest in the afternoon. Things are, thank goodness, quieting down a bit, although the builders are still in the house, doing the basement, second floor, and attic apartments. Only one other couple living here, on the ground floor, and the lady in the attic. How glad I am we are entrenched! . . .

Tonight we're relaxing to the point of going to a movie, part of *Ivan the Terrible*, with Dido and Bill.

My book should come out sometime next autumn—I hope in October—and be fat, with 50 poems in it.*

We love hearing about the gallivantings of Sappho and her new rabbity escort. We saw little black kittens in a pet shop window and had to hurry past, because they only reminded us there was One Sappho and all others mere flashy copies. . . .

Love, Sivvy

FEBRUARY 25, 1960

Dearest Mother,

I have been having a pleasant day in bed, resting and reading. Ted and I are alternating, one day each a week, until we are fully recovered from the strain of the last months and the settling in. He had his day Sunday. The one in bed orders what is desired for meals, reads, writes and sleeps. Now I am dressed and up and feeling much refreshed. Ted has made a beef stew, which is simmering ready for our supper; and we are going afterwards to the center of London to see Ibsen's *Rosmersholm*, something I have been looking forward to for a long time: my first Ibsen play seen staged. I find I am made much happier by tragedy, good tragedy, classic tragedy, in movies and on stage than by so-called "hilarious musicals and/or farces." We saw Brendan Behan's musical, "The Hostage," a while back and were both bored and depressed by what the audience lapped up as funny, very tawdry and puerile wit, no plot, etc. Tragedy, on the other hand, really purifies and liberates me.

Last night Ted gave a reading of his poems at the Oxford Poetry Society. We left after lunch by train, a one hour and 15 minutes' trip. I had never been to Oxford at all, so we went a few hours early and, though it was a cold, bleak, inhospitable day, walked about the black stone, antique lanes and into the little green courts of one or two colleges. The architecture is immensely impressive; much more of it than at Cambridge; the eating places, superb; and the atmosphere a

---

* *The Colossus and Other Poems*, London: Heinemann, 1962, has fifty poems.
  The Colossus and Other Poems, New York: Alfred A. Knopf, 1962, has forty poems.

really awesome, cloistered one. The only trouble . . . was the terribly noisy roar of traffic, out-of-town traffic, on the main crossroads —so dense I hestitated to cross the street. None of the country and open sky spilling into everything as there is in Cambridge, but very much of a big city. Yet, once in a little crooked college court, the sounds of the modern world vanish by magic. I think both Ted and I would like to have gone to Oxford, too.

We had a small tea while Ted ordered the list of his poems. His book, *Lupercal*, officially out March 18 [I wonder if the baby will coincide!), came the day before—his six copies—very conveniently. They've changed the blue of the cover to green, which put us off, and the red on the jacket and the purple on the cover are a bit of a clash to my morbidly sensitive eye, but looking at the book without the jacket, it is a handsome affair. . . .

My obliging editor at Heinemann said to tell him my birthday and he will try to get my publication date as close to that as possible. The gallantry of the British! . . .

In two days N/R will be eight months, starting on the ninth. I am at last finding some leisure for reading, and Bill Merwin is supplying me with American history books. Hope to be writing soon again, too. I feel much freer (and appreciated, by publishers, at least) here to write than I ever did in America. I hope our mail-to-be-forwarded is lessening! We look forward now to living and writing in seclusion and skimming the cream off London periodically.

. . . Now we are "at home," London is a delight.

x x x Sivvy

THURSDAY EVENING
MARCH 3, 1960

Dear Mother,
    . . . I really put my foot down about visitors now. I get tired easily and like the house to myself so I can cook, read, write, or rest when I please. I have really been strained living out of suitcases on shipboard, at Ted's crowded home, and then in and out of boarding houses in London and with the Huwses, so that I have no desire for people sleeping in my living room or causing me extra cooking or housework. Ted's sister is also coming to London this weekend, but she will stay with a girl friend. I feel most like walking, reading, and musing by myself now after three long months of enforced external, exerting and extrovert living.

Monday we went to a buffet with David and Barbara Ross at which Luke, Danny and Helga and others were present—most of the crowd that published the one and only issue of the *Botolph's Review*, where I first saw Ted's poems and at the celebration of which I first met him. David Ross, the editor, very young (24), a stockbroker and diabetic, quiet and nice, has a son; Luke is to sail for New Orleans, March 18—his wife will have a baby in May; of course, the Huwses have their Magdalene, and we are about to have our Nicholas/Rebecca. Amusing to see what paternal and familial fates have, four years later, fallen on such once-confirmed bachelors!

Tuesday we had lunch with two of Ted's editors from Faber (after my relaxation classes at my Clinic) and dined sumptuously in a Soho Greek restaurant, blissfully ignoring prices . . . They are working on getting an illustrator for Ted's children's book, and we have our fingers crossed. They've written to our First Choice, and if he did it, it should sell marvelously. I won't breathe his name until we hear definitely; he may, of course, refuse to do it as he has no end of assignments.

Wednesday evening we went for cocktails with John Lehmann, editor of the *London* magazine, who reminisced about his memories of Virginia Woolf, et al. I met the popular British Oxford graduate–poetess, Elizabeth Jennings, a Catholic, who reads for a London publishing house and lives in a convent while here, returning to her rooms in Oxford on weekends to write (she has three volumes out). We got along very well. [*Met*] a lawyer-poet-novelist, Roy Fuller, and lady novelist–reviewer, Christine Brooke-Rose. I must get them all in my diary. Very pleasant time. Lehmann is publishing my "Daughters of Blossom Street" (changed from "This Earth Our Hospital") sometime this spring . . . I just got the proofs. He's also taken two more poems. . . .

. . . Went to my doctor again today, and he let me listen to the baby's heartbeat! I was so excited. He said the baby is in fine position. I like him much better than any doctor I had in America. All shots— whooping cough, scarlet fever, diphtheria, polio—are given free and Health Visitors tell you when to get what. I won't go to the Clinic, but will have my doctor give them. I couldn't have kinder or better care.

. . . We hope to get our phone in next week and will call you as soon as the baby is born to announce your Grandmotherhood.

Having my book accepted here is very consoling at this time of change and anticipation. Ironically, two other British publishers (one from the Oxford University Press) have asked to see a book since I signed my contract. I hope some American press will see fit to take it eventually.

x x x Sivvy

Dear Mother,

. . . Here there has been not a whiff of snow all winter, and I am homesick for it. The last four months seem like an endless, drawn-out, grey-brown November. Ted and I went for a walk on Primrose Hill this noon after lunch, and the air was mild and damply spring-like; the sun almost warm, and green buds out on all the lilac bushes; the forsythia looks about to open.

. . . Ted is, if anything, too nice to his relatives and friends, and I got weary sitting for eight hours at a stretch in our smoke-filled rooms, waiting for them to leave—impossible to nap or relax with so many people around. I feel very unlike entertaining anyone just now, simply "in-waiting," wanting to read, write in my diary, and nap. Luckily we have no more prospective visitors (knock on wood) and I have been able to lie down in the afternoons, which rests me enough to sleep at night. The baby has been growing by leaps and bounds, and the doctor said when I saw him today that it seemed to have very long legs, which accounts for the surprising occasional bumps and visible kicks which appear on my right side. . . .

x x x Sivvy

MARCH 24, 1960

Dearest Mother,

. . . Your copy of the *Ladies' Home Journal* arrived on the best possible day, Monday, when I was too miserable with my cold for anything but that. I read it from cover to cover and enjoyed it immensely. Perfect sickbed reading!

Wonderful news via telegram just came for Ted. He's got the Somerset Maugham Award for his book—about 400 pounds—just over $1,000, which has to be spent "enlarging his world-view" in about three months abroad. We are envisioning the Greek Islands next winter and all sorts of elegant sun-saturated schemes.

x x x Sivvy

SATURDAY NOON
MARCH 26, 1960

Dearest Mother,

Well, all is quiet and uneventful. I somehow imagine I should be seeing large comets or lions in the street at this point, but can't believe the baby will *ever* come. I sort of expected it early—didn't we arrive early?—and really am set on the 27th, that mystical number [*an important date for various friends and family members*] for a date now, but this waiting feels ready to go on forever. . . .

. . . A marvelous folklore library is just down the street from us. I think I'd rather live in London than anywhere in the world, *and* get a seaside cottage in Cornwall someday, too! Ted's going to work on a libretto for a modern young Chinese opera-composer we met at Yaddo. I hope that works out. . . .

Your letter about *Lupercal* arrived today, and we're so pleased you like it and that the copies came intact. Ted is now in the middle of writing on a second play, and I am convinced it is only a matter of time before he does a stageable one. We got his official letter from the Secretary of the Somerset Maugham Trust today; he's got the 1960 award "on the strength of the literary quality and promise" of *The Hawk in the Rain*. This year the Award is 500 pounds! One hundred more than usual, about $1,400. We have to spend it within two years from now by spending "at least three months outside Great Britain and Ireland, with the object, not of having a holiday abroad, but of acquainting yourself with the manners and customs of foreign nations and thereby having an opportunity to increase your experience and knowledge for your future literary benefit." So we will take the three months in the sunny south (we've thought of France, Italy, Greece) either next winter or the one after that. Ideally, we'd rent a furnished villa on the Mediterranean near a large and cosmopolitan city so I could register the baby with a doctor and have one of those foreign maid-babysitters and could have at least 4–6 hours a day free to write, too. . . .

They ask Ted to write a thank-you note to Maugham in his French Riviera villa. How I would love to meet him! I am especially partial to the French Riviera because of the relative ease in language, but Rome and environs are a possibility—an immense English-speaking civilization there.

We hear the clear song of a certain thrush at dawn each morning. The square is full of children, playing something like baseball with flat bats. The daily ice cream truck jingles to a stop and the little ones all rush up. Oh, I am so impatient!

(Monday noon, March 28) Well, I am about to go out shopping, round as ever. Since the baby did not take advantage of the significant 27th date, I am sure it will wait till April Fool's Day, just to get into the main Plath Month. [*Her father's birthday, April 13; mine, the 26th; and Warren's, the 27th.*] Ted's bought me a marvelous huge covered French earthenware casserole and I cooked a whole pile of little tough pigeons in it (9 cents each) and served them with rice, in which I stirred a delectable mixture of fried onions, garlic, raisins and blanched almond slices when it was cooked dry and fluffy. Marvelous. . . .

Yesterday, lazing in bed and leafing through the Sunday *Observer*, I came on a marvelous review of *Lupercal* by A. Alvarez, *the* intelligent reviewer (Oxford, Princeton, etc.) who had been approving, but with reservations, about *The Hawk in the Rain*. A column and a half—excerpts: "There are no influences to side-track the critic, no hesitations to reassure him. Hughes has found his own voice, created his own artistic world and has emerged as a poet of the first importance . . . What Ted Hughes has done is to take a limited, personal theme and, by an act of immensely assured poetic skill, has broadened it until it seems to touch upon nearly everything that concerns us. This is not easy poetry to read, but it is new, profound and important."

We cooed and beamed all day. At the movie everybody was reading the *Observer* and some were just at Ted's review. I turned a bit further: his picture, among the South African massacres, news about the Maugham Award and even a note about *me*—"his tall, trim American wife . . . who is a *New Yorker* poet in her own right." We'll send you copies when we get some.

Ted is being marvelously good and understanding. He's as impatient and eager as I, if that's possible. Well, keep calm for another week.

x x x Sivvy

THURSDAY EVENING
MARCH 31, 1960

Dear Mother and Warren,

. . . In her/his infinite wisdom, the baby is waiting until my cold is all gone (I'm just at the last vestiges now and feel close to my old self again), till the weather improves (it's been raw, sleety, utterly grey and nasty till today, which is green, sunny, and lambish) and till the very last touches are calmly put on the apartment. My midwife came yesterday and cheered us by laughingly predicting it would arrive at 2 a.m. Sunday; I wish it would, because she is on duty this weekend, and if I had her (there is a shift of three midwives), I'd be overjoyed. We both are very fond of her. I saw my doctor today, who examined me inside and out and said everything was ripe and ready for my having the baby in the next few days. . . .

Ted and I took a lovely, quiet walk this evening under the thin new moon, over the magic landscape of Primrose Hill and Regent's Park; all blue and misty, the buds a kind of nimbus of green on the thorn trees, daffodils and blue squills out on the lawns and the silhouettes of wood pigeons roosting in the trees. A heavenly hour of peace and easy strolling, our first in weeks. I want to have nothing to do after it comes, so am busying myself, cleaning house, etc., now. Waiting for Dot's meat loaf [*Aunt Dot's recipe*] in the oven. Will make a big fish soup tomorrow.

Ted's been getting a flood of letters from all sorts of people about his award, a real stack of mail. Two requests to give readings (one in June, with me and someone else, and one in December, which would pay about $35 for the hour), editors asking for poems, old friends stirred into writing, etc. I must type answers for him tomorrow, or they'll never get done.

Well, I'll put this aside for a day, in case I collect any more news.

On the morning of April 1, 1960, at about 3 a.m., the phone at my bedside rang. I was awake at once, grabbed the receiver, and called into it, "Hello!"

"Mother," said a tremulous voice.

"Sylvia!" I cried. "How are you!"

A click and we were disconnected. I waited a bit, then called the overseas operator, who advised me just to wait.

Wait I did, for a whole, interminable hour, walking the floor, praying, and reassuring myself with "At least, she's alive." Then the ring once more and Sylvia's voice, now clear and strong, giving me details of the baby's vital statistics. I interrupted to ask, "Is it Nicholas or Frieda Rebecca?"

"Oh, Frieda Rebecca, of course! Ein Wunderkind, Mummy. Ein Wunderkind!"

APRIL 1ST, 1:15 P.M.

P.S.

Well, just twelve hours ago I woke up groggy from two sleeping pills, after one hour's hard-won sleep, and everything began. The miraculous rapidity of the delivery amazed even my seasoned doctor and midwife, which is why I had absolutely no anesthesia. The midwife, a capable little Indian woman I had visit me once before, came on her bicycle "to see how I was getting on" about 2 a.m. and planned to see my contractions establish, leave and return after breakfast. In no time I was contracting violently with scarcely a rest. I thought the worst pains, just before the second stage of pushing began, were only the beginning and didn't see how I could last through 20 more hours of them. Suddenly, at five, she said I was fully dilated and showed me the baby's head—a crack of it—in the mirror. She called the doctor, but he was at home and had no anesthesia handy. He came about 5:30, just in time to supervise the delivery.

I looked on my stomach and saw Frieda Rebecca, white as flour with the cream that covers new babies, little funny dark squiggles of hair plastered over her head, with big, dark-blue eyes. At 5:45 exactly. The afterbirth came shortly after. Ted was there the whole time, holding my hand, rubbing my back and boiling kettles—a marvelous comfort. I couldn't take my eyes off the baby. The midwife sponged her beside the bed in my big pyrex mixing bowl, wrapped her up well, near a hot water bottle in the crib; she sucked at me a few minutes like a little expert and got a few drops of colostrum and then went to sleep.

From where I sit, propped up in bed, I can see her, pink and healthy, sound asleep. We can't imagine now having favored a boy! Ted is delighted. He'd been hypnotizing me to have a short, easy delivery. Well, it wasn't "easy," but the shortness carried me through. I slept an hour or two after calling you—feel I could get up and walk about, but am, of course, wobbly. The miracle is how after my sinus siege of two weeks and sleepless nights, I should be lucky to have only 4½ hours' labor. "A wonder child," the midwife said. Of course, of course!

Ted brought me breakfast—I'd vomited up all that meat loaf at the start of labor—and a tuna salad, cheese and V-8 lunch, which I have just finished with gusto. I feel light and thin as a feather. The baby is, as I told you, 7 pounds, 4 ounces, 21 inches long and, alas, she has my nose! On her, though, it seems quite beautiful. Well, I have never been so happy in my life. The whole American rigamarole of hospitals, doctors' bills, cuts and stitches, anesthesia, etc., seems a nightmare well left behind. The midwife came a second time at 11 a.m. and will come again at tea time to wash me and care for the baby. I'll write soon again. Love to "Grammy" and Uncle Warren from Frieda Rebecca, Ted, and your own Sivvy.

Monday noon
April 4, 1960

Dearest Mother,

Well, Rebecca is four days old, almost, and more beautiful than ever. It has been a lovely, sunny morning outside, and the trees look to be budding in the square. The baby is sleeping in the crib after being changed and bathed by the third midwife of the trio who work in my district, and I have taken my first bath, which put me in very good spirits. I don't respond well to being bedded down and enjoyed getting up last night for a candlelight dinner with Ted—an unearthly delectable veal casserole Dido Merwin brought over to heat up . . . I have a ravenous appetite, drink loads of milk and water, V-8 with gelatine to improve my nails, and orange juice. It is so wonderful not to be in the hospital, but bit by bit to slip back into my old routine as the midwife gives me the go-ahead and as I feel stronger. Just tidying up this or that while sitting on a stool or chair makes me feel pleasant. . . .

For the first week, these [home-delivered] babies tend to cry and wake at night as they are bathed in the morning and therefore drowsy all day. Rebecca is no exception and yells herself into fine red fits any time from midnight to four. So I nap in the day to make up for lost sleep and try to persuade Ted to do the same.

You should see him rocking her and singing to her! She looks so tiny against his shoulder, her four fingers just closing around one of his knuckles. Now, of course, she is sleeping like a top, rosy and pink-cheeked. Already she shows a funny independence and temper. . . . I'm allowed to go out with her if it's nice on the tenth day, and I can't wait. . . .

We are dying to hear from you and Warren about your reactions to all this. Everybody is most amazed by the rapidity of my labor, especially myself. I am sure one of the reasons I felt so well after the delivery and had no tears or anything is because I had no anesthesia and therefore was able to respond to all the directions of the doctor. And Rebecca, of course, looked lovely immediately, hasty lady that she was.

Things seem much calmer and more peaceful with the baby around than without . . . Ted will have a study and utter peace by the time I have all my strength back and am coping with baby and household. Now I rely on his cooking, shopping, going to the laundromat, etc., etc., and his help (so much better than a stranger's) will be invaluable in my quick return to normal activity.

I'll leave just a corner for Ted to say Hello. . . .

Love to you, Warren and Sappho . . .

Sivvy

Dear Mother,

Well, if I hadn't heard from you today, I was seriously thinking of disowning my nearest kin! Ted said you'd probably be so busy informing half of America of this event that you'd not get around to writing *me* for at least a month. Anyhow, your letter was so cheering it made up for the days of waiting. I actually had a dream during my nap yesterday that Ted and I were waiting for you and Warren in the Wellesley kitchen. You both came in with huge armloads of groceries (this was before I read of your forgetting the groceries last weekend). "Well, what do you *think* of it!" we called out to you. Whereupon you handed us two letters, unstamped, that you had been about to send. I still haven't heard from Warren, so get him to write in person, even if it's only a little.

The one infuriating thing about the general euphoria around here is that I have no relatives or friends of *my own* to admire the baby in person. Ted's people and friends are dear, the room is full of flowers, telegrams and cards and well wishes, but it isn't the same.

Dido Merwin has been supplying us with delicacies off and on: blanquette de veau, trout in aspic, with eyes turned to pearls and lemon slices arrayed about; and when Ted went over to dessert and to meet Bill's publisher last night, she gave him some beans in a pot and another stew to heat up. Such goodness is beyond thanks. Bill came over yesterday—my first visitor and the first to see the baby. He brought daffodils, a silver thimble for the baby and a pile of old *New Yorkers* for me, figuring with exact intuition I was ready for nothing more concentrated than first the jokes and cartoons, then the poems, then stories—short, amusing and something easy to pick up and put down.

The baby is sleeping sweetly after her 2 p.m. feeding; her little hands in the most delicate attitudes. Her ballet-like gestures with her hands are one of the loveliest things about her. I have begun changing her diapers myself now and enjoy it immensely. She is very good and quiet and seems to like moving her legs about and being bare. . . .

No more words about hormones and growth-stopping, please! [*I'd shared an endocrinologist's report on work in this field with her.*] I'm surprised at you. Tampering with nature! What an American thing to feel measuring people to ideal heights will make them happier or not interfere with other things. Whatever height Frieda Rebecca is, I shall encourage her to be proud of it. My own height, 5'9", which so depressed me once is now my delight; and I have a handsome, tall, living documentary of a husband to prove a tall girl need be nothing but fortunate in that line . . . Enough of that.

. . . Warren will be the wealthy one of us two and be able to visit you in England while we would only come to America on a paid-for reading tour or possible resident-poet year much later. I'm becoming more and more anglophilic—watch out!

Love,
Sivvy

P.S. I'm going to have *all* my babies at home; I've loved every minute of this experience!

APRIL 15, 1960

Dear Mother,

. . . These last weeks, in fact, the last month or so, have slipped by with my hardly noticing the dates, and I am eager to begin writing and thinking again. The most difficult thing is the idea of leaving the baby with a sitter. We are invited to cocktails at Faber's next Thursday from 6–8 and shall presumably meet Eliot; yet I am so reluctant to leave the baby. . . . They don't believe in bottles here at all, nor do I, and I wouldn't miss feeding her for the world. . . .

x x x Sivvy

APRIL 21, 1960

Dearest Mother,

. . . I am sitting in our sun-flooded kitchen, waiting for a pan of hash to finish cooking, planning to feed Frieda Rebecca (we are oddly enough starting to call her *Frieda!*) at two and then go out to Regent's Park for a walk and sit in the sun . . . I am just getting over my tiredness from getting up at night. During the day the baby (known informally as The Pooker, or Pooker-Pie) wakes on the clock four-hourly and at night she shows reassuring signs of sleeping for five and even an occasional 6-hour interval. She eats like a little piglet.

3:15 p.m.: I am now sitting on a bench, facing the sun in Regent's Park. They are mowing the lawns everywhere and the smell of cut grass, plants, and warm earth is delicious. Nothing is so beautiful as England in April. I only wish you were here to walk out with me—by the time you come, the baby should be toddling! I can't wait till she does laugh and communicate with us. She is so tiny still when she curls up, she almost disappears . . . Tonight I am employing the Babyminder Service for the first time from 6 to 9-ish so we can go to Faber's for cocktails, and again tomorrow at the same time, so we can go to dinner in Soho with Lee Anderson. He looks like a white-bearded Civil War general, is a poet and has a farm in America, and is over here to record British poets for Yale. Tuesday we went to lunch with two ex-Cambridge people—a girl who works for the BBC and is interested in Ted's writing a verse drama for them, and Karl Miller, literary editor of the *Spectator* . . .

Last Sunday . . . I had an immensely moving experience and attended the arrival of the Easter weekend marchers from the atomic bomb plant at Aldermason to Trafalgar Square in London. Ted and Dido had left at noon to see Bill Merwin, who was with the over 10 thousand marchers come into Hyde Park, and I left later with the baby to meet a poet-friend of Ted's, Peter Redgrove, and go to Trafalgar Square with him. He brought a carry-cot, which he is loaning us, and we carried the sleeping baby easily between us, installed the cot on the lawn of the National Gallery overlooking the fountains, pigeons, and glittering white buildings. Our corner was uncrowded, a sort of nursery, mothers giving babies bottles on blankets . . .

I saw the first of the 7-mile-long column appear—red and orange and green banners, "Ban the Bomb!" etc., shining and swaying slowly. Absolute silence. I found myself weeping to see the tan, dusty marchers, knapsacks on their backs—Quakers and Catholics, Africans and whites, Algerians and French—40 percent were London housewives. I felt proud that the baby's first real adventure should be as a protest against the insanity of world-annihilation. Already a certain percentage of unborn children are doomed by fallout and no one knows the cumulative effects of what is already poisoning the air and sea.

I hope, by the way, that neither you nor Warren will vote for Nixon. His record is atrocious from his California campaign on—a Machiavelli of the worst order. Could you find out if there is any way I can vote? I never have and feel badly to be deprived of however minute a participation in political affairs. What do you think of Kennedy? The Sharpesville massacres are causing a great stir of pity and indignation here.

. . . The days of the three last weeks have just flown without my seeming to really accomplish anything except feeding the baby and us and writing a few letters. I really long for a house here near the park and must learn from you how one sets about committing oneself to a house. I want lots of rooms so we can have more children; I would so like about four. I hate to be limited by money and space!

x x x Sivvy

APRIL 26, 1960

HAPPY BIRTHDAY!!! HAPPY BIRTHDAY!!!

Dear Mother and Warren,

It was wonderful to hear your voices Sunday. Ted shouted "Many happy returns" into the phone, but I guess it was after you had been cut off. I am always sad at what little can be said on the phone—the main thing is hearing voices. You sounded so close. I had Rebecca in my arms all the time I was talking. How I wish you were here to admire her! To other people she must just be an ordinary baby, but I would love to have an admiring grandmother and uncle appreciate her unique and absolutely marvelous qualities! I shall send the snapshots, if any come out, as a belated birthday token. . . . I don't know how I can wait till next summer for the prospect of seeing you! Hearing your voice makes me feel your absence more; you feel so close it seems you should be able to drop right over.

. . . I'm going to try a "relief bottle" for the baby one evening this week preparatory to our dinner at T. S. Eliot's May 4th, so I won't have to rush home then. Just us, the Stephen Spenders and the Eliots! The Faber cocktail party was great fun. The first time I had really dressed up for ages. Everyone marveled I had had a baby just three weeks ago. I met a lively American girl on a 2-year fellowship to Cambridge whose path crossed mine often in America. Faber is doing her first novel, and I invited her and her Indian poet friend to a spaghetti supper in early May. Met an old college-mate of Ted's, now a TV producer of arty programs, drank champagne and felt very grand and proud of Ted.

Got a very nice letter from Edward Weeks at the *Atlantic* and have finally by doggedness broken through the Iron Curtain raised by Peter Davison's coming into power as Advisor on Poems. They accepted two—the best of the sheaf I sent, gratifyingly enough, one of them the first in my book and written to the baby while I was at Yaddo. I'll get $75 for each, which is nice. Knew Peter was behind my rejections, oddly enough—he fancies himself as a poet, as you know—but felt once he thought he'd shown off his power and glory, he would find it difficult or pointless to keep rejecting my good things, and so it has come to pass. . . .

Ted joins in sending lots of love to you both.

x x x Sivvy

Dear Mother,

How wonderful Sappho is going to have kittens. Oh, I wish we could somehow have one of them. You must describe each one in detail and note the day of their birth. We are very excited about this. So proud Warren has a scholarship next year. . . .

Yesterday the proofs of my book *The Colossus* came in a paper binding. We are so excited. The book will look handsome, 88 pages long. The poems look so beautifully *final*.

Had dinner at an excellent Indian restaurant with Peter and Jane Davison Monday at the expense of the *Atlantic*. Peter is worse than ever. He was furious (although he tried to conceal this) that I'd sent my stories and poems directly to Edward Weeks and not through him. I figured he'd been behind the rejections of my things, as since he came on, not one of my pieces had been taken and he is very jealous, as he now considers himself a real poet. Evidently his job is furthered by "bringing writers in," but I was there before he came. He also bragged about his work in the most puerile way. Said he read Ted's story in *Harper's*, "the issue before the issue with a poem of mine in it," and as we left them on the bus, he yelled desperately after us, "Look for the *Hudson Review*; I have a long poem coming out in it." Pity and shame kept me from yelling back, "I have four coming out in it." . . . He can't bear to hear about our work, so of course we tell him nothing.

Last night at Eliot's was magnificent. By a miracle I got the baby bathed and fed, me bathed and dressed . . . and the baby-minder instructed about the baby's relief bottle (she takes all 6 ounces beautifully; Ted tried her out on her first bottle while I was at the Olivier play to see if it would work). We took a taxi, as it was rush hour and the place a hard one to get to. A beautiful green May evening. Passed through streets I'd never seen: Little Venice, houses mirrored in a still green canal, Palace Gardens, streets with large pastel stucco houses with gardens, and the street lined with pink and white flowering trees. We saw a FOR SALE sign and promised ourselves we'd make a symbolic effort to inquire about it. Oddly enough, the more we set our sights on, the more good fortune occurs. No harm in dreaming: I see a lawn full of babies and descendants of Sappho—and a bookcase full of books!

The Eliots live in a surprisingly drab brick building on the first floor—yet a comfortable, lavish apartment. His Yorkshire wife, Valerie, is handsome, blond and rosy. He was marvelous. Put us immediately at ease. We exchanged American travel experiences; had sherry by the coal fire. I felt to be sitting next to a descended god; he has such a nimbus of greatness about him. His wife showed me his baby and little-boy pictures in their bedroom. He was handsome from the start. Wonderfully wry and humorous.

Then the Spenders arrived; he handsome and white-haired, and she . . . lean, vibrant, talkative, lovely. Her name is Natasha Litvin, and she is a concert pianist. Talk was intimate gossip about Stravinsky, Auden, Virginia Woolf, D. H. Lawrence. I was fascinated. Floated in to dinner, sat between Eliot and Spender, rapturously, and got along very well. Both of them, of course, were instrumental in Ted's getting his Guggenheim and his book printed.

Much love to you, Warren, Sappho and embryos.

x x x Sivvy

MAY 11, 1960

Dear Mother,

Ted is starting to work regularly over in Merwin's study, which is a great relief for both of us. It is impossible for him to work in this little place with me cleaning and caring for the baby, and when he is out, I have the living room and desk to myself and can get my work done . . . I find my first concern is that Ted has peace and quiet. I am happy then and don't mind that my own taking up of writing comes a few weeks later . . .

. . . Ted got a very touching letter from Somerset Maugham at his Riviera villa in answer to his thanks for the award. Maugham said he was "thrilled" at Ted's response. The award has been going on for many years, and Ted is only "the third person nice enough to write him"! He hopes to meet Ted when he comes to London in October. We were very excited and moved by this. As Maugham says, he is an old man. How easy it is to underestimate the needs of the great to be appreciated. I rather hope Ted can strike up a relationship with him like mine with Mrs. Prouty.

Perhaps the happiest evening we've spent in ages was Monday

Sylvia with Frieda at Stonehenge, May 1960 (photo: Anne Davidow Goodman)

night. I had Ann Davidow and her fiancé, Leo Goodman, for dinner. Remember Ann? She would have been my dearest friend at Smith if she hadn't left . . . She and I took up where we left off ten years ago. She graduated from the University of Chicago and has had her first children's book (she's primarily an artist) accepted by Grosset & Dunlap: *Let's Draw.* I have so missed a good American girl friend! Leo was a wonder: handsome, blond, blue-eyed and Jewish, on a Guggenheim at Cambridge, to be visiting professor at Columbia next year in mathematical statistics, very warm-hearted—that unique combination of the intellectual and loving-lovable Jew. He'd just been visiting his family in Israel and had fascinating and moving stories to tell. He was at Cambridge on a Fulbright in Ted's time, though they never met. Oddly enough, astrologically, Leo (his middle name means *Lion* in Hebrew, too) *is* a Leo, as Ted is—a very powerful and successful sign, and Ann, with her birthday on October 26, is practically my Scorpio twin. We all got along marvelously and hope to see more of them before Ann returns to America. . . .

When is Sappho due for her accouchement? I do hope she has as easy a time as I did. . . .

Lots of love,
Sivvy

MAY 21, 1960

Dearest Mother,

. . . Ted made his second BBC program this week, a recording of his story "The Rain Horse," a program which should bring in over $100 or so, with its rebroadcasting payment. Very nice. He has several projects going with them now—possibly a verse play when he finishes it (he's doing another now), a poem and talk for high school students with other poets and critics, a long poem, etc. The BBC is the one organization that pays excellently for poetry—$3 a minute for a reading, something like that. I got $70 for my story in the *London* magazine out this month, which I'll send on soon. My tattooing story should be out in the autumn *Sewanee Review.*

I am itching to get writing again and feel I shall do much better now I have a baby. Our life seems to have broadened and deepened wonderfully with her. Yesterday Faber sent on an envelope jammed with reviews of Ted's book, excellent without exception; all remarking how much better it is than his first, good though that was, etc. I revel in such clippings. He works mornings and afternoons at Merwin's study now and things are settling down. I am just crawling out from under the mountain of baby notifications, thank-you letters and answers to Ted's voluminous correspondence since his book and Maugham prize . . .

Ann Davidow and Leo Goodman drove us on a day's trip to Stonehenge a week ago. It was an exquisite day, and we passed through beautiful country, all the immense chestnut trees in bloom, golden laburnum, rhododendrons banking the road like a bower. The baby was angelic: I fed her once in the car on the way and once sitting in a grassy ditch of buttercups the Druids thoughtfully provided just outside the circle of gigantic, ominous upright stones . . .

x x x Sivvy

MAY 30, 1960

Dear Mother,

Congratulations to Sappho via you about her triplets! Ted and I were delighted with your descriptive letter about her successful confinement and only heart-broken we can't have one of the kittens if not the mother herself. Do keep us posted on their development. How superb the little all-black one must be! . . .

I hope you won't give our number or address to any more people . . . because it simply puts us in the position of refusing to go out (it's too expensive in time and money) and conspicuously not inviting anyone over because if we don't firmly put our feet down, we will become simply a way-station for all sorts of travelers. The baby's feedings and keeping the house clean, cooking, and taking care of Ted's voluminous mail, plus my own, have driven me so I care only for carving out hours where I can start on my own writing.

. . . After this month we are not going to give any poetry readings unless we are paid for them, for it is too expensive to hire sitters, etc. . . . This may seem drastic to you, but even a modest fame brings flocks of letters, requests, schoolgirls asking for "the author's own analysis of the symbols in his stories," etc., ad nauseam. If Ted didn't have his study, he'd be distracted by the phone, the mail, and odd callers so he'd get no work done at all. And as his secretary and my own, I have a personal reason for being strict. So please help us by not steering anyone our way.

. . . Ted's mother and Aunt Hilda are coming on a London tour this weekend and will drop in Saturday and Sunday—the first relatives to see the baby. I am so pleased *they* are coming! . . .

x x x x x x Sivvy

JUNE 11, 1960

Dearest Mother and Warren,

I'm sure I haven't written for ages. I've been going through a rather tired spell, and am just now catching up with rest again. It is now 10:30; my housework is done, and I look forward to a peaceful morning at home, reading and writing, since it is a grey, rainy day out.

Ted's mother and Aunt Hilda came down to London last weekend on a holiday tour via bus, very nice for us, since they stayed at a hotel and had most of their meals on the tour. They came over Saturday evening and again Sunday afternoon—we went to sit in the Merwins' garden—and stayed for dinner. Ted and I used their coming as a spur to finish up the house. I did a spring cleaning, scrubbing all the bookshelves and cupboards, etc., and he painted the little hall and one wall of the kitchen a marvelous vermillion, which just picked out the vermillion in the kitchen wallpaper and acts on me as a color-tonic. I can hardly stop looking at it, eating it up. I am so influenced by colors and textures. The red looks superb with the black-marbled linoleum, white woodwork and dark green cord curtains.

All we need do now is hang the last of our Baskins [*the artist Leonard Baskin had been a good friend at Smith*] . . . I'm very glad Ted attracts artist admirers, a much nicer crew than writers.

As I say, Ted's been getting all sorts of requests. One just came from a boys' school in Canterbury for a reading (with fee and accommodation) next fall. I hope to go along with the Pooker to see that lovely town. Of course, his animal poems are naturals for reading to young people. Ted wrote out a 10-page single-space sheaf of notes explaining his poems for Mrs. Prouty, which I've typed up and sent off. She is so willing to try them out, we wanted to give her all the help necessary.

You will probably get a letter from Ted's mother about her visit. I could see the dear woman was trying to notice everything, what I wore and all, to tell you. The baby was very good on the whole. . . .

Did I tell you we've seen the black-and-white line drawings for his [*Ted's*] children's book? [Meet My Folks]? Very fine and witty, for college people as well as children, I feel. We'll get reams of copies and have fun giving them to the Aldriches and all our other friends: a real gift book. I can't wait to see the book itself. Ted got a very heartening notice from Faber in the mail today: his book is selling so steadily and well (for poetry) that they are doing a second printing of it! So soon! We are delighted.

The marvelous box of baby things arrived this morning. They are darling. I held them up in front of her and she gooed at them. I think you are dressing her for your arrival next summer . . . You have no idea how much it means to me to dress her in partly American clothes . . .

Love from us all,
Sivvy

JUNE 24, 1960

Dear Mother,

. . . Last night Ted and I went to a cocktail party at Faber & Faber, given for W. H. Auden. I drank champagne with the appreciation of a housewife on an evening off from the smell of sour milk and diapers. During the course of the party, Charles Monteith, one of the Faber board, beckoned me out into the hall. There Ted stood, flanked by T. S. Eliot, W. H. Auden, Louis MacNiece on the one hand and Stephen Spender on the other, having his photograph taken. "Three generations of Faber poets there," Charles observed. "Wonderful!" Of course, I was immensely proud. Ted looked very at home among the great.

Then we went to the Institute of Contemporary Arts and read our poems to an audience of about 25–30 young people with another poet (or, rather, non-poet; very dull).

. . . We love hearing about the progress of Sappho's babies; they seem to be having about the same care as our own.

. . . After a midnight curfew like last night, getting up at 6 a.m. to feed Frieda (yes, we call her that now and it seems to suit her; we did really intend to name her after Aunt Frieda; she can take Rebecca if she goes through a romantic stage), I am exhausted by noon. I have kept up a schedule this week of going over to the study in the mornings, Ted giving Frieda her morning cereal, which holds her till I come back.

I am at the depressing, painful stage of trying to start writing after a long spell of silence, but the mornings at the study are very peaceful to my soul, and I am infinitely lucky we can work things out so I get a solid hunk of time off, or, rather, time on, a day. Ted goes in the afternoons. He has written three or four very good poems toward a third book. Now he is out at a rare book dealer's who is going to sell the manuscripts of his two books to the University of Indiana, we hope, for a few hundred dollars. Of course, they'll be worth more later, but he'll have other manuscripts then, and we can do with the money now, skimping along as we are on the end of the Guggenheim, which ended officially May 31.

Glad you liked the *New Yorker* poem. I should have another about women in a Spanish fishing village coming out this summer. Now I need to write some more I can sell to them. Ted is a marvel of understanding—strongly behind my having 3–4 hours of writing and study time a day. And he is wonderful with the baby, who dotes on him.

Well, I shall sign off for now with love to you, Warren, Sappho and progeny.

Your own,
Sivvy

June 30, 1960

Dear Mother,

. . . Something odd happened to me today which both elated and depressed me. I was walking the baby about the neighborhood after her injection; the air too cold and windy to go far, and half-dreamily let my feet carry me down a road I'd never been down before. I came up another street I seldom if ever use a block away and saw a house being painted and papered with a FREEHOLD FOR SALE sign. Now "Freehold" houses (outright yours after buying) are rare in London— most have 99-year leases from an agency which keeps ownership . . . In our area, really quite slummy, there is great opportunity to get a house for less than it will be in even a few years, as it is just beginning to be fancied up.

I was so excited about this house, 41 Fitzroy Road, *the street where Yeats lived,* and one end of it showing the green of Primrose Hill, that I ran home with the carriage and called Ted up at his study. He came to have a look at it. I have been thinking ahead a good deal, and this house had just the right number of rooms, built on the narrow plan of the houses here, at the end of a row joined together (very good, quiet on one side), and instead of backing onto another row, overlooking a charming Mews in back, only one floor high, so light floods in.

. . . Well, of course I had visions of a study for Ted in the attic there, a study for me, a bedroom for us, a nursery for the baby, and a room for guests (you) now and the next baby (babies). Plus the dear garden to hang laundry in and put playpens in (it's a walled garden). Such a house, behind the posh Regent's Park Road, yet part of an area not done-up as yet, on a corner, overlooking such a marvelous prospect, is just the Thing. I feel after our 3-year lease here (we could easily sublet this place), I simply don't want to move into rented rooms again. And Ted needs a study, and the baby will need a room. . . . This place is priced at 9,250 pounds (multiply by $2.80 for dollars).

. . . Ted, of course, is much more hesitant than I to commit himself. I just don't want to touch that $5,000 in our bank [*the money they'd earned from their writing*] and am loath to jeopardize Ted's writing, which he has just got going. One of us will probably have to take a job this fall in any case as we are stretching the Guggenheim out till September 1. Well, I am so tempted to somehow get hold of this place. London is the one place in Europe we could both easily get work and live cheaply in. I am thinking of work myself, if Ted would just feed the baby her noon meal, so he could write (I'll spill this over onto a second letter . . .) and earn us something. Have you, by the way, any ideas or suggestions. I do so miss somebody who has had experience in these matters to talk it all over with.

x x x Sivvy

Here's the second installment of my air letter and the note asking to withdraw $1,000 from our Wellesley savings . . . Anyhow, somebody else will probably snap the house up. But we will have to think seriously of committing ourselves to a house in a year or two. To complicate matters, Ted (and this is a secret; don't let him or anyone know I've mentioned this) has signified a real desire to take a degree in zoology here in London, an external course at the University. Naturally, this would be very difficult in any circumstances, especially if we were still bleeding rent to landlords. But I do so wish I could see a way clear for him to do it. It would be a job he could give his heart to and not the fancy literary white-collar work or English teaching which would make him unhappy. Refer to this as The Plan if you write me about it . . .

Well, tell me what you think about all my ramblings . . .

Love,
Sivvy

P.S. Ted's been offered 160 pounds (about $450) for his manuscripts. . . .

Dear Mother,

It was good to get your letter with the nice reactions about Frieda's pictures. I hope the clipping I sent you of Ted enshrined between The Great amuses you, too. He heard definitely this week that Indiana University is buying the manuscripts of his first two books, which is good. Also, even better news came this week: the BBC Third Programme has accepted his second verse play, "The House of Aries," for production this coming fall. Ted wrote the play in the three months after Frieda arrived—amazing when you consider the confusion and weariness of those early days. It is a marvelously funny, moving and serious play, full of superb speakable poetry, about a revolution overtaking a sleepy little village. The scene is in the bedridden Mayor's house. It is relatively short, about 70 typewritten double-spaced pages, and, with a little cutting, should take about an hour on the radio. We are really thrilled by this early commercial acceptance of his dramatic verse. He has scrapped the first play, "The House of Taurus," which really was only a rough, rather unpoetic draft, or redraft, of a theme from the *Bacchae* with an antiquated social message.

Interestingly enough, your letter about your dream of Ted's satire on Khrushchev arrived just before the BBC acceptance and one of the main characters in this play is the revolutionary Captain, a profoundly analyzed military figure. So you are prophetic! I hope his next play may see the stage . . .

The BBC has also asked to see some poems of mine for a program of New Poetry, which is kind of them, and I hope they take something . . . The Third Programme is a real blessing, and they pay wonderfully, about $3 a minute for poetry.

. . . Leo Goodman, Ann Davidow's genius, drove us to see *Roots*, the middle part of a working-class trilogy by one of the very new young British playwrights. Very realistic, down to the eating of ice cream and pouring potato water out of the potatoes. I kept thinking how much more amusing a play Ted could have done.

Eliot has offered to read and discuss any plays in verse Ted does, which is highly kind of him. My one aim is to keep Ted writing full-time. When I think how easily his uncle could help him until he gets making money, I see red . . .

x x x Sivvy

Dear Mother,

I have a feeling I haven't written for ages, so probably haven't. Ted is off for the afternoon with his friend, Danny Huws, to look for some sturdy wooden chairs for us in the antique and junk dealers in Portobello Road, and Frieda is woo-wooing in bed after her lunch feed, preparatory to dropping off for her afternoon nap . . . I have been getting little surprises ready for Ted's birthday tomorrow—a Fortnum and Mason chicken pie, expensive, but which he loves, a bottle of white wine, a photograph album in which I've pasted all our good pictures and written notes under them to encourage us to take more, a jar of maple syrup, and an original (!) painting in bright colors and ink of a sort of Aztec king done by the owner of our local art gallery, and I feel marked down for me by his wife out of kindness—this last being the main item. If it's nice I hope to go on a picnic with him and Frieda in Hampstead Heath or just Primrose Hill . . .

Friday I think we'll pack off to Yorkshire. Ted is a bit homesick for the moors, and I think both of us would benefit with a change. With luck and an express train, the trip should only take half a day. We'll come down again next Wednesday, in time for Frieda's vaccination Thursday. . . .

. . . We had lunch with one of the editors of the *Texas Quarterly* last Saturday at his rented rooms, with several other people. He is a professor and a charming, odd man. In addition to taking $100 worth of poems from the two of us, he is buying one of Ted's stories . . . for $100 also. He asked us to bring Frieda, and she was very good, sleeping the whole time. That evening a friend of Ted's sister, a young Hungarian poet and playwright, took us to dinner at a good Hungarian restaurant. I went off on my own last night to save the price of a babysitter and saw Laurence Olivier in the movie of *The Entertainer*. An amazing part for him, very much the un-hero.

Warren was so good to write us on the day of the publication of Ted's book. Odd how he describes his dates by height! I have a kind of running graph in my mind of their heights and nothing else. . . . As you were reading your World War II book about Auschwitz, I was finishing Alan Moorehead's *Gallipoli*: absolutely fascinating and terrifying. One senses the awful stupidity of generals (all these were safe on islands and boats and utterly out of communication with the soldiers) and the criminal negligence of politicians in this greatest fiasco of the first World War. Ted's father fought at Gallipoli, and a diary in his breast pocket stopped a bullet, so I felt incalculably lucky as I read of the mammoth, pointless slaughters that he survived and fathered the one husband I could imagine.

I am trying to have a rigid housework schedule—laundry and market Monday, iron Tuesday, etc., to counteract the otherwise helterskelter days. When one only has one's own inclination to consult, it is too easy to procrastinate. I am managing a fair amount of time for reading—just finished translating a play by Sartre, *Le Diable et Le Bon Dieu*—but have had little energy for writing in anything but my diary and a few light poems, two of which I think *The New Yorker* will take. My manuscript of poems should come back to you from the Yale contest, which I didn't win this year; the editor likes witty, light verse and I guess mine's too serious for him. Keep the manuscript and use it for scrap. I do feel sorry no publisher in America seems to want my book, for I am sure it is better than most first books, but I am glad it will come out here. . . .

Love to all,
Sivvy

HEBDEN BRIDGE
YORKSHIRE, ENGLAND
AUGUST 27, 1960

Dear Mother,

Ted and I have been up here in Yorkshire for a week now, and I am just beginning to feel that deep, peaceful energy that comes from having completely unwound and caught up on months of fatigue. We have been simply eating, sleeping, and taking long walks. I think you would love it up here—the unique combination of breathtaking scenery and invigorating air and *no* tourists.

Ted's cousin Vicky drove us to Whitby, a British seaside resort, for a day and a night. We took the baby, who is a very good traveler. . . . There is something depressingly mucky about English sea resorts. Of course, the weather is hardly ever sheer fair, so most people are in woolen suits and coats and tinted plastic raincoats. The sand is muddy and dirty. The working class is also dirty, strewing candy papers, gum and cigarette wrappers.

My favorite beach in the world is Nauset, and my heart aches for it. I don't know, but there is something *clean* about New England sand, no matter how crowded.

. . . Ted's Uncle Walter, with his curious habits, had for some reason—probably secretly admiring Ted's sticking to his chosen way of life—stuffed about $150 into his pocket one night we were out at the local pub, playing darts with him and Ted's dad, so we did not feel the strain of a holiday eating into our strict monthly budget.

Ted's mother has a lovely little garden up here—daisies, roses, poppies, brightly surviving in the lee of a black stone wall. I prefer this landscape and air to the sea. If only we had a house to ourselves . . . in a similar lonely spot, we could get an immense deal done. As Ted says, most people's problem is lack of ideas, while his is that he has so many ideas and no really settled quiet place to write them. We're going to ask the lady in the attic above us if he can work there while she's at her job. . . .

. . . I really hunger for a study of my own out of hearing of the nursery where I could be alone with my thoughts for a few hours a day. I really believe I could do some good stories if I had a stretch of time without distractions. . . .

. . . Lots of love to you, Warren, and Sappho . . .

x x Sivvy

CHALCOT SQUARE
LONDON, ENGLAND
AUGUST 31, 1960

Dear Mother,

. . . Ted has asked the kindly bohemian Mrs. Morton, who works as French translator at the telephone exchange, if he can use her room upstairs to write in while she's out. She was agreeable and he is up there now. We'll leave her a bottle of sherry every now and then as a thanks token . . . He just has to pop down when I call for lunch. A lifesaver. He says it's much more quiet and peaceful without all the distracting books and giddy hairdresser sublessees at the Merwins'. She leaves at 7:30 and is back at 5:30, so he has a good day.

I wish you could see the mail he gets! Italian translators, asking the British Council to speak to him, American editors over here hoping to meet him, magazines and newspapers panting for his poems and stories. He has already sold his five or six new poems several times over. He wants to work on a 3-act play now. He read his speech from his BBC play wonderfully over the radio, and I can't wait to hear it produced there this fall. There is a fantastic market for plays in London—all youngish authors.

All he needs is one really good, successful play, and we would have a good start. Our wish now is to get a car, a beach-wagony affair, tour Cornwall and Devon and buy a spreading country house with some land and settle down to write and raise a family. Once he has a successful play produced, we could do this; and then buy a Hampstead-London house overlooking the Heath if we ever got really wealthy. I'm sure we could do a great deal in the peace of the country—a London house is simply out of our reach now. We'd ideally like to buy outright, or as nearly so as possible, to cut rent and rates. Well, since being in London, we've made the equivalent of $1,250 in pounds, which is nice, not counting what we sent you in dollars, which we pretend doesn't exist. . . .

. . . I wish you'd spend half as much time in your afternoons playing with women's magazine stories, with feeling. Get a plot, imagine it in several scenes, with a character changing through events and finding something out about life and resolving problems. I'll edit anything you do for what it's worth. I bet if you pretended *this* was the way you had to earn some money, you'd turn out two or three things in the year. Why don't you try? . . . Start with the things you know, your friends' stories, and pare them objectively to have a beginning, middle and end—not just to copy the long span of life. You could do it; and I bet once you started, you'd have fun. You might start with someone resembling yourself, only with young children . . . whose job is threatened and work it out via another character. Call it *The Question Mark*. What do you think? Make use of the old adage you taught me: "Get your hero/heroine up a tree; fling stones at him/her, then have him extricate himself." People "identify" with people in trouble, people wrestling with problems! Get to it, mummy!

x x x Sivvy

Tuesday morning
September 13, 1960

Dear Mother,

. . . I have a poem about the baby in this month's *Atlantic* and Ted has a wonderful review of his book by Stanley Kunitz in the book section of this month's *Harper's*. . . .

. . . Tell us when you think you would be coming over here next summer and how long you could stay. We are cudgeling our brains to think of the best time to take our three months in Europe and probably will try this next March, April, and May. Then we would have some money left over, we hope, to live on the summer you came . . . Ted works five days a week in the lady's living room upstairs, a very quiet place, but is dependent on her kindness and he needs a study, so do I, and a yard for the children to play in. Well, these are all hopeful projects. . . .

Ted's radio play is so queer and interesting that I'm dying to see this next one, which came to him in a dream.

We left the baby with a girl at Merwins' and wangled a pass to the Picasso exhibit again (we had to go separately before) Sunday morning when it was only open to a few people with passes, not the 6,000-a-day, and had it all to ourselves. Met our friend and professor at Harvard, Jack Sweeney, who recorded us for the Lamont Library, and he is due any minute for a visit to see the baby. We'll lunch with him tomorrow.

. . . How I wish you had a country place near here. I envy my neighbors who have English country grandmothers and are always exchanging visits. Ted and your beautiful granddaughter join in sending much love—

Sivvy

September 23, 1960

Dear Mother,

Hello! . . .

. . . Last night Ted and I went to John Lehmann's fashionable house overlooking a green crescent in Kensington for drinks (it happened to be champagne, we were lucky). He's editor of the *London* magazine, where we both publish a good deal, and is very odd and nice. I met my young publisher there and Ted, the writer P. H. Newby on the BBC who had accepted his play. The little balcony was open and the evening pleasant. Ted's play is being broadcast twice late this fall here, and his translation of 100 lines or so of the *Odyssey*, too, as part of a series done by about a dozen different people. He found a word for word literal translation and made poetry of it. He's also been asked to be one of three editors of an annual anthology of poems that carries a fee of about $70, which is nice.

I have just enrolled today at the Berlitz School here for lessons in beginning Italian, as Ted, I think, would most like to go to Italy for his Maugham award, and I definitely want to be able to speak and read Italian to profit by this . . . If I get on well and like their methods, I might try classes in German or French . . . My first lesson is next week. I am also investigating the extension courses at London University, which I am too late to register for this year, but which I would like to get into next year. . . .

x x Sivvy

Dear Mother,

. . . Do you know anyone whose radio can get the BBC? It would be so nice for you to hear it. In Yorkshire we sat round at tea with all the relatives, tuned in and heard Ted reading two of his poems, one of them a speech from the play, which was lovely. He is also grunting over an article for *The Nation* on the Arnold Wesker trilogy of plays which we enjoyed seeing here this summer. He was originally going to refuse to do the article, but I felt it was because he, out of his great modesty, felt he didn't know enough about the American theatre of the 30's and Clifford Odets' plays (also, about Jews and Communists), so I very slowly persuaded him to take a day or two to read Odets at the British Museum and that his own instinctive reactions were better than most garbled criticism I had read. I also bought Penguin paperback editions of the two plays in print.

Usually I let his judgment be the final arbiter on such matters, but here I felt he'd be glad he'd done an article which is right up his alley. Wesker is just my age, and his play *Roots*, the middle of the trilogy, is about Norfolk farmers and full of good things. It's coming to America this year, so see it if it comes to Boston. Although *The Nation* pays very little, both of us admire the magazine very much . . .

Ted is slaving on these bits now to clear the decks for his own play, "The Calm," which sounds marvelously exciting, very fully realized. One success could buy us a house! It's a gamble and takes faith, but Ted has every reason to feel he can do it. When Charles Monteith at Faber had lunch with Ted and Thom Gunn last week, he said, "Tom Eliot is delighted with the drawings and poems in *Meet My Folks*"! I can't wait to see the book; it is scheduled for Spring 1961, about in time for Frieda's first birthday. . . .

London is inexhaustible. Although I'd very much like to have a house in Cornwall, I would have to have some arrangement whereby we'd be in London half a year and there half a year . . . Oh, well. I am much more a city-dweller than Ted. . . .

When I get really proficient in Italian (I'll take another course after this one right up to the time we go abroad), I want to start conversational German and spend our next vacation in Austria—perhaps visiting that inn you spoke of. My ambition now is to get three European languages really well—a unique chance, living so close to Europe. I've always wanted to be able to speak and read several languages and with the reasonableness [*in cost*] of these Berlitz courses, I can.

Oh, I would LOVE a subscription to *The New Yorker*. Ironically, I dreamed of getting one last night before your letter came. Well, best love to you, Warren, and dear Sappho.

x x x Sivvy

SATURDAY MORNING
OCTOBER 8, 1960

Dearest Mother,

. . . Ted is going to buy a cheap radio this week. His story "The Rain Horse" is going to be broadcast over the BBC again next week and his translation of a section of the *Odyssey* in a series of twelve translations by various people, and, in November and December, his play, which I have just finished typing up in final revised form. So I don't want to miss any of these. And the Third Programme has a lot I want to listen to—plays in French, too.

I have a new and exciting hobby. You will laugh. . . . I went downtown and bought three 2-yard lengths of material—one bright red Viyella (at $1.50 a yard), one bright blue linen, and one soft Wedgwood blue flannel with stylized white little flowers on it (both at about 50 cents a yard). I also bought a dress pattern and nightgown pattern (*Simplicity*). Yesterday I completely cut out and basted the little nightgown, in a one-year size. It is exquisite. . . . I pinned the little nightgown together to see what it would be like, and it's a little fairytale thing. . . . My next purchase that I'll save up for is a sewing machine! I don't know when anything has given me as much pleasure as putting together the flannel nighty for Frieda—the pieces are so little, they are very quickly done. If I practice a lot now, I'll probably be able to make most of her clothes when she goes to school. The London stores are full of marvellous fabrics . . .

Ted and I agreed that when we're wealthy, we will buy a loom, a kiln, and a book press and go into handcrafts (where the materials are expensive) and teach our children these things. We feel they are the most satisfying things in the world to do. I am awfully proud of making clothes for little Frieda. . . .

By the way, the Poets' Theater in Cambridge [*Massachusetts*] writes that they are planning to "do" Ted's play this month. We don't know whether this means just to give it a reading or to produce it, and we have airmailed them the revised version. Could you—in the guise of an interested person only—call up or get a copy of their season's program and find if it's going to be produced and then go to it and report to us? We want a secret, incognito eye to see what havoc they wreak on it since we are not there to check . . . Love from us all; keep away from germs!

Sivvy

WEDNESDAY
OCTOBER 26, 1960

Dear Mother,

Well, I sent off a heavy packet of two books—one for you and one for Warren—by surface mail yesterday. I would have sent them by air, but the price, even book rate, was prohibitive as the books are fat and weigh a good deal. I am touched that my publisher got them out in my birthday week after I told him how superstitious I was. I hope the two printing errors toward the end don't upset you as much as they did me! I've marked the corrections in your books and am appalled that after several proofreadings I was guilty of letting them get through, but Ted has reassured me about them and you do, too. I am delighted with the color of the cover—the rich, green oblong, white jacket and black-and-white lettering—and the way the green cover inside matches with the gold letters. It is a nice fat book which takes up ¾ of an inch on the shelf, and I think they did a handsome job of it. . . .

. . . I am scheduled to go to the British Broadcasting Company and record two of my new poems (post-book) which they finally accepted after rejecting two groups from my book. I am very pleased about this. One poem is a monologue from the point of view of a man about the flowers in the lady's room upstairs (where he isn't working any more—her visitors are something she wants to keep secret. . . .) The other poem is about candles and reminiscences of grammy and grampy in Austria spoken while nursing Frieda by candlelight at 2 a.m. I'm very fond of it.

Last night Ted and I went to dinner at Stephen Spender's house with an artist; the poet Louis MacNiece and one of his girl friends, the novelist, ageing, with violet-white hair, Rosamond Lehmann (one of the well-known Lehmann family—her brother John being editor of the *London* magazine and her sister Beatrix being an actress). Their conversation is fascinating—all about Virginia Woolf, what Hugh Gaitskell said to Stephen in Piccadilly that morning, why Wystan (W. H. Auden) likes this book or that, how Lloyd George broke Spender's father's heart, and such-like. Rosamond Lehmann's childhood was spent among such house visitors as Browning, Schumann—or at least among memories of their visits—that whole old world surrounding them like a vision. . . .

Ted's income from the BBC this year has been as good as a salary—we've about $1,600 in the bank here from our English writing, and he has an exciting prospect of doing broadcasts for school children, which would go all over England with no paper correcting or the personal drag of actual classroom teaching . . . Love to you and Warrie from Ted, Frieda, and me.

Our names for our next three children, by the way, are Megan (for a girl), Nicholas, and Jacob. How do you like them?

x x x Sivvy

Dear Mother,

I think this birthday has been the best of all. I woke yesterday morning to find myself lying surrounded by interesting knobbly brown parcels, a German coffee cake with a candle lit in the middle of it, and Frieda sitting at my side, supported by Ted, holding the morning's mail and a bar of my favorite German chocolate. Ted really knocked himself out; I have a new badly needed pair of red plush slippers lined with white fuzzy wool, *two* pairs of plastic overshoes, one for heels, as Ted wanted me to have something easily carried about for this showery London weather, a Fortnum & Mason chicken pie (our standby for special occasions), a bottle of pink champagne, the Tolkien trilogy, *Lord of the Rings* (adult version and extension of our beloved Hobbit) . . . and three wonderful slabs of strange cheeses for us to test: a gooey ripe Brie, a superbly mouldy blue Stilton, and a fat, round Wensleydale in a cloth sack all its own. I loved the cards and letters from you and Warren. I consider the load of pajamas for Frieda my present from you—I'd so much rather get something for her. . . .

. . . Tuesday night we are going to the annual Guinness Awards champagne party (the award Ted got while in America), which should be fun. Hope you get my book in good order. Tell me what you think of it. Lots of love to you and Warren,

Sivvy

Dear Mother,

I'm enclosing two of the latest shots of the Pooker, alias Bunzo Bun . . . She sings now, a little high voice and funny look. . . .

I gather you are going to the reading of Ted's play. Do let us know what you think of it . . . He is now working on the rewriting of the libretto of the Tibetan Book of the Dead for that Chinese composer. He is very encouraged about it and really mastering it now. I think we'll go up to Yorkshire over the weekend, as he has been asked to be present at a literary luncheon in Leeds about northern writers which will be put on television with John Betjemann's program. I hope he gets his face into the screen. Then he has a lecture at the University in Hull.

. . . Had a lovely dinner the other night with a young couple around the corner in Chalcot Crescent—where we'd love to live if only a house came up—quiet, pretty, with nice professional families— and neighbors of theirs, a lively older couple on the BBC. I am immensely fond of this neighborhood! Love to all.

x x x Sivvy

P.S. Got a Press ticket from Stephen Spender for the last day of the Lady Chatterley trials at the Old Bailey—very exciting—especially with the surprising verdict of "not guilty"! So *Penguin Books* can publish the unexpurgated edition—a heartening advance for D. H. Lawrence's writings!

SATURDAY, NOVEMBER 19, 1960

Dear Mother and Warren,

I feel I haven't written you for ages, which is probably true. Frieda has been teething . . . and cries off and on all night—great miserable yowls impossible to ignore, and the one thing to comfort her is to nurse her . . . I got a sort of soothing syrup from the doctor and tried children's aspirin in orange juice, but nothing seems to stop her 2–3 a.m. crying bout. I'll probably see the doctor again this week . . .

I don't know if I said in my last letter that my book costs about $2.15 (15 shillings) here, very reasonable compared to American prices, and my publisher is William Heinemann . . . Since I got no prize or any American publisher, they haven't bothered to advertise it, so I probably won't make a penny on it unless I get some award later to call it to the public's attention—the 10 copies I ordered more than cancelled out my tiny pre-publication sale. Well, it's a nice gift book . . . My publisher thought the acknowledgments were super-fluous—only one or two magazines require them, and usually they are put in as a kind of courtesy to the magazines and bolstering of the writer's ego. I'm glad they didn't—my list was so long, it would have looked ostentatious. Both of us are getting more retiring about blazoning biographies and publication-notices everywhere.

. . . Ted has finished with his scheduled talks, lectures and commissions at last and is now free to work on his three-act play, and I shall see he is kept clear of all distractions. His broadcast translation of a passage from the *Odyssey* was very well reviewed in the Sunday papers, and I am going to hear myself read two poems over the radio Sunday night . . .

I hate to bother you about this again, but *could* you look around once more for the yellow paperbound Speedwriting book, or beg, borrow or steal another copy and airmail it to me? I have a chance at quite an amusing job later this year if I brush up my Speedwriting, which stood me in excellent stead with that exacting head of Harvard's Sanskrit Department . . . I'm dying to get hold of it. . . .

. . . Much love to you both from the three of us.

Sivvy

November 25, 1960

Dear Mother,

First of all, tell Warren how proud Ted and I are that he passed his Orals! From our permanent vacation over here, he sounds to be performing Herculean labors. How much chance is there that he might come to London for that conference? Can he apply for it? We would be overwhelmed with joy if he could come. He would be knocked silly by little Frieda. . . .

Mrs. Prouty sent me a cheque for $150 to celebrate the publication of my book, the dear. I won't earn another thing on that, so we're putting it toward current expenses. Ted has the best story he's done yet, about a fat man shooting rabbits at harvest-time, accepted by the BBC today, which will mean a nice sum. He'll read it, and then it will probably be played twice, once in Christmas week. I'm going to send it to magazines in America now. . . .

Helga Huws had a baby this week, her second daughter, Lucy Teresa. I visited her at the hospital and saw the little thing in the nursery—made me want another *really* small one immediately. I would so like a permanent spacious place where I could have as many children as I wanted!

Let us know how Ted's play sounds.

Lots of love,
Sivvy

November 28, 1960

Dearest Mother,

I'm sitting here in the late evening, curtains drawn, the little Pifco warming the room cheerily, in my bathrobe, on one of Ted's rare nights out. He has driven to Coventry with Dido Merwin and John Whiting, a playwright, to see Bill Merwin's play at the repertory theatre there, *The Golden West*.

Bill is in America, collecting thousands on lectures and readings. Ted left about three and won't be home till 3 or 4 a.m. as it's a long drive, so I've had one of my rare, rare times to myself. I realize how crowded we are here when I am alone for a bit, enjoying every minute of it, feeling inclined to do little secret things I like . . .

I am now working very hard on something I never really attacked right—women's magazine stories. Very rusty and awkward on my first, I got into the swing and am half through my second with a plot for a third . . . I also have a fine, lively agent (who wrote me about a story of mine in the *London* magazine) whom I have not met and who is affiliated with one of the best NYC agencies, and so, after I get my earliest acceptances in the many women's weeklies here, they'll send any stuff good enough to the *Saturday Evening Post*, etc. For the first time, I feel I know where I'm going . . .

x x x Sivvy

[Undated; written about December 17, 1960]

Dear Mother and Warren,

I am writing this on the eve of our departure to Yorkshire. Both of us are dying to go, recharge our batteries and come back ready for intense work by New Year's Day, brimful of energy to carry out our projected ideas. I am writing in a litter of BBC contracts, Christmas cards, and Frieda's winter clothes, having just read a poem for a book review of my book over the radio (which will be broadcast next week, a day after Ted's story, "The Harvesting"). . . .

Don't take his elaborate metaphysical explanations too seriously and *don't show them to anyone.* He is so critical of the play—which I think reads perfectly as a symbolic invasion of private lives and dreams by mechanical war-law and inhumanity such as is behind the germ-warfare laboratory in Maryland—that he feels a need to invent elaborate disguises as a smokescreen for it.

Both of us have emerged with heads above water after a deeply demanding year and are eager to plunge into our "new" lives of writing and private forays on London's wonders. . . . I've sent lots of [*Christmas*] cards and in many enclosed my poem about a "Winter Ship" off T-Wharf . . .

We got a long, marvelous letter from Mrs. Prouty and have sent her off a card with letters and poems from each of us. I am *so* pleased her reaction to my book has been so enthusiastic. I only hope I get a women's story or two published in time for her to see them [*Mrs. Prouty died in 1974*], as I think that would please her most of all.

. . . I am very excited that children seem to be an impetus to my writing, and it is only the lack of space that stands in my way. As soon as I start selling women's magazine stories, I could afford a half-day babysitter or something equivalent to do the drudge-work. I think Ted and I will probably decide to appear on a radio program called "Two of a Kind," an interview series with husbands and wives who have the same profession.

(Keep after that Speedwriting book. All sorts of queer part-time jobs crop up here.)

Oh, how I'm longing for the deep dreamless sleeps of Yorkshire! We're both so tense we need to unwind for weeks. We'll be back here by New Year's Day.

I've got my first two *New Yorkers* already and revel in them. It's like getting a fresh present from you every week!

Much, much love to you and a thousand Christmas wishes.

Your own Sivvy

HEBDEN BRIDGE
YORKSHIRE, ENGLAND
DECEMBER 24, 1960

Dear Mother and Warren,

Happy Christmas Eve. Ted and I have been up here in Yorkshire for a week now, and I am writing in the calm before the crowded 3-day holiday. The sun has burned through the mists, and grey sheep are grazing on the field in front of my window. . . . Ted looks ten years younger. His decision to refuse speaking engagements and cumbersome commissions has relieved both of us. He refused a request to appear on TV as "poet of the year," much to his mother's disappointment, but I understand very well how public life appalls him. He is upstairs now working on his full-length play.

I hope you enjoyed that *Sunday Observer* review about my book . . . I was very encouraged by it. We enjoyed listening to Ted's story Saturday and my book reviewed Sunday along with Pasternak, E. E. Cummings, Betjemann, and others and I reading one of the poems. I hope I can persuade the BBC to accept a program about young American women poets which I am drawing up, now that they seem willing enough to record my odd accent.

I've had a very heartening letter from my young agent, who liked my second women's magazine story very much and has sent it out. I probably won't hear about either of these first two for weeks, but am beginning a longer, more ambitious one today about a girl who falls in love with a beautiful old house and manages finally to possess it. . . . I'll have a story in the *LHJournal* or *SatEvePost* yet.

Ted and I wrote out the plot for a romance set up here on the moors, and we have two more coming up—a suspense story about an art gallery (I'll do research on forgeries, lost old masters and quiz our artist–gallery-owner friends on this) and one about a lady astrologer for which Ted is going to work out horoscopes. The wonderful thing about these stories is that I can do them by perspiration, not inspiration—so I can work on them while Frieda is playing in the room . . . My agent wants me to come in and talk to her again—she knows all the editors and magazines, and her practical know-how is extremely helpful. As soon as I am good enough, she'll send my things to their New York counterpart. I'm heartened she thinks my first two *real* attempts are good enough to send around here.

Ted and I have had some wonderful moor walks, 10-mile or so hikes, and the air here is superb. Do plan to stay in England *at least a month* this summer. Ideally, we'd like you and Frieda to get acquainted by your staying near us and having lunch and suppers with us, then maybe we could go off to Ireland or France for a week while you lived at our place with Frieda . . . Then, later, we could all go up to Yorkshire for a week, where you could stay at a nearby inn . . . I wish I had some of my own relatives to admire Frieda. *Is* there any chance of Warren's coming to that conference in London?

Do make a final search for that bright yellow paperback Speedwriting book! . . . I am so frustrated without it as in a few days I could get my speed back and apply for one of these part-time jobs as secretary to a woman journalist or architect or such that come up on occasion. I just feel if I walked into the house I could put my hand on it.

In future years, if you want an easy solution for presents to us, you might send on, piece by piece, my favorite children's books—that big orange "Cuckoo Clock" for one and my beloved *Red* books—*Mary Poppins,* I'd love her books, too.

Hope your packages arrived all right.

x x x Sivvy

Dearest Mother,

. . . I'm eagerly awaiting word about my two ladies' magazine stories (which my agent, at least, is delighted with) and working on a longer third. I've also been asked to edit an American supplement of modern poetry by a critical magazine here and to allow two poems from *The Colossus* to be published in a British anthology of modern British poetry, because I "live in England, am married to an Englishman, and the editor admires my work." . . .

We are planning an absolutely unsocial, quiet, hardworking winter here now. I have been bothered lately by what my doctor calls a "grumbling appendix"—occasional periods of sharpish pain, which then go away, but my appendix is extremely tender to touch. I am thinking seriously of asking him to let me have it out at some convenient time (if that's ever convenient!) this spring, as I have nightmares about going to Europe on our Maugham grant, getting a rupture and either dying for lack of hospital care or being cut up by amateurs, infected, ad infinitum. Don't you think it would be advisable to have it out now? I feel I'm living with a time-bomb as it is. Have you any idea how long one is hospitalized, how painful it is, etc.? Naturally, one is reluctant to get oneself in for an operation like that if one isn't forced to it, but I don't want to worry about rupture in Europe or during pregnancy. Encourage me, and I'll have it out with my doctor. I'd wait, of course, till Frieda was fully weaned and I was in good health . . .

x x x Sivvy

Dearest Mother,

. . . You are a genius to locate a Speedwriting book! I don't know whatever could have happened to the one I had. In any case, I'll guard these with my life—they will probably come in handy more than once. I'm really an awful correspondent this Christmas, I've felt so blue with these repeated sinus colds. . . . I am going to have an interview with a surgeon on Friday, the 13th (I hope the verdict is more auspicious than the day) about my appendix, and I suppose my job is to convince him it should come out before I go to Europe. I hope you second me in this, as I find it a bit hard to more or less volunteer for an operation of any sort that isn't an emergency necessity. Do encourage me, I feel the lack of some relative or friend to bolster my morale! . . .

Had a very sweet British poet, Thom Gunn, who is teaching at Berkeley, for lunch yesterday, passing through London on *his* Maugham award. I wish he lived near us; he is a rare, unaffected, kind young chap. Next week Ted and I are recording a radio program of 20 minutes' interview, called "Two of a Kind"—about our both being poets—and Ted's doing a program for the Caribbean services. Now he's typing out two children's programs—one about writing a novel (which he tried successfully with his Cambridge schoolboys) and the other a personal reminiscence about how catching animals turned into writing poems. He and Frieda are my two angels—I don't know how I ever managed without them.

x x x to you, Warrie and Sappho—
Sivvy

Dearest Mother,

Well, your letters have kept coming and coming and increasing my morale immensely through a rather glum period and now I am recovered enough to write letters, I realize how long a silence I've plunged into . . . I've embarked, with Ted's help, on a drastic program to pull my health up from the low midwinter slump of cold after cold, and am eating big breakfasts (oatmeal, griddles, bacon, etc., with lots of citrus juices), tender steaks, salads, and drinking the cream from the tops of our bottles, along with iron and vitamin pills . . . I feel immensely homesick when you talk of white snow! All we've had here since October is grey rain. . . .

I'm *so* looking forward to next summer. *Could* you possibly alter your flight time to cover August 20? (You better sit down, now, perhaps!) The reason I'm asking is that I discovered today your second grandchild is due about then, and I'd be overjoyed to have you there to meet Nicholas/Megan when he or she arrives!

. . . The way things look now, I will probably have my appendix out sometime in February (my doctor advised an early date as I'm pregnant and says there's absolutely no danger), rest all March, and head to Southern Europe for April, May and the greater part of June on the Maugham grant. Then here for a leisurely July with you (a week or two in France for us, perhaps), savoring Frieda and being together. I wish the four of us could manage a trip to the Scilly Isles, which we hear are beautiful, but that would probably mean reservations way in advance. *Do* tell me you'll try to stay to see the new baby!!!

I've taken on a temporary part-time job which is lots of fun to keep me from brooding about my hospital sojourn, which I don't look at all forward to. If you know anyone who's had an appendix out, do reassure me. I have a mortal fear of being cut open or having anesthesia. I don't know how I can stand being away from the baby two weeks—that will be the hardest thing of all; she is prettier and more adorable every day.

Anyhow, my job is from 1–5:30 and involves copy-editing and page layout for the big spring issue of *The Bookseller*, a trade organ which comes out weekly but has two big biannual issues full of ads and bibliography of *all* coming books in England, plus 150 pages [*of*] editorial sections (fiction, biography, children's books, etc.) with 400 or so pictures. I've been rewriting picture captions and a lot of publicity department biographical material from all the various publishers. The editor was pleased enough to let me lay out the whole children's section of pictures and galley proofs (18 pages), where I had the fun of pasting the notice of Ted's children's book in a prominent position! . . .

Oh, how I look forward to your coming! My heart lifts now that the year swings toward it . . . Do tell me you're happy about our coming baby! We already love it. A big hug for you and Warren.

x x x Sivvy

Dear Mother,

. . . I went to see my doctor this morning, and he predicts August 17 for the baby's arrival, Ted's birthday. How I wish you could switch to a flight to cover that date! It would be such fun having you come to see one baby and go away having seen two.

. . . My afternoon job is very pleasant and I have done about 60 pages of layout now, which I enjoy very much—balancing the pictures and photographs and jacket designs on double-page spreads, ordering the publishers according to importance and pasting the galleys into place. I get to do all the little rush jobs of typing as my speed is the marvel of the office where the few others hunt-and-peck, and I sound like a steam engine in contrast. My afternoons out have helped Ted really plow into his play, and I think this one will probably be really stageable. He's full of ideas and in wonderful form.

We heard our 20-minute broadcast, "Poets in Partnership" ["*Two of a Kind*" *show*] this Tuesday morning, where an acquaintance of ours on the BBC asked us questions, and we ended by reading a poem each—quite amusing. . . .

We have as names the old Nicholas Farrar and the new Megan Emily (I like Meg as a nickname, don't you? Anyway, get used to it. The Emily is a feminizing of daddy's Emil and also for E. Dickinson and E. Brontë). . . .

Ted and I went to a little party last night to meet the American poet I admire next to Robert Lowell—Ted (for Theodore) Roethke. I've always wanted to meet him, as I find he is my influence. Ted gave me his collection *Words for the Wind* this Christmas and it's marvelous. Look it up in the library. I think you would like the greenhouse poems at the front very much. He's a big, blond, Swedish-looking man, much younger-seeming than his 52 years . . . Ted and I got on well with him and hope to see him again.

I should probably go into hospital at the end of this month. My doctor says it's the best time, after my first 3 months [of] pregnancy, and perfectly safe.

. . . I'm looking most forward to Italy and practicing my Italian . . . I'm in much better spirits with the promise of spring and summer and your coming. You will be mad for Frieda; she's the prettiest little girl I've ever seen and sweet as can be. I want a house big enough for *at least* four!

Roethke said any time Ted wants to teach at Washington State to give him a nod, so in a few years we'll, no doubt, make another American year! Lots of love to you and dear Warren.

x x x Sivvy

MONDAY, FEBRUARY 6, 1961

Dearest Mother,

I feel awful to write you now after I must have set you to changing your plans and probably telling Warren and your friends about our expecting another baby, because I lost the little baby this morning and feel really terrible about it.

The lady doctor on my panel came about nine after Ted called in and will come again tomorrow, so I am in the best of hands, although I am extremely unhappy about the whole thing.

I looked so forward to sharing a new little baby with you and felt that some good fate had made this one to coincide with your visit. I am as sorry about disappointing you as anything else, for I'm sure you were thinking of the birth as joyously as I was.

The doctor said one in four babies miscarry and that most of these have no explanation, so I hope to be in the middle of another pregnancy when you come anyway. Luckily I have little Frieda in all her beauty to console me by laughing and singing "Lalala" or I don't know what I'd do. I'm staying in bed, and Ted is taking wonderful care of me. He is the most blessed, kind person in the world, and we are thinking of postponing our Italian trip till next fall as Frieda will be walking by then, and perhaps giving ourselves a two-week holiday in the Scilly Isles this April, if we get some of the money that Ted's applied for from the Royal Literary Fund, which is supposed to aid "distressed authors" with family difficulties.

All weekend, while I was in the shadow of this, he gave me poems to type and generally distracted me . . . I have, as you may imagine, an immense sympathy for Dotty now [*my sister, who had had three miscarriages and could have no children of her own*], and as I grow older feel very desirous of keeping in touch with my near kin. When you come this summer, we shall have lovely times with Frieda, and I hope I'll be safely on with another Nicholas/Megan.

I've been commissioned to write a poem for the summer festival of poetry here, which is an honor as only about a dozen are invited to contribute, so I'll try to plunge into work too, now, as it is a good cure for brooding.

Do keep in touch with Mrs. Prouty. I wouldn't mind your mentioning this to her in a casual way; it would probably be better for her to hear of it from you than me. I always make it a point to sound cheerful and wanting for nothing when I write her.

Do write and cheer me up.

Lots of love,
Sivvy

THURSDAY
FEBRUARY 9, 1961

Dearest Mother,

I do hope the sad news in my last letter didn't cast you down too much. I foresaw how you'd enjoy sharing the good news with all our friends and relatives and only hope it hasn't been too hard to contradict our optimistic plans. I hadn't told anyone over here, thank goodness, so I don't have to suffer people commiserating with me, which I couldn't stand just now. As the doctor said, it will probably just mean having a baby in late autumn instead of late summer. All I can say is that you better start saving for another trip another summer, and I'll make sure I can produce a new baby for you then! . . . Megan isn't pronounced Mee-gan, by the way, but Meg'-un, with a short "e." Forget about *King Lear!*

. . . I'm feeling pretty well back to normal now, and my daily routine with Frieda and Ted keeps me from being too blue. Ted's been extravagant and bought us tickets to *The Duchess of Malfi*, Webster's wonderful play, starring Dame Peggy Ashcroft, tomorrow night, so we're looking forward to that . . . He's writing magnificently on his full-length play, and it is the best thing he's done. Probably good enough to get a *full* production at the Poets' Theater [*Cambridge, Mass.*] and, we hope, to be staged somewhere here. If all goes well, he should finish it in a month or so. He's also writing a lot of very lively, amusing, colorful poems and has ideas for stories and another children's book. I feel so proud, coming on reviews of him here and there, "Ted Hughes, the well-known poet" and so on. We have just heard from Yale that they are going to produce a full record of Ted reading his poems in their new series, with his picture on the jacket. They've only about twenty poets on their list so far, so this is very nice. Get your friends to buy copies when it comes out! . . .

. . . Ted joins me in sending you lots of love. *Is* there really a chance of Warren's coming to England this fall? I'd like to make sure of being here if there is!

Love,
Sivvy

Dear Mother,

By the time you get this letter, I shall probably have had my appendix out and be well on the road to recovery. I got my "invitation" to come to hospital this afternoon, so I imagine I shall be operated on sometime tomorrow. It's the 27th [*her birthday was October 27th*] so I hope it's a lucky day for me. I've had this hanging over my head for almost two months now and shall be very glad to get rid of it.

I've got all the house in order, supplies in for Ted; and yesterday I baked banana bread, Tollhouse cookies, and today am making apricot tarts and griddle batter, so he shall have something to go on with. . . .

As if to cheer me up, I got an airmail special-delivery letter from the *Atlantic*, accepting a 50-line poem I did as an exercise called "Words for a Nursery," spoken in the person of a right hand, with 5 syllables to a line, 5 stanzas, and 10 lines to a stanza. *Very fingery.* I imagine that will bring in about $75. I have started writing poems again and hope I can keep right on through my hospital period. I'm bringing a notebook in with me as you (and Ted) suggested to occupy myself by taking down impressions. . . .

I probably told you about Ted and me doing a recorded interview for a BBC radio program, called "Two of a Kind," a couple of weeks ago . . . Well, they broadcasted part of it again on the Sunday following on the weekly roundup program, and evidently it was used as a "model" for the Talks producers, for they decided to give it a full rebroadcast after that on the weekend . . . which doubles the $75 fee. We got some funny letters, among them one offering us a big house and garden (I'm not quite clear under just what circumstances) since I had said our dream was to have a place big enough so we could yell from one end to the other without hearing each other. . . .

Lots of love,
Sivvy

Dear Mother,

I am writing this to you propped up in my hospital bed less than 24 hours after my operation, which I had Tuesday about 11 a.m., instead of Monday as I thought. I must have really been secretly worried about my appendix a good deal of the time, as now that it is gone, I feel nothing but immense relief and pleasant prospects ahead. The worst part was coming in Sunday night and finding I had to wait a day longer than I thought, being "under observation" Sunday night and Monday. The progress they've made since I had my tonsils out in anesthetics is wonderful. I had an injection in my ward bed which dried up all my saliva and made me pleasantly drowsy. A very handsome young lady anesthetist introduced herself to me and said I'd see her later. She gave me an arm-shot in the anteroom which blacked me out completely. I drowsed pleasantly the rest of the day after I had the shot of painkiller and was ready to see dear Ted when he came during visiting hours in the evening, bearing a jar of freshly squeezed orange juice, a pint of milk, and a big bunch of hothouse grapes—none of which they've let me touch yet. . . . The food is pretty awful, but Ted brought me two huge rare steak sandwiches . . . and a tin of Tollhouse cookies, which I'll eat later on.

He is an absolute angel. To see him come in at visiting hours, about twice as tall as all the little, stumpy people, with his handsome, kind, smiling face is the most beautiful sight in the world to me. He is finishing his play and taking admirable care of little Frieda.

. . . On my first night here (Monday), Ted was able to bring me an exciting air letter from *The New Yorker*, offering me one of their coveted "first reading" contracts for the next year! This means I have to let them have the first reading of all my poems and only send poems elsewhere if they reject them. I had to laugh, as I send all my poems there first anyway. I get $100 (enclosed) for simply *signing* the agreement, 25 percent more per poem accepted, plus what they call a "cost-of-living" bonus on work accepted, amounting to about 35 percent *more* per year, plus a higher base rate of pay for any work they consider of *exceptional* value. The contracts are renewable each year at their discretion. How's that! As you may imagine, I've been reading and rereading the letter, which came at the most opportunely cheering moment.

I am in a modern wing of this hospital—all freshly painted pink walls, pink and green flowered bed curtains and brand-new lavatories, full of light and air—an immense improvement over that grim ward at the Newton-Wellesley where Ted and I visited you! The nurses are all young, pretty, and cheerful . . . I am in a big ward, divided by a glass and wood partition with about 17 beds on my side. The women at my end are young and cheerful. One has a T.B. knee; three had bunion operations; a couple are in plaster casts. I'm really as serious a case as any of them—a great relief to me, for I dreaded a ward of really sick people lying about and groaning all the time.

Later: Now Teddy has come, so I shall sign off. With much love to you and Warrie—

Sylvia

MONDAY, MARCH 6, 1961

Dear Mother,

I am writing propped up in my hospital bed, six days now after my operation. My stitches are "pulling" and itching, but the nurses say that's a sign I'm healed . . . I'm hoping I may get rid of them today. Actually, I feel I've been having an amazing holiday! I haven't been free of the baby one day for a whole year, and I must say I have secretly enjoyed having meals in bed, backrubs, and nothing to do but read (I've discovered Agatha Christie—*just* the thing for hospital reading—I am a who-dun-it fan now), gossip, and look at my table of flowers sent by Ted's parents, Ted, Helga Huws, and Charles Monteith, Ted's editor at Faber's. Of course, *before* my operation I was too tense to enjoy much and for two days after, I felt pretty shaky since they starve you for about 40 hours before and after; but I was walking around the ward on my third day and gossiping with everyone.

The British have an amazing "stiff upper-lipness"; they don't fuss or complain or whine, except in a joking way, and even women in toe-to-shoulder casts discuss family, newspaper topics and so on with amazing resoluteness. I've been filling my notebook with impressions and character studies. Now I am mobile, I make a daily journey round the 28-bed ward, stopping and gossiping. This is much appreciated by the bedridden women, who regard me as a sort of ward newspaper, and I learn a great deal, for they are all dying to talk about themselves and their medical involvements. The nurses are very young, fresh, sweet as can be; the Sister (head nurse), lenient, wise and humorous, and all the other women and girls wonderfully full of kindness and cheer. The ward . . . overlooks, on my side, a pleasant park with antique gravestones . . . so aesthetically I feel happy . . . The food is pretty flat and dull, but each day Ted brings me a jar of fresh orange juice, a pint of creamy milk, and a steak sandwich or a salad, so I'm coming along fine. I feel better than I have since the baby was born, and immensely relieved to get rid of this troublesome appendix, which has probably been poisoning me for some time. The ward doctor said I'm fine inside—perfectly healthy in every way, so that's a relief. I've been on a strong diet of iron and vitamin pills and haven't had a cold since that ghastly Christmas interval.

. . . Ted has been an angel. I sense he is eager for me to come home and little remarks like "I seem to be eating a lot of bread" and "Doesn't the Pooker make a lot of dirty pots" tell me he is wearying of the domestic routine. Poor dear! I'd like to know how many men would take over as willingly and lovingly as he has! Plus bringing me little treats every night.

Fortunately there seem to be only two "serious" cases now—a brain operation, who still is in a coma after half a week with tubes in her nose and a skull-sock on her head, and an old lady run over by a car with both legs broken, who keeps shouting, "Police, policeman, get me out of here" and calling the nurses "devils who are trying to murder me" and knocking the medicine out of their hands. Her moans, "Oh, how I suffer," are very theatrical; and as she is shrewd all day, picking up the least whisper, and as they give her drugs for pain, I think most of this is an act for attention. I find all of us are more entertained than annoyed by this as our days are otherwise routine, and she adds a good bit of color with her curses and sudden crashes as she flings glasses of medicine about.

Anyhow, I shall be glad as anything to get out. . . .

Lots of love, Sivvy (your appendix-less daughter)

CHALCOT SQUARE
LONDON, ENGLAND
MARCH 17, 1961

Dear Mother,

A thousand apologies for this great gap between my letters. I have been so heartened by yours and say with great pleasure, "In three months from tomorrow you will arrive," over and over. I have been in a kind of grisly coma these last ten days and fit for little but vegetating . . . My stitches came out Tuesday the 7th (the worst bit of all—I hated the niggling twinges of each of the nine, plus the pulling off of a large plaster bandage, much more than the actual operative experience), and I was let go home Wednesday the 8th, with strict orders not to do any lifting or heavy work for two weeks but to "behave like a lady," or I'd feel as if run over by a small bus, etc., etc.

. . . The most difficult part has been this home convalescing. Poor

Ted insists he *likes* doing all the baby-lifting and laundry-bring and so on, but he's been at it over a month now since my miscarriage, and I do think it bothers *me* more than him. I'm a model convalescent if I'm waited on by anonymous people whose *job* it is, but very bad at sitting loose-handed about our own small rooms. I also found it awfully depressing to rise on a sunny day and think: now I'll bake some tea-bread, wash my hair, write some letters, and then feel unlike lifting a finger. And poor Frieda decided to teethe some more the minute I got back, so we've been sleeping in fits and starts. I must say that the last six months I have felt slapped down each time I lifted my head up and don't know what I'd have done if Ted hadn't been more than saintly and the baby adorable and charming. I write you about this *now it's over* and not in the midst of it.

Luckily, for all my misfortunes, I have a surprising resilience and today, 2½ weeks after my op., feel very close to a self I haven't been for some time and full of hope. The weather is amazing: real June days. I've been up on the Hill each day with Frieda out on the grass on a blanket, lying in the clear sun, and tomorrow start going over to the Merwins' study in the morning again. I hope to be able to *use* these three months, until you come, writing.

Well, I have sat round "like a lady" and this Tuesday go back for a checkup. After my appointment at the main hospital with the surgeon whose name was over my bed, I saw no more of him and was "done" by his deputies in the hospital annex, who checked up on me. I didn't care; I was admirably treated, and the nurses and other patients were sweethearts and my 3-inch herringbone is very neat.

One thing this experience has pressed on me is our very definite need for a house by 1962. Then Ted could work off in a study while I had temporary help do house-drudging during baby-confinements and any illness that comes up and not feel guilty at using Ted's noble kindness. A house and a car. We have everything else, and that's all we need to make the fullest life possible for both of us . . . Actually the most wonderful thing you could do for us would be to live here with Frieda for two weeks while we had our first *real* vacation in France with the Merwins . . .

I so appreciated your $10: Ted got me, on my orders, a stack of D. H. Lawrence—novels, stories, and travel books, which I've been reading . . . I'll use the remains to buy a fine art book when I take my first trip downtown. . . .

x x x to you both,
Sivvy

Dearest Mother,

. . . Ted's children's poems came out in the *Times* yesterday (three of them), and I'm enclosing a clipping. We are delighted at the advance publicity for his book, which should be out within a month. He also had a letter from Lord David Cecil, saying he'd been awarded the Hawthornden Prize for *Lupercal* for 1960—it's a very prestigeful fiction and/or poetry award here—gold medal, and, I think, 100 pounds. Dom Moraes, the young Indian poet, got it some years ago and the young writer Alan Sillitoe, whose first novel was made into a movie. The presentation is around the end of May, so it should get into the papers about then and is a very good way to keep up his book sales. We figured he's earned about $1,500 from the BBC alone this year, which we hope to keep up. He's had the outline of another hour-drama accepted, and they seem eager to take anything he does. . . .

We are very happy, looking forward to getting a small station wagon hopefully before you come. Then we can really take advantage of our life: going on country and Cornwall trips when other people have to work, avoiding traffic and holidayers and being portable with babies. We want to take the wagon when we go to Europe on the Maugham grant, which we are seriously thinking of postponing until next spring—the latest time possible.

Ted brought me a little bouquet of yellow primroses yesterday with a handsome edition of the *Oxford Book of Wild Flowers*—the remains of that kind $10 you sent. He is the sweetest, most thoughtful person in the world. I have had a rather glum winter, and he has tirelessly stood by and cheered me up in every conceivable way.

. . . Keep well and rested!

Lots of love,
Sivvy

Dear Mother,

. . . Luckily Ted's book comes out this month, so we're blowing ourselves to a great stack of copies and sending them to all those good people we've been wanting so much to do something for. We may not have much money, but we'll always have plenty of books!

. . . We've been very hectically busy lately—a spate of seeing people, poets paying Ted pilgrimages, movies, plays, teas. Tomorrow we do a joint broadcast over the BBC for America (it's called "The

London Echo"), reading poems and talking about our childhoods. It's supposed to come out over a lot of networks in America. Next week Ted goes on the BBC television for about 7 minutes, talking about his children's book. Probably they'll flash a drawing on the screen while he reads the poem to go with it. I'm glad he'll do this as I think it may magnify the book sales considerably and the reason he consented is because it's not a "literary pose." . . . I've asked to come along and see it as we don't have a set, so it should be fun.

Best of all, he's just been commissioned by Peter Hall (Director of the Royal Shakespeare Theatre and husband of Leslie Caron) for a play for their London company. This is an incredible stroke of luck, as only very well-known playwrights have been commissioned so far, and it means the play Ted is working on will have the best reading and if it's good enough to produce, the best cast and production it could have.

We are thrilled by this—we have yet to hear just how much money it is—because it means that Ted's plays will go straight to the best director in England for a reading, and even if this one isn't accepted (we have to keep telling ourselves this to calm down, because we think it's a superb play, which we'll be sending to the Poets' Theater as well, so you may have a chance to see it, too!), the next ones, no doubt, will be. Oh, you wait, we'll be wealthy yet. . . .

Lots of love,
Sivvy

APRIL 21, 1961

Dear Mother,

. . . I am working fiendishly at the Merwins' study seven mornings a week, as they are coming home at the end of May, and I've a lot I want to finish before then. I have found that the whole clue to my happiness is to have four to five hours perfectly free and uninterrupted to write in the first thing in the morning—no phones, doorbells or baby. Then I come home in a wonderful temper and dispatch all the household jobs in no time. Thank goodness, the Merwins are going to France shortly after they come home, so I hope to have the study till next fall. . . .

I'm trying to get the bulk of my writing done before you come, but even if I work in the mornings, we'll have the whole rest of the day together, and you could take Frieda to the park in the mornings . . . less than two months! I am looking so forward to showing you everything and having you see your beautiful granddaughter! . . .

I'm enclosing the poems and article on him [Ted] that came out in last Sunday's *Observer* . . . It is so marvelous having married Ted with no money and nothing in print and then having all my best intuitions prove true! Our life together is happier than I ever believed possible, and the only momentary snags are material ones—our lack of a house is the one thing we want to change. I want Ted to have a study where he doesn't have to move his papers or be bothered when there are visitors and where I can have an upstairs room in peace in the morning while someone minds the children in the basement nursery. Then, too, we'll be able to plan a year in America . . .

I feel so fine now this appendix worry is over and Frieda is safely a year old, I want to consolidate my health and work in the coming year. We have good friends here, most of them our age, and the older people we know are influential and benevolent, so I feel very much at home. The BBC really supports us. Our income from them in the past year has bought us our car.

Do keep in good health, now, mummy, and have a Happy Happy Birthday!

Lots of love,
Sivvy

MAY 1, 1961

GOOD NEWS   GOOD NEWS   GOOD NEWS!

Dear Mother,

I hoped it would come by your birthday, but here it is on May Day instead.

ALFRED KNOPF will publish *The Colossus* in America!

This is no doubt what Mrs. Prouty's account was about. They wrote me an optimistic letter about a month ago, and I guess I shouldn't have mentioned it to her until it was definite, so I decided not to jinx my luck and to keep quiet until I heard definitely, which I did today.

Knopf wanted me to revise the book—leave out about ten poems, especially those in the last sequence. Well, by a miracle of intuition I guessed (unintentionally) the exact ten *they* would have left out— they wanted me to choose independently. I am delighted. I can correct my typing mistakes and leave out the poems that have been criticized to good purpose here, making a total of 40 instead of 50 in the book—40 being the usual length for volumes.

After all my fiddlings and discouragements from the little publishers, it is an immense joy to have what I consider THE publisher accept my book for America with such enthusiasm. They "sincerely doubt a better first volume will be published this year."

Now you will be able to have a really "perfect" book to buy at Hathaway House Bookstore, see reviewed, etc., etc. It is like having a second book come out—this one, the Ideal. Ever since their first letter came (I had a "night of inspiration"), I have been writing seven mornings a week at the Merwins' study and have done better things than ever before, so it is obvious that this American acceptance is a great tonic.

I don't know just when it will appear over there, but I'll keep you posted.

LOTS OF LOVE,
Sivvy

MAY 8, 1961

Dear Mother,

. . . Ted's just had his story "Snow" accepted in America by *Harper's Bazaar,* the very fancy fashion magazine, so we should have another check to round out our 7th thousand [*writing money*] to send pretty soon.

We are both working very hard. Ted is typing his five-act play and has got over the 100-page mark, and I've finished my commissioned poems for the summer poetry festival at the Mermaid Theatre and everybody seems very pleased with them. . . .

. . . I know just what supper you're going to have on your arrival!

x x x Sivvy

JUNE 6, 1961

Dear Mother and Warren,

You have no idea how happy your wonderful letter made us! I have been hoping and hoping Warren would come [*in early fall*], and now my wish is granted! We shall sample good restaurants in Soho and there should be some good plays on then . . .

. . . I think you'll be a lot more comfortable at the Merwins'. It is *so* near, and Dido's room is so lovely, and Molly, the little Australian hairdresser [*roomer at the Merwins'*] is at work all day. I'll be working in the study over there in the morning and Ted in the afternoon, and then there won't be a mile trek every time you want to rest or get something. . . .

Ted went to receive his 100 pounds Hawthornden Award last Wednesday; the speech given by the poet C. Day Lewis, who is charming.

Yesterday morning I spent at the BBC, recording a 25-minute program of my poems and commentary . . . for my "Living Poet" program in July. There is a Living Poet every month, and I am on a list of Americans among Robert Lowell, Stanley Kunitz, and Theodore Roethke, which I find quite an honor. We'll miss the program as we'll be in France, but you must listen and tell us how it is. Got $60 for the morning's work and will be paid for the poems separately. . . .

The one thing I long for now is a house! As soon as our income tax for this year is cleared in the U.K., we will see how much of a mortgage the St. Pancras Council would give us and try to line a place up by winter here. As Ted says, he could treble his income as soon as he has a study where he could keep his papers and not be interrupted, and I also could afford a morning babyminder and am interested in working on a novel. Then, too, you and Warren could count on a guest room . . . Oh, it would be so nice if you could plan six weeks over here every summer! If you just had to save up for the round-trip fare and we had a guest room, you'd have next to no other expenses, and then Ted and I could take an annual two-week holiday in the middle of your stay while you got re-acquainted with your grandchildren.

I feel I haven't had a proper holiday for four or five years. Our summer in Northampton was depressing, and our tour around America magnificent but the pace tiring [she had started her first pregnancy] and since the baby's come, I haven't had a day off. The thought of going off alone with Ted for two weeks is just heaven. We have reservations for June 30 to July 14 and plan to take a little five- or six-day trip alone in France before going to the Merwins'. I think you will be very comfortable here with the baby—I have a 3-day-a-week diaper service, a laundromat is around the corner and all shops, and she is so pretty and funny you will just adore her. Yesterday she took down a saucer from the kitchen shelf and put it on the floor. Then she took down a cup and put it on the saucer. Then she picked up the cup and pretended to sip, put it back in the saucer and burst out laughing in pleasure at herself. This must result from a year of watching us drink tea!

Lots of love to you both,
Sivvy

Dear Mother,

I am delighted by your two good letters so full of Frieda. I loved hearing every word about her. Already she seems like a different child, she is growing so fast, and while I am having a wonderfully restful time, I miss her immensely. The Merwins' farm is idyllic, with a superb view, plum trees, country milk, butter and eggs, a billion stars overhead, cowbells tinkling all night softly; and Dido is the world's best cook.

They made the whole place over from a pile of bramble-covered stone, and it is full of antique furniture salvaged from peasants' barns, stripped of varnish and waxed to a satin finish.

Ted is so rested it does my heart good. I am tan, at last, from sunbathing on the geranium-lined terrace and relieved for a time to be completely free of mail, phone calls, and London. Today we are going to a local market fair.

I am glad to hear you are taking in a play. . . . Do take it easy. Yorkshire should be a nice rest for you. I am so renewed I am dying to take care of Frieda again. We'll be home in time for supper Friday, the 14th, I imagine, and plan to leave for Yorkshire very early the following Tuesday for a good week.

After we come back to London, Ted and I may go to Devon for a day or so to look at houses. I would so like to have a place lined up before we go to Italy this fall. . . .

See you in a week. Keep us posted . . .

Love,
Sivvy

The following is a letter I wrote to Warren during my visit to England.

JULY 30, 1961

Dear Warren,

. . . [Sylvia] has been awarded first prize in the Cheltenham Festival Contest (75 pounds!).

On Thursday the two [of them] took off for Devon—southwest from London—a trip of five hours by car. They have been sending for real estate listings since early spring and had selected eight places to visit—all sounding lush. While they were gone, I lived at their apartment, of course, and Frieda decided to cut her 12th tooth. Neither of us slept much as a result, although she was not ill at all—just wakeful.

Well, Sivvy and Ted returned at midnight Friday, exhausted. Seven of the eight houses were impossible. Some actually ruins. But the third place they saw on Friday morning they fell in love with, and if all is correct legally, I guess they are going to purchase it. It is the ancient (yes!) house of Sir and Lady Arundel, who were there to show them about. From Sivvy's description, I gathered the following statistics: The main house has nine rooms, a wine cellar, and a small attic. The great lawn . . . in front, leading from a wall 9 feet high, is kept cut by a neighbor who uses his mower on it, getting the grass in return for his services. All one can see from the road is the thatched (honest!) roof. There is a cobblestone court, a good stable to use as garage and a "cottage" of two rooms and a toilet (used for servants' quarters in the past) that is in great need of repair. There are three acres of land—all walled in—an apple orchard, cherry trees, blackberry and raspberry bushes, a place that once was used for a tennis court, where they are thinking of making a yard for Frieda. The land backs onto a church; the village is close by. Lady Arundel will recommend her charwoman and a midwife in the village. . . . If all goes through, Sivvy and family expect to be in Devon when you come.

If I remember all they told me correctly, they are one hour's drive from Exeter—a largish town—and one hour's drive from the coast, where there are supposed to be beautiful beaches. The countryside is lushly beautiful; the climate, while there is much rain at times, is very mild and has clear sunny weather, too.

If it is all they say and dream it is, I hope they can move there soon, and will do everything I can to help make this possible. . . .

The Arundels impressed Sivvy and Ted very favorably and seemed to be anxious to get people who would have a sense of the historic value of the site and place. (There is a Roman mound there!) As the Sir and Lady have recently bought a much larger place, they are apparently not short of cash, but they don't want the extra responsibility of the property.

I wish I could see it, but Ted and Sylvia are glad (I sense) that the distance makes this impossible right now. They don't mind your seeing it, but said that I would find flaws that they intend to eradicate by the time I come to visit next summer. (!)

Both Edith [Ted's mother] and I are each loaning them 500 pounds

*so that they won't be snowed under by the terrible interest rate, 6½
percent; that is, each of us is loaning $1,400. I was willing to take the
whole mortgage at 3 percent, but Ted would not listen to it, and I
admire him for his determination to be as independent as possible.*
 . . . Love to you and Margaret [Warren's fiancée].

Mom

CHALCOT SQUARE
LONDON, ENGLAND
AUGUST 7, 1951

Dear Mother,

 . . . I am a bit overcome by the prospect of moving everything, but our possessions will seem very small compared to the
house itself. We shall have to furnish one room at a time. I am a bit
homesick for London, as I always am before leaving a place, but
welcome the space and country peace for the next few years. Ted is in
seventh heaven. We have been working, alternating my mornings and
his afternoons at the Merwins' study, and this works out beautifully
as neither of us wants to work the whole day at a desk.

 Your presence is everywhere and your good influence, too. I am
taking about five vitamins a day, a long walk with Frieda every afternoon, and feeding her chopped meat and potato . . .

 I shall be so happy to get to the house and start fixing it up. It is
basically such a beautiful place, and now you will have a lovely country house to visit next summer! I look forward to sampling our
apples, making sauce, and anticipating our bank of spring daffodils. I
think both of us will produce lots of work. Italy is, of course, something I just won't think of until it comes, but we hope to save half of
the money of the grant and certainly can use it.

 . . . We look so forward to seeing Warren!

 We miss you immensely and count on seeing you next summer.
Thanks so much for making our trips and house-finding a possibility.

Lots of love,
Sivvy

AUGUST 13, 1961

Dear Mother,

 A thousand thanks for the $5,880 check which arrived this week
and for your own $1,400 loan (no need to put "gift" on this as loans
are untaxable) . . .

Ted and I are seriously thinking of giving up the Somerset Maugham award, unless, of course, they'll give us another 2-year extension. The prospect of cramming in a trip to Europe after a move to a house which will need a lot of attention and before a second baby just doesn't seem worth 500 pounds, even though we were hoping to save half of it. Both of us feel we could get enough writing done if we had a relatively peaceful fall to make up for not taking the grant and feel an immense pressure lifted not to have to go abroad. We've had enough of moving around to last for years. . . .

We put an ad in the paper for our flat (with a $280 fee for "fixtures and fittings" to cover the cost of our decorating, lino [*linoleum*], shelves, and solicitor's fees, and to deter an avalanche of people—the custom here) and had eight responses and two couples who arrived and decided they wanted it at the same time. Very awkward, especially as Ted and I liked one couple—the boy, a young Canadian poet [*David Wevill and his wife Assia*]; the girl, a German-Russian whom we identified with. As they were too slow and polite to speak up, officially the other chill, busybody man got it by sitting down and immediately writing out a check. We felt so badly we tore up his check that night and told him we were staying and then dug up the other couple and said they could have it. So I hope our [*Devon*] move goes through. The couple are coming to supper this week.

. . . Keep your fingers crossed for us [*the house!*]

Love to you and Warren,

Sivvy

LONDON N.W. 1
AUGUST 25, 1961

Dear Mother and Warren,

It was lovely to get your letters—especially yours, Warren, telling us about coming to Devon on the ninth of September!

Ted's children's broadcasts on the BBC have been very enthusiastically received and he has an open ticket there to do as much as he wants, plus an invitation to do occasional editing on the Children's Page of the Sunday *Times* . . . and several other editing jobs, not to mention his wanting to finish a story collection which Faber's is eagerly awaiting. I have never seen him so happy. Both of us feel a wonderful deep-breathing sense of joy at the peaceful, secluded life opening up for us and delighted that our children will have such a wonderful place to live and play in. . . .

I had a very nice letter from Alfred Knopf (my lady editor there), saying my book of poems (40 poems, a much more concise, tight book) is due out in Spring 1962. I feel very excited filling out the Knopf Author's Forms after all these years of wishing I could get a book published by them!

. . . I can't wait to see what it *feels* like to live [*in Devon*]. I shall investigate about a Bendix, mother, as soon as I can, as it would be absolute heaven to get one before the new baby comes. . . . I'm really sick of lugging great loads to the laundromat each week . . .

We've been having farewell dinners with our closest friends here. We know a few quite marvelous couples—a Portuguese poet and exile and his wonderful, vital wife, and Alan Sillitoe, the young and famous author of the novel *Saturday Night and Sunday Morning* (made into a movie) and his American wife, and, of course, our nice neighbors. Fortunately, we are on the holiday route to Cornwall, so stand a chance of seeing them about once a year. . . .

I am going out tomorrow to look for a second-hand sewing machine like the one I've borrowed from Dido.

It is wonderful, paradoxically, not to have the strain of going to Italy on top of us any more. The money we hoped to save out of it just wasn't worth it to us. Now we shall be able to write all fall in peace before the new baby arrives and get a lot done. We'll probably set you to minding Frieda in the mornings, Warren! I imagine baby sitters will be harder to get in the country.

Lots of love from us 3, Sivvy

PART SEVEN

September 4, 1961–February 4, 1963

The move to Devon delighted Sylvia and aroused all her homemaking instincts. Although there was, of course, no central heating and a great deal of work to be done, the thatched-roof house was their first real home, a place that in time could be made both beautiful and comfortable.

However, the ecstasy that followed the birth of Nicholas Farrar on January 17, 1962, and the blooming of their gardens after a long, harsh winter was completely dissipated by the end of June. The marriage grew seriously troubled.

DEVON, ENGLAND
SEPTEMBER 4, 1961

Dear Mother,

Well, I am writing this from my big "back kitchen" (not really a kitchen, for I cook and wash up in a small room across the hall) . . . surrounded by my copper saucepans and the Dutch tea set you brought, all displayed in the various lovely nooks and crannies. A large coal stove warms this room and keeps all the water piping hot (although we can switch on hot water independently of it in the electric immersion heater upstairs); and, at last, I have all the room I could wish for and a perfect place for everything. My pewter looks beautiful in the parlor, where Ted is building bookshelves.

We moved without mishap on Thursday, our furniture just fitting in the small mover's van (the move cost just under $100), and had a fine, hot, sunny, blue day for it. Ever since a fog has shrouded us in; just as well, for we have been unpacking, scrubbing, painting and working hard indoors. The house surprised us—everything seemed so much better than we had remembered it—new discoveries on every side. The Arundels had left it clean-swept and shining. The wood-worm people were just finishing work, so there is the fading aroma of their disinfectants.

The place is like a person; it responds to the slightest touch and looks wonderful immediately. I have a nice, round dining table we are "storing" for the couple who have moved into our London flat, and we eat on this in the big back room, which has light-green linoleum on the floor, cream wood paneling to shoulder height, and the pink-washed walls that go throughout the house . . . There's lots of space for Frieda to run about and play and spill things here—really the heart-room of the house, with the toasty coal stove Ted keeps burning.

Across the back hall, which is of finely cobbled stone, one of the best touches, is my compact work kitchen—my gas stove . . . loads of shelves and a low, ancient sink, which I am going to have changed to a modern unit immediately. . . .

We've been so busy indoors that we've hardly had time to do more than survey our grounds (the main crop of which is stinging nettles at present, and, of course, apples). I went out with Frieda and got a big basket of windfalls for applesauce, enough blackberries for two breakfast bowls, and about five pounds of fine potatoes from a hill of them someone had forgotten to dig up. I have the place full of flowers —great peach-colored gladiolas, hot-red and orange and yellow zinnias. The front flower gardens are weedy, but full of petunias, zinnias, and a couple of good rosebushes. My whole spirit has expanded immensely—I don't have that crowded, harassed feeling I've had in all the small places I've lived in before. Frieda adores it here. The house has only one shallow step to get down from the back court into the back hall and another shallow step into the front garden, so she can run in and out easily with no danger of falls, and she loves tramping through the big rooms. She needs two naps a day again, she gets so tired with all this exercise.

What is so heavenly here is the utter peace. Very nice tradespeople, a retired couple from London at the end of our drive (who brought a tray of tea the day we moved in), and curious and amiable natives . . .

I am going to a pre-natal clinic at the doctor's up the street to get myself on his panel. This is a wonderful place to have babies in.

. . . We can't wait for you to see it. Wish you could come in the spring. We have piles of lilac bushes (which I hadn't noticed before), daffodils, laburnum, cherry, apple, honeysuckle, and the place must be legendarily charming then. Ted has a superb attic study under the thatched eaves. I have chosen the best front bedroom for my study. . . .

x x x Sivvy

Dear Mother,

It seems strange to think that Warren will reach you before this letter does, though both depart on the same day. We saw him off at the little . . . station this morning at 11:30 after a breakfast of orange juice, fried egg and crispy potatoes and apple cake, and the house seems very lonesome without him. He has been really a wonderful part of the family—sanding an immense elm plank which will make me my first real capacious writing table, discovering a set of wooden blocks in the cottage attic and cleaning them up for Frieda, chopping wood, mowing the lawn, and, in general, making himself useful.

We've had a lot of fun while he was here—explored the Exeter Cathedral, took a picnic to Tintagel (very commercial) and found a high cowfield nearby, overlooking the sea, to eat it in. Drove to an auction at which we bought a little (4′ × 6′) Indian rug for Frieda's room, and ate out at our local inn, the Burton Hall Arms (a roast beef dinner for just over $1 a person), which gave me a welcome respite from cooking . . .

After a Saturday-Sunday visit this week from a very sweet young Portuguese couple we knew in London, things should quiet down. Ted has the most wonderful attic study, very warm under the peak of the thatch and over the hot water boiler. He looks happier and better every day. I never have known such satisfaction just seeing him revel in this place and leading, at last, exactly the life he wants.

I adore my own study, and after I get my great plank table, paint the woodwork white, get a rug and maybe an upholstered armchair, it will be heavenly . . .

Oh, saw my doctor . . . whose surgery is three houses up across the street (!) and his marvelous midwife-nurse, whom I liked immediately. I look forward to my home delivery here now, these two people being very important in my life—I couldn't be better pleased with them. I just love it here and look so forward to your coming over and enjoying it with us next summer. Much love from us 3.

Sivvy

Dearest Mother and Warren,

. . . The days have just flown since I last wrote, and we have established a very pleasant rhythm here. Right after breakfast I go up to my study to work at the marvelous 6-foot natural wood table (which you helped finish, Warren) while Ted carpenters or gardens in the back with Frieda along. He gives her lunch and puts her to bed about noon, and I come down and make *our* lunch and by the time I am through picking up the house and doing dishes, Frieda is up and out front with me, gardening, mending, or whatever, and Ted is in his study. Thus both of us get half a day out of doors and half a day writing (which is all either of us wants) and Frieda is out all the time. . . .

My cleaning woman is a blessing. She does the upstairs Tuesday and the downstairs Thursday, plus almost all the ironing. She, Nancy Axworthy, is more accustomed to the house than I as she has worked here eleven years. Her husband is a carpenter and evidently a town figure—one of the church bellringers, assistant head of the fire brigade, woodworking teacher at a night class. Nancy is a sweet, fresh-faced, healthy person, and the midwife said that when the new baby comes, she'll probably be happy to come for a few more hours a week and help with washing up and so on. I feel very lucky!

[UNDATED; END OF SEPT., 1961]

Friday: . . . Ted has planted winter lettuce and is digging a big strawberry bed. He has made my desk, a sewing table, a baby gate for the stair—is a natural carpenter! We are so happy. Seventy-two apple trees!

For Christmas do you think our American Santa might dig up some seeds for *real American corn* (I hear Country Gentleman is good—the Merwins have it in France) and Kentucky Wonder beans, or some good thin green pole bean. Nothing like that here—only thick, broad beans and corn for pigs.

Had a wonderful letter from Mrs. Prouty, enclosing a check as a housewarming gift . . . I had been feeling a bit blue because I just didn't feel I could go out and get a really fine rug or two (bedroom and living room are the two places I need them for most) with our mountain of moving-in expenses, including a bill of close to $300 from our lawyers for a multitude of fees. But *now* I can add her check to grampy's and get something really good.

Ted has been driving 35 miles to the BBC station at Plymouth to record four small programs for the "Woman's Hour." I am immensely relieved there are recording stations here, for we shall start some income again. He is finishing a radio play for the Third Programme, and *Vogue* wants a children's poem for $50, and there is the series of the *Times* Children's Pages, so no lack of assignments.

I am very encouraged by selling my first women's magazine story; my second hasn't sold yet, but the fiction editor of one of the two big women's weeklies here wants to see me and talk over their requirements on the strength of it. So I shall push this. I'll get into the *Ladies' Home Journal* yet! . . .

Lots of love,
Sivvy

OCTOBER 6, 1961 (FRIDAY)

Dear Mother,

It is just past ten and I am sitting downstairs in the big kitchen this morning, with the Aga cooker (coal-burning) Ted stoked earlier warming the place cosily and Frieda running to and from her playroom with new toys to potter about my feet. Ted is off for most of the day to . . . shop in Exeter and join the libraries there, so I have a day to catch up on baking and mending. I have been working in my study till noon every morning . . . and will be seeing the Fiction Editor [*of a women's magazine*] . . . when I go to London at the end of the month to pick up my 75 pounds poetry prize at the Guinness party and see my publisher.

Ted had a day in London this Tuesday, leaving the house at 5:30 a.m., catching the 6:30 express from Exeter and getting in in time for a long day of recording at the BBC, with a posh lunch in Soho with the head of the Arts Council, for whom he will be co-judge of the next two years' Poetry Book Society Selections [for about $150 a year). Ted is almost through with his new radio play, and we feel we are really beginning to produce things. . . .

Frieda responds more and more to her life here. She is delighted with her big playroom, the bay window of which I use for my sewing table. Ted is going to build some shelves in an alcove for her toys so she can have them all arranged in full view instead of jumbled together. She is incredibly neat—picks up every little crumb she drops and gives it to us and tries to sweep up anything spilt with a dustpan or sponge.

Lots of love from all of us.

Sivvy

OCTOBER 13, 1961

Dear Mother,

. . . I've decided the best way to grow into the community here is to go to our local Anglican church and maybe belong to its monthly mothers' group. I wrote the rector—a Protestant Irishman with a very broad background (Chicago, Africa)—about this, and he came and said he'd go through the creed and order of service with me, but that I'd be welcome (I'm afraid I could never stomach the Trinity and all that!) to come in the spirit of my own Unitarian beliefs.

I like the idea of Frieda going to Sunday School next door. The church is "low" (like our Episcopal Church, I guess) and has a champion crew of eight bellringers who delight us every Sunday . . .

I'm having Mrs. Hamilton, the wife of the dead coffee plantation owner and local power, to tea today. She is old, booming, half-deaf, with a dachshund named Pixie. I'm having Ted come to help me out! He's just finished the radio play he's been working on, and I've a couple of good poems.

Lots of love,
Sivvy

OCTOBER 22, 1961

Dear Mother,

. . . I have delayed my usual Friday letter because I, too, have been feeling tired this last week or so . . . It seems impossible one can get tired doing something one loves to do, but I suppose writing is strenuous, and I should consider my mornings at my desk as work, rather than play. We do go to bed in good time—lights out by 10:30, and Frieda generally lets us sleep till 8-ish. I guess the baby is getting perceptibly heavy now, too. . . .

Frieda is sweeter and more winsome than ever. She gets the best of each of us, I think—neither of us having to mind her when we want to write, but while we're doing things she can watch and participate in. I went out to see the two of them in the garden this morning, and Ted was planting strawberries, and Frieda was following him with her little shovel, religiously imitating his every gesture, looking like an elf in that wonderful cotton red coat and hood you sent. . . .

So glad you liked "Snow." I haven't seen *Harper's Bazaar* yet. Hope they send us a copy. Actually, I think you're closest to Ted's meaning—it's not a philosophical equation so much as just the *feeling* of being lost and struggling against terrific unknowns and odds, something most people feel at one time or another. I find it the most compelling of Ted's stories because it *fits* one's own experience so beautifully. It's incredible how moving it is, with just one character, the snow and the chair, but I feel it has a deep psychic insight into the soul's battles.

If you happen to think of it, could you pack me off a *Ladies' Home Journal* or two? I get homesick for it; it has an Americanness which I feel a need to dip into, *now I'm in exile,* and especially as I'm writing for women's magazines in a small way now. I shall have fulfilled a very long-time ambition if a story of mine ever makes the *LHJ.*

Later: A wild blowy night, with gusts of rain. Went to my first Anglican service with the lively retired London couple down the lane. It's a sweet little church, and I found the service so strange. I suppose it would be very familiar to you, like a sort of watered-down Catholic service. The choir and congregation singing is amazingly strong and good for the small number of people there, and I do like hymn singing. I think I will probably go to Evensong off and on and then send Frieda to Sunday School. I'm sure as she starts thinking for herself, she will drift away from the church, but I know how incredibly powerful the words of that little Christian prayer, "God is my help in every need," which you taught us has been at odd moments of my life, so think it will do her good to feel part of this spiritual community. I must say I think I am a pagan-Unitarian at best! The songs, psalms, responses and prayers are fine, but the sermon! . . . It's a pity there aren't more fiery intellectuals in the ministry. It seems to draw meek, safe, platitudinous souls who I am sure would not face the lions in the Roman arena at any cost . . .

Love,
x x x Sivvy

OCTOBER 26, 1961

Dear Mother,

. . . Ted has written a lovely poem about the Loch Ness Monster for *Vogue* (a children's poem) over here, the British edition, and has got a pile of children's books on animals coming from the *New Statesman* for him to review. They are sending *me* a pile of bright children's picture books to review as well (since I modestly said that was my level at present)—all free and to keep. I am quite pleased, because I think I can judge the art work pretty well and am delighted to tuck these away to bring out later for Frieda—about $15 worth.

We got our copy of *Harper's Bazaar* today. Isn't it amazing, Robert Lowell, Marianne Moore, and Ted in the middle of all those fancy corsets! Lucky for us they have piles of money. The "sophisticated" audience thus has fashion, plus cocktail-party-gossip talk and "name writers"—usually only a 2-page spread, you'll notice, so it doesn't strain the brain. The editors are generally very brainy women and the fashion blurbs written by Phi Beta Kappa English majors. Poor things.

Later: I am sitting in our "parlor" at the very little bureau-type desk Ted bought at an auction last week for $15. It's rather like yours, with three drawers and a slant top that opens out to write on and pigeonholes for letters. I love it.

OCTOBER 30, 1961

I go to London tomorrow to collect my 75-pound prize and see the women's magazine editor and leave my manuscripts with the book-dealer who bought Ted's on the chance they might sell them. I am going to the theatre Wednesday on your birthday money and shall have a nice meal beforehand. I thought you'd be pleased at my spending it that way. I look forward to the treat, as I don't imagine I'll have another chance at a fling till you come next summer.

Had a lovely birthday. Ted bought me a lot of fancy cans of octopus and caviar at a delicatessen, two poetry books, a Parker pen, and a big wicker basket for my laundry . . . We've got about 50 children's books to review in all now, a real gift, because we can't review more than ten apiece—everything from *The Cat in the Hat Comes Back* to the story of Elsa, the lioness and her cubs. A good $50 to $60 worth. My acquisitive soul rejoices.

Well, I hope the Strontium 90 level doesn't go up too high in milk. I've been very gloomy about the bomb news; of course, the Americans have contributed to the poisonous level. The fallout-shelter craze in America sounds mad. Well, I would rather be in Devon, where I am in the country, than anywhere else just now. Keep well!

x x x Sivvy

NOVEMBER 5, 1961

Dear Mother,

. . . I stayed two nights [*in London*] with our friends, the Sillitoes. The first night I went to the Guinness party and was, to my surprise, called on to read my poem with the regular Guinness winners, which included Robert Graves in the fabulous Goldsmiths hall in the City, although my prize was for another and much smaller contest. And I picked up my 75-pound check; then had a little supper with my publisher . . . The next day was all business. I typed my children's book review at the Sillitoes', saw the very encouraging women's magazine editor, had lunch with another pregnant lady poet I met at the Guinness party, dropped some manuscripts at an agent's in hopes of selling them at an American university, and had a bit of tea before the two plays by the young American playwright Edward Albee. London is very tiring when one doesn't have a place of one's own, and the getting about a Herculean task. I found myself criticizing the soot and the horrid suburbs and the exhaust, dying to get home to clear air and my own acres and two darlings. Ted and Frieda met me at the station, Thursday afternoon, my train exactly on time. None of us had been able to eat or sleep very well apart, and now we are all thriving again.

. . . The next five months are grim ones. I always feel sorry to have the summertime change, with the dark evenings closing in in midafternoon, and will try to lay in some physical comforts this month—the best insurance against gloominess for me. It's incredible to think that *carpets* can create a state of mind, but I am so suggestible to colors and textures that I'm sure a red carpet would keep me forever optimistic. . . .

. . . We have really done a great deal since we have come these last few months. I have to keep myself from asking that everything be done at once. The whole house, for example, needs replastering, as much of the plaster is dry and crumbly behind the paper, but except for one or two spots, we should be all right for several years yet. And I'll be going to Exeter in the next week or ten days to price rugs and buy curtain material. . . .

Went to the Anglican chapel evensong again tonight. It's a peaceful little well on Sunday evenings, and I do love the organ, the bellringing and hymn singing, and muse on the stained-glass windows during the awful sermons. The three windows, lit up on Sunday evenings, look so pretty from our house through the silhouettes of the trees. You'll have a *real* rest and holiday when you visit us this time, sitting out on our lilac-sheltered lawn in a deck chair with the babies playing, *no* steps or traffic, only country noises. Lots of love to you and Warren.

x x x Sivvy

Dear Mother,

I hardly know where to begin. Your good bonus letter came today, and all sorts of nice things have been happening. Ted woke up this morning and said, "I dreamed you had won a $25 prize for your story about 'Johnny Panic.' " Well, I went downstairs and found out I had won a Saxton grant for $2,000! I have been waiting for over half a year to hear from them, and as both Ted and I have been rejected by them (Ted because he was published by Harper's and they give the grant) and I because I applied for poetry and they don't like to give money for poetry, I had no hope. Well, I applied for a grant for prose this time and got the amount I asked for (I had it figured so I wouldn't have to work and could have a nanny and household help, etc.). They pay in quarterly installments as parts of a project are completed, so I should get my first lot in a week or two! It is an absolute lifesaver. . . .

Life in town has been more and more fun. They had a Hunt Meet in the square yesterday: all the local fox hunters in red jackets, brass buttons and velvet caps, drinking whisky on horseback, all sorts of fascinating faces, and a pack of spotted, sulphurous dogs. A toot of a horn and they galloped off. We took Frieda to watch and she loved it. Oddly moving, in spite of our sympathy for foxes.

We went for a long walk with Frieda first thing in the morning, it was so lovely—the hedgerows a tapestry of oak leaves, holly, fern, blackberry leaves all intertwined; the green hills dotted with sheep and cows, and the pink-plaster farms very antique. Frieda is a great walker, as you know. . . .

Tell Warren *The New Yorker* just bought a poem of mine I wrote here called "Blackberrying," about the day we all went blackberrying together down the land that sloped to the sea . . . I don't know when they'll print "Tulips"—probably in the season. I'll send for a copy of my awful first ladies' magazine story—very stiff and amateurish. It came out my birthday week. I got a very sweet fan letter for it in which the woman, also a writer, took me for an expert on Canada and Whitby, the sailing port I visited for a day. Very flattering! . . .

x x x Sivvy

Dear Mother,

. . . Don't worry about my taking on anything with the Saxton. Just between the two of us (and don't tell anyone), I figured nothing was so sure to stop my writing as a grant to do a specific project that had to be turned in at the end with quarterly reports—so I finished a batch of stuff this last year, tied it up in four parcels and have it ready to report on bit by bit as required. Thus I don't need to write a word if I don't feel like it. Of course, the grant is supposed to help you *do* writing and is not for writing you've done, but I will do what I can and feel like doing, while my conscience is perfectly free in knowing my assignments are done. Guggenheims, such as Ted had, are much easier. They ask for no reports or work; once you get it, you're perfectly free. Anyhow, I'd never have applied for a Saxton unless I'd gotten something ready; I don't believe in getting money for something you haven't done yet—it's too nerve-wracking. . . .

Did I tell you I got 100 pounds ($280) for about 130 pages of poetry manuscript of mine from a bookseller in London who is buying stuff for the University of Indiana? They'd already bought about 160 pounds' worth of Ted's stuff, and he got 80 pounds from some other dealer, so we've made a good bit off our scrap paper. Needless to say, this comes in very handy just now.

Take care of yourself these grim, dark days. Love to you and Warren.

                                        x x Sivvy

Dear Mother,

It is a marvelous, crisp, clear December morning, and I am sitting in the front room with Ted and Frieda, overlooking our acre of grasses, which are white with frost. After a week of black, wet, sunless weather, everything seems suddenly bright and Christmasy. I am trying to get off the bulk of my American Christmas cards by ordinary mail today, so I will be a bit saving.

The reason I haven't written for so long is probably quite silly, but I got so awfully depressed two weeks ago by reading two issues of *The Nation*—"Juggernaut, the Warfare State"—all about the terrifying marriage of big business and the military in America and the forces of the John Birch Society, etc.; and then another article about the repulsive shelter craze for fallout, all very factual, documented, and true, that I simply couldn't sleep for nights with all the warlike talk in the papers, such as Kennedy saying Khrushchev would "have no place to hide," and the armed forces manuals indoctrinating soldiers about the "inevitable" war with our "implacable foe" . . . I began to wonder if there was any point in trying to bring up children in such a mad, self-destructive world. The sad thing is that the power for destruction is real and universal, and the profession of generals, who, on retirement, become board heads of the missile plants [to which] they have been feeding orders. I am also horrified at the U.S. selling missiles (without warheads) to Germany, awarding former German officers medals. As the reporter for the liberal Frankfurt paper says, coming back to America from his native Germany, it is as if he hadn't been away. Well, I got so discouraged about all this that I didn't feel like writing anybody anything. Ted has been very comforting and so has Frieda. One of the most distressing features about all this is the public announcements of Americans arming against each other—the citizens of Nevada announcing they will turn out bombed and ill people from Los Angeles into the desert (all this official), and ministers and priests preaching that it is all right to shoot neighbors who try to come into one's bomb shelters. Thank goodness there is none of this idiotic shelter business in England. I just wish England had the sense to be neutral, for it is quite obvious that she would be "obliterated" in any nuclear war, and for this reason I am very much behind the nuclear disarmers here. Anyway, I think it appalling that the shelter system in America should be allowed to fall into the hands of the advertisers—the more money you spend, the likelier you are to survive, etc., when 59 percent of taxes go for military spending already. . . . Well, I am over the worst of my furore about all this. Each day seems doubly precious to me, because I am so happy here with my lovely home and dear Ted and Frieda. I just wish all the destructive people could be sent to the moon. . . .

. . . Today came a big Christmas parcel from you with the two *Ladies' Home Journal* magazines, which I fell upon with joy—that magazine has so much Americana, I love it. Look forward to a good read by the wood fire tonight and to trying the luscious recipes. Recipes in English women's magazines are for things like "Lard and Stale Bread Pie, garnished with Cold Pigs Feet" or "Left-Over Pot Roast in Aspic."

. . . I feel so thwarted not to be giving out anything but cards . . . as I love buying presents for people, but we have felt we need to really pinch this year to weather the piles of bills for plumbers, electricians, extra heaters, coal, land tax, house tax, solicitors, surveyors, movers, and all the mountainous things. As if to sanction our move, we have been *very* lucky in earning money this fall—my Saxton, in four installments, is ample to live on . . . Each September we plan to pay you and Ted's parents back each $280 of your loan, which has been such a help in saving us tons of mortgage interest . . .

We have two more Pifcos (electric heaters), making four now. The cold is bitter. Even my midwife said it was too Spartan for a new baby and to warm things up. The halls are hopeless, of course, but the Pifcos do a wonderful job in closed-off rooms. The cold seems to keep us healthy—not one of us has been taken with a cold yet (knock on wood). We look fat as bears with all our sweaters, but I find this nippy air very bracing and so does Frieda. Her fat cheeks bloom, even though her breath comes out in little puffs. Much healthier than the overheating we had in America . . .

We had a lovely time laughing over the take-off issue of *Mademoiselle*; and now I am embedded with the *Journals*, especially delighted with the apple-recipe issue. . . .

I hope Warren is having a peaceful and pleasant year and isn't too overworked. I feel dreadfully lazy myself. I really write terribly little. I remember before Frieda came, I was like this; quite cowlike and interested suddenly in soppy women's magazines and cooking and sewing. Then a month or so afterwards I did some of my best poems.

I rely on your letters—you are wonderful to keep them so frequent in spite of your load of work and being sick. All of us send love.

Sivvy

DECEMBER 15, 1961

Dear Mother and Warren,

It seems impossible that it is only ten days to Christmas. I have been so immersed in household fixing and thinking of the arrival of the new baby that I've done little but get off a few cards . . .

. . . I can't tell you how much we like it here. The town itself is fascinating—a solid body of inter-related locals (very curious), then all these odd peripheral people—Londoners, ex-Cockneys, Irish. I look forward to getting to know them slowly. There's the bank manager's wife, the doctor and his family, and the redoubtable nurse who doesn't miss an addition in every house visit. The bank manager's wife has a daughter of fifteen in Oxford and says there are no children her age here at all. But I should be much luckier. Every time I visit the doctor's surgery, I see a raft of new babies; most of them very attractive little things.

. . . It will be our first Christmas on our own as heads of a family, and I want to keep all *our* old traditions alive. (I wish I had a Springerle [*patterned rolling*] pin!) We ate a batch of apricot "half-moons" last night—how I love them. . . .

In spite of our fabulous bills, back taxes, and National Health, we are doing surprisingly well. My *New Yorker* contract for poems was renewed for another year, and I've been asked to be one of the three judges for the Guinness contest I won this year. Ted and Frieda send lots of love and so do I.

x x x Sivvy

Friday, December 29, 1961

Dear Mother,

I am sitting in our living room by a crackling wood fire, our mantel still gay with red candles and about fifty Christmas cards; our fat little tree with its silver birds and tinsel and spice-cake hearts still up, and the new, red corduroy curtains I have just finished drawn, making the room bright and cheerful, like the inside of a Valentine . . .

The midwife suggested I get a thermometer to see the temperature of the new baby's room. I was amazed. The general level of the house—in halls and unheated rooms—is about 40° (38° in our bedroom in the morning!). An electric heater gets it feeling very hot at 50°–55° . . . It all depends on what one gets used to.

. . . Our Christmas was the happiest and fullest I have ever known . . . We trimmed the tree and set out our amazing stacks of gifts on Christmas Eve. Then Christmas Day we started the three of us off with our daily ration of soup plates of hot oatmeal (something you and grammy taught me), then led Frieda into the living room, which she had not seen in its decorated state. I wish you could have seen her face! . . .

. . . The Fox Book Ted had to read immediately. He said it was the most beautiful children's book he had seen; and it means so much to me, being set in New England. His very favorite presents were the Fox Book and Warren's tools, which he hasn't put down since he got them. He's been fitting in the staircase carpet clips with them today and says they're marvelous and "very American," meaning streamlined.

. . . I spent the rest of Christmas making my first simply beautiful golden-brown turkey with your bread dressing, creamed brussels sprouts and chestnuts, swede (like squash, orange), giblet gravy and apple pies with our last and preciously saved own apples. We all three had a fine feast in the midafternoon, with little Frieda spooning up everything. Then a quiet evening by the fire. . . .

x x x Sivvy

DECEMBER 29, 1961
(SECOND INSTALLMENT)

Dear Mother,

. . . All through this I've not said anything about Warren's engagement. How wonderful! I wish he and Maggie would visit us after they're married. They could stay at the local inn we dined at if they found our place too noisy with babies, as they well might! Do send a glossy of Margaret's Bachrach picture. I'm sure we'll love her . . . What fun for you to have all the traditional trappings for one of your two children (diamond ring, Bachrach, and, I imagine, a very formal wedding) . . . Wish so much I could attend. Do you think it will be this June? You must give me some notion of what they'd like for a present. . . .

We've had two days of storybook weather. The merest dusting of snow on everything, china-blue skies, rosy hilltops; new lambs in the fields. It's the second coldest winter this century, the farmers say. Took Frieda for little trots on Dartmoor this week. . . . You should see her mother her babies—feed them her biscuits, hold up a clock to their ear so they can hear it tick, cover them up. They couldn't have come at a better time to get her used to the baby idea. She is so *loving;* I'm sure she gets it from us! . . .

x x x Sivvy

JANUARY 12, 1962

Dear Mother,

Well, Nicholas/Megan was officially due yesterday, and no sign. So this baby will probably delay a few days like Frieda and keep us all in suspense. I've so enjoyed your long, newsy letters! I've felt lazier and lazier and more and more cowlike . . . I've given up all pretence of working in my study these last weeks; I am simply too ponderous. . . .

Ted and his poet-twin here, Thom Gunn (who actually lives and teaches in Berkeley), are bringing out an anthology by half a dozen American poets for Faber. Faber is also bringing out a paperback edition of their own selected poems.

My little shilling anthology of American poets I edited for the *Critical Quarterly* here has got very good reviews and seems to be selling well.

Each day I bake something to hide away for Ted and Frieda when I'm recovering from the new baby. I have a box of sand tarts cut in shapes, trimmed with cherries and almonds, a box of Tollhouse cookies and a fruitcake. Tomorrow I'll try an apple pie with the very last of our apples.

I hope Warren takes all I write you for himself, too. I love hearing about Aunt Maggie. We'd so like to see them here. Don't worry about money for them! Ted and I had *nothing* when we got married and no prospects. And in five years all our most far-fetched dreams have come true. . . .

. . . I am having the baby in the guest room, where you'll be, and we have fixed it up quite comfortably, although the old rug is shabby. We've painted the floor, and I've made curtains.

. . . Of course, Frieda will remember you! Deep down, if not obviously . . . I'll write Dot and everyone as soon as the baby comes.

Lots of love,

Sivvy

JANUARY 18, 1962
5 P.M.

Dear Mother,

By now I hope you have received the telegram Ted sent this morning with the good news of the arrival of our first son, Nicholas Farrar Hughes (I almost wrote Nicholas/Megan!), last night at 5 minutes to midnight, making another 17th date in our family, after Ted's August 17. I am sitting in bed, feeling fine and refreshed after an afternoon's nap; Nicholas in a carry-cot at my side, getting pinker and pinker. He looked very swarthy to me when he arrived, like a wrinkled, cross, old boxer, and still is a Farrar type, although Ted suggests his head shape resembles Daddy's. Now he has turned quite pink and translucent.

All during the delivery, I felt it would be a boy—my notions that he was a much bigger and heavier baby proved true and no illusion— he weighed in at 9 pounds, 11 ounces, compared to Frieda's ladylike 7 pounds, 4 ounces, and I had a lot more work with him than with her.

Woke at 4 a.m. the morning of the 17th with niggly contractions that came and went all day while I did as much cooking as I could till 5 p.m., just after Frieda went to bed, when they started to get very strong. I had a visit from both midwife and doctor during the day —both very kindly and encouraging. Then at 8:30, when the contractions were established at every 5 minutes, Ted called the midwife. She brought a cylinder of gas and air, and she sat on one side of the bed and Ted on the other, gossiping pleasantly together . . . while I breathed in my mask whenever I had a strong contraction and joined in the conversation. I had used up the cylinder and was just beginning to push down when the baby stuck and the membranes didn't break. Then at 5 minutes to 12, as the doctor was on his way over, this great bluish, glistening boy shot out onto the bed in a tidal wave of water that drenched all four of us to the skin, howling lustily. It was an amazing sight. I immediately sat up and felt wonderful—no tears, nothing.

It is heavenly to be in my own home—I'm in the guest room, which is ideal. Beautiful clear dawn; a full moon tonight in our huge elm. Everybody . . . turned to stare at Ted when he came into town. Rose Key, our cottage neighbor, brought a little knitted suit and the banker's wife sent a card and a towel. I gave the midwife my traditional carrot cake. She is a wonderful woman. You should see her with Frieda (we showed Frieda the baby this morning and she was terribly excited). The midwife and Frieda come in and "help" as the midwife fixes the baby, advising me to share the tasks, even if it takes longer. I didn't even know Frieda could understand, but she did everything the midwife said—held the safety pins, kissed the baby, helped wrap him up and then sat and held him all by herself! She was just bursting with pride. . . .

Now everything is quiet and peaceful, and Ted is heating the vichysoisse and apple pie I made to tide us over.

Later: Saturday, January 20. I have today marked as a red-letter day because your exams will be over as well as all that extra work for your courses. I'm sure I've been as concerned for you about this as you've been about me and the baby. Hope all went well and that you have a lovely dinner at Dot's. Loved the news clipping of Margaret. I look so forward to an amiable sister-in-law! . . . I only wish I could share in the fun and plans for the wedding.

. . . After both Ted's and my first shock at having a boy, we think he is marvelous. He did look grim and cross at first, his head all dented where he had caught high up and had to really push to get out, but overnight his head and features altered. Already I can sense a very different temperament from Frieda's—where she is almost hysterically impatient, he is calm and steady, with big dark eyes and a ruddy complection. Very restful and dear.

Well, Ted's going to post before the weekend, so I'll say goodbye for now. Do write me lots of newsy letters now you are more free.

Lots of love,

Sivvy

JANUARY 24, 1962

Dear Mother,

Well, Nicholas is a week old, and I have spent my first whole day up. Things have calmed down considerably, and by next week I think we will be placidly back to schedule. I had a rather tiring week as the first night the baby came, I couldn't sleep for excitement, and the nights after that the baby cried all night (I suppose this is the one advantage of a hospital or a home nurse!), but now he is settling down to more of a schedule and the doctor gave me a couple of relaxing pills to get me to sleep till I got rested again. It is wonderful having all this room so Ted could have an unbroken night in our room and be ready to cope with Frieda . . . the next day. Now I am cooking again, sitting on my stool. I shall go on having my nap every afternoon and sitting in my study in the morning. This morning I took a hot bath first thing, put on proper clothes and feel very fresh. I simply wore through the seams of all the underwear and maternity skirts and tights I wore in the last months and looked like a great, patchy monster at the end. It is heavenly to have a whole wardrobe to choose from again. . . .

SATURDAY [JANUARY 27]

Interrupted by a nasty bout of milk fever—a temperature of over 103 for two nights—much worse than that I had with Frieda. . . . They are shocked if you take *your own* temperature here. Finally the doctor came across with some shots of penicillin—I'm sure if I'd had them immediately, I'd not have got so burned out, but this is not London. Now, at last, I am cool again, if a bit spent. Believe me, I shed some tears for our "grammy" [*me*]. Ted's been a saint, minding Frieda all day, making me mushrooms on toast, fresh green salads and chicken broth. I hope when you come, we can give him a 6-week holiday from any baby care. He needs it—and we both need a few day excursions off on our own, fishing or boating.

Margaret's exquisite sweater set arrived; I think it's the sweetest I've seen. If Warren makes her anywhere near as happy as Ted has made me, she will be the second happiest girl in the world.

x x x Sivvy

JANUARY 31, 1962

Dearest Mother,

. . . The two enclosed checks are part of this incredible yearly contract I have with *The New Yorker*, not for any special poem. The smaller is the "cost-of-living adjustment" for the last quarter, and the larger, the adjustment of the cost-of-living adjustment for the whole year (for which I've already had some checks). I think this must be some marvelous scheme on their part to avoid income tax. If I get all this for the few old poems I send, I imagine the fiction writers must be able to buy penthouses! I just hope I can get back to writing poems soon again. . . .

. . . Ted is brimming with ideas for plays, books, etc. And getting interesting books to review from his friend at the *New Statesman*—one on the six great snakes of the world, for example. . . .

. . . I have got awfully homesick for you since the last baby—and for the Cape and deep snow and such things. Can't wait for your visit.

Love to all,

Sivvy

P.S. My book should be coming out from Knopf on April 23, in time for your birthday. And I should have six poems in a paperback anthology there in May by Meridian Books—*New Poets of England and America:* 2nd selection. Ted's in it, too.

FEBRUARY 7, 1962

Dear Mother,

Thank you a thousand times for sending the bras and briefs; you got just what I wanted. I suppose it seems silly to ask you to go downtown for me on another continent, but you have no idea how much it meant. I won't be able to shop for weeks yet, when the baby is on a more fixed schedule, and small things still loom very large. I get so impatient with myself, chafing to do a hundred things that have piled up and barely managing one or two. Nicholas is very good during the night at last, waking like clockwork at 2 a.m. and 6 a.m. with no crying in between . . . Tell Warren to get a big house with a soundproof bedroom before he has a baby; I'm sure the night waking and crying would knock him out.

. . . Perhaps at the end of the month I shall be back in my study again. Ted is still taking the brunt of Frieda, who needs watching every minute. Her favorite trick is peeling our poor wallpaper off the wall—there are so many cracks she can get her fingernails in—and then running and pointing to it, saying, "Bah Poo!" in outraged tones, as if somebody else has done it. She has, since I was down and out with the baby, discovered how to throw things down the toilet, tear up minute bits of paper or cotton and sprinkle them over the red hall carpet, uproot bulbs from flower pots, draw on the walls with coal . . . Now that the baby is getting toward a four- rather than a three-hour schedule, I should be freer to keep an eye on her.

I am still delighted with my foresight at getting all the quarterly assignments for my grant done and packaged ahead. I do hope to get back to writing soon, though.

I am taking all those bottles of vitamins you sent and wonder if it isn't the combination of them, especially the Vitamin C, which has kept me without a cold so far this winter (knock on wood). Oh, how I look forward to your visit! How I envy girls whose mothers can just drop in on them. I long to have a day or two on jaunts with just Ted—we can hardly see each other over the mountains of diapers and demands of babies. . . .

Ted's play was beautifully produced and he is so full of ideas for others. He is also reviewing animal books fairly regularly for the *New Statesman* and going on with his broadcasts for children, which have been very enthusiastically received.

I am so longing for spring. I miss the American snow, which at least makes a new, clean, exciting season out of winter, instead of this six months' cooping-up of damp and rain and blackness we get here —like the six months Persephone had to spend with Pluto.

. . . You and Warren will just have to come over here often enough to keep me from getting too homesick and get to know the babies as they grow up. . . .

x x x Sivvy

Dear Mother,

. . . I seem to need to sleep all the time, so drop back after feeding Nicholas at six and don't get up till after nine, then the day is a whirlwind of baths, laundry, meals, feedings, and, bang, it is time for bed! . . . I seem to need twice as much sleep as normal people and [*am*] unable to function efficiently if [*I*] have a bad night . . .

Nicholas is absolutely darling. He seems so far advanced as a baby . . . lifts his head and turns it from side to side when lying down. He has great, very dark blue eyes, which focus and follow your face or the light . . . He has a real little-boy look, and his fuzz of brown baby hair looks like a crewcut. His eyebrows are strange—a quite black curved line over each eye, very handsome. I imagine he will have a rather dark, handsome, craggy face, although now he is soft as a peach. You'll enjoy seeing him still at a real baby stage when you come . . .

. . . We have gorgeous big double snowdrops in bloom, a scattering of primroses, and countless daffodil sprouts. When the apple trees bloom, I am just going to take Frieda and Nicholas and lie in the orchard all day! . . .

Much love to all,

Sivvy

Dear Mother,

The bitter cold of winter has descended upon us again, after a longish lull . . . yet, our first daffodil bloomed this week—we keep puffing out to look at it and admire it. Ted has planted several nut, plum, pear and peach trees he ordered this week, and yesterday Frieda and I went out for a brisk hour to pull up the dead annual shoots in the garden . . . I find being outdoors gardening an immense relaxation and hope we have some success with our fruit, vegetables, and flowers.

I am feeling in fine shape again, having made a much more rapid recovery than when I had Frieda, partly because Nicholas is so little trouble. He only cries when he is hungry and loves being sat up and talked to. He smiled a few times at me this week and is so sweet—a little sweet-smelling peach. I feel I really *enjoy* him—none of the harassment and worry of Frieda's colic and my inexperience. I love playing with him, and I also am rested enough to find energy to play with Frieda in the second half of the day, concentrating my attention on her then. . . . She is very radiant now. . . .

I am immensely grateful for the BBC Third Programme and have sent for two booklets for two language courses that begin this week, one in German and one in French. They have exercises and pronunciation, and I find them excellent. . . .

Do thank Aunt Marion for me for the check for the baby and the *Woman's Day* magazines. . . . I am looking so forward to your coming. I have Nancy a third morning a week now for two hours of ironing, so I am free of most drudgery except that of cooking, washing up, and baby tending, all of which I more or less enjoy, so we should be free to sit in the garden and play with the babies much of the time. Love to all.

x x x Sivvy

MARCH 4, 1962

Dear Mother,

. . . I am managing to get about two and a bit more hours in my study in the mornings and hope to make it four when I can face getting up at six, which I hope will be as soon as Nicholas stops waking for a night feeding. The day seems to just fly by after noon, though, and I am lucky if I get a fraction of the baking or letter writing or reading or studying done that I want to . . . In six more weeks the time will change, and we'll have the lovely long days again. . . .

I am hoping the next installments of my grant in May and August carry us over the first year's hump of major expense for furnishings and repairs; it couldn't have come at a better time. I am getting very excited about the possibilities of our garden and hope we can conquer our nightly enemies, the snails.

I am beginning work on something amusing which I hope turns into a book (novel), but may be just happy piddling. I find long things much easier on my nature than poems—not so intensely demanding or depressing if not brought off. Luckily the English will publish almost anything in the way of a novel, so I have hope. It's almost April! Take care.

Lots of love,

Sivvy

Dear Mother,

. . . I was so touched to think I shall have your lovely Bavarian
china—that's the set with the dark-green background on the border,
isn't it? One feels a girl is the one to appreciate the domestic things,
for she is the one who uses them. I know I shall reserve my treasures
for Frieda. I am getting very sentimental about family things. For
instance, someday I hope to be well-off enough to send for grammy's
desk. I'd like it to be Frieda's little desk. I have such happy memories
of it and could never find anything with such associations—it's close
to priceless.

. . . I look so forward to your visit this summer, I can hardly sit
still. It is a red-letter occasion for me, because for the first time I shall
be sharing *my house,* which you were so instrumental in enabling us
to find last summer and to buy! I just adore the place. I picked our
very first bouquet of daffodils yesterday and put them in a glass and
brought them up to Ted's study with his tea.

I'm sure you'll find us very rough, still, although we are wonderfully civilized compared to when Warren was here. . . . The playroom (where I am typing) is a fun room. I look forward to filling it
with handpainted furniture, chest for toys and the like. I want to
paint them white with a design of hearts and flowers, have an old
piano and so on. A real rumpus room. Now it's just bare boards and
deck chairs and a welter of Frieda's toys. . . .

We're arranging to have the children baptized on Sunday afternoon, March 25, by the way. Although I honestly dislike, or rather,
scorn the rector. I told you about his ghastly H-bomb sermon, didn't
I, where he said this was the happy prospect of the Second Coming
and how lucky we Christians were compared to the stupid pacifists
and humanists and "educated pagans" who feared being incinerated,
etc., etc. I have not been to church since. I felt it was a sin to support
such insanity even by my presence. But I think I shall let the children
go to Sunday School. Marcia Plumer sent me a copy of a wonderful
sermon on fallout shelters by her local Unitarian minister, which
made me weep. I'd really be a church-goer if I was back in Wellesley . . . —the Unitarian Church is my church. How I miss it! There
is just no *choice* here. It's this church or nothing. If only there were
no *sermon,* I could justify going to the ceremony with my own reservations. Oh well.

As I say, we are still rough—very creaky floors, leaky faucets,
peeling paper and plaster and so on. But the house has a real, gen-

erous, warm *soul* to it, and responds so beautifully to any care we take. I so enjoy sitting here, watching the sun set behind the church. I think I will go just wild when our trees start blooming. There are fat buds on the lilac. I think the most exciting thing to me is *owning flowers and trees!*

Nicholas is immensely strong. He holds his head up for ages, like a Sphinx, looking round—the result of my keeping him on his stomach. I think his eyes may be hazel, like Ted's—they are a deep slate-blue now. I love him so dearly. I think having babies is really the happiest experience of my life. I would just like to go on and on.

. . . I am enjoying my slender foothold in my study in the morning again. It makes all the difference in my day. I still get tired by tea time and have spells of impatience for not doing all I want in the way of study and reading. But my mornings are as peaceful as church-going—the red plush rug and all and the feeling that nothing else but writing and thinking is done there . . .

I have the queerest feeling of having been reborn with Frieda—it's as if my real, rich, happy life only started just about then. I suppose it's a case of knowing what one wants. I never really knew before. I hope I shall always be a "young" mother like you. I think working or having any sort of career keeps one young longer. I feel I'm just beginning at writing, too. Doing prose is much easier on me; the concentration spreads out over a large area and doesn't stand or fall on one day's work, like a poem.

. . . Well, I must get supper for my family. Lots of love from us all.

Sivvy

March 27, 1962

Dearest Mother,

So nice to get your happy springy letter! I have been suffering from the March megrims—we seem to have had nothing but a horrid, raw, damp east wind (which blows around our antique back door and straight through the house) for the last month. March is the worst month when it is mean; it seems one has used up all one's resistance to winter and is left vulnerable. Just when I was most dismal, we had one glorious sunny day when I had the babies out and ate out and gardened from sunrise till sunset. We all got little sunburns and felt wonderful. Then the cold and grey closed in again.

I am becoming a devout gardener—knowing nothing about it. It is so soothing and kindly to work in the earth, pruning, digging, cutting grass. Ted is doing wonders with the back, which will be our vegetable garden, digging and fertilizing it. . . .

. . . I am thinking of learning to ride horseback at one of the local riding schools about here. I anticipate Frieda and Nicholas learning to ride, or wanting to, and would like to be practically grounded myself. But this is as yet just a notion. I mean straight riding—no jumping or hopping or skipping. Life begins at 30!

Keep me posted on all the wedding plans. Is there any chance of Warren and Maggie ever getting over here?

Lots of love to all,

Sivvy

April 8, 1962

Dear Mother,

Honestly, the reason I have been so slow in writing is that I have said to myself, "I will write tomorrow; then it is sure to be a sunny day and how cheerful I will be." Believe it or not, we haven't seen the sun for *three weeks* . . . At least, it is supposed to have been the coldest March in over 70 years. We are also having our floors done . . . workmen hacking about. They have cemented the playroom and this week will cement the floors in the downstairs hall. I just learned that it will take two weeks for the cement to dry properly before the lino can be put down. So by your birthday, I expect things will be settled. I have been painting odd bits of grubby wood furniture—a table, a chair—white, with designs, very primitive, of hearts and flowers, which cheers me up and should look gay in the playroom. . . .

Now that the weather is going to be supposedly more springlike, we shall have some friends down from London, so I shall have some company. A young American boy and his wife are coming Tuesday, he to do a BBC interview with me for a series on why Americans stay in England. It better be sunny by the time he comes, or I won't have so many reasons! . . . I have just got winter-tired these last days—don't want to see another dish or cook another meal.

My poetry book is officially due out May 14. It is very handsome, as I believe you'll think when you see it—no errors in this one. Knopf seem very enthusiastic about it. Ted's children's programs are so wonderfully received, he has a running request for as many as he can provide . . .

Well, I hope by the time I write again I may have all my seeds planted and be out with my babies. Our daffodils and jonquils are wonderful. I've picked about 300 these last two weeks and they're only beginning. Once a week I pick for myself and once a week to sell at the stands. Lots of love to you and Warren.

Sivvy

APRIL 16, 1962

Dearest Mother,

. . . I am now awaiting Ted's return from a day-trip to London where he is making a BBC broadcast, a recording, and seeing Leonard Baskin's show of engravings, for which he has been asked to write the foreword—an honor we think. I have a nice big Irish stew ready, with cheese dumplings, which he likes . . .

I never dreamed it was possible to get such joy out of babies. I do think mine are special. We had a young American I know and his British wife down last week, and they brought an acquaintance with two of the most ghastly children I've ever seen—two girls of five and six. They had no inner life, no notion of obedience, and descended shrieking on Frieda's toys, running up and down through the house with mucky boots . . . they kept sneaking up to peer in the rooms and at the baby, though they'd been told repeatedly not to. They almost knocked us out. How I believe in firm, loving discipline! . . . Now we are planning to have several couples we like down in the next month. Honestly, I wish you knew how much I miss Warren and Margaret! I already love Maggie sight unseen from what I've heard of her, and think of what lovely times we could all have together. I have such lovely children and such a lovely home now, I only long to share them with loving relatives . . .

So glad you liked the poems in *Poetry*. I don't feel they're my best, but it's nice to get the "exercises" published, too. The "News from Home" is, of course, your letters, which I look forward to above all . . .

How I wish you could see us now with all the daffodils. I pick about 600 a week for market and friends and notice no diminishing. They are so heavenly. We even had an antiquarian come to visit our Ancient Mound last Sunday!

x x x Sivvy

Dearest Mother,

How I wish you could see us now! I am sitting out in a deck chair in shorts in heavenly hot sun, smelling the pungent box bushes at our door and the freshly mown and plowed tennis court; Baby Nick (as Frieda and, therefore, we now call him) asleep among the daisies in his pram; Frieda so excited she can hardly nap; and Ted out back, beaming among the few strawberry plants that survived the late frosts. On Easter Sunday the world relented and spring arrived. Our daffodils are in full bloom; we picked about 1,000 this week, and I look out over a literal sea of several thousand more. I keep finding new treasures: little yellow and pink primroses and grape hyacinths opening in a grassy tangle by the lilac hedge, the spikes of lily-of-the-valley poking through a heap of dead brambles. I think I would like nothing better than to grow flowers and vegetables. I have such spring fever, I can hardly think straight. I am dying for you to come and to see it all through your eyes. I got your room all fixed up and cleaned yesterday. Two months seems such a long way away!

Hilda and Vicky stayed with us over Easter. We were very surprised they did not bring Ted's parents, but hope Uncle Walter may bring them later. Evidently the long winter, arthritis, and the prospect of the day's trip put Edith off . . . Hilda and Vicky pitched right in with dishes and cleaning, so were no extra work; they are both very lively and nice . . .

My book should be out in America May 14. Do send any clippings of reviews, however bad. How I would love Mrs. Prouty to come. We have a very fine, pompous hotel in town on the hill . . . Do tell her! . . .

You must be full of plans for Warren's wedding. How soon could they think of coming? I wish *somebody* could come around Easter next year to admire the daffodils. Of course, early September is lovely, with apple pie every day for breakfast . . .

I wouldn't leave this place for a million dollars. It is a miracle we found it, and you were instrumental in minding Frieda and freeing us at just that time . . .

Lots and lots of love,

Sivvy

Dear Mother,

These photographs are meant for a late birthday surprise. We took them Easter Sunday, the first day of real spring. I think you can see some of the reason I am so happy. This is just the very smallest corner of our daffodils. Frieda is an expert at picking handsome bouquets—you simply mention the word "daffodil," and she is off. You will love the children. Nicholas smiles and laughs, and is wonderfully responsive to attention and kind words; Frieda thirsts for knowledge and laps up every word you tell her . . .

. . . Now it is spring, it is just heaven here. I never dreamed it was possible to be so happy. . . .

We have the Sillitoes here now—Alan, his American writer-wife Ruth and their month-old son, David. They are marvelous guests— Ruth helps cook, Alan washes up; they take walks on their own, and our life proceeds as usual. I don't feel a drudge, because they chip in, and I work in my study as usual in the mornings . . .

Our daffodils are waning, but our cherry trees are coming into bloom—better than Washington! Bright red leaves and fluffy, round, pink blossoms. It is like a little garden of Eden. Lots of love to everybody.

x x Sivvy

Dear Mother,

I hope by now you have received the color photos and have some idea of our lovely daffodils that have now vanished. We earned about $17 or so by selling them, very small in amount, but we are proud of it because it makes it seem as if the place is "earning." If we have a good apple harvest, we should earn some more . . .

My book officially comes out in America today. Do clip and send any reviews you see, however bad. Criticism encourages me as much as praise. . . .

We have a nice young Canadian poet and his very attractive, intelligent wife coming down for this weekend—they're the ones who took over our lease for the London flat. Then Ted's parents will probably be driven down by his Uncle Walter for the next weekend . . .

Nicholas has, for some reason, been crying at night, so I am rather weary. I think my firm resistance to the long, hard winter has hit me now that it is nicer and I can relax. I just don't want to do a thing, or rather, I *want* to, but don't feel like it. I have had my mending stacked up for months and am tired of my own cooking, with no energy to try any of the exotic recipes I get in my beloved [Ladies Home] *Journal*. O pooh. We have huge amounts of wonderful legendary rhubarb, which we inherited. Have you any canning advice? Maybe you will supervise some of my canning this summer. We have a fine, dark "wine cellar" which asks to be crammed with bright glass jars full of good things . . .

Love to all,
x x x Sivvy

June 7, 1962

Dear Mother,

Forgive me, forgive me for what must seem a huge silence. I have reached, I think, the last of my "guests" with six days of Ted's mother, father, and Uncle Walt. That is partly why I have been so quiet. They were the end of a long string . . . Ted's mother stayed with us and the men stayed up at the Burton Hall hotel . . . I made a few big meals for everyone, and we ate at least half of our dinners out. Mrs. Hughes is very sweet and did a whole pile of darning on Ted's socks (!), which I have no patience for. As she sends him these big wool things, she is an expert at doing it, and I felt it was a good way for her to feel useful with no real strain. They went on car-jaunts with Walt and were immensely impressed and proud of our place. I am glad they, like you, have had a part in helping us get it.

This is the *fourth* day in a row of absolutely halcyon, blue, clear hot weather. I took off from my study the last three days and had a little Lookout Farm. I weeded all our onions and spinach and lettuce—out in the garden from sunrise to sunset, immensely happy, with Frieda digging in a little space, "helping," and Nicholas in the pram sunbathing. This is the richest and happiest time of my life. The babies are so beautiful. . . .

Just now the two laburnum trees are in full bloom and sit right in front of my study window. Isn't it odd that I've written about Golden Rain Trees in my book and now have *six*—two out front and at the side of my study and the rest about. I am praying some apple bloom hangs on till you come. I can't wait to see the place through your eyes. Work inside the house has come to a standstill with the demands of the big gardens, so I hope you'll overlook minor cracks and peelings. . . .

I'd like to get into a long work, which I've been unable to do with all the spring interruptions of other people. O it is so beautiful here. Bring Bermuda shorts for wear about the garden; we're pretty private. (Of course, no one wears them in town!) And one warm outfit. Thanks a million for the molasses! I've made mountains of gingerbread. I'm learning to do gros point tapestry for cushion and seat covers. Wonderfully calming.

I hope Warren and Margaret got our little telegram of good wishes, which I sent to the New York address. [*Warren and Margaret were married June 2, 1962.*] . . . I felt very, very sorry for myself at not being at the wedding and look forward to a full account from you in the next day or so. Even down to the last minute I considered squandering our savings and flying over by jet! Tell me all about it!

We've been doing quite well (although we don't seem to be working). I've had a long poem (about 378 lines!) for three voices accepted by the BBC Third Programme (three women in a maternity ward, inspired by a Bergman film), which will be produced by the same man who does Ted's plays and who'll be down here to discuss production with me!

Ted did a beautiful program on a marvelous young British poet, Keith Douglas, killed in the last war, saying how shocking it was no book of his was in print. In the next mail he got grateful letters and inscribed books from the poet's 75-year-old, impoverished mother and a suggestion from a publisher that Ted write the foreword to a new edition of the book. Both of us mourn this poet immensely and feel he would have been like a lovely big brother to us. His death is really a terrible blow and we are trying to resurrect his image and poems in this way.

I have been asked to do a short talk for a program called "The World of Books," and Ted's children's programs are classics. . . . His radio play, "The Wound," will be broadcast a third time this summer (which means another blessed $300 out of the blue). We are trying to save a bit now while I still have one more installment of my grant. Perhaps in a couple of years, we'll do a poetry reading tour in America and earn a great pot. They pay one to two hundred dollars a night!

Love to All the Plaths,
Sivvy

Dear Mother,

Well, this is the last letter I will be writing before you come! . . . I have been working so hard physically out in the garden that I am inarticulate and ready for bed by evening, hence my long silences. I don't know when I've been so happy or felt so well. These last few days I have been weeding our strawberry patch and setting the runners, just as I did on Lookout Farm, and at night I shut my eyes and see the beautiful little plants with the starry flowers and beginning berries. I love this outdoor work and feel I am really getting in condition. . . .

Today, guess what, we became *beekeepers!* We went to the local meeting last week (attended by the rector, the midwife, and assorted beekeeping people from neighboring villages) to watch a Mr. Pollard make three hives out of one (by transferring his queen cells) under the supervision of the official Government bee-man. We all wore masks and it was thrilling. It is expensive to start beekeeping (over $50 outlay), but Mr. Pollard let us have an old hive for nothing, which we painted white and green, and today he brought over the swarm of docile Italian hybrid bees we ordered and installed them. We placed the hive in a sheltered out-of-the-way spot in the orchard—the bees were furious from being in a box. Ted had only put a handkerchief over his head where the hat should go in the bee-mask, and the bees crawled into his hair, and he flew off with half-a-dozen stings. I didn't get stung at all, and when I went back to the hive later, I was delighted to see bees entering with pollen sacs full and leaving with them empty—at least I *think* that's what they were doing. I feel very ignorant, but shall try to read up and learn all I can. If we're lucky, we'll have our own honey, too! Lots of people are really big keepers in town with a dozen to twenty hives, so we shall not be short of advice. When we have our first honey, I think we shall get half a dozen hens.

Luckily I have lots and lots of work to do, like painting furniture and weeding, because I am so excited about your coming I can't sit still! I wish now you had seen the house in its raw state so you would see how much we have done. Of course, there is still an immense deal to do, and my eyes are full of five-year plans. . . .

Frieda and Nicholas are getting brown and are so wonderful I can't believe it. They are such happy healthy babies. I adore every minute of them.

Ted and I are arranging a day in London about a week after you come to do a broadcast, see an art exhibit, and, maybe, a foreign movie. It's exciting as a safari to Africa to me to think of a day away! . . .

When you come, I really must sit in my study in the mornings! Six weeks seems such a short time. I realize how terribly much I have missed you (and Warren, too!) now that the time draws close to see you again.

Lots of love and a smooth trip!

Fond wishes from us all,
Sivvy

The welcome I received when I arrived the third week in June was heartwarming. The threshold to the guest room I was to occupy had an enameled pink heart and a garland of flowers painted on it. Frieda recognized me; "Baby Nick" went happily into my arms.

After the first few days, however, I sensed a tension between Sylvia and Ted that troubled me. On July 9, when Sylvia and I left Ted with the children in order to drive to Exeter for shopping and lunch, Sylvia said proudly, "I have everything in life I've ever wanted: a wonderful husband, two adorable children, a lovely home, and my writing." Yet the marriage was seriously troubled, and there was a great deal of anxiety in the air. Ted had been seeing someone else, and Sylvia's jealousy was very intense.

I thought it best to leave and took a room with the midwife, planning to remain there until the time of my scheduled return to the U.S.A. I visited the house daily and spent a great deal of time with the children.

When I left on August 4, 1962, the four of them were together, waiting for my train to pull out of the station. The two parents were watching me stonily—Nick was the only one with a smile. It was the last time I saw Sylvia.

Soon afterward Mrs. Prouty and her sister-in-law arrived in London and invited Sylvia and Ted to join them there. To avoid difficult explanations, Sylvia and Ted, for the time being, put their marital torments aside, and together made the trip to join Mrs. Prouty for what she had planned to be a gala occasion.

Dear Mother,

. . . We did go to London, had cocktails, dinner, and saw Agatha Christie's *Mousetrap*, a play which has run for over ten years. Mrs. Prouty put us up at her hotel, the Connaught, and it is the loveliest hotel I've ever stayed in—very intimate, clean, yet antique-feeling. No great impersonal grandeur . . . It was wonderful to see Mrs. Prouty again . . . She asked Ted and me about our work with her usual insight. She means an immense deal to me. I hope you drop over to see her now and then; her loneliness must be appalling.

. . . We now have with us a young American writer, who was evicted from his London flat, and his wife. They are fantastically neurotic. She has dozens of illnesses, all untreatable because she has decided she is allergic to any medicine that might help. For instance, she has ulcers, she says, yet claims she can't swallow milk; and has migraine, but is allergic to codeine; and she is fanatic about food . . . They are living in the guest room—I said we would take them in rent-free for a month or six weeks until they were rested enough to look for another flat if they would help pay for the food and help with the children. However, when they took over the day we were in London, it nearly killed them. They have said they will stay while we go to Ireland, which would be wonderful as the children get on beautifully with them, but I have grave doubts as to their staying power. I shall ask them to tell me now, so I can hire a nurse if necessary. I simply must go to Ireland and sail for a week. Mrs. Prouty is scheduled to come to dinner here, Sunday, September 9, and we hope to leave the next day.

It was very kind of you, Warren and Margaret to remember Ted's birthday.

I have seen the doctor's wife, whom I *very* much like, about riding lessons . . . and we may take them together. Someday I would like a pony for Frieda.

Lots of love to all,
Sivvy

These letters were, of course, written under great strain. They were meant, as were her many phone calls to me during this period, to reassure herself as well. They are desperate letters, and their very desperation make it difficult to read them with any objectivity; I could not, at the time. But I must ask the reader to remember the circumstances in which they were written and to remember also that they represent one side of an extremely complex situation.

Dear Mother,

. . . I hope you will not be too surprised or shocked when I say I am going to try to get a legal separation from Ted. I do not believe in divorce and would never think of this, but I simply cannot go on living the degraded and agonized life I have been living, which has stopped my writing and just about ruined my sleep and my health. . . .

. . . I feel I need a legal settlement so I can count on so much a week for groceries and bills and the freedom to build up the happy, pleasant life I feel it in myself to make and would but for him . . .

I have too much at stake and am too rich a person to live as a martyr . . . I want a clean break, so I can breathe and laugh and enjoy myself again.

The woman Winifred [*the midwife*] got for me came one morning, then sent her husband to say it was too hard work. Well, I have Kathy for the time being and really couldn't afford anyone else now.

The kindest and most helpful thing you can do is send some warm articles of clothing for Frieda at Christmas. I have plenty for Nicholas, AND a big bottle of Vitamin C tablets for me . . . I can't afford another cold like this one.

I do hope Warren and dear Maggie will plan to come in Spring and that I can have Marty and Mike Plumer as well. I try to see the Comptons weekly and have met some nice couples with children there.

I would, by the way, appreciate it if you would tell no one but perhaps Margaret and Warren of this and perhaps better not even them. It is a private matter and I do not want people who would never see me anyway to know of it. So do keep it to yourself.

I am actually doing some writing now Kathy is here, so there is hope. And I feel if I can spend the winter in the sun in Spain, I may regain the weight and health I have lost this last six months. I meant you to have such a lovely stay; I can never say how sorry I am you did not have the lovely reveling and rest I meant you to have . . .

Tell Dotty [*my sister*] to go on writing me; she means a very great deal to me. I love you all very very much and am in need of nothing and am desirous of nothing but staying in this friendly town and my home with my dear children. I am getting estimates about rebuilding the cottage so I someday can install a nanny and lead a freer life.

Lots of love,
Sivvy

Dear Mother,

Thank you for your letter . . . The children are fine. Nicholas has cut his first tooth and is the most energetic, bouncy child imaginable. He crawls all over the playroom, playing with Frieda's blocks, much to her consternation. "Put in pen, put in pram," she tells me to do with him and gathers all the toys he seems to like in a little heap out of his reach . . .

I had a wonderful four days in Ireland, treated to oysters and Guinness and brown bread in Dublin by Jack and Marie Sweeney of the Lamont Library, Harvard; then two eggs, homemade butter and warm milk straight from the cows every breakfast in wild Connemara, about 50 miles from Galway. . . . My happiness was compounded of the sailing, the fishing, the sea, and the kind people and wonderful cooking of an Irish woman from whom I bought a beautiful handknit sweater . . . I also was very lucky in finding a woman after my own heart, one of the sturdy, independent horse-and-whisky set, with a beautiful cottage (turf fires—the most comfortable and savory fire imaginable), her own TT-tested cows and butter churn which she will rent to me for December through February and show me all the sea walks. Spain is out of the question. . . . I think this Irish woman and I speak the same language—she will live next door in a cottage of hers. She loves children, and I have no desire to be in a country, alone, where I do not even speak the language. I will try to rent [*the house*] for these months. . . . I want to be where no possessions remind me of the past and by the sea, which is for me the great healer. . . .

. . . I must at all costs make over the cottage and get a live-in nanny next spring so I can start trying to write and get my independence again . . . Love to Warren and Maggie—

Sylvia

Actually, this emphasis on her lack of funds may have been an exaggeration intended to convey her sense of urgency. Ted Hughes says that he borrowed money from his family when he left and between September and early February gave her over £900.

Dear Mother,

I feel I owe you a happier letter than my last one. Now that I have come to my decision to get a legal separation and have an appointment with an immensely kind-sounding lawyer in London tomorrow (recommended to me by my equally kind accountant), I begin to see that life is not over for me. It is the uncertainty, week after week, that has been such a torture. And, of course, the desire to hang on to the last to see if something, anything, could be salvaged. I am just as glad the final blows have been delivered . . .

It is a beautiful day here, clear and blue. I got this nanny back for today and tomorrow. She is a whiz, and I see what a heaven my life could be if I had a good live-in nanny. I am eating my first warm meal since I've come back—having an *impersonal* person in the house is a great help. I went up to Winifred's [*the midwife*] for three hours the night I realized Ted wasn't coming back, and she was a great help . . . Since I made the decision, miraculously, my own life, my wholeness, has been seeping back. I will try to rent [*the house*] for the winter and go to Ireland—this is a dream of mine—to purge myself of this awful experience by the wild beauty I found there, and the children would thrive. Quite practically, I have no money to go farther. I have put all my earnings this summer in a separate account, the checking account is at zero, and there are 300 pounds I have taken from our joint savings—just about the last of them—as Ted said at one point I could, as some recompense for my lost nanny-grant, to build over the cottage. This is a *must*. Also getting a TV for a nanny. I can't have one live in this house or I could have no guests, and I do want to entertain what friends and relatives I have as often as I can. I dream of Warren and Maggie! I would love to go on a skiing holiday in the Tyrol with them someday. I just read about it in the paper. And then if I do a novel or two, I might apply for a Guggenheim to go to Rome with a nanny and the children. Right now I have no money, but if I get the cottage done this winter while I'm away, I might sink all my savings in a nanny for a year. My writing should be able to get her the next year . . .

If I hit it lucky, I might even be able to take a London flat and send the children to the fine free schools there and enjoy the London people (I would *starve* intellectually here), renting [*the house*] for the winter, and come down here on holidays and in the spring for the long summer holiday. I feel when the children are school-age, I want to be able to afford this. Some lucky break—like writing a couple of *New Yorker* stories in Ireland or a play for the BBC (I've got lots of fan mail for the half-hour interview I did on why I stayed in England . . .)—could make this life a reality. But first the cottage, then the nanny. I'll have to do this out of my own small pocket, as I imagine Ted will only have to pay for the children. . . .

Took Frieda to the playground again today. She is talking wonderfully, says names. I'm getting her two kittens from Mrs. MacNamara next week and trying to go somewhere, on some visit every afternoon with them, to keep busy. Lots of love to you, Warren, and Maggie.

Sylvia

SEPTEMBER 26, 1962

Dear Mother,

I went up to London to the solicitor yesterday—a very harrowing but necessary experience. Not knowing where Ted is, except in London . . . I hope he will . . . settle out of court and agree to an allowance . . .

The laws, of course, are awful: a wife is allowed one third of her husband's income, and if he doesn't pay up, the suing is long and costly. If a wife earns anything, her income is included in his and she ends up paying for everything. The humiliation of being penniless and begging money from deaf ears is too much. I shall just have to invest everything with courage in the cottage and the nanny for a year and write like mad. Try to get clear . . . Together we earned about $7,000 this year, a fine salary, I earning one third. Now it is all gone. . . . I shall be penalized for earning, or, if I don't earn, have to beg. Well, I choose the former . . .

Thank God the solicitor said I could take the children to Ireland. I am hoping to let this place, but must go even if I can't. . . .

I am sorry to be so worrying at this time when your own concerns are so pressing, but I must get control of my life, the little I have left.

With love,
Sivvy

SEPTEMBER 29, 1962

Dearest Mother,

It is going on 6:30 in the morning, and I am warm in my study, Pifco going, with my first cup of morning coffee. Winifred, for all her lack of imagination, is full of good sense, and I love her for it. She is very busy, so after my one 3-hour evening session with her when deciding what to do, I only will see her briefly for social occasions and practical questions. It was *she* who suggested that when I wake up early and am unable to sleep, I come in and work on my novel before the babies get up . . . Well, of course, just now my emotions are such that "working on my novel" is so difficult as to be almost impossible, but I actually did do three pages yesterday and hope to work into it, first numbly, then with feeling.

It is the evenings here, after the children are in bed, that are the worst, so I might as well get rid of them by going to bed. I feel pretty good in the morning, and my days are, thank goodness, busy. I find that by eating my meals with Frieda in the kitchen it is easier to eat something, and every day I religiously make tea in the nursery at four, try to invite someone or take them to see someone, so each day I have a time with other people who know nothing or, at least, who are darling, like the Comptons.

I do have to take sleeping pills, but they are, just now, a necessary evil and enable me to sleep deeply and then do some writing and feel energetic during the day if I drink lots of coffee right on waking . . .

The solicitor says I am within my legal right and to draw all money out of our joint accounts and put them in accounts of my own since my husband has deserted me . . . So do send me that $500 "gift" and another $500 at Christmas, if I need it. I have to make an outlay for the cottage this winter and get a nanny in the spring. Having the nanny here from the agency made me realize what heaven it would be, and I don't break down with someone else around.

Love,
Sivvy

OCTOBER 9, 1962

Dear Mother,

I don't know where to begin. I just can't take the $50. [*I finally persuaded her to do so, monthly, and I opened a joint account in a London bank, so she could use it in any emergency, hoping she would consider returning to the United States. We, as a family, were prepared to set her up in her own apartment here.*]

. . . Just sold a long *New Yorker* poem. I'll get by. Ted has agreed to give us 1,000 pounds a year maintenance. This will just take care of rates, heat, light, food, with 200 pounds for the children's clothing and upkeep expenses. I want nothing for me. I'll pay the upkeep and gas and taxes on the car, Ted's life insurance (which is made out to me and will be a kind of pension . . .) and for nannies. Right now I get up a couple of hours before the babies and write. I've got to . . . I've made out accounts, and it is a scrape . . . I pray he will sign the maintenance . . .

I am getting a divorce. It is the only thing. . . .

I should say right away America is out for me. I want to make my life in England. If I start running now, I will never stop. I shall hear of Ted all my life, of his success, his genius . . . I must make a life all my own as fast as I can . . . the flesh has dropped from my bones. But I am a fighter. Money is my only way to fight myself into a new life. I know pretty much what I want . . .

[*Eventually*] I want to have a flat in London, where the cultural life is what I am starved for . . . Also, as you can see, I haven't the strength to see you for some time. The horror of what you saw and what I saw you see last summer is between us and I cannot face you again until I have a new life; it would be too great a strain. I would give heaven and earth to have a visit from Aunt Dot or Warren and Margaret. Can the latter come in spring?

The shock to me has been an enormity. . . . I was very stupid, very happy . . . no time . . . to make any plans of my own. As you may imagine, the court case is for me to appear in, not he. A necessary evil . . .

. . . Dot's letter a great consolation. Reassure me she'll accept the divorce [*she is a devout Catholic*] and not stop her kindness for that. I have *no one.* . . . Stuck down here as into a sack, I fight for air and freedom and the culture and the libraries of a city.

Do you suppose either Warren or Aunt Dot could fly over to be with me for a few days when I have to face the court? I don't know whether it will be this autumn (I doubt it, alas) or next spring, but I will need protection. I look to Warren so, now that I have no man, no adviser. He was so good and sweet here . . .

Everything is breaking—my dinner set cracking in half, the health inspector says the cottage should be demolished—there is no hope for it, so I shall have to do over the long, unfinished room in the house instead. Even my beloved bees set upon me today when I numbly knocked aside their sugar feeder, and I am all over stings . . .

I must get to London next fall. . . .

Please tell Warren to write and say he and Maggie will come in spring. In Ireland I feel I may find my soul, and in London next fall, my brain, and maybe in heaven what was my heart.

Love,
S

Dear Mother,

Your nice fat letter received with many thanks. Do tear up my last one. It was written at what was probably my all-time low, and I have [had] an incredible change of spirit; I am joyous, happier than I have been for ages. . . .

It is *over*. My life can begin . . . I am having the long room made over, new floors and will furnish it as a bed-sitting room with TV. I hope to keep this (very expensive) nanny until Ted's Aunt Hilda comes, as she hopes to, at the end of November, to accompany me to Ireland . . . Ted does want the divorce, thank goodness, so it shouldn't be difficult . . . [In] Ireland—in my darling cottage from December 1 to February 28—I should recover on the milk from TT-tested cows (hope to learn to milk them myself), homemade bread, and the sea!

Every morning, when my sleeping pill wears off, I am up about five, in my study with coffee, writing like mad—have managed a poem a day before breakfast. All book poems. Terrific stuff, as if domesticity had choked me. As soon as the nanny comes and I know I've got a stretch of guaranteed time, I'll finish the novel. I have forty children's picture books at my side to review for the leftish weekly I've done for them before—*Horton Hatches the Egg* among them! So send no children's books; I've mountains.

Nick has two teeth, stands, sits, and is an *angel*. Ted had cut Frieda's hair short and it looks marvellous, no mess, no straggle. She has two kittens from Mrs. MacNamara: Tiger-Pieker and Skunky-Bunks; the first a tiger, the second black and white. She adores them, croons "Rock-a-bye baby, when the bough breaks" at them. They're very good for her now.

Did you see my poem "Blackberries" in the September 15 *New Yorker*? Wrote that when Warren was here last year . . . Hope, when free, to write myself out of this hole . . .

. . . I need a bloody holiday. Ireland is heaven, utterly unspoiled, emerald sea washing in fingers among green fields, white sand, wild coast, cows, friendly people, honey-tasting whisky, peat (turf) fires that smell like spiced bread—thank God, I found it. Just in time.

I go riding tomorrow; love it. Shall send Frieda and Nick to church in London, not here! I miss *brains*, hate this cow life, am dying to surround myself with intelligent, good people. I'll have a salon in London. I am a famous poetess here—mentioned this week in *The*

Listener as one of the half-dozen women who will last—including Marianne Moore and the Brontës!

x x x Sivvy

P.S. Forget about the court case—I'll manage that fine alone. Every experience is grist for a novelist.

OCTOBER 12, 1962

Dearest Warren and Maggie,

Your lovely letter arrived today and cheered me immensely. How often I have thought of you both! I have been through the most incredible hell for six months, influenza, the lot, and amazingly enough, now . . . to have something *definite* . . . the release in my energy is enormous . . .

The one thing I retain is love for and admiration of [*Ted's*] writing. I know he is a genius, and for a genius there are no bonds and no bounds. . . . It is hurtful to be ditched . . . but thank God I have my own work. If I did not have that I do not know what I would do. I have a considerable reputation over here and am writing from dawn to when the babes wake, a poem a day, and they are terrific.

So glad you are behind me on the nanny, Warren. I am and have been an intelligent woman, and this year of country life has been, for me, a cultural death. No plays, films, art shows, books, people! . . . Now I am stuck; but not for long. I plan to go to Ireland to a lovely cottage by the sea from December to February to recover my health and my heart, then return here for spring and summer, see you and Maggie I hope and pray, my good friends, the Alan Sillitoes (now, alas, in Tangier for a year), and Marty and Mike Plumer if they come. The loneliness here now is appalling. Then I shall fight for a London flat . . . I shall be able to do free-lance broadcasting, reviewing, and have a circle of intellectual friends in London. I loved living there and never wanted to leave. You can imagine how ironic it is to me that Ted is now living there, after he said it was "death" to him . . . I will try to finish my novel and a second book of poems by Christmas. I think I'll be a pretty good novelist, very funny—my stuff makes me laugh and laugh, and if I can laugh now it must be hellishly funny stuff.

I wish you would both consider going on a holiday to Germany and Austria when you come. You should know some lovely places in the Tyrol, and I would love to go with you! I just dread ever going on a holiday alone. I could leave the babies with the nanny for a couple of weeks, and you could begin and end your stay here. I would be very cheerful and entertaining by then, I promise you.

Just now I am a bit of a wreck, bones literally sticking out all over and great, black shadows under my eyes from sleeping pills, a smoker's hack (I actually took up smoking the past month out of desperation—my solicitor started it by offering me a cigarette, and I practically burned off all my eyebrows, I was so upset and forgot it was lit! But now I've stopped). I do hope Dotty isn't going to snub me because of the divorce, although I know Catholics think it's a sin. Her support has been marvelous for me. I hope you can tactfully convey to mother, Warren, that we should not meet for at least a year . . . when I am happy in my new London life. After this summer, I just could not bear to see her; it would be too painful and recall too much. So you and dear Maggie, whom I already love, come instead.

Tell me you'll consider taking (I mean escorting! I'll have money!) me to Austria with you, even if you don't, so I'll have that to look forward to. I've had nothing to look forward to for so long! The half year ahead seems like a lifetime, and the half behind an endless hell. Your letters are like glühwein to me. (I *must* really learn German. I want above all to speak it.) Do write me again. So proud of your Chicago speech, Warren! I want both you and Maggie henceforth to consider yourselves godparents to both Frieda and Nick. Lord knows, they need as many as they can have, and the best! Lots of love to you both.

Sivvy

OCTOBER 16, 1962

Dear Mother,

I am writing with my old fever of 101° alternating with chills back. I must have someone with me for the next two months to mind the babies while I get my health back and try to write . . . I need help very much just now. Home is impossible. I can go nowhere with the children, and I am ill, and it would be psychologially the worst thing to see you now or to go home. I have free doctor's care here, cheap help *possible* though not now available, and a home I love and will want to return to in summer to get ready to leap to London. To make a new life. I am a writer . . . I am a genius of a writer; I have it in me. I am writing the best poems of my life; they will make my name. I could finish the novel in *six weeks* of day-long work. I have a gift of an inspiration for another.

Got a $100 "birthday present" from Dotty today; $300 from Mrs. Prouty. Thank God.

Very bad luck with nanny agency; a bitch of a woman is coming tomorrow from them; doesn't want to cook, do any breakfast or tea, wondered if there was a butler. Ten pounds a week. If I had time to get a *good nanny*, possibly an Irish girl to come home with me, I could get on with my life . . . I feel only a lust to study, write, get my brain back and practice my craft.

I have, if you want to know, already had my first novel finished and accepted—it is a secret, and I am on my second. My third—the idea—came this week.

After Ted left with all his clothes and things, I piled the children and two cats in the car and drove to stay with a . . . couple I know in St. Ives, Cornwall—the most heavenly gold sands by emerald sea. Discovered Cornwall, exhausted but happy, my first independent act! I have no desire but to build a new life. Must *start here.* When I have my second book of poems done, my third novel, and the children are of age, I may well try a year of creative-writing lecturing in America and a Cape Cod summer. But not just now. I must not go back to the womb or retreat. I must make steps *out,* like Cornwall, like Ireland.

Please share this letter with Dotty and Mrs. Prouty. *I am all right.* . . . Could either Dot or Margaret spare me six weeks. I can get no good nanny sight unseen; I could pay board and room, travel expenses and Irish fares. I am as bereft now as ever . . . I must have someone I love . . . to protect me, for my flu with my weight loss and the daily assault of practical nastiness—this nanny sounds as if she will leave in a day or so . . . has made me need immediate help. Know my only problems now are *practical:* money and health back, a good young girl or nanny, willing to muck in and cook, which I could afford once I got writing. The strain of facing suing . . . for support, with the cruel laws here, is something I need to put off just now.

I'm getting an unlisted phone put in as soon as possible so I can call out; you shall have the number.

The babes are beautiful, though Frieda has regressed; the pussies help. I cannot come home. I need someone to cover my getting to Ireland. I can't rely on any nanny at this short notice—I just can't interview them. Do let me know what you all think. The life in Ireland is very healthful; the place, a dream; the sea, a blessing. I must get out of England. I am . . . full of plans, but do need help for the next two months. I am fighting now against hard odds and alone.

x x x Sivvy

Dear Mother,

Mention has been made of my coming home for Christmas, which, alas, this year is impossible from every angle, psychological, health, babies, money. I gathered from Dot's letter you might all chip in to do this. Do you suppose instead there is any possibility of your chipping in and sending me Maggie? By next spring I should have my health back, the prospect of visits from friends . . . Could she come *now* instead of then? I already love her; she would be such *fun* and love the babies. We could go to Ireland together and get me settled in, and she could fly home from Dublin well before Christmas. Do I sound mad? Taking or wanting to take Warren's new wife? Just for a few weeks! How I need a free sister! We could go on jaunts, eat together; I have all the cleaning done and someone who'll mind the babies nine hours a week.

I need someone from *home*. A defender. . . . I have a fever now, so I am a bit delirious. I . . . work from 4 a.m. to 8 a.m. On the next few months depend my future and my *health* . . .

. . . I dread the nanny who is coming tonight; she sounded such a bitch over the phone, so snotty, wanting a "cook," etc. I simply can't afford these high fees and a *bad,* lazy nanny. It's the worst thing for the children, these changes. If only Maggie could come for six weeks, then I could get settled in Ireland and look around for an Irish girl. I would have a blood ally . . . Do see if Maggie and Warren could make this great and temporary sacrifice. I am fine in mind and spirit, but wasted and ill in flesh. I love you all.

Sivvy

[*On receiving the above letter, I cabled Mrs. Winifred Davies, Sylvia's midwife and friend:* "Please see Sylvia now and get woman for her. Salary paid here. Writing."]

Dear Mother,

Do ignore my last letters! I honestly must have been delirious to think I could uproot other people's lives to poultice my own. It was the bloody fever that just finished me. I went to the doctor—no medication, of course—then to bed at 8 p.m. Yesterday I was much better. The Health Visitor came to see Nicholas and gaped at me: "My,

Mrs. Hughes, you've lost weight!" I told her I was up at 4 a.m. every morning, writing till the babies woke, and she looked concerned. I guess my predicament is an astounding one, a deserted wife knocked out by flu with two babies and a full-time job!

Anyhow, Winifred, bless her, came round last night with some hopeful news—a young, 22-year-old nurse nearby would "love" to live in till mid-December, visit home one day a week, etc. I could propose the Irish trip after she'd settled in; she thought she'd be game. She'd want to be home for Christmas and have to go back to London as staff nurse in January, but it's this limbo through to Ireland I've got to settle. Evidently they'll invite me round to tea to discuss business—about 5 guineas a week ($15) plus board and room should be okay, Winifred thinks. *Half* of the fee for the bastardly nanny who arrived last night. She's an old, snobby snoop, and I can't wait to get rid of her. It's cost $10 just to *hire* her through this fancy agency, which in desperation I've had to use—I just don't have time to shop around . . . Hilda, Ted's aunt, wrote today about coming down soon, so I shall tell her I've been ordered to have a live-in nurse . . . since I've been flattened by influenza . . . no hurt feelings.

The weather has been heavenly. Fog mornings, but clear, sunny, blue days after. I have a bad cough and shall get my lungs x-rayed as soon as I can and my teeth seen to. Up at 5 a.m. today. I am writing very good poems. The BBC has just accepted a very long one which I'll go up to record . . . I need time to breathe, sun, recover my flesh. I have enough ideas and subjects to last me a year or more! *Must* get a permanent girl or nanny after this young nurse (whose father writes children's books and whose mother is the secretary of the local bee-keepers' club). She sounds nice. Everybody here very good to me, as if they knew or guessed my problem . . . I shall live on here and eventually in London, happy in my own life and career and babies . . . I love it here, even in the midst of this. I see it is imperative to have a faithful girl or woman living *in* with me, so I can go off for a job or a visit at the drop of a hat and write full time. *Then* I can enjoy the babies. It is lucky I don't have to work out. . . .

. . . being utterly cut off from culture, plays, libraries, people, work, resources, my writing stopped and my grant gone . . . I shall never forget and shall commemorate in my next novel.

. . . I love and live for letters.

x x x Sivvy

Dear Warren,

Your welcome letter arrived today, together with a very sweet and moving letter from Clem [*Warren's Exeter and Harvard roommate*]. I certainly want to see his father [*an attorney in London at this time*]. As it happens, the BBC has taken a long, gruesome poem of mine, so I can go up to record it during his stay, expenses paid, and a *good* local temporary nanny is imminent, thanks to the efforts of blessed Winifred Davies, our midwife. I have a horror now (don't tell mother) whom I shall fire tomorrow—she is a snobby, snoopy old bitch and has upset my faithful cleaner, Nancy, and the babies and me and is terribly expensive. I got her from the same agency as my young dream-nanny who came while I was in Ireland; have resolved *never* to get someone sight unseen again . . . I know just what I need, what I want, what I must work for. *Please* convince mother of this. She identifies much too much with me, and you must help her see how starting my own life in the most difficult place—here—not running, is the only sane thing to do. I love England, love [*this place*] for *summers*, want to live in London in fall and winter so the children can go to the fine free schools and I can have the free-lance jobs and cultural variety and stimulus which is food for my year-long culture-starved soul.

I fear I wrote two worrying letters to mother this week when I was desperate . . . Do try to convince mother I am cured. I am only in danger physically, mentally I am sound, fine, and writing the best ever, free from 4 a.m. to 8 a.m. each day. I did not tell Mother that I almost died from influenza, that is why I begged to see Maggie. I thought a loving . . . sister-in-law whom I already love dearly would protect me from further assaults while I got back my weight, my health. But now I am better and if this local nanny comes through and covers my trip to Ireland, I should be safe for a while.

. . . I am a writer and that is all I want to do. Over here I can earn quite a bit from the radio, live on little, get free medical care, and have had my first novel accepted (this is a secret; it is a pot-boiler and no one must read it!) and am ready to finish a second the minute I get a live-in nanny . . .

I *must* have someone live in or otherwise I don't eat and can go nowhere. By next fall I hope to have earned and written my way to a flat in London where my starved mind can thrive and grow. My God, Warren, imagine yourself on an endless potato farm, forever deprived of your computers, friends, relatives and only potato people in sight. I am an intellectual at heart. This will be a fine summer house for the children, but the schools are awful; they must go to school in London. Do reassure mother. I hope my new nanny will want to manage Ireland.

x x x Sivvy

October 21, 1962

Dear Mother,

Will you please, for goodness sake, stop bothering poor Winifred Davies! . . . She is busier than either you or I and is helping me as much as she can and knows and sees my situation much better than you can . . . she came over this afternoon and said you sent her some wire to tell me to "keep the nanny" . . . Please do understand that while I am very very grateful indeed for financial help from people who *have* money . . . and while I should be glad for the odd birthday and Christmas present from you, I want no monthly dole, especially not from you. You can help me best by saving your money for your own retirement . . .

I am even enjoying my rather frustrating (culturally and humanly) exile now. I am doing a poem a morning, great things, and as soon as the nurse settles, shall try to draft this terrific second [*third*] novel that I'm dying to do. Don't talk to me about the world needing cheerful stuff! What the person out of Belsen—physical or psychological—wants is nobody saying the birdies still go tweet-tweet, but the full knowledge that somebody else has been there and knows the *worst*, just what it is like. It is much more help for me, for example, to know that people are divorced and go through hell, than to hear about happy marriages. Let the *Ladies' Home Journal* blither about *those*.

I know just what I want and want to do. I made a roast beef, potato and corn dinner with apple cake today; had the bank manager's handsome 14-year-old son and a school friend in—they had Ted's poems in class. They were charming.

I dearly love the people I know in town, but they are no life. I am itching for museums, language study, intellectual and artistic friends. I am well liked here, in spite of my weirdness, I think, though, of course, everybody eventually comes round to "Where is Mr. Hughes?" . . .

I adore the babies and am glad to have them, even though now they make my life fantastically difficult. If I can just financially get through this year, I should have *time* to get a good nanny . . . The worst difficulty is that Ted is at the peak of his fame and all his friends are the ones who employ me. But I can manage that, too.

Had a lovely afternoon out with the children, mowing the lawn, Frieda playing with the cats and a stick, and Nick laughing wildly at them all. *He* is a sunshine; Frieda gets awfully whiney, but that is because of the big changes. Let me know roughly when and for how long Warren and Maggie can come next spring, so I can start planning a rota of guests! Love to all.

Sylvia

OCTOBER 23, 1962

Dear Mother,

Please forgive my grumpy, sick letters of last week. The return of my fever, . . . [*and*] the hideous nanny from whom I expected help, . . . combined to make me feel the nadir had been reached. Now everything is, by comparison, almost miraculous. I hardly dare breathe. Winifred found me the prettiest, sweetest local children's nurse, age 22, who lives in the most gorgeous house at Belstone, just overlooking Dartmoor, who is coming in days until she goes back in December to be staff nurse at a famous children's hospital in central London. She has been here two days, from 8:30 to 6, and the difference in my life is a wonder. I *think* she will go to Ireland and see me settled in. With her it would be a lark. I see now just what I need—not professional nannies (who are snotty and expensive) but an adventurous, young, cheerful girl (to whom my life and travel would be *fun*) to take complete care of the children, eat with me at midday—an "au pair" girl, as they say here, "one of the family." . . . I *love* Susan O'Neill-Roe, she is a dear with the children. I come down and cook us a big hot lunch and we and Frieda eat together in the playroom. Then I lie down for an hour's nap. I make a pot of tea in midafternoon and chat over a cup. O it is *ideal.* And Nancy does the cleaning. I am so happy and doing so much work, just in these two days, I can hardly believe it. My study is the warmest, brightest room in the house. After Susan goes in the evening, I come up with a tray of supper and work again, surrounded by books, photos, cartoons and poems pinned to the wall.

I have put my house deeds in our local bank under my name with Ted's life insurance policy and the fire insurance policy. . . . I am having a heater put in the car and shall now start all my arrangements for the formidable trip to Galway through the AA.

Susan is coming up overnight while I go to London for a few days next week to record a poem for the BBC . . . and, hopefully, to see the head of the British Arts Council who has just put an exciting job in my way. There is to be another big Poetry Festival in London this July at the Royal Court Theatre (a big, famous, adventurous theater) for a week. I've been asked to organize, present, and take part in the American night! It means I'd have to be an actress-hostess of sorts. A fantastic challenge—me, on the professional stage, in London. But I think I shall undertake it. By next spring I *should* have managed to come up with a live-in girl, and this Arts Council man I think will help throw a few jobs my way when he knows my predicament and sees I am willing to tackle everything. Don't you think I should do it?

O the package came today, too! How wonderful. I am *mad* for Nick's fuzzy red pants and the blue sweater set. Thank Dot a million times. And the pastels, both sorts! O mother, I shall find time to use them, too. I must be one of the most creative people in the world. I *must* keep a live-in girl so I can get myself back to the live, lively, always learning and developing person I was! I want to study, learn history, politics, languages, travel. I want to be the most loving and fascinating mother in the world. London, a flat, is my aim, and I shall, in spite of all the obstacles that rear, have that; and Frieda and Nick shall have the intelligences of the day as their visitors, and I the Salon that I will deserve. I am *glad* this happened and happened *now*. I shall be a rich, active woman . . . I am so glad to have *Ship of Fools*. I have been dying to read it. I shall bring it for wild, wet nights in Ireland.

Now do write Winifred and thank her a thousand times for obtaining this girl for me at the most difficult and necessary period of my life. I feel this London trip will do me a power of good—I shall cram in every film and play I can . . . I should love to use your birthday check on a Chagford dress. I want some of those hair-grips—copper or wood, a curved oval, with a kind of pike through it—for the back of my hair and to get the front cut in a professional fringe, so the front looks short and fashionable and I can have a crown of braid or chignon at the back. I shall have to take all my hems up. Almost all my clothes are ten years old! Just wait till I hit London . . .

Love to Dot, Warren and Maggie, too.

Sivvy

Dearest Warren and Maggie,

Just a short letter to say how immensely grateful I was to feel you both so thoroughly behind me that you would consider uprooting your lives for our sake! Thank goodness, it won't in any way be advisable or necessary. My main setback was having this awful shock . . . come the week after my influenza with no time or energy to do all I had to do to keep going on a day-to-day basis, let alone cope with the endless practical ruins . . . Ever since the 22-year-old children's nurse, Susan O'Neill-Roe, has been coming days from 8:30 to 6, my life has been heaven . . .

. . . the critic of the *Observer* is giving me an afternoon at his home to hear me read all my new poems! He is *the* opinion-maker in poetry over here, A. Alvarez, and says I'm the first woman poet he's taken seriously since Emily Dickinson! Needless to say, I'm delighted.

Now can you possibly get mother to stop worrying so much? . . . I do think I have adjusted to *very* unpleasant circumstances very fast . . . and am now very busy, but fine, knowing just where I want to go. I have a gorgeous, plush house hired in Ireland, *much* cosier, smaller and easier to manage than this, sheltered, with a lovely woman, the owner, in a cottage next door, willing to babysit and help shop, etc. . . .

It is very important for me to make new discoveries now, and I am very stable and practical and cautious and thoroughly investigated this house and surroundings before hiring it. I need to get away from here for a change, after the hell of this summer, and am lucky to have such a delightful place fall into my lap. As I said to mother, winter can't at the North Pole be worse than here! . . .

. . . I've not had a holiday on my own for two years, and as you may imagine, after these events, the court trial ahead, heaven knows when . . . I shall *need* a holiday on my own, preferably with two lovely people like you! I adore you both, have the gorgeous wedding picture on my desk where I can see it as I work. Do write.

Lots of love,

Sivvy

Dear Mother,

Thank you for your last letter. This time I shall accept the much-traveled $50 as a birthday present. I shall buy a dress, have my "fringe" cut and get a copper hair thong [*barette with removable pin*]. I shall try and do this in London next week, so you can imagine me having fun . . .

On my birthday, if it's nice, I'll be at my horseback riding lesson—I'm "rising to the trot" very well now, tell Dotty and Nancy; they'll know what I mean. My riding mistress thinks I'm very good.

Forget about the novel [The Bell Jar] and tell no one of it. It's a pot-boiler and just practice.

I am immensely moved by Warren and Maggie being willing to uproot themselves to help, and so glad this won't in any way be necessary. They are just darling, and I hope they'll come for a *holiday* next spring . . .

Now stop trying to get me to write about "decent courageous people"—read the *Ladies' Home Journal* for those! . . . I believe in going through and facing the worst, not hiding from it. That is why I am going to London this week, partly, to face all the people we know and tell them happily and squarely I am divorcing Ted, so they won't picture me as a poor country wife. I am not going to steer clear of these professional acquaintances just because they know or because I may meet Ted with someone else . . .

Now don't you all feel helpless any more. I am helped very much by letters, the birthday checks.

Love to all,

Sivvy

London, England
November 7, 1962

Dear Mother,

I am writing from London, so happy I can hardly speak. I *think* I have found a place. I had resigned myself to paying high sums for a furnished place for the winter while I looked for an unfurnished one with a longish lease that I could then furnish and let for fabulous rates in spring and summer while I was [*in Devon*]. By an absolute *fluke* I walked by *the* street and *the* house (with Primrose Hill at the end) where I've always wanted to live. The house had builders in it and a sign, "Flats to Let"; I flew upstairs. *Just* right (unfurnished), on two floors with three bedrooms upstairs, lounge, kitchen and bath downstairs *and* a balcony garden! Flew to the agents—hundreds of people ahead of me, I thought, as always. It seems I have a *chance!* And guess what, it is *W. B. Yeats' house*—with a blue plaque over the door, saying he lived there! And in the district of my old doctors and in the street [where] I would want to *buy* a house if I ever had a smash-hit novel.

I am now waiting for the tedious approval of the owner and for my references to go through. Ted is behind me in this; he took me round looking at places. Now he sees he has nothing to fear from me—no scenes or vengefulness . . .

I am now staying with a wonderful Portuguese couple, the girl a friend of Ted's girl friend, and they see how I am, full of interest in my own life, and are amazed, as everyone is, at my complete lack of jealousy or sorrow. I amaze myself. It is my *work* that does it, my sense of myself as a writer, which Mrs. Prouty above all understands. My hours of solitude in my study are my most precious, those, and the hours I spend with my darling babies. I am, I think, and will be when I get this London flat (I hope) arranged, the happiest of women . . .

I am so happy and full of fun and ideas and love. I shall be a marvelous mother and regret nothing. I have two beautiful children and the chance, after this hard, tight year, of a fine career—schools and London in winter, [*the house in Devon*], daffodils, horse riding and the beautiful beaches for the children in summer. Pray for this flat coming through. I would try to get a 5-year lease. Then, in five years, I hope to be rich enough to buy a house in London, rent flats at the bottom and live at the top, rent *my* furnished part in summer—so easy here, it is a sure income. I have real business sense. I am just short of capital right now. I would be right around the corner from Katherine Frankfort, etc., whom I'm so fond of, by the Hill, by the Zoo—minutes from BBC! *And* in the house of a famous poet, so my work should be blessed. Even if I *don't* get this place, I should be able to get one like it near it sooner or later. It's about time my native luck returned! *And* I have, on the advice of Katherine Frankfort, applied for an au pair girl, preferably German. They get only two pounds (about $5) a week, plus board and room, and are students, wanting to be part of the family. They would mind the babies mornings and study at classes afternoons and babysit nights with one day off. *Just* what I want—for I want to devote myself to the babies afternoons myself, take them to teas and visits and walks.

Mrs. Prouty called me. I was thrilled. I am dedicating my second book of poems (almost done) to Frieda and Nicholas in England . . . I'll dedicate it to her in America if it gets taken there.

I have found a *fabulous* hairdresser . . . —Doctor Webb's wife, of whom I'm very fond, told me of her. I had my fringe cut just before I came up to London in the most fashionable style—high on top, curling down round the ears—and kept my long coronet in back. It looks fabulous and the cut, shampoo and set was only $1.50. From the front I look to have short hair, and from the back, a coronet . . . Ted didn't even recognize me at the train station! My morale is so much improved—I did it on your cheque. Men stare at me in the street now; I look very . . . fashionable. Now I shall get a Christmas dress for myself with the rest of the money. I hope to be able to move up here before Christmas. I shall get toys for Frieda and Nick with your money at Hamley's.

When I appear at the Royal Court this summer, I shall be a knock-out. My haircut gives me such new confidence, truck drivers whistle, and so on, it's amazing. I am so happy back in London; and when I came to my beloved Primrose Hill, with the golden leaves, I was full of such joy. *That* is my other home, the place I am happiest in the world besides my beloved [*house in Devon*].

If I get the lease now, I should be able to write for five years and save up to buy a house there, and then the children would have the best of both worlds.

Living apart from Ted is wonderful—I am no longer in his shadow, and it is heaven to be liked for myself alone, knowing what I want. I may even borrow a table for my flat from Ted's girl—I could be gracious to her now and kindly. She has only her high-paid ad agency job, her vanity . . . and everybody wants to be a writer . . . I may be poor in bank funds, but I am so much richer in every other way, I envy them nothing. My babies and my writing are my life and let them have affairs and parties, poof! . . . Love to Warren and Maggie. Wish me luck.

Sivvy

NOVEMBER 19, 1962

Dear Mother,

Thanks for your good letter. I haven't written sooner because I have been fantastically busy. My correspondence alone would keep a full-time secretary going—I've had letters from a physiotherapist asking for a copy of a poem about living in a plaster cast to read to her patients and just now a fan letter from an Australian gynecologist who heard from a "colleague in London" about my maternity ward poem for three voices on the BBC and wanted a copy as he'd done a life-long study on miscarriages. I am thrilled. The medical profession has always intrigued me most of all, and the hospital and doctors and nurses are central in all my work. I'm hoping to get my dear Susan O'Neill-Roe to take me into her Children's Hospital when we're both in London.

Just now is "one of those weeks"—Susan has a week off in London, my local babysitter is out with flu, Nancy is moving from one house to one next door and all three of us have colds. In spite of it, I am happier than ever before in my life. . . .

Well, I have finished a second book of poems in this last month— 30 new poems—and the minute I get a mother's helper in London, I will do novel after novel. Even in the greatest worry and adversity, . . . I have discovered it [her own talent] in time to make some thing of it.

I took Mrs. Prouty's first check, as she said to, and went to the Jaeger shop in Exeter. It is my shop. I bought an absolutely gorgeous camel suit . . . and matching camel sweater, a black sweater, black and heavenly blue tweed skirt, dark-green cardigan, red wool skirt, and in St. Ives got a big pewter bracelet, pewter hair clasp, pewter earrings and blue enameled necklace. All my clothes dated from Smith, were yards too long and bored me to death. I am going to get a new black leather bag, gloves, and shoes and just take my new things to London. I feel like a new woman in them and go each week to have my hair shampooed and set in neighboring Winkleigh for under $1! My new independence delights me. I have learned from Nancy how to keep the big coal stove going in the kitchen, and it is heavenly, heats all the water, dries all the clothes immediately and is like the heart of the house—even Ted couldn't keep it going overnight . . . I love [the house] and am going to see that gradually my dream of it comes true. . . .

I am in an agony of suspense about the flat. I was first on the list of applicants! Already I have met an offer for 50 pounds more a year, now they have sent out for my "references"; in other words, to solicitor, banker, accountant, to see if I can afford it. I had the uncanny feeling I had got in touch with Yeats' spirit (he was a sort of medium himself) when I went to his tower in Ireland. I opened a book of his plays in front of Susan as a joke for a "message" and read, "Get wine and food to give you strength and courage, and I will get the house ready." Isn't that fantastic?

I would have to get a stove and new furnishings. Then I could rent it out by the week at fantastic rates in the summer when I was [*in Devon*] and almost *cover* the year's rent! . . .

I will die if my references say I'm too poor! Living in Yeats' house would be an incredibly moving thing for me.

I didn't tell you of my thumb—it's now healed—because Dr. Webb made a botch of it. It is now deformed, because he did not put a proper bandage on it or even a tape to hold the top in place, nor *look* at it for ten days . . . I went back to my darling Regent Street doctor, who fixed it properly, as much as he could. He saved the top, although the side is gone . . .

Have some fascinating historical biographies from the *New Statesman* to review; am sending the almost full-page children's book review to Mrs. Prouty. Got $50 from Dot—bless her; will write her.

Love to all,

Sivvy

THANKSGIVING DAY, 1962

Dear Mother,

It is perfect Thanksgiving weather—how I miss that holiday! I'll have chicken fricassee today. Susan comes back tonight, thank God. It has been absolute hell . . . me with a bad cold, unimproved by having to lug coal buckets and ash bins . . . It is enough to drive me up the wall.

I am desperate to get the flat. I called up today and found they were boggling over my "recent" references—only good for the last eighteen months. So I gave your name (*Professor* A. S. Plath) as a guarantor and security and offered to pay the year's rent in advance out of sheer impatience. I hope you don't mind and will put on a good front for the agents if they write you. I have so much against me—being a writer, the ex-wife of a successful writer, being an American, young, etc., etc. This was my one lucky break—finding this flat—and I've got to get it. I simply can't get help here in the country; and the minute they sense they are really needed, like this week, they desert. Besides, they are lazy bastards. I work like a navvy day-in day-out without rest or holiday, and they sit and watch "telly." I am dying to be *able* to work at writing, and now I am just up to my ears with this coming move and haven't time to write at all.

I have written Mrs. Prouty, yesterday, enclosing a copy of my children's book review, telling her about the lovely Jaeger clothes I bought with her first cheque and asking if I may dedicate this second [*third*] novel I am desperate to finish this winter to her, as she has been such a great help and knows what I am working against.

This year will be the hardest financially in my life (I hope) as I have to make bold and considered investments, as in this flat, in order to enable me to work toward a future . . .

It is so frustrating to feel that with time to study and work lovingly at my books I could do something considerable, while now I have my back to the wall and not even time to *read* a book. So anything I may turn out just now is merely potboiling . . .

Love,

Sivvy

November 29, 1962

Dear Mother,

I was so glad to have your letter saying you got *my* letter. I think I will get the flat and hope to move in about December 17. They are at the "draft-contract" stage; it is all so slow and Dickensian . . . The chance at this place (I'll take a 5-year lease) is fantastic. It is like a weird dream come true. *My* dream is to sell a novel to the movies and bribe the owner to sell me the house; I *want* that house. I am sending back your bank book; I shall have no need for it and no need to use it as security for the flat . . .

I am back with my panel of blessed, excellent doctors. I can't wait. I have been culture-starved so long, utterly alone, that these last weeks are a torture of impatience. Winifred has been wonderful. I had her and her son Garnett over for a very special dinner last night, Sue here as well. Everybody had a lovely time . . .

When I get safely into this flat, I shall be the happiest person in the world. I shall apply immediately for a live-in mother's help and get cracking on my novel. I hope to finish it by the date of that contest you sent information of; even if I don't win, which I won't, it will be an incentive. This experience, I think, will prove all for the best—I have grown up amazingly. Did I say *I* was taking out the policy on Ted's life because if *I* pay, I get about 10 thousand pounds at the end of 30 years if he lives. I'll need a pension of some sort, and this is the only way I can think of doing it . . .

. . . *Stunned* to get a check for about $700 from Aunt Dot today. . . . I just burst into tears at her sweet letter, I was so moved by that and the story of the check. [*Dorothy's "before-marriage"* savings had been put into U.S. Series E bonds with the intention of keeping them for "something very special." She wrote that she felt Sylvia was just that.] . . . Once I am in London . . . working, I expect to be self-sufficient . . . I'll be in London again this week to arrange a stove, straw mats, phone, etc., for the flat, and to see a man for lunch about a reading at an Arts Centre in Stevenage—the man I am working with for the Royal Court Theatre Night put him in touch with me. Once I get started, I should be able to get lots of speaking engagements. It will be lovely to have *both* Susan and Garnett in London and coming to tea. . . . I am so fond of them both.

My solicitor is gathering the evidence necessary for a Divorce Petition. I think there should be no trouble as Ted is very cooperative . . .

. . . I am very smug at a review of the most fascinating book I've just done—*Lord Byron's Wife*. I am very lucky to get it; it costs $6.50, a fortune here, and all the big papers have already given it full-page treatment. I've been asked to do it for the *New Statesman* by a friend of ours who is literary editor and who knew I'd love to get my hands on it . . . Shall send this to Mrs. Prouty, too. Have asked if I can dedicate my second novel to her—the one I hope to finish this winter. Hope she agrees. Don't worry about my paying bills. I pay them immediately; always have.

Love to all,

Sylvia

In December she closed the large house in Devon and moved with the children to a flat in Yeats's former home in London, where, for a brief time, she responded excitedly to the cultural stimulation of the city. Then the worst cold, snowstorms, and blackouts in over a hundred years engulfed London for months; Sylvia fought off flu; the children had coughs and colds.

In spite of all this, she continued the writing she had started in Devon. She began at 4 A.M. each morning to pour forth magnificently structured poems, renouncing the subservient female role, yet holding to the triumphant note of maternal creativity in her scorn of "barrenness."

Feeling she needed a backlog of funds to prepare for the sterile periods every writer dreads, she had earlier sent out The Bell Jar *for publication, stipulating that it appear under a pseudonym in the firm belief that this would fully protect her from disclosure.*

By the time the novel appeared in the London bookstores, she was

Sylvia and Frieda in Devon, December 1962

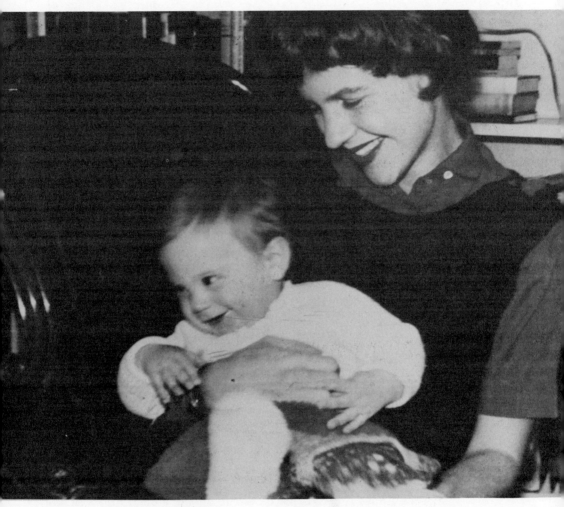

Sylvia and Nick, December 1962

ill, exhausted, and overwhelmed by the responsibilities she had to shoulder alone—the care of the children, the bitter cold and darkness of the winter, and the terrible solitude she faced nightly.

Despite the strong support of her friends, her sure knowledge of the importance of her new writing, her deep love for the children, supportive letters from her beloved psychiatrist Dr. B., the hope of a reconciliation with Ted, and endless offers from her family to help her weather her crisis—her tremendous courage began to wear thin.

FITZROY ROAD
LONDON, ENGLAND
DECEMBER 14, 1962

Dear Dotty,

It was so wonderful to hear your voice over the phone, sounding just as if you were next door!* I was so excited about getting the flat—everybody says it was a miracle, including my solicitor—and here I am, in my favorite house in my favorite neighborhood, happy as a clam! The children are thrilled, too. Frieda has been dying to go to the Zoo, two minutes away, and I took her and Nick day before yesterday. She was fascinated by the owls that "had bottoms just like Frieda," the lions, the new baby elephant and the penguins swimming round. She is such fun, such company, and Nick is the sturdiest, handsomest little boy imaginable; he just laughs and chuckles all the time. They are so good. I put them into the same cot in the morning, and all I hear is laughs till I've got breakfast. I am dying to take them round to all my old friends here, all of whom have had new babies. It is like a village—so many shop people remembered me and welcomed me back! It is heaven to be surrounded by *people* and to know as soon as I get my phone, I'll have all sorts of friends dropping round and be able to go out. Imagine, I've not seen a movie for two years! I am just starved for fun and chat. The country is lovely in spring and summer, but my work and dearest friends are in London.

Already I have two BBC broadcasts to do and a poetry reading and then this big American poetry night to [be] produced at one of the most famous theatres here this spring, a real great job. I am delighted you think I have an English accent, Dotty. Everybody over here thinks I come from the Deep *South;* they think my American accent is so broad!

---

* On December 11, 1962, as I was chatting with my sister in the kitchen of her home, the phone rang. Sylvia called us, her voice musical and lilting. She told us she and the children were well and that she was looking forward to moving to London within a day or two.

I am now in the little limbo between mother's helps. My dear nurse saw me through to a day after my move and then went on a deserved holiday before she starts work as an operating threatre nurse at a children's hospital near here this January . . . I love her like a younger sister for what she's been through with me. I was in London all through the smog, making the final arrangements for a gas stove, electricity to be connected, a phone (which will take ages here) and signing the lease. It was incredible [*the fog*], thick white for five days. You couldn't see your hand before your face and you can imagine what it was to get around. All the busses were stopped at one point. But I did it. And then I came home and in four days did all the packing and closing up . . . —you can imagine what *that* involved! I spent a day stringing all my onions and brought a load up with a load of my own potatoes, apples, honey, and holly. I am very proud of my gardening and hope to plant a lot of stuff next spring down there, too, and keep my bees going.

I got off the leading rein on my horse [*Ariel*] just before I left and have had some heavenly rides under the moors. I hope Frieda and Nick learn to ride very young. I seem to get on with the horse, I must say, and my riding mistress is very pleased. You can imagine what a relief riding has been through all this trouble, having to take on all a man's responsibilities as well as a woman's. Well, after I get this lovely flat all fixed up—and your "investment," bless it, is making that possible *right now*—I shall know what I'm doing for the next five years and can maybe take a little rest! Right now I hardly have time for a cup of tea, I have so many irons in the fire!

I got your dear letter today and went out and bought steak and lamb chops. Now I've finally got here, after half a year of being stuck and not knowing if I ever could manage it, I am so happy I am ravenous and eat like a horse. I hope to get off sleeping pills as soon as I get through the first week or so fixing this place up. I must say they have kept me going; otherwise I'd have been awake all night, and one is just no good without sleep. I wish you'd talk mother out of worrying. Hard work never killed anybody, and I think hardship can be a good thing. It has certainly taught me to be self-reliant, and I'm a lot happier because of it! . . . I am fine and happy and so are the babies. . . . Now I am settling in, I shall write once a week. I am with the babies all the time and they are angels. . . .

I hope by the New Year to have this place pretty well furnished and cosy and get a mother's help to live in by then. And then I should be able to really get on with my career. It is lucky I can write at home, because then I don't miss any of the babies' antics. I just adore them.

I must say there is *nothing* like American clothes. Everybody here envies my American babies' clothes. You have no notion how much your cheery letters mean! My nurse has taken some color shots of me and the babes that I hope will come out. I'll send them on as soon as they do.

Love to all,

Sivvy

DECEMBER 14, 1962

Dear Mother,

Well, here I am! Safely in Yeats' house! I can just about allow myself time for a cup of tea and a bit of letter writing after the immensity of the move—closing up [*the Devon house*] and opening this place. And I can truly say I have never been so happy in my life. I just sit thinking, Whew! I have done it! And beaming. Shall I write a poem, shall I paint a floor, shall I hug a baby? Everything is such fun, such an adventure, and if I feel this way *now*, with everything bare and to be painted and curtains to be made, etc., what will I feel when I get the flat as I dream it to be. Blessed Susan stayed with me through the move up and a day after, so I could make innumerable dashes into town ordering and buying the most necessary things . . .

We had a lovely drive up—a clear, crisp blue day. . . . I arrived here to find no gas stove in and no electricity connected! As I dashed out, Susan nobly holding the babies in the car, to drive to the gas board, I left my keys in the open flat and the door blew shut! Well, it was a comedy of errors. The obliging gas boys climbed on the roof and jimmied a window and installed the stove—the Devon mover did it all by candlelight (which I had the foresight to bring)—and by getting laryngitis, I persuaded the electricity people to connect us up—the agents hadn't sent them the right keys. The minute this was over, everything went swimmingly. I was dumbfounded at the people who remembered me—you, too. The laundromat couple rushed up; they had been in Boston since we last met; they wanted to be remembered to you. The people at the little dairy-grocery shook hands and remembered me by *name*, and the *nappy*-service man I called up remembered me and welcomed me back! Well, it was like coming home to a small, loving village. I haven't had a second to see Katherine Frankfort or Lorna Secker-Walker yet, both of whom have had

Sylvia and Nick in Devon, December 1962

new babies, I've been so busy on my own with Frieda and Nick. I can only work evenings at the house and writing when I have no help.

So the next five years of my life look heavenly—school terms in London, summer in Devon. I only pray I earn enough by then to offer the widow who owns this place so much she'll sell it to me. I feel Yeats' spirit blessing me. Imagine, a Roman Catholic priest at Oxford, also a poet, is writing me and blessing me, too! He is an American teacher-priest who likes my poems and sent me his for criticism. I thought this would please Dot.

The first letter through my door was from my publishers. I spent last night writing a long broadcast of all my new poems to submit to an interested man at the BBC and have a commission to do a program on the influence of my childhood landscape—the sea. Oslo, Norway, radio wants to translate and do my "Three Women" program set in the maternity ward and A. Alvarez, the best poetry critic here, thinks my second book, which I've just finished, should win the Pulitzer Prize. Of course, it won't, but it's encouraging to have somebody so brilliant think so. As soon as I get my mother's help (I hope early in January), I'll finish my second novel. I *am* writing these "potboilers" under a pseudonym [*Victoria Lucas*]!

. . . I took Frieda and Nick to the Zoo and had a heavenly time. Nick slept, but Frieda was thrilled . . . They are so happy and laughing, we have such fun. F. does her puzzle in 5 seconds, reads books with me and *loves* coloring. I'm going to make their bedroom—the biggest—a playroom, too. I brought the Geegee horse and the favorite toys. My bedroom will be my study; it faces the rising sun, as does the kitchen.

Viewed the full moon from my little "balcony" in sheer joy. It is so *light* here. The only real job is painting the floors. I've ordered rugs and mats. I *adore* planning the furnishing. You were very wise about ordering a double bed [*in view of future subletting*]—I'll get one. I have a single on loan from a Portuguese friend. The cats are being fed by friends in Devon.

. . . A big bouquet of my own beautiful green and white holly with red berries is in my newly polished pewter set. I am so happy, I just skip round. *Please* tell darling Dotty her blessed "investment" is enabling me to furnish the flat straight out instead of poem by poem, as I'd thought . . . I had the darlingest young solicitor at my firm do the lease business for me—we were exchanging advice about kinds of paint at the end. Everybody—Frank, Dot, Mrs. Prouty—says you worry if I don't write. For goodness sake, remember no news is good

news and my work is so constant I barely have a second to fry a
steak . . .

Lots and lots of love to all,

Your happy Sivvy

P.S. Have told Mrs. P. I would like to dedicate my second novel
to her. She wanted to be sure I was dedicating something to you, so I
said I was dedicating my third book of poems to you—I'm dedicating
the second one I've just finished to Frieda and Nick, as many poems
in it are to them, and I'm sure you approve! Don't want Mrs. Prouty
to feel I'm "expecting" anything, though!

DECEMBER 21, 1962

Dear Mother,

I do hope *these* pictures convince you of the health and happiness
of us three! Susan took them and for Christmas blew up four big
ones for me. Here, Frieda and I are having a December picnic in St.
Ives, Cornwall.

I have never been so happy in my life. By some miracle *everybody*
has delivered and done everything for me before Christmas, their usual
"after Christmas" excuses melting miraculously away. I have fresh
white walls in the lounge, pine bookcases, rush matting which looks
very fine with my straw Hong Kong chairs and the little glass-topped
table, also straw and black iron in which I can put flowerpots and
currently have a lilac hyacinth. I have found the most fantastic
store—Dickens and Jones—which knocks Harrod's out the window. I
spent the rest of Mrs. Prouty's clothes money and feel and look like a
million. Got a Florence-Italy blue and white velvet overblouse, a deep
brown velvet Italian shirt, black fake-fur toreador pants, a straight
black velvet skirt and metallic blue-and-black French top. One or two
other outfits made me drool, notably some Irish-weave shirts—I love
everything Irish, as you may imagine. But I stopped at a Viennese
black leather jerkin. I haven't had a new wardrobe for over seven
years, and it's done wonders for my morale. You should see me nip-
ping round London in the car! I'm a real Londoner at heart; I love
Fitzroy Road and this house above all.

. . . Got in my old Doris, who loves the children, so I could see a
marvelous new Ingmar Bergman movie . . . Will have Christmas
dinner with this lovely Portuguese couple who've been putting me up
on my London visits . . . Just had two long bee poems accepted by

the *Atlantic* and have been asked to judge the Cheltenham poetry contest again this year. I am in heaven. . . . Everybody tells me his life story and warms up to me and the babies right away. Life is such fun.

Katherine is finding out about a little nursery school round the corner where I might send Frieda mornings. The weather has been blue and springlike, and I go out every day with the babies. Still have the babies' floors to paint, the "au pair's" floors, the hall floors and three unpainted wood bureaus. *Blue* is my new color, royal, midnight (not aqua!). Ted never liked blue, and I am a really blue-period person now. With lilac and apple green accents.

If you ever want to make another hit, send some more kitty balloons! I read a picture book with Frieda every night. My bedroom has yellow and white wallpaper, straw mat, black floor borders and gold lampshade—bee colors—and the sun rises over an 18th century engraving . . . I'd like to live in this flat forever . . . Lots of love to you, Warren, and Maggie. Tell everyone of my move; hence no cards this year. I've not had a second . . .

Sivvy

WEDNESDAY, DECEMBER 26, 1962

Dear Mother,

. . . It is amazing how much my new hairdo and new clothes have done for my rather shattered morale. I had a lovely tea with the Frankforts, with the two beautiful blond Secker-Walker children and their parents (they live two houses down from our Chalcot Square place) . . . and some others . . . I plan to throw myself into painting the rest of the upstairs floors this week so I can give myself the treat of applying for an au pair first thing in the new year. I have been resting a bit the last few days. We went for Christmas dinner with a very nice Portuguese couple in Hampstead. They cooked a goose which they lit with cognac and gave Frieda a tiny toy piano that plays simple songs and Nick a rubber rabbit. I thought the outfits for Nick and Frieda which Warren and Maggie sent just lovely; do thank them for me. I have been so preoccupied I have barely had time to cook. The little nursery school just round the corner takes children from 9:30 to 12:30, and I shall try Frieda at it next week. She seems to blossom on outside experiences with other children, and I think she needs this. . . .

I am hoping the BBC accepts my 20-minute program of new poetry

—the producer thinks they are wonderful, but the Board still has to approve. Then I have the commission for a program on my childhood landscape, or in my case, seascape. Did I tell you Mrs. Prouty sent $100? And bless you for your $50. I have double expenses just now—the closing expenses [*in Devon*] and the rather large opening ones here, but once I am settled here, it will be five years' blessed security and peace and *no more floor painting!* All of which is much to look forward to and in which time I should have produed a lot of work.

How lucky I am to have two beautiful babies and work! Both of them have colds, which makes them fussy, but I keep them warmly dressed and they take long naps. Did Maggie knit that gorgeous blue sweater for Frieda? Their color pictures are lovely—Frieda has claimed them. She says of every sweater, "Grammy made that." Frieda loves the little mouse that came in Warren's parcel. She came in holding a rusk in her hands just as the mouse is holding the corn and said, "Like mouse." She is unique in seeing resemblances to things. Just now I held her up to see a fine snow falling and she said, "Like Tomten book," which is about a little Scandinavian dwarf on a farm in the snow. I took the very favorite picture books to London, and we "read" one each day. I am enjoying just sitting about with the children and making tea and breathing a little. I don't feel to have had a holiday for years!

Nick is wonderfully happy and strong. . . .

Well, I hope to drop over to the Frankforts a bit later this evening for a "Boxing Day" supper with them . . . I naturally do get a bit homesick for relatives and was grateful to have Christmas dinner out with friends. Frieda did very much enjoy opening presents, but is much too young to grasp more than that "Santa brought it for Frieda." She is very encouraging about my painting floors, getting up and praising me in her little treble each day, "Good mummy, paint floors all clean for Frieda." She is such a joy . . .

It is now snowing very prettily, crisp and dry, like an engraving out of Dickens.

Lots of love to all,

Sylvia

JANUARY 2, 1963

Dear Mother,

. . . Probably you have heard we've had fantastic snow here—my first in all my years in England. I heard Devon was completely cut off by 20-foot drifts, and they were dropping bread and milk by helicopter! Well, I just got out in time. The English, of course, have no snow plows, because this only happens once every five years, or ten. So the streets are great mills of sludge which freezes and melts and freezes. One could cheerfully use a dog sled, and I wish I had a sled for Frieda, for they are sledding on Primrose Hill; it looks so pretty! I am trying her at the little nursery school around the corner where Katherine Frankfort sends her boys, three hours a morning, five days a week for just over $4. They drink cocoa and play. Some mornings she is more tearful than others, but she does need to be free of mummy for some time, and I need desperately to have time to work. I put Nick down for a nap, which he's ready for by then, having been up and playing and shaking his cot since six.

I have a BBC assignment to do "live" next Thursday night, reviewing a book of American poems on a weekly "New Comment" program, so my being back is already getting round.

It takes months to get a phone here, but once I get all these things done, I'll be set for five years and one can do a lot in that time . . . The car is really snowed up. I don't want to use it until some of this Arctic is thawed.

The wonderful package from Dot and you came the day after Boxing Day, which is the holiday the day after Christmas. *Much* better then! I was astounded at all the toys and beautiful clothes! Nick *loves* the baby doll, which he seems to think is another of his own sort, and he chews the little mouse Warren sent as a cat would . . . I am so glad Grampy could spend Christmas Day [*he came from a nursing home*] with you. Do give my love to Uncle Frank and Louise—I believe I wrote them thanking them for their $25 cheque, but thank them again for me, anyway.

It is such a relief to be back with my wonderful and understanding Doctor Horder. He has given me a very good tonic to help me eat more, is checking my weight—I lost about 20 pounds this summer—and has sent me to have a chest x-ray after hearing of my 103° fevers, so I am in the best of hands . . .

. . . Love to Warren, Maggie and Dot and Joe.

x x x Sivvy

WEDNESDAY, JANUARY 16, 1963

Dear Mother,

Thanks very much for your letter and the cheque. I am slowly pulling out of the flu, but the weakness and tiredness following it makes me cross. I had a day nurse for a week when I was worst and the children had high fevers (little Frieda got a ghastly rash, which turned out to be an allergy to penicillin, which she can't have), but then the nurse got a cold and went home, just as well, for she used up that $50 cheque; they are very expensive. The children are themselves again, thank goodness. . . .

The weather has been filthy, with all the heaped snow freezing so the roads are narrow ruts, and I have been very gloomy with the long wait for a phone, which I *hope* to get by the end of the month after two months' wait, which makes me feel cut off, along with the lack of an "au pair." I did interview a very nice German girl of eighteen from Berlin whom I wanted and engaged, but her employer is making difficulties for her leaving . . . I hope to goodness I hear this week that she is coming. Then I should feel cheered to cook a bit more; I've been so weak I've just wanted boiled eggs and chicken broth.

I did get out for a small BBC job the other night, very pleasant, reviewing a book of American poetry, and was entertained with drinks and sandwiches; and I have a commission for a funny article which I just haven't had time or energy to think of.

I still need to sew the bedroom curtains, have some made for the big front room windows and get a stair carpet and oddments. It is so hard to get out to shop with the babies, but I've decided to use the agency babyminders, who are very good, though expensive, for a few nights out this week. A very sweet couple have invited me to dinner tomorrow and me and the babies to dinner Sunday, and I think I may go to a play with this Portuguese girl.

I just haven't felt to have any *identity* under the steamroller of decisions and responsibilities of this last half year, with the babies a constant demand. Once I have an "au pair," the flat finished—after all, it is furnishing for at least five years and should always be my "London furniture," so it is an investment—and a phone and routine, I should be better, I think.

. . . But I get strength from hearing about other people having similar problems and hope I can earn enough by writing to pay about half the expenses. It is the *starting* from scratch that is so hard—this first year. And then if, I keep thinking, if only I could have some windfall, like doing a really successful novel, and *buy* this house, this ghastly vision of rent bleeding away year after year would vanish, and I could almost be self-supporting with rent from the other two flats—that is my dream. How I would *like* to be self-supporting on my writing! But I need *time*.

I guess I just need somebody to cheer me up by saying I've done all right so far.

Ironically there have been electric strikes and every so often all the lights and heaters go out for hours; children freeze; dinners are stopped; there are mad rushes for candles.

Sue and her sweet boyfriend, Corin, took me out to a movie the other night, and I realized what I have missed most, apart from the peace to write, is company—doing things with other people.

Thank goodness, I got out of Devon in time. I would have been buried forever under this record 20-foot snowfall with no way to dig myself out. Nancy is feeding the cats; I sent her a $15 cheque.

. . . I was very lucky in calling the Home Help Service, which sends out cleaners to sick or old people, and got a wonderful vigorous woman, named Mrs. Vigors (!), who had the place gleaming in about two hours. I got a terrific lift from it and hope I can persuade her to come to me on her own Saturdays after I no longer qualify as a person in need. It is very hard to get good cleaners here, and she has two young girls and is very good with the babies.

Do give my best love to Dot and Joe and Warren and Margaret. I hope to write in a week or so saying I have got this au pair—she left some of her stuff and seemed a very nice, cheerful girl whom the children liked.

Love to all,

Sivvy

Letter written by Patty Goodall to my friend Mrs. William Norton. She knew it would reassure me.

JANUARY 19, 1963

Dear Aunt Mildred,

Having a pretty good idea how anxious you and Mrs. Plath must be about Sylvia (I know my mother would feel the same way about me!), I dashed off a note to her [*Sylvia*] immediately, suggesting that I drop in on her Saturday, January 19. I did mention that I had heard from you . . . I hid my mission further by stating that John would be taking Susie to the Zoo in nearby Regent's Park while she and I visited and that I felt in great need to chat with someone who was not only American also, but who knew my family.

It was a bitter cold day, but the bright smile and eager American expression that greeted us as Sylvia opened the door made the visit already worth while. John had seriously intended continuing on to the

Park, but Sylvia urged him strongly to stay and for the next hour or so we sat and drank tea and NEVER STOPPED TALKING! She seemed well, as did the children, but apparently they had had a bad bout with the flu. There is a lot of this about, and it does bring with it very high fevers. At one point all three were down at once, but, as Sylvia says, her doctor is an absolute Saint, giving them every attention and care. She feels very tied down with two children and no one to look after them when she needs to go out, but she is looking for a foreign girl to live in . . .

Frieda is a darling little girl with the biggest blue eyes I have ever seen. Nicholas was in his playpen, adding to the conversation occasionally with a deep chuckle. Sylvia says he possesses a wonderfully happy disposition, and he certainly seemed quite content to chuckle away while our Susie patted him on the head and stole his biscuit.

Saturday was the dreariest of winter days, yet inside her flat life seemed warm and cheery . . . Of course, we never finished our conversation, but I do hope to see more of her soon. John is off to the States in a week or so for a short business trip, and I am hoping Sylvia will come to dinner one night to keep me company. She hopes to have her phone installed soon, but whether she will or not is anyone's guess. Things move slowly in England! However, there is always the mail, and I really would love to see more of her.

I just as soon Sylvia didn't know that I reported back to you about our visit. I would rather she think that I came simply because I needed and wanted to meet her—certainly our future meetings will be because she is interesting, fun, and full of charm.

Sylvia is still continuing with her writing and seems to recently have had some success in publishing a book. Whether this is intended to be passed on, I don't know, but will leave it up to you whether to tell Mrs. Plath. Perhaps she knows. Sylvia seemed shy about the subject, saying it was being published under an assumed name—I didn't question her further . . .

I must dash in order to get news to you right away. I am so pleased you wrote me, and, incidentally, pleased to have added another Aunt and Uncle.

Love,

Patty

Dear Mother,

Thanks so much for your letters. I got a sweet letter from Dotty and a lovely hood and mittens for Nick from Warren and Margaret. I just haven't written anybody because I have been feeling a bit grim—the upheaval over, I am seeing the finality of it all, and being catapulted from the cowlike happiness of maternity into loneliness and grim problems is no fun. I got a sweet letter from the Nortons and an absolutely wonderful, understanding one from Betty Aldrich. Marty Plumer is coming over at the end of March, which should be cheering . . .

I have absolutely no desire ever to return to America. Not now, anyway. I have my beautiful country house, the car, and London is the one city of the world I'd like to live in with its fine doctors, nice neighbors, parks, theatres and the BBC. There is nothing like the BBC in America—over there they do not publish my stuff as they do here, my poems and novel. I have done a commissioned article for *Punch* on my schooldays and have a chance for three weeks in May to be on the BBC Critics program at about $150 a week, a fantastic break I hope I can make good on. Each critic sees the same play, art show, book, radio broadcast each week and discusses it. I am hoping it will finish furnishing this place, and I can go to [Devon] right after. Ask Marty for a copy of the details of the two places and the rent, and maybe you could circulate them among your professor friends, too.

I appreciate your desire to see Frieda, but if you can imagine the emotional upset she has been through in losing her father and moving, you will see what an incredible idea it is to take her away by jet to America. I am her one security and to uproot her would be thoughtless and cruel, however sweetly you treated her at the other end. I could never afford to live in America—I get the best of doctors' care here perfectly free, and with children this is a great blessing. Also, Ted sees the children once a week and this makes him more responsible about our allowance . . . I shall simply have to fight it out on my own over here. Maybe someday I can manage holidays in Europe with the children . . . The children need me most right now, and so I shall try to go on for the next few years writing mornings, being with them afternoons and seeing friends or studying and reading evenings.

My German "au pair" is food-fussy and boy-gaga, but I am doing my best to discipline her. She does give me some peace mornings and

Sylvia, her children, and her mother in Devon, July 1962

a few free evenings, but I'll have to think up something new for the country as these girls don't want to be so far away from London.

I am going to start seeing a woman doctor, free on the National Health, to whom I've been referred by my very good local doctor, which should help me weather this difficult time. Give my love to all.

Sivvy

On February 12, 1963, my sister received a cablegram from Ted, telling us "Sylvia died yesterday" and giving details of the time and place of the funeral service.

Her physical energies had been depleted by illness, anxiety and over-work, and although she had for so long managed to be gallant and equal to the life-experience, some darker day than usual had temporarily made it seem impossible to pursue.

List of Poems

Index of First Lines

HB10E